El Salvador in the Aftermath of Peace

THE ETHNOGRAPHY OF POLITICAL VIOLENCE

Cynthia Keppley Mahmood, Series Editor

A complete list of books in the series is available from the publisher.

El Salvador in the Aftermath of Peace

Crime, Uncertainty, and the Transition to Democracy

Ellen Moodie

PENN

University of Pennsylvania Press

Philadelphia

Published by
University of Pennsylvania Press
Philadelphia, Pennsylvania 19104-4112

Printed in the United States of America on acid-free paper

10 9 8 7 6 5 4 3 2 1

Library of Congress Cataloging-in-Publication Data
Moodie, Ellen.
  El Salvador in the aftermath of peace / Ellen Moodie.
      p.   cm.—(Ethnography of political violence)
  Includes bibliographical references and index.
  ISBN 978-0-8122-4228-7 (alk. paper)
    1. Violence—El Salvador.   2. El Salvador—Social conditions.   3. Crime—El Salvador.   4. El Salvador—Politics and government—1992–   I. Title.
HN190.Z9V550   2010
303.6'209728409049—dc22   2009029043

Contents

Introduction

Peace officially arrived in El Salvador on 16 January 1992. That day representatives of the government and the Farabundo Martí National Liberation Front (Frente Farabundo Martí para la Liberación Nacional, FMLN) signed accords in Chapultepec Castle in Mexico City. The agreement, brokered by the United Nations, ended nearly twelve years of a civil war often characterized as one of the last battles of the Cold War. The United States had sent the country $6 billion in economic, military, and covert aid.[1] At least 75,000 Salvadorans died in the conflict, and more than a million were displaced. Nearly 20 percent had left their country.

Postconflict policy analysts have called the Salvadoran case among the most successful peace agreements in the post–Cold War period.[2] The cease-fire held. The FMLN became a legal political party. Military, judicial, and electoral institutions were reformed. An Office of Human Rights Counsel was established and a Truth Commission formed. Limited agrarian reform was granted.

To former guerrillas, thwarted from challenging the country's unjust economic structure, the crucial aspect of the accords became the founding of a civilian police force trained in human rights.[3] To financial elites in the country, the key element of the agreements was the (image of the) opening up of a clean, calm space for investment. To many social scientists, peace activists, and other observers, the most important achievement was that electoral competition prevailed over arms. Democracy, it seemed, had triumphed.[4]

This story of the successful arrival of peace and democracy after a violent civil war has been the standard representation of El Salvador. This story is true.

Other stories circulated in the Central American country of six million in the years after the peace accords. Stories shared across kitchen tables, on street corners, on local television newscasts, and in newspapers. Many belie the kind of success trumpeted by the United Nations and the Salvadoran state. They tell of conflict and violence and danger around every corner. They are also true.

This book examines stories of daily life shared by people living a stunted transition to democracy. It explores how many urban Salvadorans came to talk of the "peace" as "worse than the war." In the immediate years after the 1992 peace agreements, many versions of that phrase echoed across the country's capital, San Salvador. Throughout the next decade, intensifying insecurity circulated in common talk, seeped into public discourse, and crowded mass media.

I arrived in El Salvador in 1993. I expected to learn about peace. But I quickly realized that I was witnessing a fragmented postwar staging of frustrated hopes. What I found there was not peace. It wasn't war, either. It was something else, something somehow more sinister, less knowable. This mystery, this unpredictable new mode of danger, only amplified anxiety. The most visible reason for this sentiment was the rising crime rate. Over the next decade and beyond, I would listen to hundreds of stories about postwar insecurity. I eventually began to record and analyze experiences told by urban Salvadorans of diverse backgrounds and perspectives. These crime stories, these narrative fragments of people's lives, form the core of this book.

Crime stories occur at the intersection of self and other, citizen and state, the powerful and powerless. Sharing them became a key way to talk about and evaluate the postwar transition in El Salvador. These stories oriented people, shaping the way they experienced not only their encounters with postwar violence, but also their encounters with the concept of democracy, both in the free-market present and in the remembered Cold War-era past—as well as in imagined future possibilities. How this happens tells us something about operations of knowledge production, agency, power, resistance, cooptation, optimism, dreams, and disenchantment.

With this book I pursue three goals. First, I follow the peace process ethnographically. Researchers have examined many aspects of the Salvadoran case: negotiations, institution-building, construction of democratic and human rights practices, and transitions in social movements.[5] I spoke to few actors directly involved in these processes. Rather, I listened to a range of "ordinary" citizens telling stories as they struggled to get by in disturbing new circumstances. By ordinary citizens, I generally mean people without much wealth and structural access to power, though some Salvadorans I talked to were more comfortably situated than others, and a couple I knew could easily make a few phone calls to well-placed officials if they ever got into trouble.[6] By focusing on a predominant form of storytelling circulating in the first decade after the war ended, I illustrate how public sentiment and political feelings can cohere around a common narrative of national life.

Second, I examine how practices of violence, and how criminalized individuals, are imagined and interpreted in a postconflict environment—how new forms of knowledge production emerge out of a sense of *not-knowing*. The democratic transition produced a new coding of violence. While during the war, the default assumption was that just about all violence emanated from some ideological conflict—that it was "political"—after the war, the crime was often assumed to be "common," random acts of violation aiming for simple material gain. This recalibration had consequences, reorienting the population to different ways of interacting with the world. Sharing crime stories, I argue, helped produce new postwar social imaginaries. The concept of social imaginary I define with the help of philosopher Charles Taylor: "Ways people imagine their social existence, how they fit together with others, how things go on between them and their fellows, the expectations that are normally met, and the deeper normative notions and images that underlie these exchanges."[7] After the war, the old expectations about social existence became unhinged. People sought new orientations toward those around them.

And so, third, I analyze *how* such reorientation happens. In El Salvador, postwar crime stories generated, and also were generated through, an emergent structure of feeling. More and more, people were narrating danger in terms of personal experience, rather than in terms of the public violence of war. This sense of separateness could supplant orientations toward collectivities. It could displace people's attachments to social movements struggling for change, and indeed also attachments to an ethic of obligation, of social care, to larger communities. As in so many places, whether post-authoritarian Brazil or post-socialist Poland, such shifting subjectivities helped reconfigure the relationship between the government and the governed. In the years after the Salvadoran civil war, this process helped create an era of what critics have called market democracy, structured around individual responsibility for the management of risk.

In sum, I propose that examining narratives of violent events large and small—their form, content, connections, communicability, the cartographies they project[8]—can shed light on how changes in state structure and historical circumstance impinge on, and help shape, lived experience and social subjectivities.

*   *   *

From guerrilla to banditry?

The anxiety so many Salvadorans expressed through crime stories during the early years of "peace" was not only about rising violence. After all, the nation had just endured twelve years of war. In part it was that it felt like a *different* violence, less knowable. In retrospect, many people thought they had figured out how to avoid problems during the conflict. They may have stayed out of certain areas; they may have shunned anything smelling of politics; they may have stopped wearing red. And after the war? These same techniques did not necessarily work. Not that they truly worked during the war, either, as the frequently cited cipher of 75,000 war dead reminded them.

Violence was not the only aspect of life that was transforming. Even before the war was over, the state began implementing structural adjustment policies to remake the economy. Everything seemed to be changing; Salvadorans cross-referenced post-1992 phenomena in many ways. They witnessed (reprivatized) banks open new branches under new names. They watched as new television sets, which migrant relatives brought with them on flights to the big new international airport, could be tuned to an increasing number of commercial television stations. They tried to make their way to work as thousands and thousands of imported vehicles, from dented pickups to late model SUVs, jammed the streets and newly paved highways—and traffic fatality rates spiraled up. And they saw exclusive, walled neighborhoods crop up in matters of weeks over the fallow coffee plantations that no longer girded the national economy.

None of this apparent postwar prosperity seemed to have anything to do with known or knowable national production, such as the coffee, sugar, cotton, and other industries upon which past fortunes were made. But it was just as unevenly distributed as in the past (and, indeed, after 1994, growth slowed considerably).[9] Instead money seemed to spring from invisible sources, from remittances sent by absent migrants' labor elsewhere, from the investments of faceless foreign speculators, from rumored narco-trafficking and endemic corruption. In the logic of this simultaneity, many Salvadorans correlated excess wealth with the transformation in forms of public violence, from categories of war and insurgency to classes of "common" and organized crime.

After 1992, the international reporters who had come for the war began to leave El Salvador. They returned only for scheduled events (elections, commemorations) or disasters (plane crashes, hurricanes, earthquakes). For much of the next decade, the kind of violence that garnered world attention

drew the journalists to other spots. But, as this book shows, violence continued to fill El Salvador's domestic mass media. Crime narratives, largely
defined, as we shall see, as *not war* but also *not political*, dominated public
discourse in the 1990s: they filled daily news, overflowed daily talk. If during the 1980s, the airwaves told people about the atrocities of war, in the
1990s, the news detailed atrocities of peace. Television programs much more
than newspapers communicated—graphically—most news to Salvadorans
after the war.[10] There were the daily body counts, with lingering views of
bleeding, tattoo-covered cadavers in the streets, blood-covered lumps in
bus aisles and stiff bloated corpses in coffins surrounded by weeping aunts
and mothers. (Just as common were shots of mutilated traffic casualties and
muddy drowning victims.) There were ongoing stories, unresolved myster-
ies that, thanks to modern video camera technology, were repeated over and
over across the small screens. Sometimes, alarmingly often in fact, police—
the peace-negotiated, human rights-trained police—were implicated these
incidents.[11]

The fact that some police crimes were making it into the media, and
to the courts, marked a change. Everyday experience told most people that
during the war, the state security apparatus committed many atrocities—
many more, people believed, than common criminals or the guerrilla forces
committed. The UN Truth Commission confirmed that view in 1993. Some
critics argue that the amnesty President Alfredo Cristiani (1989–94) and
the Legislative Assembly quickly granted to those implicated in the report
(in which 85 percent of human rights violations were attributed to agents
of the state, allied paramilitary groups, and death squads and 5 percent to
leftist guerrillas)[12] set the stage for continued impunity of most criminals,
perpetuating many people's distrust in state authorities.[13]

Most crime, however, still did not make it to the mass media, nor did
it involve police—even as authorities. Those were the stories I listened to
for the next dozen years in El Salvador. Everyday conversation overflowed
with all kinds of stories, of course, not just those of violence. The personal
experience stories I heard people sharing in San Salvador in the mid-1990s
homed in on danger and threats, perils presented by other people and institutions (though in each crime story the way these threats were portrayed
and perceived varied with the social position of the teller). Talk of crime and
violence was a subset of these kinds of conversations. Though I separate out
stories in this book analytically, their effects must be considered within a
larger narrated/narrative world. Every society has its own speech genres and
registers, its own ideologies about language.[14]

Salvadorans telling crime stories in the postwar decade were not often confessional, in my experience, not the way a North American in my circle of friends might be, even with relative strangers and acquaintances. No, San Salvadorans talking about change might begin with grumbling complaints about everyday inconveniences. A talk session in the decade after the war usually began at the end of a darkening workday, over a bitter beer or instant coffee or bubbling yellow Kolashampán, a popular Salvadoran soda. Stoplights don't work. Strikes block traffic. Another bus breaks down right in the middle of the Boulevard de los Heroes. The customs officer demands bribes. People did not often focus on challenges to the state, which many of them saw as already deeply corrupt; rather, they tended to worry about challenges to their own safety, security, well-being.[15] So conversation very often got around to money. Prices rising—gas or electricity or beans. The newly privatized telephone services ripping people off. The background buzz of the constantly "on" television might draw some in for a moment, to listen to President Calderón Sol (1994–99) make some pronouncement about reforming the judicial reform. Or to hear national football team coach Milovan Djoric, a Serbian from then-Yugoslavia, explain in stumbling Spanish the latest failure. Or to watch another reenactment of a murder on the sensational *CuatroVisión* news show. And then, of course, there would be the crime stories.

Crime stories produced for and presented on the news diverge from the crime stories told about personal experiences. One important difference lies in the primary source of information. The first voices heard in most mass media crime stories are almost always the police, focusing on suspects' offenses. The law is the principal prism through which people see crime in the media.[16] This is so even if witnesses are recruited to speak, even if family members cry out to reporters' microphones—as they frequently did in the 1990s in El Salvador—"He didn't have any enemies!" This is so even as police line up suspects before the cameras, though in El Salvador they usually covered their heads with their T-shirts. Only gang members defied this pattern, glaring at the nation.

The cultural theorist Stuart Hall and his cohort have argued that mass-mediated crime stories are a key site in which the state manufactures public consent on issues of security. Such accounts are less open to alternative viewpoints than are other news subjects.[17] The 1978 volume *Policing the Crisis* examines "moral panics" through a study of media coverage of an alleged rise in the "new" crime of "mugging" in England. "Moral panics" occur "when the official reaction to a person, groups of persons or series of events is out of all proportion to the actual threat offered, when 'experts,' in the form of police chiefs, the judiciary, politicians and editors *perceive* the threat in all but identical terms, and appear to talk 'with one voice'." [18] Agents believed responsible for the perceived threats are social deviant "folk devils." [19] Of course, what "out of proportion" meant in 1970s Britain undoubtedly veers far from what it meant in 1990s El Salvador.[20] Could anxiety about postwar crime in El Salvador have been a form of moral panic? Crime statistics are not reliable; often officials and mass media did seem to speak in one voice; and by the late 1990s tattooed gangbangers had become Central American folk devils. But there seems little doubt that violence was something to worry about for anyone who ventured into the streets of San Salvador. What would be the proper proportion of concern?

Certainly the mass media help shape the way such concerns manifest. Building on some of these ideas and critiques, the linguistic anthropologist Charles L. Briggs has developed a concept of "communicable cartographies" in his analysis of readers' interpretations of violence in the Venezuelan mass media. He describes how media narratives project "a small set of shared and predictable circuits, . . . creating subject positions, arranging them in spatial, moral and legal terms, and making only a very limited range of responses thinkable." [21] Salvadorans' responses to violence, like most people's, are usually limited by convention and "common sense." But most news consumers in the immediate postwar years did not fully trust what they read and heard. The newspapers, owned by generations of prominent families, were associated with the past, with traditional structures of power. Though one powerful mogul dominated television programming, people tended believe broadcast news slightly more than they did print media. TV had emerged as a fresh protagonist during the war.[22] And, at least in the first moments after the peace accords, a number of Salvadorans hoped that a newly energetic public sphere—the icon of democracy, after all—might tell them things worth knowing.

The crime stories I heard in conversation and interviews usually derived from personal experience. People also repeated others' accounts. Folklorist Eleanor Wachs, who listened to New York City residents' narratives of experiences with crime during the 1970s, distinguishes what she calls "crime-victim stories" from "crime narratives" through their different centers: crime-victim stories portray the victim as a hero or heroine, whereas crime narratives, recounted by offenders (and, I would add, law enforcement officials), focus on the crime itself.[23] While I appreciate this distinction, I want to avoid the binary reproduced in this terminology. Storied experience varies widely, from self-portraits of clever heroes to bumbling clowns to traumatized victims. So, like Briggs, I prefer to call these narratives simply "crime stories."[24]

I initially structured my formal fieldwork project as comprising a rather minimal circuit between conversational, "face-to-face" stories, and mass-mediated accounts. I thus balanced my research design between the poles of rapidly mutating "hot" everyday talk (and its approximation in recorded interviews) and the entextualized meanings from newspapers and television news. By "entextualization," I mean the movements of detached fragments of texts (stories and bits of stories that are retold) through transformations in genre (from one kind of situation to another).[25] Soon, however, I saw limits to this plan. These accounts are not separately narrated and constructed. They do not originate in individual experience even as their narrations spring from what appear to be discrete moments. They are always already intertextual, meaning that no stories are innocent: they inevitably are structured through past texts, engaged in an "implicit or hidden dialogue" among the "communicable cartographies" of intersecting textual surfaces (whether TV news stories, personal narratives, political slogans, poetry, sermons, etc.).[26]

One crucial textual surface intersecting with the conversational genre of crime storytelling is that of spiritual faith, whether versions of Latin American Roman Catholicism, rising forms of Salvadoran Pentecostalism, or Western conceptions of Buddhism. During the war, narratives linking to biblical stories could reveal reasons for, and even benefits of, persecution, at least for believers involved in the revolutionary struggle and influenced by liberation theology.[27] But after the war, as well, many tellers drew from their religious background as they structured their crime experiences into stories. Even the smallest encounter with danger could push a person into a contemplation of the possibility of death. And this, I suggest, is why crime storytelling, at least in postwar San Salvador through the 1990s, did not fully map onto the hegemonic institutional discourse so common in news accounts. Whether imbued with skepticism or anxiety, such awareness becomes "embedded within a frayed everyday life," as the anthropologist Veena Das writes, "so that guarantees of belonging to larger entities such as communities or the state are not capable of erasing the hurts or providing a means of repairing this sense of being betrayed by the everyday."[28] At the same time, sharing crime stories in San Salvador in the late 1990s worked to remake worlds, to reach beyond postwar betrayal and link listeners to each other. In this way crime stories, small as they may be, link to larger life histories, indeed to the more celebrated Central American war-era genres of *testimonio*, in which witnessing political repression and terror was seen as "a key form of approaching and transforming reality." [29]

As "articles of faith," as stories that hint at (or shout out) the closeness of death, then, crime stories are practically readymade for circulation. They are eminently tellable, detachable things that can easily be recontextualized into new situations. Public circulation is possible because of the doubled quality of stories. They are both *about* the world and *part of* it. [30] This quality is most apparent in the reflexivity crucial to circulating discourse. As speakers comment on the stories they tell and hear and read (whether from a black-and-white newspaper article dryly punctuated by the phrase "police said" or the breathy, ephemeral performance of a vivid personal narrative), they turn them into ritualized, normalized "things," "standard versions," that become circulable and communicable. [31] It is in this very reiterability that the potential for change in ways of thinking inheres. As the text-things move across genres, as they are retold in new contexts, they inevitably mutate. They transform with the circumstances. These changes both constitute and reflect new understandings, new orientations, new knowledges. [32]

Like so many people of my generation who became interested in Central America, my attachment to the place, and its people, has roots in my involvement in solidarity movements and protest against U.S. foreign policy during the late 1970s and 1980s. I am still a little awed by my former self's odd dedication to a country she had never visited. I spent part of one summer with my friends Deirdre and Maura in the gentrifying streets of Hoboken, New Jersey, knocking on doors and asking for donations to help Salvadorans. (Since some of that money provided military aid to the FMLN, considered a terrorist group by the Reagan administration, under post-9/11 laws we would probably have been arrested for doing what we did. [33])

When I finally went to El Salvador, in the spring of 1993, it was with a Sister Cities group from New Jersey that supported a resettled community of former refugees in the rural department of Chalatenango. We all went to see the heralded new "peace." I had made that first trip as somewhat of a romantic activist—perhaps seeking a utopian scenario, much like that theorized by my friend Rosario Montoya of her expectations as she carried out fieldwork in a onetime "model" socialist village in Sandinista Nicaragua in the late 1980s. [34] What I remember most about that trip was a massive march across the hot, dusty city from the hospital chapel where Archbishop

Óscar Arnulfo Romero had been assassinated in 1980, to the steps of the still earthquake-shuttered Metropolitan Cathedral in the San Salvador city center, where he is buried. At that very spot, about forty mourners of 50,000 who had gathered for Romero's funeral mass died after soldiers launched bombs and then opened fire into the panicked crowds. That in 1993 we could wave FMLN flags freely seemed a joyous affirmation of emancipatory possibilities, of hopes for democracy.

The "violence after the violence" that engulfed the country in peace was not what we had expected, not what anyone had predicted. I had been accepted to graduate school in anthropology at the University of Michigan just before that trip, so I arrived in Ann Arbor in the fall of 1993 looking for tools to understand the new situation in El Salvador—to explain El Salvador in the aftermath of peace.

I carried out more than four years of fieldwork in stints varying from two weeks to two years between 1994 and 2008. Though I first hoped to work in a mountain village that had felt the brunt of war, early on in my research I settled in the sprawling, unevenly developed metropolitan area of San Salvador. Typical of urban anthropologists, I traveled from neighborhood to neighborhood, event to event, following different paths and footsteps throughout the city.[35] Many routes I took were lined by thick exhaust and great waves of heat rising from metal and cement. Loud horns and squealing brakes and wheels punctuated my journeys. San Salvador is not terribly amenable to wandering. It is not easy to make your way through it all, or to get to know a broad swath of people. I quickly learned the bus routes (despite warnings by a burly military type at a U.S. Embassy orientation for Fulbright scholars about the risks of such travel) and moved around largely on public transportation during my first few years there. For a time I drove a Honda Civic across the rapidly changing city streets (during a massive road reconstruction phase, funded with loans tied to neoliberal development projects). With friends and allies, I learned shortcuts and less trafficked routes. Likewise, I made my way into a series of interpersonal networks. Like the anthropologist James Ferguson in the urban anonymity of Kitwe, Zambia, I knew some people quite well, some in passing, others in specific, detailed ways about some small part of their lives (such as their crime story or their expertise on police). I, too, have often been "obliged to hazard various ideas about the larger configurations that framed people's lives."[36]

Between August 1997 and August 1999, I tape-recorded seventy-five conversations with diverse San Salvadoran men and women—people from densely packed concrete-block barrios covered with gang graffiti and people living in the exclusive enclaves on the shady skirts of the two-hump volcano that looms over the city from the west. I read and heard hundreds more such narratives of violence in daily news and in conversation with friends, neighbors, and strangers in bank lines and bus stops. I met many of the storytellers socially (in the gym, at a cooking class, at the university cafeteria, at a photocopier in a stationery store, at a news conference, at someone's house) or else a mutual friend made the match. Most of the people involved in this study loosely connect with at least one of four networks living across the San Salvador metropolitan area: (1) those linked to a gym in an elite neighborhood of the Colonia Escalón, branching out to friends of my ebullient exercise buddy Ondina Ochoa (I have changed all names, following common ethnographic practice to protect confidentiality), mostly well-off business owners or professionals from "known" families; (2) those linked to my very social real estate agent/English teacher/marijuana connoisseur friend Eduardo "Guayo" Esquivel (his friends nicknamed him "Alcalde," or "Mayor," because like a politician he was endlessly greeting acquaintances in public), middle-class professionals, working-class employees, and some slackers of mixed social class; (3) those linked to a Roman Catholic church in a neighborhood of Reparto Los Santos II deep in the densely populated working-class city of Soyapango, especially friends and family of the generous, ribald Caro Portillo de Mejía and Carlos Mejía, working class and poor, small- and micro-business owners; and (4) those connected to my poker-faced partner Evert Antonio, in a working-class neighborhood of Santa Tecla and in several San Salvador sports federations, working class and poor, students and employees.

Over time, I became closer to some people and lost contact with others. In my first trip to El Salvador with the New Jersey Sister Cities group, I met many FMLN supporters, and I kept in touch with several of them over the years.[37] In my next trips, for three months in 1994 and a year in 1995–96, while living with working-class relatives of migrant friends in New Jersey, I audited seminars in journalism and history at the University of El Salvador, volunteered at some feminist organizations and worked in the small house that served as first location of the Museum of the Word and Image, founded by the former FMLN *compa* (comrade) Santiago (Carlos Henríquez Consalvi), the voice of the underground Radio Venceremos. I returned to live in El Salvador for two more full years, between 1997 and 1999, and rented a small house in Santa Tecla. Near the end of the 1990s, I taught at the American School and at an English-language college for monied students in San Salvador. With time, as my networks widened, I realized that there were only a few degrees of separation between the wealthiest and the poorest people in San Salvador.[38]

In the methodology sections of social science research proposals, the kind of work I did would be qualified as "unstructured interviews," with a loose list of questions altered according to the situation. The interviews were modeled on everyday conversations, built up from quotidian experience and carried on through local discourse genres in particular Salvadoran speech communities. The interview is, after all, iconic of conversation, even as it is imbued with its own particular power relations and awkwardness.[39]

I recorded narratives in interview situations in homes of storytellers or homes of their friends, as well as in restaurants, cafés, parks, or on the perimeter of a church, depending on the speakers' preferences and our mutual convenience. I also took notes as soon as I could after the fact if I happened to be present when people told each other stories. The stories I tape-recorded and quote directly in this book are not precise examples of "spontaneous" experience-telling (emergent without the anthropologist asking awkwardly, "Have you had any experiences with crime?"). But in the mid- to late 1990s it seemed as if that question was always already half there, hanging in the air, ready to be revived at the latest gossip. Conversations were always turning to crime. People would often introduce it by bringing up specific incidents— "Tengo la ultima [I've got the latest]," as my father-in-law Don Antonio would say wryly before launching into the day's tale. Other people would step in after the first story with their own news. In the end, I was convinced that much more than gossip was happening in the exchange of crime stories at that historical moment. Most crime stories told after the signing of the peace accords were related in what I have come to see as a postwar mode of performance.

After more than three years of listening to and participating in a discourse of decline and dread, I almost forgot what a paradox it seemed—"peace" worse than war. So the first few times I shared this research on the aftermath of peace with people in the United States, I was surprised at the resistance, even rejection, I sometimes encountered. I have a clear memory of the brisk winter day I met with a well-known social scientist, an expert on revolutions, who had done some research on Central America (and had been in El Salvador in 1987 and 1990, during the war). He seemed to refuse to believe what I heard Salvadorans saying. He insisted I must not have understood them. "You can't compare bombs with, with—burglaries!" he sputtered. I tried to explain that as an interpretive anthropologist my goal wasn't to calibrate whether postwar conditions were empirically worse (though if the criterion was simply the murder rate, indeed the situation was "worse," or at least "the same" [40]). But he was a respected scholar.[41] I wondered if I had put words in people's mouths—if I had framed things in a way that compelled them to partake in my (outsider) vision of their world. Had *I* suggested to them that it was worse now than (during or before) the war? Had they echoed my words, whether in a sort of empty urge toward conversational continuity or in an effort to "help" me in my research? But I had not gone to El Salvador intending to impugn the peace. And I was not the only person to report this perspective. Other anthropologists and journalists have found versions of this same kind of sentiment. Irina Carlota Silber, for example, in her moving work among former guerrillas in Chalatenango, suggests that rural men and women's theories of violence circulate through the language of "estamos peor que antes (We are worse off than before [the war])."[42]

It was easy to get people talking about El Salvador's crime and violence in general. But they were not always comfortable discussing their own lives. At the very least, most of the working-, middle-, and upper-class people I lived with in different parts of the San Salvador metropolitan area did not like telling others many personal details about themselves. Distrust was everywhere: distrust of me, distrust of being studied, distrust of questions, certainly distrust of tape recorders picking up every syllable to be taken to unknown regions—or, better said, to regions known for their links to imperial power structures.[43] I found that that distrust could be mitigated but not dissipated through introductions by close friends, or longtime contact with slow rapport building.[44] In San Salvador, even those people, the majority in my orbit, who had not been direct participants in the conflict of the 1980s—even the teenagers and children—shared common social memory of the conflict. They knew, for example, what an *oreja* was (literally ear, meaning an informer). I often heard the terms *cuilio* (cop, originally from slang referring to rural patrols) and *guachimán* (street language that means finger-pointing servant—a servile henchman) used to the same ends. (This curb on what was seen as collaboration, or lack of confidence in authorities, caused many problems for court trials after the war. Many witnesses were afraid to testify.)

Simply put, very few people I knew in San Salvador liked others to know their "business." They called other Salvadorans especially *chambroso* (gossipy), as if that were a uniquely Salvadoran trait. For example, when my schoolteacher friend Maru got a visa to visit the United States to attend her sister Gertrudis's wedding to a white North American, she told her mother not to tell anyone in their home village of Cacaopera ("They'll think I have money," she said; a few days later, "They'll all ask me to bring something up with me"). My partner Evert remembers his mother admonishing him when he was a child not to yell out her shopping lists as he ran to the small *tienda* (shop) down the narrow, ear-lined passageway: "How many eggs?! Did you want salt, too, or just sugar?!" ("Why should the whole world know what we eat?"—what we buy, how much or little money we have to buy it, etc.—she reasoned.) Years later, when she used to return to El Salvador from Los Angeles to visit, she would refuse to tell her family what day she was to arrive. They only knew when she called from the airport.

And so I had to "learn how to ask" in culturally appropriate ways.[45] Direct questions rarely seemed to work among Salvadorans. Evert, listening to my ideas about a particular story, more than once told me that a speaker "te dio paja" (essentially, "bullshitted you"). That, I told him, isn't the point in studying narratives. What is important is that people imagined a common shape of their world. What is important is that the stories had patterns— and that they were seen (or rather, heard) as *possible* in the postwar world. They created convictions, social facts, structures of feelings, senses of reality that had effects. They had consequences in and on the world. Consciousness cannot be false in that sense.

We cannot deny how our own lenses shape the way we see. Mine happen to be green, peering out of a pale white (or, often in El Salvador, sweating red) face. At the end of one hot day during my first fieldwork stint in 1994 I had gone to a large *tienda* to ask, through the barred window so typical of neighborhood shops, for a cardboard box. While I was chatting with the friendly owner, I tried not to notice that one of the ever-present *bolos* (drunks) was staring at me. Suddenly he burst out, "Do you see the same as we do with those green eyes?"

I almost answered tersely, "Well of course!" But then I stopped and smiled. "I don't know. I've never seen out of any other eyes!" Everyone laughed. I felt relieved, accepted for my difference, at least for the moment among the *bolos* and other various *tienda* loiterers.

My gringa green eyes ("like dollars" some would say[46]) inevitably shape the truth I seek. I hope what emerges is a dialogic truth, "'negotiated' out of a vibrant cacophony of voices contesting, combating, sharing, and sometimes drowning each other out," in the words of Nancy Scheper-Hughes, the medical anthropologist who has written fiercely against human suffering. She contrasts the negotiated truth with "experiential truth," experienced as true while not necessarily historically verifiable (as with the crime stories I heard).[47] Somewhere in there is the kind of "truth" one speaks to power. It is this truth, about who lives and who dies, that underlies all the other forms, even if it is always deferred in liberal, and neoliberal, democracies.[48]

El Salvador was an iconic place in the 1980s, its death squads and peasant movements galvanizing global solidarity and inspiring scholars and journalists and others to write against terror. Its peace accords, at the end of the Cold War, offered a satisfying sense of finality to that world metanarrative. For many it ended there. This book begins at that moment of international closure. It asks, like an insistent child who does not want to sleep when the book closes at bedtime, "But what happened next?"

This answer, it turns out, is not so simple. Describing the aftermath of peace, this book tells a story that moves from the production of knowing to the production of *not-knowing*; from the determined presentation of coherence in the postwar world by authoritative state and global entities, to its unraveling in everyday life as ordinary Salvadorans confronted radical uncertainty.

Chapter 1, "Big Stories and the Stories Behind the Stories," explores the narratives that hegemonic forces attempted to impose as sure knowledge on the nation and its history. This effort to construct coherence drew on longer historical arcs. As such the chapter maps the ethnographic and historical setting of the book.

Chapter 2, "Critical Code-Switching and the State of Unexception," considers the war-postwar cusp, when meanings of violent acts were in flux and knowledge of how the world worked was shifting. The dominant discourse insisted that the violence filling the front pages after the war was something different from before—that it signified rupture rather than continuity. The chapter argues that the state (dominated by an emergent transnational faction of elites) tried to manufacture knowledge that would shape a vigorous market logic in the nation. Parsing violent incidents as individual acts, as unconnected to social relations or political conditions, could help rupture the old revolutionary and solidary social imaginaries—and could help reconstruct how people envisioned their rights and responsibilities toward each other in a mode of neoliberal rationality that would facilitate transnational free-trade currents.

Chapter 3, "'Today They Rob You and They Kill You,'" moves from portrayals of knowledge produced through the larger stories told by those in power to scrutinize the knowledge emergent in the conversational crime stories that circulated in the 1990s. Many San Salvadorans' stories offered on-the-ground knowledge production of the postwar world: the stories they told each other indicate that they theorized the changes not in terms of war to peace, but in terms of shifting forms of enacting violence. The chapter compares dramatic stories that speakers shared as they collaborated in imagining new ways to respond to new techniques of danger.

The core of Chapter 4, "Adventure Time in San Salvador," is a single narrative that breaks down all the certainties deployed in postwar knowledge production. It describes a young woman's experience with violence, kidnapping, and near-rape. At the core of this trauma is a production of intimate self-knowledge. It focuses on a fear of bodily violation. The analysis considers how the speaker, Marielena, positions herself, her interlocutors, and other figures in and outside the communities she constructs in her talk. A central feature of the narrative is its rethinking of certainty about the democratic triumph in the nation, on levels both above and below the threshold of awareness. The analysis shows how notions of solidarity and community are intertwined with changing historical ideas about nation, race, gender, and class.

Chapter 5, "Democratic Disenchantment," explores meanings of democracy to Salvadorans in a post-civil war world and in the larger post-Cold War environment. The meanings veer far from the proclamations described in the first two chapters of the book. Throughout the 1990s in San Salvador, many of the stories—the crime stories—about the postwar moment incorporated, in more or less subtle ways, a critique of the state as it purported to be democratizing. I develop this critique as a form of "democratic disenchantment." Crime stories could not overcome the determined knowledge production of the state; rather, they mourned a kind of community that many had felt, paradoxically, in the midst of war. They evinced a sense of tremendous loss of the hopes for a future after war.

Finally, Chapter 6, "Unknowing the Other," directly confronts the sense of unknowing that underlies so much anxiety in postwar, free-market El Salvador. It moves from the local analysis of violent forms (the "robbing and killing") to the imagining of violent essences (the "they" who do it). The search for the material manifestation of criminality became an obsession in postwar San Salvador. Hard, visible clues, especially those repeated in crime stories and news programs as information, became signs pointing to danger. Attached to bodies in certain classed and raced configurations, these characteristics became (re)essentialized as "criminal." Drawing on material ranging from archives in the 1930s to interviews in the late 1990s, this chapter offers historical precedents to more recent discussions on gangs and hardline anti-gang laws that form part of a global antiterrorism discourse—and that threaten the political climate that would nourish a fledgling democracy.

The Epilogue reflects on shifting conditions of possibility for change, for hope, and even for democracy in El Salvador long after global eyes have turned elsewhere.

Today El Salvador has returned to its peripheral place in the world order. It only gets noticed in moments of crisis. The revolutionary poet Roque Dalton's writing of a half century ago is full of bemused observations on the insignificance and even absurdity of his native country. In exile in Prague, homesick, Dalton wrote these words:

> Todo es posible en un pais como éste
> que entre otras cosas, tiene el nombre más risible del mundo:
> cualquiera diría que se trata de un hospital o de un remolcador.

> [Everything is possible in a country like this
> that has, among other things, the funniest name in the world:
> anyone would say it must be a hospital or a tugboat].[49]

I did not want to write a book about crime stories in El Salvador in order to reiterate a familiar image of the country *as* a crime story. It is, rather, the other side of Dalton's poem that keeps me returning—that dry, sly humor in the midst of crisis shared by so many Salvadorans.[50] *Everything is possible in a country like this*. Not only war, not only horror, not only suffering. El Salvador may not have achieved *peace*—it remains an aspiration there as everywhere else. But the place abounds with courage—and wit—and hope. Crime stories told among Salvadorans may describe ongoing violence. But they also tell of strength, resilience, and survival. They refuse to give up.

Chapter 1
Big Stories and the Stories Behind the Stories

You have to go back. It's urgent.

As soon as we got to Cacaopera, they told me. They didn't say who had called. Or why. All afternoon that day back in June 1994, I had been riding around in the bed of a rattling pickup truck with four or five San Salvador friends who had invited me to their home village. I still have the pictures I took. Laughing children running alongside us on dirt roads shouting their greetings, "¡Salud! ¡Salud!" Grandmothers hanging wet socks off the sides of sad adobe houses shadowed by sagging palms. Foregrounds of brilliant flowering trees whose names I didn't know, backgrounds of thickly forested mountains where I imagined abandoned guerrilla camps. Somewhere along the way my borrowed baseball cap had flown off. My hair was a tangled mess. My face was covered with a thick layer of grit.

I don't remember now why we arrived so late in the evening in Cacaopera, in the mountainous northeastern department of Morazán. During the 1980s civil war, part of the region had been a guerrilla zone controlled by the People's Revolutionary Army (ERP), one of the five factions that united in late 1980 to launch an insurgency as the Farabundo Martí National Liberation front (FMLN). That particular day might have been the time the group of us slogged through the muddy paths of some nearby *cantones* (hamlets), stopping at door after door. We were seeking someone's brother's ex-wife's family whose address we didn't know to deliver a package carried by a visiting migrant friend of a relative back in New Jersey. By the time we reached Ernesto's house, it was eight or nine P.M., long dark. That cryptic communication demanding my urgent return had been delivered, Ernesto said, by la Niña Luisa, his elderly cousin.[1] He said he thought that Luisa's neighbor—with one of the few telephones in their part of the village—had brought *her* the message. By then, it was too late to knock on either of their doors to find out anything more. And the local office of the national telephone company (ANTEL), where many people made their calls, had closed for the night.

All we knew was that I had to go back to San Salvador.

I guessed the message was from María Eugenia (Maru), a daughter of Niña Luisa. I had met Maru, the sister of a friend in North Bergen, New Jersey, the year before, during my first trip to the small Central American country. When I returned to El Salvador, she invited me to stay with her in the small cinderblock house her sister Gertrudis had bought with money earned cleaning other people's houses in wealthy New York City suburbs.

Why hadn't Maru said anything more? The next morning I agonized the full five hours back to San Salvador. I imagined worse and worse scenarios as the first bus groaned and farted its way down the mountain pass to San Francisco Gotera, as the next one barreled nonchalantly over the broken roads to San Miguel, and as the third creaked slowly over the Lempa Rivera and past the volcanos and fields near the towns of San Vicente and Cojutepeque. San Salvador's sprawling metropolis of two million arrived in our nostrils before we saw it, in the thick exhaust of the traffic jams on the Boulevard del Ejército (Army Boulevard, a continuation of the Pan-American Highway). There the trees morphed into factories, their walls splattered with a hybrid mix of early flashes of hieroglyphic gang graffiti—"MS-13" (standing for Mara Salvatrucha, the now well-known transnational gang)—and the slogans echoing war resistance—"Calderón Sol es escuadronero" ("Calderón Sol is a death squad member"; the graffiti refers to the former mayor of San Salvador, a member of the dominant, right-wing party ARENA, the Nationalist Republican Alliance [Alianza Republicana Nacionalista], who had just been elected president). Then came the corrugated metal-roofed neighborhoods of the hunched cities of Ilopango and Soyapango. It was Saturday morning. The whole world was up, selling, watching, buying, mothers and children with mangos and plantains and avocados and pineapples arranged on banana leaves along the road, men and women with newspapers and brooms and flowers walking among the cars and trucks and buses gunning at the stoplights.

The fourth leg of the trip was on a dented Bluebird-type city bus that would have reminded me of my childhood rides to school through Indiana cornfields if it weren't for the crucifix and image of martyred Archbishop Óscar Arnulfo Romero gazing at the passengers from the front. I got out at the stop by the furniture factory near the Residencial Holanda, a newer working-class neighborhood named for the estate that once stood there.

Maru appeared at a neighbor's door just as I was trudging up the last few steep meters.

"Maru!" I shouted. "What happened!?"

She ran down to me. "It's okay, it's okay." She wasn't one to yell her business in the streets. "It's just—I was robbed. They even got my key. I couldn't get into the house." [2] I had the only spare.

A Little Mugging

Looking back, that urgent return to the city, that abrupt truncation of my palm-lined fieldwork fantasy, became my arrival scene.[3] The anxiety I felt, the *not knowing* what would come next, may be a common condition for an uneasy foreign fieldworker. But it was also a widespread way of being for many nervous Salvadorans in the first few years after the country's civil war ended in 1992. So many people were conscious of not knowing what to expect back then. They recognized the loss of context, the failure of trusted categories, even if the categories had been built up from the perversions of war, even if the "pathologies of the state [had acquired] a life in the everyday."[4] (Now you probably could carry a book-filled backpack on the bus without fear—in the past university students were instantly suspected of subversion. But would you sit next to a baggy-pantsed kid with glaring eyes? Could he be one of those gang members who by the mid-1990s were mobbing the mass media—or was he just a sullen teen mimicking MTV?) My forced return, then—and my need to *know* even as I dreaded what I might learn—is the first story behind the story. It marked my settlement into the meddlesome, presumptuous, and often naïvely optimistic discipline of sociocultural anthropology in its self-doubting late twentieth-century version. It was also how I began to dwell, awkwardly, in and on the urban chaos and gritty charisma of San Salvador, El Salvador. And it was on that very day I joined Maru, and countless other Salvadorans, in telling and listening to crime stories while grasping at the murk of the aftermath of war. Or, perhaps better said, grasping at the murk of the aftermath of a peace declared to much fanfare just two years earlier.[5]

Back in June 1994, I didn't seize on that key to comprehending the postwar moment. I didn't write much about Maru's mugging in my field notes. Why should I have been concerned with the affairs of pickpockets and muggers? The Salvadoran papers and TV may have been spreading more and more alarming information on what was being called *delincuencia común* (common crime). But, I reasoned—much like UN observers surveilling the early implementation of the peace accords—what transcendental meaning could there be in the theft of a few colones and a house key?[6] What consequence could a swift street robbery possibly have for someone like Maru, after her brother-in-law had slipped into *el monte* in the early 1980s (to the bush, as they said about those who joined the guerrilla forces) and her sister had fled two thousand miles north from Cacaopera, Morazán, to North Bergen, New Jersey, leaving her at the age of fifteen to take charge of her two small nieces? The big story, I believed, the story that mattered, was the war and its end. That was why I had first visited El Salvador, after all, arriving with a bright-eyed delegation from New Jersey to see our Sister City, a resettled village in a once wartorn rural area.

But that little mugging *had* meant something to Maru. She had not wanted to tell anyone in Cacaopera. They worry too much about her already, she explained. But she talked in San Salvador. I must have heard her story five or six times that week, as she repeated it to neighbors over coffee or to friends on the telephone she covered with a tiny yellow towel. I remember it well.[7] It conformed to a kind of Salvadoran postwar "standard version" crime story, happening unexpectedly, and forcing changes in understandings and habits to adjust to a new climate of risk.[8] Here is how it went: About six in the evening—sundown—at the Plaza Libertad in the city center, Maru got off the bus as usual in order to board another on her way home from classes at the University of El Salvador. (Afterward she found a new route, longer but thought safer.) A girl, a teenager, no one you would look at twice, bumped into her. Maru turned. A group of girls swarmed her. One scraped a blade against her stomach. She demanded cash. Maru protested. They grabbed her backpack. They ran.

In the years after the peace accords, crime stories both like and unlike Maru's moved through San Salvador, across the country, indeed over the globe as Salvadorans continued to migrate elsewhere. As these fragments of experience began to accumulate, to acquire patterns in social and individual memory, people started saying, "It's worse than the war." Whether they described muggings or kidnappings, the stories fit into a series of bigger stories—the story of the democratic transition, the story of the war and the peace process, the story of twentieth-century postcolonial and anti-imperial resistance, the story of a new free-market global economic order. In order to understand processes of knowledge production in postwar El Salvador, emerging from a feeling of *not-knowing* the new situation, we must grapple with these big stories. They are the uneven foundation on which any sense of the present is built—and through which conditions for possibilities of change emerge. After all, men and women can change the world, but not just as they please—not under circumstances they choose, but, as Marx put it, "under circumstances existing already, given and transmitted from the past." And the past, in El Salvador, weighs like a nightmare.[9]

Some stories of the past constructed coherence in familiar historical arcs. There is that of violent El Salvador, a place of chaos and carnage. Other stories have faded under the weight of hegemonic versions of events. The story of Salvadoran struggles for democracy, surging in key moments through the twentieth century, has usually been swallowed into a dominant historical plot of fifty relentless years of authoritarianism leading inevitably to the war. In this chapter, we will explore some of the larger narratives in which many Salvadorans' experiences are embedded—the big stories, and the stories behind the stories.[10]

Land, Coffee, and a Massacre

One big story reverberates through twentieth-century Salvadoran history: the massacre of 10,000 indigenous and ladino (non-Indian) peasants who participated in a Communist-led uprising in 1932.[11] The Matanza, it is called. That moment of horror, that nightmare, starts with the rise of coffee as El Salvador's main export. The account usually given is one of dispossessed Indians forced into landlessness and peonage by a greedy, rising oligarchy that wanted to insert El Salvador into the rising world economy of the late nineteenth century. The "grain of gold," or coffee, thrived on the rich volcanic soils where Indians had planted maize and beans. So the rich took the lands in the name of progress, and paid peasants (a pittance) to harvest the beans a few months a year. After the worldwide depression hit, the hungry masses rose up in desperation—only to be cut down by a savage military.

This account is still the dominant narrative. The big story. But it gets it wrong. What happened is not merely a familiar Latin American tale of elite greed and repressive military violence. It is also a story of the first experiences of popular sovereignty and democratic hopes in El Salvador. It is true that in 1881 and 1882 the Liberal government divided up corporate rights to communal lands. But the principal motive for this privatization was not just a land grab enabling the rise of the coffee aristocracy, as popular histories would have it (and as Marxist theories of primitive accumulation would insist). Historian Aldo Lauria-Santiago has shown that an important goal was to nudge peasants into a new economic order, to get them to participate in the expanding commodity market.[12] Partition aimed in part to turn Indians ("perceived as having no interest in accumulating wealth") into productive, individualistic entrepreneurs.[13] The number of landholding peasants did increase. In the first years after land reform, small farms were more common in many areas than haciendas or plantations. But through the 1920s the power of the agrofinancial oligarchy grew in a land boom linked to increasing international commodity prices. A rising class of coffee barons seized more and more land. Indebtedness of the smaller property holders also fed the land grab, especially after the decline in coffee prices that began in 1927.[14]

The state may have sought to modernize its peasants, prodding them toward productive roles in the market economy. But it also needed workers from which to extract the surplus labor that creates value. When it privatized the land, it also passed new criminal laws, and directed the (itinerant, mostly privately paid) police force to gather up vagrants and debtors and send them to work the fields. To justify these tactics, the country's leaders pointed to the need to discipline the Indians, whose perceived lack of work ethic they blamed for El Salvador's backwardness. The liberal rhetoric of individual freedom, in other words, was frequently lost in the quest for economic growth. When the National Guard was formed in 1912 as El Salvador's first permanent system of state vigilance, its primary mission was to defend agrarian interests. The more prosperous landowners billeted Guardsmen on their estates.[15] The country was run by a small group of landholding families—many (largely European and some Middle Eastern) immigrants of whose names still reverberate powerfully today. To them the national interest and coffee profits were one and the same.

Then, in 1927, one member of the ruling elite challenged the repressive system of government in his country. As a candidate, Pío Romero Bosque, brother-in-law of the president, had been considered a safe choice by the Meléndez-Quiñonez political dynasty that had ruled for fifteen years. But a large contingent of artisans and workers, listening to his words of change and progress, also supported him. Once elected, Romero Bosque quickly broke from the regime, quite likely in part for personal reasons.[16] He started by lifting the state of siege that had dominated the decade. What followed was the rise of a civil society unprecedented in El Salvador's history.[17] Rural and urban workers began organizing openly. The emergent news media began to disseminate more diverse views.

In 1930, Romero Bosque refused to anoint a successor. Five new political parties competed in the country's first (reasonably) free elections. Arturo

Araujo, a landowner with progressive ideals, won. His election raised hopes across the country. But the timing was bad, very bad. The October 1929 Wall Street crash had changed everything. El Salvador's national income had dropped by half after coffee prices began falling. A third of the tenant farmers had been forced off their land. Popular unrest increased. Labor unions and student syndicates called for massive strikes. The chaos forced Araujo to declare martial law. The military overthrew his government in December, and hardline General Maximiliano Hernández Martínez (known by his maternal surname, Martínez) took over.

For six weeks after the coup, Indian and ladino peasants and workers, many affiliated with Communist Party-linked groups, organized a series of strikes and protests. On 22 January 1932, they launched a well-planned uprising, attacking army garrisons, telegraph offices, and city halls and briefly holding a dozen towns in the western, coffee-growing region.[18] The rebels killed no more than fifteen to twenty people. But Martínez responded with what has been described as hysteria. He ordered the immediate executions of insurgents. Soldiers killed far more than those who had participated in the uprising. Most of the victims were indigenous, though ladinos likely made up half the rebels.[19] The massacre devastated indigenous communities. It also demolished political dissent. Martínez's rule began fifty years of direct military rule characterized by coercive labor practices and repressive policing.

Among those killed was a young man and Communist Party leader from a landowning family, Agustín Farabundo Martí, whose name would be taken up by the FMLN a half century later. The remembered event would also play a central role in the formation of ARENA, the right-wing party founded in 1980 that won the presidency in 1989 and stayed in power for twenty years. ARENA opened each new presidential campaign in the town of Izalco, the symbolic center of the massacre, where candidates declared, "Here we buried communism!"[20]

The Matanza became a central reference in Salvadoran history, *the* big story, interpreted and reinterpreted according to the contingencies of the political moment. For the political left, it has served as a story of class warfare, demonstrating the ruthless nature of El Salvador's bourgeoisie and military. More recently it has become a tale of racism and genocide. For the political right, the story of 1932 became a cautionary tale that the state would trundle out whenever deemed necessary—especially when agrarian reform, or any kind of redistribution of power or resources, threatened. The specter of communism condensed into an image of the peasantry rising up with machetes—or what has been called the *indio comunista*.[21] Such views would harden in the 1960s and 1970s, merging threats of peasant organizations, workers' unions, priests and nuns and guerrillas into an outlaw specter of criminals and terrorists. These figures inevitably haunted crime stories that circulated in a newly democratizing El Salvador of the 1990s.

Democracy, Prosperity, and Security

In the immediate post-civil war years, social scientists and journalists discussing the transition would lament El Salvador's authoritarian political culture. "El Salvador is not a case of re-democratization; there was no legacy of democratic institutions to draw on," they asserted.[22] For most of its history it has been ruled by "a self-serving oligarchy allied with a praetorian military," they declared.[23] To these experts the big story is a tragic one, defined by El Salvador's lack. But a lack of democratic tradition of governance does not purge political feelings in the population. It does not preclude democratic desires. The continually thwarted struggle for democracy may be the biggest story in twentieth-century Salvadoran history.

As the buildup to the 1932 uprising shows, the possibilities of liberatory politics have overtaken popular imagination at several critical junctures in Salvadoran history. Another important episode of democratic aspirations and political opening occurred twelve years after the Matanza. The people rose up to overthrow Martínez. This was the same time, 1944, that Guatemalans deposed their own dictator, Jorge Ubico, and launched a democratic decade known as "The Ten Years of Spring." El Salvador enjoyed only five months of such a spring. In May, Martínez stepped down under pressure from a coalition of state employees, professionals, and urban workers who collaborated in Gandhi-inspired actions of noncooperation, refusing to attend work or school. Then in October, the military staged another coup. The new government quashed the opposition and clamped down on dissent.[24] The country had to wait twenty years for another upsurge of democratic desires.

What incites democratic desires in a place with no firm democratic tradition? Indeed, what kinds of democracy have Salvadorans desired? This question is important for understanding expectations after the 1992 peace accords—for grasping how the Salvadoran story was supposed to "end." Political scientists tend to delimit democracy in their taxonomy of political forms as comprising regular, competitive elections with universal suffrage, as well as political accountability of the state to the population. But, as historian Greg Grandin reminds us, when the United Nations was founded in 1945 democracy was broadly seen as entailing both human freedom and social equality. In his own research Grandin has worked with Guatemalans struggling against "daily traps of humiliation and savagery" of an exclusionary, exploitative society. In the mid-twentieth century, he argues, they shared "a commonsensical understanding of democracy not as a procedural constitutionalism but as the felt experience of individual sovereignty and social solidarity." [25]

The post-World War II global wave of anticolonial resistance inspired many Central Americans. In El Salvador it shaped political commitments of a generation of educated middle-class young people born about the time of the Matanza. Many of them came of age with the overthrow of Martínez—only to see the military coup five months later. They then watched the decade-long rise of democracy in Guatemala—only to see it killed by a CIA-backed coup in 1954. The sensibilities born of these experiences are documented through the writings of a group of politically engaged artists called the "Committed Generation." The poet Roque Dalton coined the name in an editorial in which he insists that art and literature must change the world. Dalton, a committed Communist Party member, would be arrested several times—charged with organizing student protests on one occasion, and found with the "communist propaganda" of a book of poetry by Cuban Nicolás Guillén on another—before going into exile in 1961. [26]

The 1959 Cuban revolution inspired political movements throughout the region. In 1961, a group of Nicaraguan intellectuals formed the Sandinista Front for National Liberation (Frente Sandinista de Liberación Nacional; FSLN); they spent nearly two decades planning for a popular revolution and insurrection that would lead to the overthrow of dictator Anastasio Somoza in 1979. The Guatemalan insurgency arose in that moment as well; in April 1961 students and members of the outlawed Communist Party marched in Guatemala City's streets to protest their government's participation in training Cuban exile mercenaries for the Bay of Pigs invasion. Three protestors were killed when the military opened fire.

While political ideas of democracy were growing and sometimes radicalizing among activist Latin Americans, the concept was being deployed in rather different ways in powerful global institutions of the Cold War. Democracy there functioned as the simple antithesis to an ominous gray image of Soviet communism. Primarily as *not-communism*, it promoted individualism, property rights, and free-market economics. Promoting this perspective became an urgent task to the United States after the Cuban revolution (and Bay of Pigs failure) threatened its hegemony in its own "backyard." So the Kennedy administration launched Alliance for Progress in Latin America in 1961, linking "political freedom" with capitalist economic planning, development, and the flow of foreign investments. To broaden its appeal it tolerated some welfare-state features, such as limited agrarian reform, nationalized resources such as oil, and social security systems offering limited health care and pensions. In El Salvador, Col. Julio Adalberto Rivera, who ran unopposed for the presidency in 1962 (following a military coup two years earlier), quickly "molded himself as an Alliance for Progress President."[27]

For a time the top-down modernizing vision encouraged by the United States produced strong statistics. The agro-export economy, not just coffee but also cotton and sugar, expanded. The industrial base grew, especially for manufacturing light products. The Central American Common Market (CACM) began operating in 1960, promoting an import-substitution model (in which finished goods were produced for a "domestic" market spanning Guatemala to Panama) and helping to further integrate the region into the global economy. In 1964 and 1965 El Salvador's annual economic growth rate hit 12 percent, the highest in Latin America, raising living standards among most urban groups and the rural middle and upper classes—though not among the poor majorities.[28]

El Salvador's space for democratic energy started to widen again. The electoral system changed in 1963 to permit proportional representation. This move gave opposition parties, led by the newly formed Christian Democrats, a voice in governance. State spending on education rose, with more and more literacy programs, grade schools, and universities. My friend Urias Betoel Escobar here in Illinois tells a story that shows the almost flamboyant surge of hope of that moment: one day some strangers from the capital came to his school and administered tests to all the young people in rural Santa Rosa de Lima in the eastern part of the country. They chose *him* to be one of the first music students at the Centro Nacional de Arte, though he had no training. Almost all their teachers were U.S. Peace Corps volunteers, who passed on to their students a passionate belief in possibilities for the future—it was 1968, after all. That, he laughs, was how a peasant boy from El Salvador became a trombone player in a symphony orchestra, in Costa Rica and then Colorado: the audacious optimism of that moment.

That collective energy spilled across the nation. Political activism filled the streets. It was fueled in part by a university population that quadrupled between 1960 and 1971 to more than twelve thousand. More and more labor unions formed, including the National Association of Salvadoran Educators (Asociación Nacional de Educadores Salvadorenos; ANDES-21 de Junio). Rural organizing reemerged for the first time since the 1920s. The U.S. Agency for International Development (USAID) supported peasant organizations, and the Christian Democrats and the Catholic Church launched rural cooperative programs and peasant leagues. The church, inspired by new ecclesiastical doctrines of social justice and a preferential option for the poor, sent priests and laypersons across the country. Christian base communities began to form, emphasizing reading the Bible for liberatory messages—and for the place of the poor in a big story of capitalist expansion and exploitation.

Most of the rural poor were not recruited to play classical trombone. They still had few options. Their wages stagnated, even in the years of growth. Landlessness also rose through the 1960s, from 12 to 29 percent, partly because of population growth but mainly due to greater concentration of land ownership.[29] As many as 300,000 Salvadorans migrated north to squat in more sparsely populated Honduras. Most peasants who stayed in El Salvador remained tied to a coercive labor regime that demanded their services for brief, intense periods. The percentage of rural residents dependent on temporary wage work grew from 51 to 60 percent.[30]

Astounding social and economic inequality marked El Salvador. In a slim 1964 *Life* World Library volume on Central America, a chapter called "The Great Families" points out that only in El Salvador, among the six Central American nations, was there a millionaire *class*.

> The *Catorce Grande* [Big Fourteen] . . . live the lives of men of wealth. They have lavish homes in town and imposing estates in the country. They work in fancy, air-conditioned offices and drive to work in flashy sports cars. The women wear the latest dresses from New York, Paris and Rome. . . .
>
> Members of the Catorce Grande [have] done a great deal for the Salvadoran economy. El Salvador is a highly developed country by Central American standards. . . .
>
> Until recently, however, the Catorce Grande resisted social change. It took a military dictatorship, which seized power in 1960, to force them to pay their workers of minimum wage of seventy cents a day, to reduce slum rents and to make other reforms necessary. . . .
>
> Many of the sons of the other families have returned from schools in the U.S. with the idea that Indians and *mestizos* are human beings, not animals. However, this is still a minority view.[31]

Such attitudes constituted, and were constituted through, a form of distrust that only intensified with the rising prosperity. The paramilitary networks that traditionally policed the countryside increased even during this time of democratic opening. The government may have acceded to some political liberalization, but it hardly forgot the threat of subversion. It soon began to reorganize its intelligence activities with technical assistance from the United States. Anticommunism, after all, had been the impetus for the Alliance for Progress. And the Salvadoran oligarchy, raised on stories of the terror of the subversive rebellion and the Matanza, was nothing if not anticommunist. A paramilitary network known as the Democratic Nationalist Organization (ORDEN) was founded in the mid-1960s to surveil suspicious activities in the countryside (seen in practices such as peasant organizing). Betoel Escobar, the trombone player, recalls those years as times of political liberation—but also of danger. He and his fellow students—musicians, actors, and painters—were under constant suspicion as subversives for the simple fact of studying the arts, having long hair, singing. (Ironically, the left also distrusted them, since their teachers were gringos—sure to be spies.) He recalls how, the night of one large protest rally in 1971, no one could leave the school grounds—the National Guard had surrounded them, convinced they were plotting anarchy.[32] He would go to Costa Rica the next year. He was not there when his father was taken hostage on their farm, when neighbors were murdered, their bodies left out on display. Eventually such "intelligence activities" would be centralized under the National Security Agency of El Salvador (ANSESAL), cooperating closely with the agrarian elites described in the *Life* volume. Early death-squad actions in the 1970s would be traced back to ANSESAL.[33]

Though police repression continued through the 1960s, after the civil war ended in 1992 many Salvadorans looked back on that distant decade almost fondly. "You could walk around late at night and nothing would happen to you," my father-in-law, Don Antonio, once told me. "Even rich people took the buses. President Rivera used to ride his motorcycle to church—the Don Rua—without security guards! The main problem I remember was the police. They would grab you on the street and make you pay to get out of jail, if you weren't carrying [the paper showing you paid] your *viabilidad* (street usage) taxes. Once I had to pay seven colones and fifteen centavos to get my brother out. That was two days' pay!"[34]

In 1969 the five-day war between Honduras and El Salvador broke out. Outside Central America, the conflict became known as "football war," because it erupted after hostile World Cup qualifying matches. The light-

hearted dubbing of the event as an amusing fit of pique between two peripheral little places—the only kind of story that seemed to make subaltern
states legible in the North (beyond proximity to Cold War interests)—belied
the gravity of the situation.[35] Honduras, resentful over imbalances in the
CACM, had passed a law ordering deportation of Salvadoran settlers. Many
of them were small farmers pushed from their own country by land scarcity. El Salvador responded with invasion, bombing the Honduran capital,
Tegucigalpa. Several thousand died; 100,000 deported Salvadorans were left
homeless.[36] The land tenure problem intensified. The CACM disintegrated.
Industrial production slowed. Economic growth stalled. The big story of
progress to democracy faltered.

Repression, Rumors, and Revolution

The 1972 presidential elections became a defining moment in many Salvadorans' faith in the possibility of democracy. A progressive coalition is
widely believed to have won. But the military party declared victory. Though
thousands marched in protest (130,000 gathered in a rally in the Plaza Libertad in the city center), opposition candidate Christian Democrat José
Napoleón Duarte was arrested, tortured, and forced into exile. The fraud
galvanized many activists. Some sought out the clandestine revolutionary
organizations that had been forming among student groups, labor activists,
and Christian peasant leaders. Roque Dalton returned secretly to his country to join a new group supporting armed insurrection, the ERP. (In an act
that still incites animosity among leftists in the country today, in May 1975
he would be murdered by his own comrades, some of whom accused him of
being a spy.[37]) The rise of the Salvadoran insurgency has been traced by sociologist Paul Almeida to the same political dynamic we saw between 1927
and 1932. The liberalization of the 1960s sustained growth in civil society
and social movements. In the subsequent political closure of the early 1970s,
these groups radicalized. But this time there would be no single Matanza to
silence their struggle.

Was war inevitable? Was revolution the only story that could follow?
The government, trying to stave off revolt, proposed modest land reform in
1976 (and would do so again several times). President Arturo Armando Molina promoted it as an "insurance policy" against social upheaval.[38] Landowners fought the legislation with everything they had—including death
squads, which targeted not only leftist activists but also Ministry of Agri-

culture officials. All efforts at reform failed, leading to deeper radicalization of not only peasants but also many members of the middle class. As the national crisis sharpened, the next year's presidential elections, in 1977, saw even more fraud. This time, state security forces shot at the crowd protesting the results in the Plaza Libertad. Between fifty and one hundred died.[39]

For many Salvadorans, the war had started by then. Some historians date the conflict to the January 1981 FMLN "Final Offensive," in which hundreds died. Others say it began with the 15 October 1979 military coup that overthrew the president, Gen. Carlos Humberto Romero. But people living through those events often recount episodes from the mid- or even early 1970s as part of the war. They might speak of kidnappings, such as those of businessmen Ernesto Regalado Dueñas in 1971 or Roberto Poma in 1977 (both died in guerrilla custody).[40] They might name the 30 July 1975 protest march of university students through San Salvador, in which the National Guard and Treasury Police killed at least thirty-seven.[41] Or they might point to the assassinations of priests. Between 1976 and 1977 more than twenty-five Catholic priests were imprisoned, tortured, or murdered.[42] As one saying went at the time, "Be a patriot—kill a priest."

In the 1970s, slogans and rumors circulated as information, as clues to what was happening and what would come next. Any sense of vagueness about when the war became the big story may have something to do with the lack of verifiable facts. Before the war there had been very little independent journalism in El Salvador. The mass media ignored the majority of the population. Few peasants and urban workers could afford the products advertised.[43] (Roque Dalton wrote, "Freedom of the Press/for Don Napoleón Viera Altamirano/and the Dutrizes . . . /is worth several million dollars: . . . what they receive every day from the big/retailers industrialists and ad agencies."[44]) The only television news program in the country, *Teleprensa*, largely dedicated itself to "society news." After all, only the elites and the bourgeoisie—not "the masses"—could afford televisions.[45] Most people listened to radio.

As guerrilla strength grew, censors choked the already limited dissemination of political news. "The repression was brutal," the founders of the FMLN's clandestine Radio Venceremos recall. "The written media became ineffective. If you had a (revolutionary) flyer with you, this could cost you your life."[46] Between January 1980 and June 1981, seventeen news offices and radio stations would be bombed or machine-gunned, twelve journalists would be killed, and three would be disappeared.[47] Seeking to broadcast their views, guerrillas would carry out lightning takeovers of radio stations, arriving with cassettes and guns and demanding the managers play their messages.

✦ In early 1980, National Guard major Roberto D'Aubuisson, rising star of the extreme right, organizer of death squads, and founder of the ARENA party, sent his own messages through mass media. He made several television spots in which he named priests, activists, and others as "part of El Salvador's terrorist conspiracy" planning to "deliver the country to a totalitarian regime." D'Aubuisson's targets feared for their lives. Some went into exile, some disappeared, some were found dead. The day after D'Aubuisson denounced prominent Christian Democrat Mario Zamora, on 22 February 1980, six armed, masked men broke into his home and shot him ten times.[48] Archbishop Óscar Arnulfo Romero, whose increasingly radical masses were broadcast on diocese radio, would be next.[49]

Murder of the Archbishop

It was, finally, the martyrdom of Romero that left no question about war in El Salvador. His murder was a truly big story—one that continues to be told, traveling through Vatican City as theologians and cardinals consider petitions for his sainthood. In 1980, the story brought the entire world's attention to Central America.

Romero became archbishop in February 1977, a week before the military fired at the protesters in the Plaza Libertad. He said nothing then. Two weeks after that, on 12 March, his friend Father Rutilio Grande was murdered along with a little boy and a seventy-two-year-old man. They had been traveling from Aguilares, a town where peasants had begun to participate in political organizations, to celebrate mass in El Paisnal, a rural community just north of San Salvador.

Grande's assassination transformed the archbishop. At that moment he embraced the preferential option for the poor enunciated in the 1968 Latin American Bishops' Conference in Medellín, Colombia. After the assassination, this new archbishop, originally selected for his conservatism, went to Aguilares to collect the bodies of the victims. He said, "I have the job of picking up the trampled, the corpses, and all that the persecution of the church dumps along the road on its way through."[50]

Romero brought stories of those bodies into his sermons every week. He "put their lives in his mouth." He became their voice, *la voz de los sin voz* (the voice of the voiceless). His sermons were full of what many people, especially the poor majority, saw as the reality of El Salvador, despite all state efforts to project a story of a modernizing democracy. Salvadoran Jesuit theologian Jon Sobrino writes: "In front of those who wanted to portray what they called the 'true' image of the country, Monsignor Romero answered . . . that it had all been built with blood. 'What good are beautiful highways and airports, all these beautiful skyscrapers, if they are fashioned with the clotted blood of the poor, who will never enjoy them?'"[51]

In his homilies the archbishop listed names of disappeared people. He read the names of fathers and daughters found discarded on roadsides, he repeated the names of kidnap victims. As he predicted, he became one of those names when he was murdered on 24 March 1980, shot in the chest while saying mass at the chapel in the Hospital Divina Providencia in San Salvador. The day before on the radio he had pleaded with soldiers to put down their arms rather than kill their brothers. To their leaders, he said, "In the name of God, in the name of this suffering people whose cries rise up to Heaven more urgently with each day that passes, I beseech you, I beg you, I order you to stop the repression!"[52] During his funeral mass a week later, a bomb went off in the plaza outside the Metropolitan Cathedral. Snipers shot into the crowd of 50,000. Forty died and two hundred were wounded. The investigation carried out by the Commission on the Truth for El Salvador, more than twelve years later, would conclude that D'Aubuisson had planned the murder.

More than 8,000 others died in the war that year.[53] Some victims were noncombatants, such as the three hundred Chalatenango villagers murdered in May by National Guard and ORDEN paramilitaries who suspected them of being guerrillas. They died fleeing across the Sumpul River into Honduras. The Honduran military refused to let them onto the other side.[54] Other victims were open members of the political opposition, such as six leaders of the Democratic Revolutionary Front (FDR). They were abducted from a San Salvador school one November morning by a group of Treasury Police officers. They were tortured before being murdered and dumped into public streets.[55] Though both incidents hit the international headlines, it was the December 1980 murder of three North American nuns and a religious lay worker by the National Guard that got the most global attention.[56]

Just at that time, in the last months of 1980, the FMLN was forming as a coalition of five guerrilla factions: the Popular Liberation Forces (FPL); People's Revolutionary Army (ERP); National Resistance (RN), a group that had broken off from the ERP after Roque Dalton's murder; Central American Workers' Party (PRTC); and Communist Party. It would claim to have more than 5,000 militia when in January 1981 it launched the "Final Offensive," named to emulate the May–July 1979 Sandinista Front for National Liberation action in neighboring Nicaragua. The FSLN overthrow of the dictator Anastasio Somoza had inspired the Salvadoran guerrilla combatants. After they failed to repeat the Sandinista story—they could not spark an urban popular uprising—they turned to the countryside to raise their army. Some people joined out of outrage at the increasing repression, whether against themselves or family members or priests. Others became guerrillas seeking vengeance against local landlords or ORDEN. While some combatants were forcibly recruited by the FMLN, many concluded that revolution was the only way to make change, after the failure of the reform movements of the previous decade. Political scientist Elisabeth Wood identifies a "pleasure of agency" in the moral commitment and emotional engagement of Salvadoran peasants in the insurgency.[57] The guerrilla forces, supported by a vast underground network of civilians who gave them food and supplies, eventually took about a quarter of Salvadoran territory as "liberated zones." At its height in 1984, some estimates suggest the FMLN had as many as 12,000 combatants.

The Salvadoran armed forces would also grow tremendously at that time. In one of his last acts as U.S. president, on 14 January 1981, Jimmy Carter restored military aid that had been suspended the previous month after the murders of the North American churchwomen. Carter pointed to evidence of Nicaraguan aid to the Salvadoran rebels as a reason to dispatch another $5 million to the country.[58] Over the next eleven years, the United States would send $6 billion in economic, military, and covert aid. The money would go to increase the size of the military from 15,000 to 60,000; to augment military power with helicopters and gunships; and to restructure and professionalize the forces, creating groups such as the Rapid Deployment Infantry Battalions specializing in counterinsurgency tactics. Within a year, on 11 December 1981, the first of those groups, the Atlacatl Battalion, would carry out the largest atrocity of the war, in northern Morazán. It killed more than a thousand men, women, and children in an event known as the El Mozote massacre.[59]

Hundreds of international reporters had arrived in the country by then.[60] The place became a proving ground for would-be war correspondents, much like Iraq or Afghanistan some twenty years later. At the University of Michigan in 2000 I met a journalist on a year's fellowship who, hearing about my research, told me, "Oh, yeah," he'd "done Salvador." Stories were not hard to come by, even as the Salvadoran and U.S. governments tried to deny or downplay military atrocities (most famously in the cover-up of El Mozote). Between 1979 and 1983, as many as 40,000 Salvadoran civilians, including many students and labor and religious activists, were killed.[61] The seeming clarity of the struggle—suffering peasants and workers rising up against arrogant oligarchs and generals who refused even the most modest land reform (or, conversely, communists bent on world domination invading a country determined to defend its "freedom")—caught writers' and poets' and filmmakers' imaginations and inspired a broad-based solidarity movement in the United States and Europe.[62] Many tried to tell the big story themselves. Carolyn Forché wrote a famous poem about dining with a colonel who poured a pile of dried-peach-half-like human ears from a grocery sack and said, "As for the rights of anyone, tell your people they can go fuck themselves."[63] Joan Didion and Oliver Stone produced their separate *Salvadors*, a dread-filled novelesque essay and a frenetic Hollywood movie.[64] Italian Gillo Pontecorvo, seeking a project for which he felt as much passion as he had about his anticolonial classic *The Battle of Algiers*, came close to directing a film on Romero.[65]

This was not the news the U.S. administration wanted to get out. By then the story of saving El Salvador (and redeeming U.S honor after Vietnam) had become an all-consuming project for the young neoconservative idealists who surrounded newly elected President Ronald Reagan. They aimed not only to empower the military to defeat the guerrillas, but also to establish a legitimate government through democratic elections. "The country was brought under U.S. tutelage in a manner unprecedented in Central American history, except perhaps for the U.S. occupation of Nicaragua in earlier decades of the twentieth century," sociologist William Robinson would later declare. "U.S. intervention thoroughly penetrated and transformed Salvadoran society—apart from those areas under FMLN control—from government ministries, to social service institutions, the private sector the mass media, and civil society organizations."[66]

The United States did not immediately find suitable allies in its efforts. The Christian Democrats—or the remnants left after repression and defections to the insurgency—became the "moderate" alternative to the extremists in ARENA. José Napoleón Duarte had returned from exile in Venezuela after the 15 October 1979 coup. He joined the governing military junta the following March. With massive financial support from U.S. sources, he won the 1984 presidential elections against D'Aubuisson. Some analysts date the

Salvadoran transition from this moment, even as it took seven more years and the loss of about 35,000 more lives to end the war.

Paradoxical Spaces for Stories

As Ignacio Martín-Baró, a Jesuit priest and sociologist at the Central American University (UCA), would write in 1989—shortly before his murder—the U.S.-led counterinsurgency project starting in 1983 actually opened up public dialogue in El Salvador. It offered a "paradoxical space for communication" in which many new stories could be told.[67] The newly elected Duarte needed to bolster his democratic credibility in both Salvadoran and world eyes. He began by loosening restrictions on the mass media. What followed would be called a news "boom." It started with a state-run news program that often clashed with the nation's business sector but also critiqued the government. In 1985 a commercial program called *Noticiero Al Día* debuted on Channel 12, owned by independent and politically unaffiliated businessman Jorge Zedan. It immediately drew an audience—and advertising dollars. It carried "*testimonios* by the population affected by the combat . . . [and] the voices of unions, students, combatants." Many such reports were brought in by a rising young journalist named Mauricio Funes who in 2009 would be elected president on the FMLN ticket. Much of his appeal would later be rooted in a reputation for integrity (he was never a guerrilla and only joined the party when he became a candidate).[68]

On the program, the outspoken Jesuit priest Ignacio Ellacuría, rector of the UCA (he would be killed in 1989 along with Martín-Baró) would debate rising ARENA activists. Reemergent civil-society organizations, such as labor unions and church human rights groups, would be invited to speak. When the profitability of Zedan's Channel 12 venture became clear, more news outlets followed. They began to compete with each other for stories of war. The commodity of representation of violence had found a domestic market. By 1987 one survey showed that three-quarters of San Salvador's population informed themselves by television news. Five years earlier the majority got their news from the radio.[69]

The war inspired a new kind of knowledge production in El Salvador, in which big stories could potentially be challenged through networks of news reporting. The thousands of foreign correspondents who had come for the war made an impression on young Salvadorans. Local reporters worked for the internationals as assistants, and with them as colleagues. Often, the guerrillas would speak only to international reporters, who would tip off their local colleagues to events. Despite all horrific stories of the war's savagery, then, for most of the 1980s El Salvador was never fully engulfed in what some social scientists and writers have described as a totalizing "culture of terror" or "culture of fear."[70] People wanted to *know*; navigating the atmosphere of *not-knowing* the state promulgated in its efforts to maintain political control, Salvadorans worked to decipher the traces and fragments and aporias and absences that circulated in rumors and news reports. Many of them knew how to read (or how not to read) the right-wing newspaper *El Diario de Hoy* or to listen to the dominant radio news outlet YSKL, perhaps in tandem with the clandestine Radio Venceremos. "Reality" was not fully up for grabs—even as most news media self-censored while the military watched over them.[71] This was the paradox of the war. More knowledge was being produced than ever before about, and within, their country. The war forced the development of a news media infrastructure that had never existed before.[72]

Of course, in the aftermath of disappearances and kidnappings, in the sites of ongoing repression, a more existential *not-knowing* envelops everyday living. Anthropologist Linda Green wrote of "fear as a way of life" during ethnographic fieldwork among Mayan widows in highland Guatemala in the 1980s. More than 200,000 Guatemalans were killed in the civil war between 1960 and 1996, when peace accords were signed in that country. Green vividly portrays how among the Mayan women she knew fear expanded far beyond the coordinates of formal politics, much as it did among rural Salvadorans. Violence and militarization suffused people's embodied interactions with the world. Green points to the power of ambiguity, of *not-knowing* why some people were targeted, in maintaining domination over a population's feelings and activities.[73] Susan Coutin infers the same kind of political subjectivity among Central Americans applying for refugee status in the United States in the 1980s and 1990s. During the Salvadoran and Guatemalan civil wars, she writes, "continual violence, surveillance, and interrogation made the causes of persecution unclear and defined average people as potentially subversive."[74] This uncertainty—the inability to discern precisely what actions put one at risk—is a key tactic used in state terrorism.

Spectacular acts of intimidation—massacres, abductions, torture—decreased in El Salvador after 1984, as the U.S. strategy of democracy promotion and low-intensity warfare began to show results. Human rights training seemed to limit more egregious violence (as some officers connected with major abuses were removed from their positions). The guerrillas, too, changed their strategies, breaking into small units and retreating to the countryside to engage in smaller-scale maneuvers. President Duarte proposed peace dialogues, and held several summits with the FMLN and the military. Still, the Christian Democrats lost support with continued conflict and a deteriorating economy. Many people became disillusioned with Duarte's inability to deliver promised land reform. The powerful right-wing business sector also fiercely opposed him, sure he was pro-communist. The October 1986 earthquake exacerbated the crisis, causing $1 billion in damage and destroying more than 50,000 homes. ARENA took the majority in the legislative assembly in 1988, and the presidency in 1989.

One more horrific big story would circulate globally before the war ended. On 11 November 1989, five soldiers from the Atlacatl Battalion shot and killed Martín-Baró, Ellacuría, four of their fellow Jesuit priests, and their housekeeper and her sixteen-year-old daughter, at their residence in the Pastoral Center on the UCA campus. The UN Truth Commission, noting the "nightmare image" of a bullet hole in a portrait of Monsignor Romero, called it "the final outburst of the delirium that had infected the armed forces and the innermost recesses of certain government circles."[75]

The Jesuits were massacred in the midst of a major guerrilla attack in San Salvador. The November 1989 offensive became the most powerful experience of war for many Salvadorans living in the capital. People from poor and working-class barrios of Soyapango have told me of watching hundreds of guerrillas pass by silently at dawn, of sharing their food with the *compas,* and of having to evacuate en masse with white flags after days without water or food. Wealthy Escalón residents have shared the shock of seeing dead bodies outside their gates—and the grim amusement with which they watched guerrilla combatants from the countryside peer curiously into their cabinets, confusing cat food and human food. People from other neighborhoods have described listening to bombs as they huddled inside their homes with friends and family—and then hearing rumors about the murders of the Jesuits.

The news media played a potent role in that event. The knowledge it produced would be simultaneously infused with the *not-knowing* tactic of state terror. In fact the government took over the airwaves, declaring a state of emergency. Channel 12's *Noticiero Al Día* went black rather than broadcast military-vetted information. At the same time some radios broadcast call-in programs dominated by anonymous voices demanding the murder of "the terrorists." For days reports insisted that guerrillas had killed the priests (a sign left near the bodies said, "The FMLN has executed the spies who turned on them. Victory or death. FMLN"; some crime storytellers I met nearly a decade later insisted that that version of events was true, even though two army men had been convicted of the murders in 1991 [76]).

Three days into the siege, the FMLN called for a general uprising. The people did not respond as the insurgents hoped. The military, with its air power, drove the guerrilla units out of the capital. The offensive forced all the parties to recognize a stalemate. The FMLN could not win, though the offensive proved its continuing capacity to inflict damage on centers of power. The military could not win, even though ARENA's Alfredo Cristiani had taken the presidency six months earlier. ARENA, now dominated by a faction of financial elites, wanted to make a deal; many of its leaders were more interested in getting on with business in a globalizing economy than with fighting. The U.S. Congress, pressured by constituents outraged by the killing of the Jesuits, threatened to cut military assistance. The new president, George H. W. Bush, was not sure he wanted to keep up a Cold War conflict in the face of rapidly changing geopolitics. The Berlin Wall had fallen on 9 November, 1989, just days before the San Salvador offensive.

The FMLN and the Salvadoran government would meet over a period of nearly two years to negotiate the end of the war, their discussions mediated by the United Nations. On 16 January 1992, in Chapultepec Castle in Mexico City, they signed the peace agreements.

Stories Behind the Big (Success) Story

This big story usually ends with the pronouncement of peace. Since that moment when the guerrillas and the government officials shook hands in front of the cameras, the United Nations has repeatedly pointed to the Salvadoran peacekeeping and human rights monitoring missions as "paradigmatic" and "pioneering." After the United Nations Observer Mission in El Salvador (known as ONUSAL, its Spanish acronym) shut down in 1995, the Security Council passed a resolution recognizing ONUSAL's feat in guiding El Salvador as it "evolved from a country riven by conflict into a democratic and peaceful nation."[77] The Salvadoran showcase buttressed UN Secretary-General Boutros Boutros-Ghali's vision of an activist United Nations, promoting peace through democracy around the world.[78]

Academic experts and international relations types generally have concurred that El Salvador offers one of "the most dramatic and positive recent political achievements in the Western hemisphere."[79] Such authoritative voices have largely set the tone for the production of knowledge about the Salvadoran story. Political scientist Terry Lynn Karl, for example, labeled it a "negotiated revolution" and pronounced the Central American country's experience as a model: "Future policy for dealing with regional conflicts can benefit from the experience of El Salvador."[80] The reasons for El Salvador's feats vary in analysts' accounts, but that the case is a successful one is rarely in doubt. Elisabeth Wood, for example, privileges insurgents' counterhegemonic agency as crucial in driving the government to the negotiating table. She calls El Salvador's transition a case of democracy "forged from below via a revolutionary social movement."[81] William Robinson, in contrast, sees a peace pushed by a transnational, technocratic faction of elites, who formed a "polyarchic democracy" in which a select group of leaders rule and mass participation is limited to voting.[82]

But what happened next? How was it that so very soon after such a successful conclusion to a globally storied conflict, so many Salvadorans were saying it was "worse than the war"? Why did life in peace feel (more) risky and dangerous for the majority of people in the country?[83] What kept them from recognizing El Salvador's achievement the way the experts did? One could answer, sincerely, "It's complicated." Experts in the many public seminars on violence I attended in El Salvador during the 1990s unfurled impressive multicausal charts, with arrows pointing to factors varying from unemployment to international drug trafficking to endemic acculturation to violence to broken families to lack of a history of dialogue to post-traumatic stress to indexes of economic inequality. In the United States, sensationalist media reports became fascinated with a small number of deportees with criminal records, some of whom formed transnational gangs (the most famous being the Mara Salvatrucha). All these factors undoubtedly play a part. But other stories behind the story are rarely recounted. And an important one insists that the lauded peace accords hardly represent a "negotiated revolution." In fact the agreements maintained El Salvador's unjust structures of power. Anthropologist Leigh Binford declared, succinctly, "The 1992 peace accords ended the shooting, but they did not initiate an era of greater social and economic justice."[84] Indeed, as we know, they did not even end the shooting. Risk and danger just took new forms in postwar El Salvador.

The public management of risk may have seemed to be at the core of what was negotiated in nearly two years of meetings between the FMLN and the government in 1990 and 1991. And perhaps it was. Military and police reforms dominated the talks. But not in the sense most observers (and perhaps many participants in the peace agreements) had imagined. In the simplest terms, the FMLN guerrillas had gone to war with an emancipatory politics proposing to radically restructure the economy so that Salvadorans would not have to live desperate lives constantly at risk of disaster. They could not do so, either in battle or at the negotiating table. In the end, it was ARENA that would radically restructure the economy. It was ARENA that would launch the "liberation movement"—but for elites' unconstrained accumulation of capital, not the masses' rights to inclusion.[85] Individual risk-taking and everyday insecurity, intensified but thoroughly familiar elements of late modernity's "risk climate," long part of most poor people's ontologies, became sanctified features of economic existence in El Salvador after 1992.[86]

Shock Doctrine

The peace accords marked not a beginning but a midpoint in the implementation of a series of market-oriented reforms in governance commonly known as "structural adjustment" toward a neoliberal economy. When the United States intervened in the war, it aimed to do more than merely defeat the guerrillas, more than just "save" El Salvador from communism. In fact it wanted to knock out the oligarchs as well as the rebels. It aspired to modernize the country, principally by remaking it as a model free-market democracy in which capital gained maximum mobility. The public struggles over human rights and democratic advances during the twelve-year civil war had masked processes pitched toward economic globalization.

El Salvador offers a clear case of what journalist Naomi Klein calls the "Shock Doctrine," in which societies reeling from some kind of shock are reengineered for neoliberal economics.[87] Klein's prime contemporary examples are wartorn Iraq and post-Katrina New Orleans. But as she points out, the myth of the democratic triumph of free-market capitalism had earlier taken hold elsewhere, first in Chile, then through much of Latin America. For El Salvador, William Robinson points to the year 1983, one of the bloodiest in the civil war, as the beginning of the transition to a new mode of governance. At that moment the FMLN guerrillas were on the verge of winning. Masses of Salvadorans were fleeing the chaos as internally displaced persons or refugees and migrants. That same year, a new constitution was written, preparing the country for elections.

However, the year 1983 was crucial not just because of the bloodshed, or the new constitution; it became a pivotal moment because the Foundation for Social and Economic Development (FUSADES) think tank was founded. FUSADES, funded by USAID, aimed to establish a consensus for the development of neoliberal social and economic policies.[88] The U.S. stance was that economic liberalization should accompany the counterinsurgency policy. To that end, in 1985 it began to attach conditions to support to the Salvadoran government, demanding structural adjustment toward a more open economy.[89] In 1989 ARENA's Cristiani won the presidency. His government, following a blueprint drawn up by FUSADES, immediately launched a full-blown economic liberalization program. It started by eliminating price controls, deregulating interest rates, and cutting public spending, especially in public services such as education and health care. Next it reprivatized the banks, granting autonomy to the Central Reserve Bank, a move that allowed the financial sector to concentrate its power.[90] Even before the war ended, El Salvador was well on its way to becoming a model—not of peace, at least as imagined by revolutionaries and solidarity movements, but of neoliberalism.

Neoliberalism first refers to the tenets of a Smithian market economy. It is linked to theories of Milton Friedman and a generation of University of Chicago economists who opposed interventionist Keynesian economic theories and believed fervently in the democratic possibilities of a radically free market.[91] Its earliest state practice emerged in Chile, where Friedman advised dictator Augusto Pinochet. But since the early 1980s it has taken on several new modes of meaning. The mode promoted by the International Monetary Fund (IMF) and the World Bank through the 1980s and 1990s focused on privatizing public entities, encouraging investment, and eliminating trade barriers. This is an orientation many Latin Americans know well. It echoes the impulses of liberals of the late nineteenth and early twentieth centuries. El Salvador's privatization of communal lands in 1881 and 1882, encouraging peasants to enter the market, perfectly exemplified such classic economic liberalism. The rise of neoliberalism shows once again capital's creative and flexible possibilities. It may be a global force but it constantly articulates itself with local conditions.

Neoliberalism began to take on additional qualities in the early 1990s, aiming not just to free the markets but also to substitute the market for both state and society. Since the Cold War ended, neoliberalism has intertwined with the very idea of democracy. "Democracy," anthropologist Julia Paley tells us, "is now so deeply embedded in a prolonged moment of economic and philosophical liberalism that democracy (as ideology, as experience, as expectation, as policy) is co-produced with market economics, a phenom-enon neatly captured by the phrase 'free market democracies.'"[92] (Or have we been duped into calling it democracy? After all, "A democratic election can enhance a country's credit rating, regardless of how national decisions are made," as anthropologist of Guatemala Diane Nelson cracks.[93])

Even as neoliberalism linked to democracy as a *political* form, in its more philosophical mode neoliberalism recast governing activities as *non-political* problems in need of technical solutions. It sought rationalizing, optimizing outcomes that maximized efficiency rather than expanded citizenship rights. Furthermore, in a constructivist mode, neoliberalism of the post-Cold War moment did *not* assume, as in classic liberalism, a natural tendency toward the market. Rather, it aimed to *instigate* this ostensibly apolitical market rationality in all spheres of society.

In particular it has worked as a "technology of self," fashioning the kind of "free" person desired by the market economy. It aims to produce neo-liberal citizen-subjects as unmoored, ahistorical, and risk-taking yet rational, private agents.[94] Citizens are reenvisioned as "autonomous, individual bearers of rights who 'must entrepreneurially fashion their overall personal development through wider relations to the marketplace.'"[95] In different contexts this project has played out differently, though always in the logic of global capitalism. In the United States, efforts to inculcate individual mar-ket orientations were exemplified by President Bill Clinton's 1996 welfare re-form in which moralistic "individual responsibilization" became the goal.[96] In Guatemala, such subject formation has targeted indigenous peoples in a form of "neoliberal multiculturalism" which, by granting cultural rights while denying equality, has effectively shaped forms of resistance.[97] In El Salvador, neoliberal governance has shaped and been shaped through an entrepreneurial culture focused on the informal sector, as well as by both high migration rates and high crime rates.

I recall during 1995 and 1996 after massive public-sector layoffs every-one commenting on the proliferation of *tiendas* (small shops often in peo-ple's houses) in every neighborhood, as many former state employees used their small buyouts to start their own businesses. Everywhere, people were selling *chocobananos* (frozen chocolate-covered bananas) out of new freez-ers. Or they were flipping *pupusas* (the national dish, fat tortillas stuffed with meat, beans, and/or cheese) on new grills in garages converted to picnic-table-furnished eateries. Or they were importing used car parts from North American junkyards. Or they had managed to nab some kind of job with one of the many new nongovernmental organizations unevenly carrying out some of the functions of a recalibrated state. The decline of government services and jobs intersected with increased remittances migrants sent home, encouraging more and more individualistic economic orientations. At the same time, as we will see in this book, the rise in crime and the sharing of crime stories describing new, individual ways to confront postwar risks also helped to shape this new postwar rationality.

This account of legal, political, and administrative intention should draw attention to another aspect of neoliberalism of the late twentieth and early twenty-first centuries. It is not free, in the sense understood through the concept of laissez-faire economics, in which state intervention is minimized in order to let the market do what it will. It requires concerted institutional efforts to develop. Such efforts include those imposed from the outside, as in the conditions attached to loans from the World Bank or stipulations in regional trade agreements. Within national economies, these efforts include the restructuring of the state regulatory apparatus. This neoliberalism also hardly marks a hallowed "end-of-history" form of human organization when fused with liberal democracy, as was declared to much fanfare soon after the fall of the Berlin Wall in 1989.[98] It is just another phase in capitalist expansion. If this historical articulation was not clear to economists before, by 2007 the global economic crisis and massive state intervention that followed seemed to predict the end of the neoliberalism as an ideologically radical free-market economic form. But of course the history of capital reveals it as creative, expansive, flexible, and ever articulating to changing historical conditions.[99]

Under ARENA even before the war ended, El Salvador's new economic policies quickly drew praise. In March 1991, the journal *Business America* boasted, "The El Salvadoran economy . . . has made remarkable strides in the last eighteen months thanks to a bold new stabilization and structural adjustment program." The journal claimed that the nation's growth rate had reached 3.4 percent in 1990, the highest in many years. It also pointed to an unquantified "boom" in the agricultural sector, and vague "respectable gains" in manufacturing, commercial and service sectors. It encouraged investors to explore the "wide range of Salvadoran government investment incentives and the renowned work ethic of Salvadoran laborers."[100] In an immediate post-Cold War world awash with new capitalists seeking investments for their cash, El Salvador looked like a good bet. Such news brought more international support to the country. The World Bank provided structural adjustment loan packages in 1990–91 and 1993–94. The United Nations Development Programme would later call El Salvador's structural adjustment process "one of the most aggressive of Latin America." [101] By 2001, El Salvador would finally dollarize its economy, allowing for an even freer flow of investments and migrant remittances but effectively raising the cost of living for most Salvadorans, who would say, "We're paid in colones but we have to buy in dollars."

The signing of the peace accords thus both marked a kind of artificial rupture (since the crucial economic transitions predated and presupposed an eventual "peace," long before the details were negotiated) and, in a soft parallel to the atmosphere in postsocialist states, allowed an accelerated shift to the transnational finance model of capital accumulation. Of course El Salvador had its particular differences, most notably the rising tide of migrant remittances, which held up the economy by pumping cash into consumer services and generating high savings rates in the banks.[102]

Were these neoliberal, or market, rationalities entering commonsensical ways of knowing the world in El Salvador? How did people understand and represent to each other ongoing experiences of subjectification, of political-economic oppression, of social injustice? How and when might they recognize legitimations of continuing, or growing, inequality? [103] These are some of the questions that must follow the grand pronouncement of peace at the end of the story: what happened next?

Postwar Crime Wave

In March 1994, my friend Maru had voted with a million and a half other Salvadorans in what were called the country's "elections of the century." The hyperbole referred in part to the simultaneous competition for all public offices—for the president, assembly deputies, and mayors. These were the first contests in which the FMLN participated as a legalized political party. Thousands of international observers as well as ONUSAL monitored the voting. Though they found many irregularities, they certified the contest as legitimate, if "mediocre," conducted under "appropriate conditions in terms of freedom, competitiveness and security." [104] On 1 June 1994, shortly before the truncated trip to Cacaopera that opened this chapter, Maru and I had stood together at the edge of what was then called the Hermano Lejano monument on the Boulevard de los Heroes, waving tiny paper blue-and-white Salvadoran flags with her cheering uniformed fifth-grade students.[105] We waited hours for the newly elected president, Armando Calderón Sol of ARENA (for whom she had *not* voted, Maru assured me), to pass by in a

cacophonous motorcade. Reviewing my photographs years later, I was surprised to see that the portly new president had not merely passed by but descended from his limousine and mingled with the people. He had stood just
two feet away from me. Perhaps these snapshot moments encapsulate the
"success" praised by the United Nations: after a brutal civil war there had
been a nonviolent competition for power in which the winner could safely
step out of his armored vehicle, his bodyguards in relatively inconspicuous
positions, and greet crowds.

A year after the hopes signaled by Calderón Sol's inauguration, in 1995—
just as the UN Security Council was making pronouncements about Salvadoran success—statistics suggested a cruelty in that optimism. El Salvador's
postwar violence levels matched, and perhaps surpassed, war carnage. The
attorney general's office would report 7,877 intentional homicides, a murder rate of 138.9 per 100,000 population—more than the annual wartime
violent death rate, the highest in the Americas and second only to South
Africa in the world. These dramatic figures have since been questioned (one
recent estimate suggests that the rate was about 80 per 100,000).[106] But for
most Salvadorans, usually skeptical of government data, the high figure held
unique truth-value. It was bolstered by headline after headline, all lamenting the crime wave, the crime increase, the crime surge. Such media narration helped frame the stories Salvadorans told and circulated of their own
and others' experiences with everyday insecurity. Crime stories amplified
uncertainty; talk of crime can be contagious, compelling endless analysis, obsessive interpretation, and surplus anxiety.[107] A poll just a year after
the war ended found that 73 percent of the respondents called violence the
country's principal problem—violence in the form of "crime, thievery, lack
of authority, robbery, violations and gangs"—and that 89 percent believed
crime had increased since the peace accords.[108]

These survey results would be replicated through much of the decade,
the frustration doubled by the incapacity of the public security bodies
(whether this was due to state restructuring or the endemic weakness of
the state was unclear). By 1996, 45 percent of the respondents to a national
survey agreed that people had the right to take justice into their own hands
because the government did not provide justice and security. The same proportion approved of the social cleansing of criminals by a clandestine organization called the Sombra Negra (Black Shadow). Two years later more than
half of those polled supported such vigilantism.[109] As José Miguel Cruz, the
independent director of the University Institute of Public Opinion, wrote

in 1997, "Concern about the so-called 'problem of crime' has reached such a level that Salvadorans have become more alarmed about crime than they were worried about the war in the second half of the 1980s." [110] "Peace," then, may have meant absence of war—but it did not *feel* "better" or more secure than before. It didn't mean the end of violence.

And it didn't mean justice. "Those who were excluded from judicial protection at the beginning of the war," writes legal scholar Margaret Popkin, who spent years in El Salvador supporting judicial reform, "still found themselves essentially without recourse, both for what happened to them and their families during the war and for cases that have arisen in the postwar period." [111] The judicial system's actions only exacerbated distrust in the state: statistics even fifteen years after the war ended suggest that only 3 percent of cases *that made it to the courts* ever ended in sentences. [112] The violence of the postwar period, apparently unmoored from any sense of deep motivation, any possibility of redemption, would become mere scandal. [113] It seemed to delegitimate past struggles, robbing meaning from earlier deaths in which people were portrayed as "assassinated as witnesses to faith" in Monsignor Romero's words. [114] Martyrdom such as Romero's, celebrated in the Christian theology of the popular churches, lost at least some of its sense, and the political killings their fierce purpose. [115]

It was precisely after the war, when peace was declared, that Salvadoran mass media and academics and policymakers (left and right) began to frame violence as the *problem* (rather than a symptom of ideological opposition, or of communism, or of a repressive state apparatus). Barely a day passed without some newspaper columnist agonizing over the seemingly apolitical matters of national and citizen security. *Estudios Centroamericanos*, the academic journal of the UCA, dedicated a full issue to "The Culture of Violence in El Salvador." Much of the research was funded by the Inter-American Development Bank (IADB). [116] The IADB is one of a number of institutions that sponsored forums on violence in postwar El Salvador during the 1990s: others included the World Bank, the Pan-American Health Organization, and the United Nations Development Programme, as well as national power brokers such as FUSADES. While debates about violence and policing grew in the early postwar years, the Salvadoran government itself was quite anxious at that particular moment to dismiss the disorder as an internal issue: to *state* as a state that postwar criminality was a domestic problem, unremarkable, not of concern to the international human rights community or to global investors. Political leaders' efforts to assert the state as centralized entity, exercising what Max Weber called the state's "monopoly on the legitimate use of physical force in a given territory," stumbled throughout the next decade.[117] It was only when ARENA fell behind the FMLN in the pre-election polls in mid-2003, after several years of economic decline, that it launched a very public anticrime initiative, Plan Mano Dura (Operation Iron Fist), targeting gangs. It finally declared everyday crime—at least that embodied in defiant young men who did not fit into the neoliberal economic formula—a dire threat to postwar democratic accomplishments.

In the mid-1990s, many people I knew in El Salvador, and countless media commentators and state officials, thought of the overwhelming sense of everyday danger as a postwar phenomenon rather than as a regional (or global) issue. It has since become clear that crime spikes and surges of violence were not just Salvadoran phenomena in that historical moment. By the middle of the first decade of the 2000s, "everyday violence, public insecurity and deteriorating rule of law" had become central concerns in much of Latin America.[118] This rise in criminality has coincided with democratization and structural adjustment, not just in places like El Salvador and Brazil and Haiti, but across the world, in South Africa and Russia and elsewhere.

This millennial crime wave is more than fallout of a post-Cold War economic transition. After all, as anthropologists John and Jean Comaroff contend, criminal economies are often the "most perfect expressions of the unfettered principle of supply and demand."[119] Other analysts link the problem of violence to economic globalizing processes, noting that most "national" economies have been superseded by transnational capital. They point to processes of fragmentation across the planet, to massive dislocations in the wake of collapsed imperial orders or disintegrating postcolonial states, and to a "violence of lumpenproletarianization in many of the world's urban zones."[120] Indeed theories of market efficiency tell us that some disorder is necessary. The market thrives on flexibility, insecurity, and anxiety, on unevenness of knowledge—seeking the territory or product that no one knows yet, that isn't already wired into global flows, and exploiting that disjunction.

Freedom, in post-Cold War democracies, is all about risk. Danger and disorder are not unintended but part and parcel of a market state, just as in late modernity crisis is "not merely . . . an interruption, but a more or less continuous state of affairs."[121] Marx and Engels told us a long time ago of the connection between capitalism and crisis: "Constant revolutionizing of production, uninterrupted disturbance of all social conditions, everlasting uncertainty and agitation distinguish the bourgeois epoch from all earlier ones," as they wrote in 1848. "All that is solid melts into air, all that is holy profaned." [122]

Hope and *Angstbereitschaft*

What can a little mugging mean in the midst of a dramatic reordering of social structure, at the turn of a historic epoch? Recalling Maru's bus-stop assault more than a dozen years later, even knowing now that this kind of criminality would dominate discourse within El Salvador and across the Americas through much of the 1990s, I am still struck by its banality in the context of her own life story. During the months we lived together in 1994, Maru sometimes spontaneously shared glimpses of her experiences in the war era. This was a strong, stubborn young woman who during the 1980s often traveled between Cacaopera, where her family lived in wartorn Morazán, and San Salvador, where she worked as a primary school teacher in the mornings and studied for a university degree in education in the afternoons and evenings. She boasted about challenging soldiers at the frequent military checkpoints on her trips—crossing the Lempa River, leaving the military stronghold of San Francisco Gotera—as they demanded all the bus passengers' papers and sometimes more.

"The soldiers thought we were all guerrillas," she told me. She recounted one occasion when she had registered (as required) with the military in order to get permission to bring back cement and nails to repair her mother's house. The sergeant in charge at one of the stops insisted she must be a guerrilla since "only terrorists need those kinds of things." Another time a soldier tried to accost her sexually as she sat in the back of the bus. She yelled at him—and then refused orders to get off the bus.

Whatever had or had not happened in her past, I believe that what distinguished the assault in June 1994—what made it an unexpected shock—was that Maru simply hadn't been prepared. Perhaps she lacked the right kind of *Angstbereitschaft*, or readiness for anxiety, in Freud's lexicon. Perhaps her "knowledge and sense of power *vis-à-vis* the external world," as Freud put it, limited her capacity to respond at the moment, her anxiety diffuse, paralyzing. [123] During the 1980s, as the war continued for so many years, she believed she *had* felt that she was ready for almost anything, that she knew what might happen, where it might happen, how she might avoid it, and what she might have to do if she couldn't. At least in retrospect she believed this, despite long experience living in the murk of a terrorist state. After all, she had survived. But this new mode of alarm—amid so many other transformations after the 1992 peace accords—in some strange way confounded her. And so she, like countless other Salvadorans, told her post-war crime story again and again.

Chapter 2
Critical Code-Switching and the State of Unexception

El Salvador Rebel Leader Gunned Down in Capital
SAN SALVADOR, October 26 [1993] (REUTERS)—El Salvador's delicate peace process was dealt a blow yesterday as gunmen fatally shot a mid-level leader of the country's former leftist guerrilla movement.

Rebel leaders said the killing bore the hallmarks of a premeditated, death squad-style murder and demanded the arrest of those responsible.

Francisco Velis, 37, was shot in the head at close range by unidentified gunmen shortly before 8 a.m. as he walked his one-year-old daughter in a middle-class neighborhood in the capital San Salvador.

He was the first member of the rebel leadership to be murdered since the end of the country's civil war in 1992, rebel officials said.

"Peace could go to the wall because of things like this," Francisco Jovel, a member of the Farabundo Marti National Liberation Front [FMLN]'s top five-man command, told reporters as he stood by the body.

President Alfredo Cristiani said he had ordered a specialized police unit to investigate the killing and played down its consequences.

"We don't think it is a critical situation . . . We cannot let it become a critical situation," Cristiani said at his regular Monday news conference.

The UN observer mission in El Salvador, known as ONUSAL, condemned the killing as a blow to national reconciliation.

"It harms the extraordinary atmosphere that has reigned in El Salvador," ONUSAL head Augusto Ramírez Ocampo said.

Velis was to run for the National Assembly in March 1994 legislative elections, the first the FMLN will take part in as a legal party. He was also a member of the FMLN's national council and a leader of one of the rebel front's five factions, the Central American Workers' Party.

"The method was the same as in the past, death squad

> *style. . . . Someone knows who they are," said Nidia Diaz, a fellow workers' party leader.*

"We don't think it is a critical situation. . . . We cannot let it become a critical situation." San Salvador's midday news had been filled with lurid images of the morning's featured corpse. This one the body of a former guerrilla leader, limbs splayed on the street, blood and brain bits sprayed over the sidewalk. Reports say he was walking his toddler daughter to a daycare center on a busy avenue near the University of El Salvador when two strangers, men in their twenties, walked up to him. One jammed a pistol into his head. The exploding bullet destroyed his cranium. The child stayed by her father's body drenched in blood. Two National Police officers stood nearby, oblivious: "We saw two men running, but didn't stop them since we didn't know what had happened." [1]

Cristiani's words at that regular Monday afternoon news conference are terse, tense. Just reading them, years later, mediated by tape recorders and transcriptions and reporters and editors, you can still almost feel him tightening his moustache-fringed lips. You practically sense his feet shifting behind the podium as he looks out at the dozens of news correspondents and cameras. You watch him scan familiar faces from the local media, see him note new men and women rotated in by a shrinking international press corps. And you sense him struggling mightily to corral the meaning of this inconvenient dead body. His is not an easy task: This body, after all—this man, Francisco Velis—had, for the full twelve years of civil war, fought in the guerrilla forces. He had, for more than a decade, lived as one condemned to "bare life," existing outside the law (and so defining the law, in the form of his exclusion). [2] He had been a "terrorist," "subversive," in the vocabulary circulated through the army and the government and in most of El Salvador's mass media. As such he had incited Cristiani's own political existence in the thunderous emergence of the fiercely anti-communist Nationalist Republican Alliance (ARENA) party in 1980.

"We. Cannot. Let. It. Become. A. Critical. Situation."

Let us examine Cristiani's statement. The first word, *we,* is already ambiguous. Whom was the president addressing—or rather, what kind of public did he want to call into being? His discourse attempts to effect a certain kind of subject, to interpellate listeners into a common relationship with the state's postwar political project.[3] Most immediately, Cristiani was calling upon local news consumers—Salvadoran citizens—to collaborate in their country's peace process. They must not overreact. They should let the state make the statements; let the state *state*.[4] And they should let the state finally get its mojo back, so to speak—its monopoly on the use of force. At the same time, eyeing the global audience, the people who would read and listen to many of the journalists' reports, Cristiani seemed to be pleading: Please, just as this small country is learning democracy, let's not let it *become a critical situation!*

Critical. Here the word holds at least three meanings. First, *critical* in the sense of condition: the grade of bodily risk assigned to countless gunshot victims in emergency rooms (at that very moment, October 1993, Salvadoran health workers were on strike, protesting miserable conditions in public hospitals that had undoubtedly failed many such critical cases[5]). Critical in this medical sense means, "Vital signs are unstable and not within normal limits. . . . Indicators are unfavorable."[6] Cristiani's *critical* here, however, refers not to the body of Velis but to the body of the nation—of *all* the people. Was it stable? Normal? Would it survive?

Second, there is *critical* in the sense of judging; a guerrilla force, or an opposition political party, is critical of those in power. In this context Cristiani aimed his words at national critics, as well as the world court of opinion. Don't judge us so harshly; we're a nation in transition to democracy, Cristiani was saying to the reporters. Finally, there is *critical* in the sense anthropologist Veena Das describes as "critical events": events after which new modes of action and new forms of politics emerge. Das draws from the work of historians of the French Revolution; her example is the partition of India and Pakistan.[7] The critical event of 25 October 1993, in this sense, would not be the Velis murder, but the 1980–92 civil war itself and its end. The Salvadoran president was trying to channel new modes of action and political forms ultimately produced by that critical event.

This chapter considers the war-to-postwar cusp, when meanings of violent acts were in flux and knowledge of how the world worked was shifting. Questions of inclusiveness—what does "we" mean, and who comprises the nation?—merged with concerns about critical Others—who and what threatens the nation? The previous chapter offered some of the big stories, the Salvadoran narratives of history into which people situated their experiences as crime stories after the war ended. In a moment defined by *not-knowing* what would come next, stories of the past, whether factual or mythical, helped orient people. But they could not explain everything. Growing anxiety about the new situation, and about how to maneuver in an uncertain future, gave rise to the paradoxical sentiment, "It's worse than the war." This chapter examines one way of confronting—attempting to manage—the postwar murk. It develops a theory of *critical code-switching* as a historical practice of categorizing modes of violent action, and explores what possible performative effects this naming had on Salvadoran social imaginaries.[8]

The dominant Salvadoran discourse, largely managed by people in power like Cristiani, insisted that the violence filling the front pages after the war was something different from before, that it signified rupture rather than continuity. It was no longer related to war—it no longer threatened the state—it was no longer critical. And thus it no longer required a state of exception, in the sense the philosopher Giorgio Agamben describes: the legal condition allowing eradication "not only of political adversaries but of entire categories of citizens who for some reason cannot be integrated into the political system."[9] Cristiani was in a sense declaring a state of unexception. By making this argument, the state, reestablished through the violence of war—the state, now dominated by a new transnational faction of elites hitching themselves to capital's latest, savage mode of accumulation—was trying to fabricate a sense of normality in this new form of insecurity. It was attempting to manufacture new knowledge of social relations that would shape a vigorous market logic.[10]

Parsing violent incidents as unexceptional individual acts, as unconnected to social relations or political conditions, could help rupture the old revolutionary and solidary social imaginaries. It could help reconstruct how people envisioned their rights and responsibilities toward each other. Ultimately, these efforts, resignifying violence as noncritical, helped to install the architecture of El Salvador's postwar transition, from an epoch characterized by fear of state and paramilitary and insurgent terror, as well as collective resistance, toward an era of market democracy structured around life as a series of channeled choices—around private responsibility for the management of risk. This risk is ever necessary but always unexceptional and noncritical. The nation is never in danger, just individuals. Crucially, too, this risk is unevenly distributed across genders, races, sexualities, and classes.[11] This disparity in life chances would eventually push the logic of individual risk over the edge, as within a few years racialized young men would be coded as critical national threats to be dealt with collectively, with tough laws and fierce policing.

Critical Code-Switching

During that year after the peace accords, amid growing postwar chaos, Velis's was not the first murky murder. A number of homicides had taken place of disputed classification. Were they "political" or were they "common"? Were they critical extensions of the war, or were they unfortunate, but noncritical and unexceptional, aspects of risk in any modern nation? These were the available options in common discourse. If the peace accords were to retain their aura of triumph, and if El Salvador was to join the ranks of the modern, investment-grade nations, then traces of war and indeed "politics" had to be erased. So attention turned to recategorizing acts of violence, to recoding them, in a way that established a sense of order and normativity. That sense of order was bolstered by a new discourse on technical mastery of criminal investigation, of science rather than politics. What was happening in 1993, then, was a transition in taxonomy—what I call critical code-switching.

To define critical code-switching I find the work of historian Ranajit Guha useful.[12] In his search for subaltern consciousness in colonial India, Guha distinguishes two broad codes of violence: the criminal, which he describes as conspiratorial and individualistic, and the insurgent, which is public and communal. These categories often blur—especially in moments of historical rupture. Common crime and political rebellions both have an "inversive" function, "turning things upside down." This overlap leads people to mistake one for the other. But an insurgency "extricates itself from the placenta of common crime in which it may be initially enmeshed and establishes its own identity as violence which is public, collective, and total in its modalities."[13]

This perspective has its limits; it harbors more than a few traces of a functionalist, evolutionary view.[14] It is the blurring of categories that draws my attention. Guha suggests that this confusion of codes (is it ordinary banditry—dismissible? Is it collective insurgency—a threat?) happens at specific moments of historical rupture. But if we follow Walter Benjamin's familiar observation that "the tradition of the oppressed teaches us that the 'state of emergency' in which we live is not the exception but the rule"—

then we can begin to think of codes not as occasionally overlapping stages steadfastly progressing toward more advanced forms, but power-laden categories of knowledge that fluctuate in historical moments.[15]

Postwar, post-critical event, people—especially those in power, particularly the victors aiming to write history's script—*want* to code-switch. They want to mystify the violent origins of the state, even as they simultaneously celebrate it as the basis of their power. Its pull, made mythical, becomes uncontainable. But even ordinary people—those without wealth or structural access to power—also hope to "go back" to an imagined previous moment of unity and harmony. As Nancy Scheper-Hughes writes, after war, after episodes of horror, "we expect a return to the normative, to peacetime sobriety, to notions of civil society, human rights, the sanctity of the person . . . , *habeas corpus*, and the unalienable rights to the ownership of one's body."[16]

But who are "we"? Again: What is critical?

Before we go on, I must acknowledge that this book, examining the *public* discourses of violence in El Salvador, collaborates in a conventional set of codes. Just as conversational and media discourse are conditioned by the possibilities presented by law and "common sense," so this book focuses on the categories of crime that manifest in empirically measurable bodily damage, the kind adjudicated in state courts.[17] This violence may be coded as criminal or political, intentional or random. But if we could speak outside ideology (or at least expand the ideological grounds on which we speak), we would acknowledge that all forms of violence exist on a continuum that encompasses suffering not easily qualified legally. Along with political violences and ideological targets, there are the structural violences of capitalism, or the symbolic violences of racism and sexism, or the "everyday violences" of routine practices of domestic, interpersonal, or delinquent aggression.[18] Some theorists have suggested that a widespread acceptance of interpersonal violence today in El Salvador links to the country's history of public terror and exclusion, reaching back to the repression on haciendas in the early twentieth century.[19] Whatever the origins or reasons, these other violences—Elizabeth Povinelli calls their effects the "cruddy, cumulative and corrosive aspects of life [that] have spread so deep into the everyday"[20]—are often normalized by global human rights discourses that focus on the weight of war or genocide as aberrations. But, Scheper-Hughes asks,

> What if a climate of anxious, ontological insecurity about the rights to ownership of one's body was fostered by a studied, bureaucratic indifference to the lives and deaths of "marginals," criminals and other no-

account people? What if the public routinization of daily mortifications
and little abominations, piling up like so many corpses on the social
landscape, provided the text and blueprint for what only appeared later
to be aberrant, inexplicable, and extraordinary outbreaks of state violence
against citizens?[21]

The relative valuation, and interpretation, of violence has a long and
complicated genealogy. The contemporary concept of human rights arose
in the context of sovereign abuse of power. Today, much moral indignation
of modern human rights activism addresses individual rights. Perhaps this
is not surprising; the contemporary movement, galvanized in the 1948 Universal Declaration of Human Rights, arose at the height of the Cold War, in
the context of dissidence in Communist and totalitarian regimes.[22] While it
includes references to the right to shelter, education, health care, and human
dignity, its practice and interpretation have focused on the rights to free
expression and attended closely to individual violations in the form of state-
sponsored bodily incarceration, torture, and murder. The human rights
framework connecting democracy (seen especially in terms of individual
expression) and peace thus transferred neatly to the Salvadoran war and
postwar context, in which the transition to the free-market economy called
for individual management of risk. The danger to "peace" and "democracy"
in this framework is ideology as exercised collectively, whether by the right
or the left—both by "authoritarian stagnation and revolutionary radical-
ism," as Cristiani himself would say in a speech before the United Nations a
month before Velis died.[23]

In El Salvador, it was only when citizens began to publicly denounce and
protest structural and symbolic violence that the state started to consciously
narrow the discourse on harm to a binary of criminal violences (common
versus political). As we know, in the late 1960s El Salvador (like much of
the world) was experiencing a new historical sensibility. Social movements
surged in a democratic opening. Christian base communities recognized
the structural violence in their everyday lives; labor leaders demanded less
exploitative conditions; citizens of all kinds called for more participation
in and greater access to the state. As protests, strikes, and political organizing became more confrontational, however, the Salvadoran government
and major mass media began to label defiant activity both subversion and
common crime. Such blurring can discredit actions. It can defuse efforts
for change. After 1980, however, the political project of the Salvadoran insurgency could not be denied. While the state always maintained that the

FMLN was an illegal, criminal entity, hegemonic discourse on violence essentially code-switched. After 1980, in the state of exception that defined most of the war, almost all violence in the territory was indiscriminately deemed critical. *Critical,* judging those in power and undermining the nation, and *critical,* as in critical condition, threatening the body of the nation with death. But also *critical,* as in a critical event: engendering new modes of action and politics. Almost all opposition figures thus became excluded from the nation, condemned to bare life. As political subversives they threatened the state—and so compelled responses from the military and paramilitary groups protecting state interests.

Then the peace accords were signed. The war ended. The state of exception revoked. Suddenly, the state wanted to re-code-switch and declare a state of unexception.[24] All crime was noncritical, in the three senses of the term—the state was not in jeopardy, the action did not challenge the state, and indeed the crime hardly had the weight of a critical event. This is what I am calling critical code-switching.

Irrationality to Rationality, Madness to Hope

"Even the dead will not be safe. . . ." Walter Benjamin warns us.[25] Velis's body, blood still congealing, was converted into a vehicle for ideological transformation that Monday in late October 1993. In front of all the international and Salvadoran journalists at his regular press conference, President Cristiani, in declaring the noncriticality of the corpse, partook in critical code-switching. Before the signing of the peace accords on 16 January 1992, the guerrilla's body would have been displayed as a military trophy; another terrorist down. Now, Velis had become an unfortunate victim of circumstance, shot dead while innocently dropping off his daughter at a daycare center. Cristiani's discourse was not just an attempt to leave the war behind. It hoped to channel the new mode of politics and action demanded by the critical event of the war. It worked to orchestrate citizen subjectivities into the disarticulated, individualistic ethos that characterizes a democracy in which freedom is defined through free-market economics and the logic of global capitalism.

The president's efforts at critical code-switching did not go over as smoothly as hoped. Friction filled most media reports, especially within El Salvador. FMLN leader Francisco Jovel insisted to the afternoon tabloid *El Mundo,* "This is a political assassination and there's no two ways about it.

The investigations should start from there and not do what they always do, assume it's common crime." Another former guerrilla leader, Schafik Handal, called the act an execution. He pointed out that the assassins didn't rob anything, not even Velis's car next to his body.[26] The next day in the morning papers the U.S. government and ONUSAL condemned the act. ONUSAL chief Augusto Ramírez Ocampo said the incident "saddens all of us deeply and . . . damages the extraordinary atmosphere that El Salvador has been living through."[27] The Salvadoran human rights counsel (the new post created through the peace accords) called the murder "a summary execution."[28] Soon after, the U.S. ambassador spoke up, saying that President Bill Clinton "can't accept this kind of violence." He announced the FBI was on its way.[29]

The arrival of the FBI underscored the political stakes of the homicide. But it also signaled a further attempt to depoliticize the incident—to reorient the Salvadoran population to a post-political way of thinking, divorced from collective sentiment. This mode was presented as more advanced. The FBI would bring modern ("unbiased") investigatory techniques. The Salvadoran minister of defense cautioned people to "avoid speculation and . . . act with prudence while the investigation is undertaken." The director of the National Civilian Police (Policía Nacional Civil, PNC) announced "a profound investigation," with the support of the Laboratory of Scientific Investigations of Crime. Calls came from all quarters for an exhaustive investigation.[30] Civilized scientific rigor would resolve the question. Not primitive political passions. Citizens should refrain from being critical, from being political at all, and wait for the modern, rational solution to deal with the nation's remnants of irrationality.

The status of El Salvador as a modern nation was at stake (once again). In his speech before the United Nations General Assembly the previous month, Cristiani had proclaimed, "El Salvador, for the first time in its history, is in the vigorous mainstream of modernization. . . . If we in El Salvador can testify to anything, we can testify that it is possible to move from irrationality to the deliberate construction of historical rationality."[31] Echoing the title of the Truth Commission report, *From Madness to Hope: Twelve Years of War in El Salvador* (which he had nonetheless rejected months earlier when he called for amnesty for all war criminals named), Cristiani coded El Salvador's tormented story as one of progress from barbarity to civilization.[32] The familiar Latin American narrative provided a template for the transition.[33]

As we saw in the big stories of the first chapter, El Salvador's diffident progress toward an imagined manageable, productive space, toward success as a nation, has ever sought the erasure—the expulsion, or the absorption—of the disorderly bodies of Others. For much of the country's history the Indians have been seen as the culprits holding back progress. They formed the ultimate category of person who could not be integrated.[34] In the late nineteenth century, El Salvador's rulers at first tried to assimilate them, privatizing lands and feebly encouraging indigenous peasants to join the market economy with small coffee farms.[35] Then they tried to annihilate those who remained, who were seen to refuse absorption, massacring them when President Maximiliano Hernández Martínez sent the military out to respond to the 1932 Communist-led uprising. In the postwar years, however, it was former guerrillas, ex-soldiers, vagrant youth, and other used-up men and women—testifying to El Salvador's ungovernability at a moment when the state sought international investment—who had to be managed. So the state's Others would be remade yet again, now into new, late twentieth-century models of flexible, market-oriented subjects.[36]

This matter of rebuilding the nation into a model market state exceeds discourse. After all the talk, the pronouncements, the analysis, the matter is also matter. Matter: bodies behind the discourse. Dead bodies, but also damaged ones. What to do with all the leftover bodies? In postwar El Salvador (as elsewhere) the return of battered men and women to civilian life is called "reinsertion." The word conjures images of a past unity and holism disrupted by war and irrationality. It erases any reason in the revolutionary search for an alternative to authoritarianism, capitalism, imperialism. It inscribes the insurgency that inspired so many Salvadorans to struggle for change as ahistorical pathology. That, then, is why Cristiani was insisting on the noncriticality of Francisco Velis's corpse. At stake in the postwar resignification of violence, in what I am calling critical code-switching, was the value of the peace accords as a global model. At stake was a verdict on whether the state of emergency that defined the war was an exception—or the rule.

Ambiguities of Violence

Of course all forms of violence mingle and intermix; conventionally defined "common" and "political," "random" and "organized" crime coexisted both during, and in the years immediately after, the war. News stories, narratives by Salvadorans, court cases—all demonstrate the multiplicity of classes of crime being committed during those years. Indeed Velis's killing, whether common or political, was only one murder on the news budget the day he died. *La Prensa Gráfica*'s front page on 25 October 1993 displays a gunfight between cops and thirteen members of the "Banda de Sabino," a crew of kidnappers who were accused of both abducting the daughter of a high-ranking military officer, and murdering three military men—all while dressed in stolen military uniforms. The leader, ex-FMLN member Sabino López Presa, remained at large.[37] That same day the tabloid *El Diario de Hoy* announced that out-of-control crime was forcing coffee planters to demand military protection during its harvest: "After the dissolution of the honor-able National Guard with the so-called Peace Accords, the rural zones of the country have fallen to bands of criminals who rob, murder and terrorize with impunity."[38]

An ambiguity of code imbues both cases. On the one hand, Sabino, guerrilla in soldier garb, leads a band in kidnapping and killing targets that are—coincidentally?—military. On the other, powerful coffee barons ask the state to shield them from bandits. What do we know of these rural delin-quents' class consciousness? It is hard to imagine that, after years of insur-gency, they randomly targeted wealthy landowners. If the Banda de Sabino had emerged before 1992, or if the landowners had complained of mobs ter-rorizing their territory before the peace accords, an entirely different narra-tive would have been assigned to the events. What I am suggesting, then, is that while there are obviously distinct (and ever multiple) motivations for acts of violence, it is crucial to examine the struggle to signify them, to study the attempts to fix meaning to them in particular times and places.

Look back at the Algerian revolution and its most famous global repre-sentation. Gillo Pontecorvo's film *The Battle of Algiers* starts with the coming to political consciousness of a thug. (The 1966 drama, threaded with Frantz Fanon's views on the violence of colonialism, became a training manual for the Black Panthers and the Irish Republican Army in the 1960s—and then in 2003 was screened in the Pentagon as the Iraq War deepened.) In an open-ing scene a street tough is fleeing police. He is Ali La Pointe, later described by Algerian National Liberation Front (Frente de Libération Nacionale, FLN) leader Saadi Yacef as originally "a crook, a small-time crook, a pimp and a drug pusher." Incarcerated, he is radicalized by FLN political prisoners, including Yacef. He converts from what might be called a primitive rebel, a proto-insurgent, into an anticolonial nationalist—or into a terrorist, a political criminal, in the eyes of the French colonial rulers. He becomes a fierce enforcer in the Casbah, the labyrinthine old Arab quarter of the "modern" European Algiers. His death, in a spectacular explosion set by the French counterinsurgency, ends the battle and the film. But not the revolution.[39]

Even as it takes place in an urban setting, the revolutionary trajectory portrayed in *The Battle of Algiers* fully conforms to the evolutionary model posed by historians of peasant revolutions.[40] The seeming common criminal can grow into a social bandit and then a revolutionary, as "first elements" of his thought processes mature and combine in complex formations to theorize revolt and class struggle.[41] But what happens *after* a revolution? Or what happens when a revolution fails? El Salvador's own history seems to offer only a model of silence and repression, as we have seen in the aftermath of the 1932 insurgency.[42] That revolt lasted a few days; the horrifying reprisals in which 10,000 died went on for weeks. So what happens to revolutionary consciousness—to hope for radical change—after twelve (or more) years of conflict in which 75,000 died? What happens next?

Another more recent film offers a coda to *The Battle of Algiers*, and proposes an uncomfortable answer to our question. In a post-Cold War, postrevolutionary moment, the Mexican director Alejandro González Iñárritu's *Amores Perros* suggests a murky reverse process to La Pointe's conversion. González follows a man's path from revolutionary to common criminal. A bearded vagrant known as "El Chivo" (the Goat) haunts the picture, wandering through the streets, bare life embodied. We soon learn that he survives by murdering for hire. Eventually we discover that this man had been "a normal guy" who had "one day—boom!—dump[ed] his wife and daughter and [become] a guerrilla" in the 1960s. After kidnapping a banker and bombing a shopping center in pursuit of revolutionary goals, he went to prison for twenty years.

After his release, the corrupt police officer who had arrested him discovered him living in the streets. The cop "saves" him by giving him "little jobs" as an assassin—the two hits we know about in the film are of wealthy businessmen. Unlike La Pointe, El Chivo does not die at the end. He seeks personal, individual redemption, as a father to his daughter (who thinks he is dead). In a telephone message, he tells her, "At the time, I thought there were more important things than being with you and your mother. I wanted to set the world right and then share it with you. I wound up in jail." The film, set in NAFTA-shocked, crisis-ridden 1990s Mexico City, could be seen as a hyperkinetic requiem for collective struggle—perhaps for any politics at all. All that is left, it seems, in a dangerous, risky world, is individual yearning (consumption?) and thin filial threads (property?).[43] Violence is stripped of intent, of meaning, of motivation. The movie in fact centers on the consequences of a random, if spectacular, car crash, the paradigmatic case of "meaningless" violence.[44]

It all comes down to the individual: individual redemption, individual risk, individual survival. Seen in an international human rights framework prioritizing individual freedom, as well as a historical moment proclaiming the post-Cold War "end of history" with the final fusion of capitalism and liberal democracy, the postconflict security mechanisms prescribed by the peace accords make perfect sense.[45] El Salvador's domestic security enforcement system was intensively negotiated during the peace accords; it was transformed from a structure of notorious military bodies seeking to deflect threats to the state (the National Police, Treasury Police and National Guard) into a civilian institution concerned with citizen security. The PNC stood out as a defining element of reform in the first hopeful moments of the new, postwar era. Effectively, through civilianization, violence began to be depoliticized, as violations of the law were converted into atomized, decontextualized acts. That kind of danger did not matter in international relations logic: it just threatened everyday citizens as they sought labor and sustenance. It was not seen to threaten the government, nor the institutions of the state, nor (so much) the businesses and corporations that rely on the functioning of the state.

Thus, despite the insecurity and instability that suffused everyday life in El Salvador, the discourse on Salvadoran success flowed freely both around the globe and within the country. The resignification of violence made this possible. This is apparent in critical code-switching. If the state operated as a democracy, if the war was over, then insecurity could no longer be instigated by internal "terrorists" or "insurgents" or even activists struggling for social change. As Bill Clinton had dictated upon learning of the Velis murder, "this kind of violence" was unacceptable.[46] Instead, it had to be coded as "random" or the product of an endemic, pathological (but never political) "culture of violence."

And so, standing in front of all the reporters on that hot October day, Cristiani announced that the bullet-ridden body of Francisco Velis was merely that of an ordinary man. Over the next months he would have to repeat that assertion several times, over more corpses left by a series of suspicious murders. It had to be so, if the war was truly over. Each man, before becoming a corpse, had been merely "an individual withdrawn into himself, into the confines of his private interests and private caprice," in Marx's words.[47] Velis had just been minding his own business, walking his little girl to school. He had died an ordinary death. An ordinary crime, something that would happen anywhere else, in any modern nation.

So this was not a critical situation.

"Socialism, for Me, Has Always Implied Democracy"

Just before his murder Francisco Velis shared his visions for postwar El Salvador in an interview with German writer Stefan Ueltzen.[48] Published six months after his death, the interview revealed a highly intellectual, deeply political being. Velis recognized the limits of imagining political alternatives within the state's new legal structure, in the sanctioned space of civil society. Yet he was determined not to abandon revolutionary ideals. He said he had joined the struggle as a high school student, in 1974—first the Communist Party, then the Central American Workers' Party (PRTC) (both of which became part of the FMLN in 1980). He left for the guerrilla front after his wife was assassinated in 1981. He spoke of his life as "a process of transformation of consciousness, [sometimes] with *compañeros* (comrades) integrated in the guerrilla forces or [other times] living with civilians who directly felt the effects of the war."

Through most of the published conversation he focused on his vision of political possibilities for the future. If the war was a critical event, in the sense Veena Das describes, then Velis and the demobilized, legal FMLN— like Cristiani and ARENA—aimed to foment new modes of interaction in the public sphere. Yet even as he hoped to "create a new form of politics in the country," he acknowledged that "frankly, I don't see . . . any kind of paradise for years (even if the next government *isn't* ARENA, and not because this government would be against the poor—but simply because the social and economic problems are just too complex)." He worried about the neoliberal projects ARENA had set into motion. He was alarmed at likely painful consequences of the government's recent agreements with the IMF and the World Bank. He spoke fiercely of a horizontal rather than vertical "democracy" even as he refused to renounce Marxism: "Marx's writings never opposed necessarily socialism and democracy; . . . Socialism, for me, has always implied democracy." This view does not diverge from revolutionary rhetoric in Latin America. It echoes the Sandinista experiment in neighboring Nicaragua, which sought democratic pluralism and nonaligned politics as well as a mixed economy.[49] As Greg Grandin has argued, in the twentieth century throughout the continent mass movements demanding social justice understood democracy as "the felt experience of individual sovereignty and social solidarity." [50]

And so Francisco Velis had become a candidate for the Legislative Assembly in the upcoming elections. After years of living outside the law, with the hope of "peace," he had wanted not merely to live within, but to insert himself into, the law. Perhaps for this very reason, the post-1992 Velis as a politician and public intellectual posed a greater threat to the Salvadoran ruling class than he ever had as an armed revolutionary. He neither died, as did La Pointe in the dramatic demise of *The Battle of Algiers*, nor tried to redeem himself by turning away from politics toward his progeny, as El Chivo dreamed of doing in *Amores Perros*. He wanted both activism *and* family, revolution *and* law.

Now he had become another corpse. One of hundreds and then thousands of cadavers that continued to accumulate in the weeks and months and years after the peace accords. The irony is that perhaps only in this moment, in his death, did Velis truly become incorporated into the law. If the law lives by violence, then what happened on a busy street outside a daycare center near the University of El Salvador on Monday, 25 October 1993, follows a certain fateful logic. [51] "The criminal produces not only crime," Marx once wrote, "but also the criminal law . . . [and] the professor who produces lectures on this criminal law, and even the inevitable text book . . . [and] the whole apparatus of the police and criminal justice, detectives, judges, executioners, juries, etc." [52]

For the next few years Velis's name would haunt reports and commentaries and studies of El Salvador's endemic postwar violence. It quickly showed up on the reports of ongoing surveillance of El Salvador's transition by groups such as Human Rights Watch and Amnesty International. Within a year it appeared in the report released (in July 1994) by the Joint Group for the Investigation of Politically Motivated Illegal Armed Groups, [53] a commission Cristiani had appointed a month and a half after Velis's murder, under UN pressure, to investigate the apparent resurgence of political violence in the country. Two years later the name "Velis" became associated with the corruption deep within the law itself. Nine former detectives, including a mysterious figure called "Sergeant Zaldaña," all from the police unit that investigated Velis's murder in October 1993, would themselves be charged with killing the former guerrilla leader. Later the so-called Zaldaña—actually Detective Carlos Romero Alfaro—fled the country. Someone had tipped him that he was about to be indicted as the triggerman who, like him, was missing fingers on his right hand. After the FBI arrested him in

Houston in 1995, he was extradited to El Salvador. He was finally convicted in 2001, eight years after Velis died.

The homicide continues to resurface as an index of a Salvadoran post-war matrix of law/crime/corruption. Just about the time Zaldaña was convicted, the Salvadoran novelist Horacio Castellanos Moya published a story evoking the precarious months of late 1993. He describes the killing of a certain former guerrilla "Celis" walking his three-year-old daughter to a nursery in a neighborhood near the national university. In *El arma en el hombre* (*The Weapon in the Man* [2001]), a novel of bloody, out-of-control, ostensibly apolitical postwar criminality, Castellanos Moya imagines the other side of Velis's story: that of the assassin. He describes how an alienated, demobilized sergeant known as "Robocop" (perhaps a twisted right-wing mirror image of *Amores Perros* former guerrilla El Chivo, in its disenchantment with any politics at all) becomes part of a private, clandestine security unit. He takes orders from one of his former military bosses. The orders soon spiral far beyond the polarized left-right ideology of the war.[54]

As recently as March 2007 Velis's name slipped into news about another presumed victim of Zaldaña, thirty-one-year-old banker Ramón Mauricio García Prieto Giralt. (In June 1994, García Prieto had been shot to death in front of his house in the Colonia Escalón, as his wife, holding their four-month-old son, watched.) Despite Cristiani's best efforts at critical code-switching back in 1993, the Velis case remains a symbol of the immediate postwar moment. At the fifteenth anniversary of the peace accords, the murder of a thoughtful former guerrilla who had decided to run for public office stood out as an extrajudicial execution in what some considered a continued "dirty war."[55]

"We Never Said It Was Common Crime"

Journalists vet critical code-switching, as Cristiani was well aware in that October 1993 news conference. Although "doing Salvador" had begun to lose its cachet for foreign reporters after the signing of the peace accords on 16 January 1992 (or even after 1989), corporate-contract news hounds and swashbuckling freelancers would swoop back into the Hotel Camino Real at any hint of chaos—or certain kinds of valued chaos. Mark Pedelty, explaining why reporters spurned the bloody remains of a thief cut down in 1991, points to a clear code among journalists: "The messy nature of the incident would provide political capital to no one, because it would not fit easily into the two-dimensional discourse of terrorism and human rights. Wrong body, wrong story."[56] Wrong two-dimensional discourse, it might be added. By the mid-1990s, criminals' individual motivations (political versus "common") became less important as theories of embodied deviance resurged in a public obsession with gang violence, as we shall see in Chapter 6.

Pedelty's anecdote portends emergent trends. Some accounts point to an escalation of crime rates *before* the war ended. The Salvadoran Ministry of Justice reported that crime went up 83 percent in the two years prior to the peace accords.[57] This was precisely when the ARENA government began implementing the IMF- and World Bank-promoted structural adjustment projects Velis lamented in his last interview.

During the 1980s, the news media, the government, the left—just about everyone—saw violence as war. As I noted above, for many years there was a tendency to read almost everything as "political." There was no public controversy about what caused war-era violence. People killed or disappeared would often retrospectively be assumed—at least by outsiders—to have done *something*. As one television news executive from the dominant Telecorporación Salvadoreña (TCS) told me in a confidential interview, "We never differentiated violence [during the war]. We never said it was common crime."[58] The news director of the leftist *Diario Latino* (later called *Co-Latino*) would add when we spoke a few days later: "What happened is that the coverage was directed to attacking the guerrilla. They covered up the political violence done by the government" (and ignored "other" violence that could not be attributed to the left).[59] Mauricio Funes, the Salvadoran newsman who would be elected president as the FMLN candidate in 2009, reiterated to me during several interviews he granted me in his Channel 12 news offices that he doubted there was much common crime to cover. He believed that the presence of the military and other state agents inhibited other kinds of violence.[60] Only after war, in retrospect, did differentiation of violence become important. Most other news directors, however, agreed that there had probably been a lot of common, so-called "nonpolitical," or at least non-war-related crime, "disguised" as war.[61] The lack of attention to "common crime" in the war era suggests that the postwar surge may have been more of a postwar recognition.[62]

As the first full postwar year began, on 1 January 1993, an editorialist for *La Prensa Gráfica* lamented, "The dream of living in tranquility . . . is an illusion that has little to do with reality. Today we know, after the experience of war, that it's fundamental to project an image that truly resounds with the facts of life."[63] By February, headlines announced that President

Cristiani was stationing 25,000 police in San Salvador "to confront what has been up to now an uncontrollable explosion of crime and citizen insecurity" (note the unqualified description of crime, the blurring—neither political nor common).[64] By December the situation had catapulted into crisis. *La Prensa* closed the year by editorializing, "Once the war ended, other scars of less historical density, but no less a violation against the fundamental rights of a person, have intruded on the daily reality of the Salvadorans."[65] The violation here is individualized—the fundamental rights *of a person*.

By late 1992 certain sectors of society were calling for the military to collaborate in the crime fight, despite a peace accords prohibition of soldiers intervening in domestic security.[66] (We saw this in the papers circulating on the day of Velis's murder, in calls to protect the coffee harvest.) But the soldiers would have done (and in fact did) very little to help the situation: they were trained to focus on threats to the state, and ignored most other crime. As political scientist William Stanley, who researched links between powerful elites and the military in El Salvador, tells us, "The old security forces, though effective in terrorizing the population and suppressing above-board political opposition activity, were *not* effective in controlling crime, especially organized crime."[67] Neither, it turned out, could the new, human rights-vetted National Civilian Police do much: the peace agreements may have produced institutions mildly proficient in confronting war-related destabilizing forces, but they could not effectively counter the fine grind of common crime.[68]

As the crime problem became the primary discourse of the postwar decade, many Salvadorans—like many other Latin Americans—came to believe that international covenants on "human rights" principally protected the rights of criminals rather than those of "ordinary citizens." Such discussions show presuppositions of clear, separate categories of criminality—of codes (and, for that matter, of categories of persons, to be ordered, classified, and regulated[69]). In mid-1999 I arranged a meeting with a well-connected former National Police colonel, whom I had naïvely hoped would grant me access to war-era files. He waxed nostalgic for the days when the police could arrest a person just for *seeming* suspicious. When I asked him what he meant, he could not tell me—well, he finally said after a few moments, if someone reported the suspect as suspicious. Police could gather the proof after the arrest, while they interrogated the suspect, he explained. Today, things are different, he said. He recounted a series of robberies of his family members, including the theft of his gun. "There are too many requirements for evidence," he declared. "Too many criminals go free."[70]

He likely applauded a few years later when those good old days of cop intuition trumping the rules of evidence were resuscitated. Antigang legislation passed in 2003 targeted certain visible bodies as degenerate rather than particular acts as illegal.

But back in 1993, requirements for evidence were precisely what the Cristiani administration stressed as they engaged in critical code-switching. They saw (at least a claim to respect) procedure and law, and investigation of individual crimes, as an antidote to the collective passions that ruled war. As Minister of Defense Humberto Corado Figueroa said in the aftermath of Velis's murder: it would be "lamentable" if a wave of violence followed the death, since the armed forces were seeking "to discover the material and intellectual facts, in order to submit them to the rigor of law." [71]

A Hobbesian Vision of the Nation

The ONUSAL Human Rights Division wrote of the first few months after the peace accords were signed (through 30 April 1992), "Summary executions and violent deaths . . . have continued after the cease-fire, and no effective action has been taken to put an end to them, investigate them or punish the perpetrators." [72] The Salvadoran government invoked postwar crime when justifying violations of the peace agreements less than two months after they were signed: The notorious National Guard and Treasury Police, which should have been abolished by 2 March 1992, were transferred intact into the army. "The Government defends these transfers on the grounds that . . . the rise in common crime requires it to strengthen the National Police," UN observers reported. [73]

There is a change in terminology here: from *summary executions and violent deaths* to *common crime*. A later ONUSAL report makes a similar move to distinguish war-era from postwar violence: "The situation has been aggravated by the fact that no public security plan was designed and therefore implemented for the transitional period [. . . nor were] emergency measures [taken] for combating *ordinary crime*." This move naturalizes certain forms of violence—inherent in the words "ordinary" or "common." It suggests a Hobbesian vision of the nation as a collection (but not a collectivity) of self-interested, jealous, competitive individuals, now purified from the contaminating, ideological forms of violence that had characterized the civil war. It is also a critical code-switch, a recategorizing of all violence as common, rather than political (resisting the state and laws, challenging property regimes) as in war. The problem is violence itself, as a disorderly act, rather than oppositions or ideologies usually manifested in armed resistance.

Following this same logic, scholars of war in the early 1990s focused their analytic attention on postconflict turmoil—including that of El Salvador—that could either be characterized as residue of war (the political violence decried by human rights activism) or as a technical issue of institutional competence (the neoliberal rationality encouraged by the World Bank, which has sponsored forums and studies on the issue of violence in El Salvador as elsewhere).[74] Still, in the late 1980s and early 1990s, as much of Latin America emerged from authoritarianism or war, such violence, coded as "common," as criminal delinquency, was not usually perceived as a threat to the institutions of democracy. This same attitude is reflected in a summary of El Salvador's transition written in 1995, as ONUSAL left the country—and as the national homicide rate was spiraling out of control. UN Secretary-General Boutros Boutros-Ghali did not acknowledge the contemporaneous crime wave and called early postwar violence mere "carry-over": "Rights violations [by 1993] were no longer a reflection of the will of the State but, rather, 'carry-overs' from the period prior to the Peace Agreement." [75] That same year the UN Security Council recognized ONUSAL's feat in guiding El Salvador's "evol[ution] from a country riven by conflict into a democratic and peaceful nation," [76] at the precise moment that El Salvador's murder rate would rank it among the most dangerous places on earth.[77]

It was true that the "*felt presence* of government authority and vigilance" fell dramatically in the first months after the war.[78] Suddenly there were only about 6,000 public security agents working, down from 14,000 after the National Guard and Treasury Police were finally abolished. If you tally in the 20,000–strong regular army, and as many as 30,000 part-time civil defense and village patrols in the countryside, as well as FMLN in areas the guerrillas controlled in the war, then effectively, there was an abrupt drop in policing from a war-era 75,000 to a postwar 6,000.[79]

The novel *El arma en el hombre* suggests what happened to some of those former soldiers and combatants. The trajectory of author Castellanos Moya's Robocop character, once part of an elite military squadron, shows the consequences on subjectivity of critical code-switching. Code-switching is performative—it is speech that does things, changes things. Robocop's identifications shift through the book, from an impassioned, collectively oriented war-era subject and into a depoliticized, alienated individual. He first experiences the postwar era as a momentary truce in the unfinished mission "to end the subversion once and for all"; [80] he sees the military leaders who signed the peace accords as traitors. When he signs on as an assassin, he believes he is in "a continuation of the struggle against the terrorists." [81] He finally recognizes the postwar critical code-switch in the public reaction to the assassination of "Celis": "Things had changed. A few years ago no one would have said anything if a terrorist had been wiped out, but now, with this bullshit democracy, guys like me were finding it harder and harder to do our work [of ending subversion]." [82] Eventually such thoughts disappear. Everything blurs together, common, interpersonal, political, subversive, and mercenary violence. In the book, Robocop ends up in prison in Texas, recruited by U.S. antinarcotics forces to join the "special operations" in Central America as part of the drug wars—prescient in its pre-9/11 prediction of a widening of the U.S. Empire with post-Cold War means. Robocop has become a flexible, apolitical subject, managing his options in the new market.

Crime Stories of Critical Code-Switching

"Ordinary" Salvadorans moving through their city streets in those first postwar moments soon started perceiving the world differently—and what happened next wasn't what they had imagined it would be. "There were a few months in which the army and the old security bodies were being reduced and the new National Civilian Police wasn't ready," Atilio Cárcamo (the name is changed), a lawyer who would later become a top law-enforcement official under President Francisco Flores (1999–2004), told me in a June 1998 conversation (referring to mid-1993).[83] "The country was in a phase in which really the streets belonged to the thieves and criminals, and everyone was going around watching for anything that could happen—always seeing who was ahead of you, who's behind you." I met Atilio one night with my pal Guayo at a bar—they had grown up in the same neighborhood, it turned out, but hadn't seen each other in years. Together we watched the (sanctioned violence of) Salvadoran-American lightweight boxer Carlos "El Famoso" Hernández on a big-screen television. Atilio began telling me his crime story that night, over one too many beers: we finished it with a tape recorder a few days later, in his well-appointed corporate office.

The incident happened one May 1993 evening: his nervous dread materialized when two armed men suddenly appeared in front of his car at a stoplight. He immediately accelerated his car—meaning to kill them. Though he had a certain prominence in society (his wife was related to the president), he didn't think the two men targeted him in particular. At that chaotic moment, he believed, criminals just grabbed whatever and whomever they could.

Though he thought he had hit one of the men with his car, the other man managed to shoot into the passenger window. A bullet pierced the lawyer's left thumb, snapping the tendon and breaking the bone. Atilio got to a hospital, but after the doctors treated him he fled. He was sure that the men—whom he described as "very professional"—were ex-guerrilla or ex-army. He didn't want to risk revenge by reporting the incident.

This attorney's crime story echoed accounts I heard throughout the 1990s. They exemplify the neoliberal sensibility of individual management of risk. What distinguishes such stories as Atilio's as typical of the postwar era, I suggest, is the evacuation of any sense of politics in the description. The same incident, just two years earlier, would have been narrated differently.[84] The motives of his attackers would have been described as subversive, as challenging the order of things, as part of the war.

Listen, for example, to the blurring of codes in César Ochoa's crime story.[85] He was kidnapped about the same time Atilio escaped with his broken thumb, in mid-1993. César was raised in a fairly prosperous business family (his more politically conventional sister, my gym buddy Ondina, had introduced us). He had joined the FMLN during the war but eventually went into exile in Nicaragua. He returned to El Salvador for peace. One Sunday at 5 A.M., as he was leaving home to attend a retreat of his nongovernmental organization (NGO) employer, a car pulled him over. Three men leaped out. For a moment he thought they might be from the nearby military barracks. Then one of them held a gun to his head. "The first thing they did was take my wallet. They began to take everything of value, my sunglasses and everything, insulting me. Then there wasn't any doubt that they weren't soldiers. They were criminals." They announced they were going to kidnap him and pushed him into the back seat of his own car. They told him, "Son of a bitch we got you!"

Within a half hour they would let him go. But five years later, César, despite his assertions (such as "there wasn't any doubt that they weren't soldiers"), could not quite tell a coherent story. What *were* those men? His account of the incident testifies to an ambiguity, a blurring of codes of violence. He still wondered how they passed effortlessly through a police checkpoint. It had to have looked suspicious, four men squeezed into a car—did they get through because they had signaled ahead to the police? Had they flashed their lights? They told him they were guerrillas, though they clearly weren't, to César's FMLN eyes. "I am sure they had nothing to do with the guerrilla, at that moment they were criminals, pure and simple criminals," he declared. Still, he wondered who was duping whom: "The truth is that they looked like that they were well trained. They weren't the kind of everyday thugs, they had training, the kind of weapons they had were real *weapons*. They were good machine guns. They had rifles and pistols, and combat knives, and they were in uniform, and grenades, they had hand grenades . . . I think that they had to do with organized crime. It's all made up of ex-military types. I mean I think there's a lot of people in crime who are common criminals, but the big crime, the major crime, for example people who rob banks, people who rob armored cars, or who kidnap people with money, these aren't common criminals, these are people with training, with a source of weapons, and resources, and contacts, or they're just ex-military who can work on their own or who can work linked to the military."

In descriptions of postwar El Salvador, then, whether constructed by Salvadoran officials or elites or UN observers, by journalists or former guerrillas or ex-police or novelists, we find shifting codes of public, corporal violence. In 1993, the categories still slipped precariously. But the movement of meaning of violence was slowly cohering. What was emerging was a semiotic structure meant to hold up the image of democratic success: from residual political violence, considered a carryover from war-era collectivities, to emergent and soon dominant common crime, considered individual acts of violation, even if committed by organized "professionals" or ex-combatants. It would take some time for this process of coding violence to consolidate. But when El Salvador's homicide rate hit the record books in 1995, most postwar crime had been safely sanitized in the public sphere as "apolitical" (though a parallel sphere of loudly whispered rumors insisted on other, darker realities).[86] One widely known exception, the vigilante death squad called the Sombra Negra (Black Shadow), may have comprised political (state) figures, including police officers. Their targets, however, were so-called "common" criminals and gang members, allowing the state codification of motives to stand (they may have been political, but they did not threaten the state). Of course these discourses do not congeal. They are ever shifting. In the first decade of the new century, more and more rumors of political killings in El Salvador (especially around election times) were circulating.

"A Serious Attack on the Democratic Process"

Francisco Velis was slain just hours after auxiliary San Salvador archbishop Gregorio Rosa Chávez had warned in his Sunday homily that "the bitter fruit of the death squads continue to be harvested week by week." [87] Despite (or because of?) Cristiani's attempts to corral the meaning of the corpse, the murder quickly made the international newswire updates, the global human rights alerts. The U.S. embassy in San Salvador called the assassination "an insult to those Salvadorans who have worked successfully to forge a Salvadoran peace based on democracy." Ambassador Alan Flanigan attended Velis's burial, joining UN officials and politicians from the right and left—along with demonstrators chanting, "One death more and there won't be peace." Human rights counsel Carlos Molina spoke of "a serious attack on the stability of the democratic process." [88] The conjuncture of worldwide publicity, internal and external pressure, and the presence of protestors, the U.S. Embassy, the United Nations, and a mix of Salvadoran politicians at the funeral pushed the murder beyond simple crime story to "critical situation."

Even if Cristiani had been able to control the meaning of Velis's body, other forces made the state's efforts at critical code-switching difficult. Between June and September of 1993, ONUSAL officials counted at least forty-three "summary executions," half the victims from the FMLN. The surge suggested to them "a renewal of death-squad-style assassinations [that] indicated that some groups and individuals were continuing to choose to resort to violence in order to achieve political objectives." [89] Just five days after Velis was killed, ex-FMLN commander Heleno Castro was murdered on a rural highway in Usulután. The incident appeared to be a dispute with a farmer after an accident. Immediately the state, again, insisted on asserting its new taxonomy, in stamping the act as noncritical. "It was common crime!" Óscar Santamaría, a presidential cabinet member, declared in a television interview.[90] But Gregorio Rosa Chávez grimly warned radio listeners, "These cases are not fortuitous." [91] Then it came out that another body had been discovered a few days earlier, in a car, riddled with .45–caliber bullets. The victim had been suspected of killing FMLN activist Óscar Grimaldi the previous August. The murder occurred the day he was to testify before ONUSAL.[92]

President Cristiani quickly vowed in capital letters on the front page of *La Prensa Gráfica* newspaper to apply "la mano dura" (an iron fist) to any proven political violence.[93] Soon afterwards he agreed appoint the Joint Group for the Investigation of Illegal Armed Groups. But for a time discourse surged far beyond the reach of the powerful financial class that governed the nation and dominated business and mass media, despite their determination to portray El Salvador as a rational free-market haven. "Salvador's bloody sequel!" screamed a *Miami Herald* editorial.[94] "Salvador killings bring a warning of terror," the *New York Times* warned.[95] "El Salvador's transition to democracy is under threat," the *Guardian* of London announced.[96]

And then—yet another killing. José Mario López, a well-known FMLN ex-commander and one of the founders of the National Association of Salvadoran Educators (ANDES-21 de Junio) was shot, apparently as he tried to help an elderly woman being mugged. The next morning leftist leader Nidia Díaz said in an interview program that López's homicide was a "message from people who don't want to carry out the peace accords, who don't want stability in this country."[97] Soon it seemed as if all those state efforts to sculpt individual citizen-voters out of the remnants of war-polarized *pueblo* had disintegrated. Protests began. *El Diario de Hoy*'s front page two days after the murder showed a flaming truck (a familiar image from the war) and announced, "THE MOBS ARE BACK."[98] The article took the "fact" of murder, possibly even a political murder, and effected the very world it feared: not that the death squads could be out of control, but that the "left," the unwashed masses, the uncivilized rabble—and the monstrous guerrilla force, back—could not be controlled and threatened everyone, especially the innocent.

On the next page, however, another news article took the government line: "It is proved López died at the hands of [common] assailants: the left manipulates events to justify violence."[99] The next day, President Cristiani held to his postwar critical code-switching. To *La Prensa Gráfica* he said, "Everything points to the incident being an act of common crime, because Mr. López and his bodyguard went out to help a woman who was being attacked."

Just before López's murder, President Cristiani had hosted a breakfast for foreign reporters in the presidential palace. Howard French of the *New York Times* reported the executive's critical code-switch. But the quote appeared in an article focusing on López: "'There is a huge amount of delinquency, a huge amount, but this country is different now,' Mr. Cristiani said, rejecting assertions that there had been a revival of death squad activity in El Salvador."[100] As did other reporters, however, French stressed the "circumstances suggesting execution" and the "human rights crisis." He characterized Cristiani as "show[ing] little willingness to concede a political nature to the killings" indeed decrying ONUSAL's "bias against the country's political right."

By the time López was buried, the services attended by hundreds, UN head Boutros Boutros-Ghali himself had stepped in to demand an inquiry

into the murder. Archbishop Arturo Rivera y Damas announced that Tu-
tela Legal, the Catholic Church's influential human rights office, had found
"signs of an operative" with political motivation in the assassination.[101] He
spoke of fears that violence that was "dominating" the nation would deeply
polarize the elections. "With more blood, there could be a disaster."[102]

"A Certain Improvement"

There would be more blood in the years to come, much more blood. But was
there a disaster? It depends on the code. Cristiani's attempt may have failed in
Velis's case, but by 1995, with the highest homicide rates in the hemisphere, it
seemed as if El Salvador had successfully redefined even murder by exploding
bullet to the "attenuated background conditions of ordinary life," as mun-
danely lethal as pneumonia, hemorrhagic dengue, and heart attacks.[103]

Who won, in that struggle for the power to define ways of imagining
the new Salvadoran time/space in the flux of postwar transition? ARENA
presidential candidate Armando Calderón Sol's (1993–1994) campaign did
focus on crime—but noncritical crime: "We're all going to live better!" sang
a commercial that ran in the midst of the December 1993 turbulence. "We're
going to increase the number of police agents trained and equipped to meet
our needs to come through with our mission to give us all security, both in
the city and the countryside. A country without crime is our commitment,
and united we will do it. We're going to vote for ARENA!"[104]

Soon after Calderón Sol took office, ONUSAL's human rights director,
Diego García Sayan, wrote with some relief that the narrative of the peace
process, the determined tale of progress, was righting itself. In his report for
the period from 1 March–30 June 1994, he said that the human rights situation showed "a certain improvement, in contrast to the serious problems
warned of" previously, "an indication that the overall trends of the process
seemed to be reasserting themselves."[105] For a time death threats and assassination attempts continued to be reported in the papers. Nidia Díaz, the
FMLN leader who stood by her former guerrilla *compañero* Velis's corpse in
front of news cameras, survived two attempts on her life.

The Joint Group for the Investigation of Politically Motivated Illegal
Armed Groups, which Cristiani had appointed soon after Velis's murder,
clarified some questions when it released its report in July 1994. It affirmed
that the details of Velis's assassination pointed to political motivation, but
could not make a determination in López's murder. Castro's death had al-

ready been ruled "common crime."[106] The report concludes: "The broad network of organized crime that afflicts the country, in which, the evidence shows, there is active participation of the members of the armed forces of El Salvador and the National Police, cannot be divorced from many acts of politically motivated violence."

But it points to something that neither adhered to the war-era antiterrorist model nor to the "common" category of violence: another taxonomic code coming to prominence, indicating the transition to another historical stage in the Salvadoran transition. "To be sure, political motives do not seem to constitute the sole or even the essential driving force behind these [criminal] structures, which engage predominantly in acts coming under the label of 'common crime,' but with a high degree of organization and infrastructure."[107] This "new" or newly recognized criminal form did not quite fit into the binary common-political code in which the state was toggling. Perhaps for that reason it continued to escape discursive, legal, and material containment, expanding through the decade, into the early years of the 2000s. Whatever the code, it was obvious that many of those carrying out the crime in postwar El Salvador were skilled, very skilled, likely more skilled than most of the newly trained National Civilian Police force. The sense of postwar impunity that unfurled most dramatically when Cristiani granted amnesty to those named in the Truth Commission report in early 1993 would only intensify through the decade as most crime went unreported, uninvestigated, and unresolved.

The Wounded Body Within Capitalist Rationality

If we accept the critical codes, categories of crime defining war and peace: Was Velis's murder a remnant of the past conflict? Was it a political assassination originating in Cold War ideologies held by organized collectivities? Or was it a sign of the rising, post-Cold War, neoliberal era in El Salvador, in which individuals make choices among a range of options available? The answer to the question, posed this way, is not a mere matter of detective work and police reports and then court trials and sentences, though that is certainly the solution—the technical, ostensibly apolitical response—that authorities proposed after Velis's murder. It is a matter of whether collectivities can unite in struggle, whether communities matter, indeed whether or not, as British Prime Minister Margaret Thatcher once famously declared, there is even society.[108]

Thatcher's pronouncement, made in the midst of England's own economic restructuring, may have seemed distant from El Salvador when she said it in 1987. But, as described in the first chapter, the Salvadoran transition in forms of capitalism had already begun by then, at precisely the bloodiest point of the war, when the United States set up a policy research foundation. The crisis effected what Naomi Klein has called a "softening up," like the torture of individuals, allowing the infiltration of market-based governance.[109] Within a year of the first election of the ARENA government, still two years before the war ended, its leaders reached an agreement with the IMF to expand the country's financing beyond its U.S. limits (during the 1980s, the United States sent El Salvador $3.15 billion in military and $1.1 billion in economic aid[110]). By the time of the peace accords the country was well prepared for the postwar reconstruction and the continued conversion to free-market models of capitalism.[111]

In El Salvador, then, the end of the war allowed an acceleration of the shift to a transnational finance model. The structural changes in the economy begun by ARENA technocrats as soon as they came into office in 1989 meant more than trade liberalization, more than tariff reductions, more than the privatization of state entities such as banks, more than nontraditional exports and assembly plants in free-trade zones. Cristiani and the like endeavored to incorporate these changes as the vanguard of a new, all-encompassing social imaginary. They were part of a process that would shape Salvadorans' ways of thinking about and acting upon the world. Salvadorans, after 1992, were terribly aware of "the world," of their world, as changing.[112] They were quite conscious of the *need* for a new consciousness, even if they weren't exactly sure—even if most of us in the rest of the world, too, weren't exactly sure—what that would entail. These new forms of governance became the contact point in which, in Foucault's words, "techniques of the [free, agentive] self are integrated into structures of coercion."[113] As the political theorist Wendy Brown writes, "The model neoliberal citizen"—in El Salvador, the model postwar subject—"is one who strategizes for her or himself among various options, not one who strives with others to alter or organize those options."[114] This is a key difference from the war era, when many people actively imagined other possibilities for themselves and their communities, when people collectively envisioned options transcending the limits of their experiences as well as of their nation's violent and authoritarian history.

Revolution and/or the popular movement were not the only paths Salvadorans saw to changing their conditions in the war. Individual migration became the alternative more and more people began to envision for themselves in the 1980s, at first fleeing political violence and economic devastation. Migrant labor power joined coffee and cotton as El Salvador's primary export commodities.[115] This individualized strategy for survival continued into the postwar years. By 2002, one in four Salvadoran citizens lived outside the country, most in the "Fifteenth Department" of the United States, sending remittances equivalent to 13.6 percent of the Gross National Product.[116] (By then President Francisco Flores had dollarized the economy, easing the flow of cash from abroad.) The economic infusion of remittances and other foreign capital would effect other dramatic changes as well, changes consonant with market rationality.[117]

Signs of this postwar form of knowledge production were apparent, for example, among activists in some of the leftist feminist organizations I got to know in my early days in El Salvador, in 1993 and 1994. They described having to rethink their missions after the war. As never before, they were being forced to justify their activities for their (fading) funding agencies and sponsors, mostly in Europe and the United States. This was the new audit society. "Before, there was an assumption that in the urgency of the war, our mission was clear . . ." they would say. People hadn't asked them to show receipts for acts of resistance and revolution. This was not just a Salvadoran phenomenon; in the 1980s and 1990s, a form of "transnational governance" arose in which NGOs took over a range of activities across the Global South, whether environmental education or health care or microenterprise development.[118] A "vast number of non-governmental organizations (NGOs) now pervad[e] the Third World landscape," writes Marc Edelman, who has researched widely on social movements, "some effectively building new civil society structures, others assuming functions that used to be carried out by the government, others simply providing a more or less comfortable living for their staffs and directors, who are typically professionals [who have been] 'downsized' or 'retrenched' from public sector agencies."[119]

In many ways, this new need for accountability in the transition from war made perfect sense in the seeming sobriety of the immediate postwar years. No longer part of the popular/revolutionary movement, you were no longer likely to want to overthrow the state. An NGO in postwar El Salvador was, instead, seeking "meaningful access points in the political system."[120] This new mode of strategizing, deep within former "subversive" groups, comprised a key instantiation of postwar neoliberal governmentality. The loss of solidarity, the loss of vision, and a sense of vague postwar *lack* hid behind the mask of transparent, accountable democracy. For most of the

1990s, most NGOs and social-movement organizations in El Salvador felt there was no alternative but to "devote their energies to empresarial re-engineering in the search for insertion points in the world capitalist system," in the words of Adam Flint, a sociologist whose work points to the limits of political space for social movements in 1990s El Salvador.[121] Sustained social activism reemerged only a decade after the peace accords, after a period of reorganization and in recognition of the growing threat of neoliberalism, with the massive 2002–3 "white marches" against the privatization of the Social Security system.[122]

From Radio Venceremos to Adult Contemporary

Some former guerrillas embraced the postwar free-market rationality. Within two years of Cristiani's news conference over Velis's body, FMLN leader Joaquín Villalobos would form a centrist party with other members of his faction of the FMLN. He decided that the key to change lay in civil society, through *social property*: what he conceived of as small businesses organized along cooperative principles—in which producers controlled their own means of production—yielding both development and profit along with social justice and solutions to poverty.[123] (Velis, in his interview with Ueltzen above, was likely responding to this market pragmatism.) As an early demonstration of this principle Villalobos had helped turn the guerrilla broadcaster Radio Venceremos into a largely apolitical commercial adult-contemporary music outlet in the mass-media postwar aperture. All factions of the FMLN invested in small businesses, whether shoe factories or island tourist attractions. Villalobos publicized his support for a kind of market socialism in his 1992 book *A Revolution in the Left for a Democratic Revolution*. In it he declared his own Third Way: "Without the market, social property can provide for justice at a given time, but it will not drive development or generate wealth."[124] However, his centrist Democratic Party got few votes and disappeared.

This sober sense of postwar reality would spread—imperfectly, incompletely—though mass media advertising, USAID tutorials for microdevelopment projects, newspaper columns, conversations with migrant relatives in Los Angeles and New Jersey, and so on. The former guerrillas who were running for the Legislative Assembly, such as Velis, could not help but collaborate with this new mode: Their "opposition voices," located within liberal democratic society, would often enter public awareness as individual alternative points of view, reasonable available options, *within* the market rationality of state and society. "Neoliberalism," Brown writes, "entails the erosion of oppositional political, moral or subjective claims located outside capitalist rationality but inside liberal democratic society."[125] Villalobos's descent from the mountains and entry into liberal democratic society also involved an acceptance of largely free-market logic. We will never know if Velis could have helped to conjure alternative possibilities had he lived—had he survived until 2009, when leftist politics had reemerged throughout the continent, and when the savvy center-left candidate, the television journalist Mauricio Funes, became the first FMLN president.

And so, standing there before all the national and international news correspondents at his regular weekly news conference in 1993, a year and a half after he had signed peace accords, Alfredo Cristiani was doing much more than refuting another left-wing accusation of state barbarity. He was doing far more than rubbing out a residual war-era structure of feeling about collective action and shared community imaginaries. By insisting that the murder of Francisco Velis was a noncritical, ordinary crime—something that would happen anywhere else, in any modern state, on the streets of New York or Los Angeles or Munich or Moscow—Cristiani was precisely placing the wounded body *within* capitalist rationality, encompassing it *within* the emergent free-market logic. In his critical code-switching, he was calling attention to change, to transformation, from war to peace—from barbarism to civilization. He was also attempting to redefine the democratic polity as coterminous with capitalism, without any legitimate place from which to critique it. Casting the murder as a crime against an *ordinary* individual not only defines the act as apolitical but suggests that the principal motivation within the system is one of strategizing for profit, of taking an entrepreneurial risk—as the state's imagined "common" criminal-assailant must have done. This mentality is of course not new in El Salvador or in most of Latin America. The new valence lies perhaps in its starkness.

In the decade and a half after the peace accords, El Salvador's postwar criminality, coded as noncritical, as ordinary, as (perhaps bad) individual choices among available options, fit into a straightforward capitalist rationality, and aligned itself snugly with the emergent post-Cold War liberal democratic ethos of a "free" society of equals. There were no alternatives. Engels, commenting on exploding crime rates in newly industrializing, nakedly exploitative capitalist societies of mid-nineteenth-century Europe, once said: "Present-day society, which breeds hostility between individual man and everyone else, thus produces a social war of all against all which inevitably in individual cases, notably among uneducated people, assumes a brutal, barbarously violent form—that of crime." [126] And so as in many societies undergoing a shift in phases of economic production—to the savage capitalism in the 1990s and the early years of the 2000s—public attention began to obsess on street crime, especially, as we shall see, in the surplus of men like Castellanos Moya's "Robocop" (and his younger brothers and cousins): insolent in their excess, refusing to disappear even as economic equations rendered them bare-life biopolitical debris, latter-day lumpen-proletariat. Excluded from the model post-Cold War free-market state, they crowded into the crime stories that had begun to narrate the postwar nation as "worse than the war."

Chapter 3
"Today They Rob You and They Kill You"

Salvadoran postwar crime stories incited, and also were incited through, an acute sense of insecurity. In an atmosphere of unknowing, of wondering what would come next, people described postwar danger in terms of increasingly personal, or private, experience. This way of thinking contrasted with how many Salvadorans had conceived of war-era violence, as fueled by socially motivated passion, patriotism, and nationalism, whether from the left or right. It also contrasted with an imagined community of affect and meaning, of social care, produced through the violence, such as the murder of Archbishop Óscar Arnulfo Romero.[1] After the war, the social imaginary of class conflict that had girded much knowledge of the war, and defined a seemingly clear *us* versus a well demarcated *them*, seemed to recede in the concerns of everyday living.

In the previous chapter we saw that just after the war, this production of knowledge about the new era's risk—as something to manage individually, as part of an ideological society of equals—contributed to the transition to post-Cold War global capitalist logic. One (unstable) effect of this ideological discourse was the fabrication of a flexible, reflexive free-market postwar subject in the 1990s. We saw how the state worked to instigate this rationality through techniques of governance, including critical code-switching. By renaming "political" violence as common, noncritical crime, the sovereign, President Alfredo Cristiani, in effect declared a state of unexception. But how did changes in people's orientation to the world occur? We must look to everyday interactions to see the effects, and side effects, of government.[2] The premise of this book is that crime stories became media for urban Salvadorans' negotiations of meanings of the postwar moment. Both below and above the threshold of awareness, they helped shape the way people experienced and felt about their encounters with violence in the present and in the past. They also influenced conditions for the possibility of effecting change in the postrevolutionary and apparently post-ideological world. Salvadoran postwar crime stories were thus a barometer of the post-Cold War changes, of the transition to free-market democracy. They could also function to critique those changes. And they helped advance the changes.

We have seen the critique in the way the "worse than the war" sentiment traveled through crime stories. The emergence of this feeling might be traced through a process in literary theorist Lauren Berlant's notion of "cruel optimism," which, as she puts it, "names a relation of attachment to compromised conditions of possibility."[3] The object to which so many Salvadorans had been attached in the immediate postwar years was the cluster of promises embedded in ideas of democracy. People's desires for democracy were enigmatic but enduring. Many saw their struggles for social justice or for the nation, or even just their survival through the hardships of the war era, as attached to a vision of a better future coded as democratic. But even before the war ended, as we know, the conditions for the possibility for the inclusive democracy so many had imagined had been deeply compromised through the Salvadoran state's commitment to a free-market model. The postwar sense of disillusionment, then, indexed much more than crime rates.

This chapter offers two key arguments about correlations among crime stories, citizen subjectivities, and postwar transformation. First, the chapter investigates how the "worse than" theme infused crime stories—at the very moment when hopes for democracy had been raised. State actors' attempts to exchange the meaning of violence tied into larger efforts to remake citizen subjectivities. In their stories Salvadorans often echoed the state discourse on critical code-switching. But the rising "worse than the war" sentiment showed that many people rejected the way the state framed violence. Rather than registering progress from an alarmed state of exception to one of normative unexception, many people's crime stories in the 1990s portrayed an increasingly critical situation in the country. I qualify this sense, emergent through crime stories, as a "structure of feeling," as defined by Raymond Williams: "thought as felt and feeling as thought: practical consciousness of a present kind, in a living and interrelating continuity."[4]

The second half of this chapter offers a fine-grained analysis of two interspersed and contrasting crime story narratives, attempting to trace a route toward the production of postwar subjectivities. Emergent in the affective and ideological space created by the "worse than" sentiment, crime stories rejected any simplistic binary of violence entailed in a practice of critical code-switching. Rather, they produced practical knowledge of how to manage—and potentially transform—social relations. Postwar crime stories instructed listeners that the very way the world was available as a space for action was changing. People had to reorient themselves, their bodies, their intentions.[5] This chapter's title, "Today they rob you and they kill you," is an evaluation of changing forms of action, comparing imagined past behaviors with present modes (in other words, yesterday they just robbed you). Sharing this message, creating new knowledge, San Salvador crime storytellers worked to reshape new selves for the postwar world.

The nature of this knowledge and the shape of subjectivities varied according to class, gender, and generation.[6] Don Mauricio, a wealthy, middle-aged businessman I met in the gym, for example, loudly bemoaned the increasing dangers of going to his beach house at La Libertad, just south of the capital, with so many thieves lurking about.[7] And Dayana, a woman in her early twenties I got to know after she knocked on my door offering to wash my clothes, confided to me that she had to lock her young children alone in her *champa* (shack) in Las Margaritas, a crowded nearby slum, while she sought work. Gang members might molest them, or worse, she intimated.[8] Still, postwar crime stories circulating in the immediate years after the peace accords did not usually highlight discrepancies among diverse experiences. They constructed a common consciousness of "new" individual strategies to manage the postwar threats.

As they produced commonly shared knowledge, crime stories became a site of potential transformation. All stories are performative, in the sense conceived of in speech-act theory. They "do things with words," as in explicit speech acts such as "I promise."[9] The words, and the linguistic forms containing them, can change the world rather than merely represent or inform. The very contour of the 1990s Salvadoran crime-story genre acted to create knowledge and instigate subjectivities, as the narratives became "standardized," reiterable, compelling their own reproduction. The important thing is that they always were capable of slippage, of opening to something else, as they teetered at the edge of an unknown *next*.[10]

"Even More Terrible"

"It's strange," Nelson said, enunciating precisely for the tape recorder. "After the peace accords, it's even more terrible."[11]

Nelson Gutiérrez was thirty-two when we spoke in late 1998. He worked developing film in a camera shop. He lived with his mother in the middle of the congested, industrial city of Soyapango, a site that in the previous quarter-century had drawn many thousands of rural Salvadorans fleeing war and hunger. The population had swelled from about 43,000 in 1971 to a projected 290,000 by 2003.[12] The city straddles the nation's main eastern route, the Pan-American Highway, called the Boulevard del Ejército there—we passed through it earlier in this book, when I described my panicked trip back to San Salvador from Cacaopera in the eastern department of Morazán. Soyapango habitually hit the headlines in the decade after the war, especially with gang violence. Salvadorans from other parts of the metropolitan area often saw it as a space of danger.

Nelson and I had our first conversation after mass at a Roman Catholic church. We balanced our Styrofoam cups of hot chocolate with sweet *semita* and *milhojas* cakes as we sought a shady corner to talk. The church's services took place under a corrugated-metal shelter that only partly covered an open-air sanctuary. Parishioners were raising money for a new building. For the moment, though, during the guitar-accompanied singing, sermonizing, and praying, latecomers at the edges (often including me) scooted their plastic chairs through the hour-long service to avoid the shifting sun.

Although I had asked him about postwar crime, Nelson started by telling me about his younger brother's disappearance in 1982. The brother had left school at fourteen. He began working as a carpenter to help their single mother and five siblings. One day he did not come home. They never found him. They thought the guerrilla forces or the army might have grabbed him. For more than a year, their mother traveled east and west, checking unidentified bodies for scraps of the last clothes she saw her son wear. Back then, Nelson explained, "cadavers appeared right and left, everywhere, so my mother went around hoping to find him even if [his body] was thrown into a ditch, in pieces, you know, because really that's how they found cadavers, mutilated." But after asking around, Nelson guessed his brother had been caught up in a problem with drug traffickers who had "used him." He stressed, though, "It was just marijuana, not like today with all the coke everywhere."

After we speculated on the possibility that his brother was still alive—that maybe he had fled north—I asked Nelson what changes he had seen since the end of the war.

"It's strange. Before, before the peace accords, I was assaulted twice. One of those times it was an awful experience . . . I could even have been killed, but something intervened somehow and it didn't happen. But after the peace accords it's even more terrible [*más tremendo todavía*]. After the peace accords, the peace accords of—of—ninety, uh, uh . . ."

"Ninety-two?" I prompted.

"Ninety-two, after the peace accords I've only had the experience, the bad experience, well, to have been assaulted twice, but this time—" he paused.

"The truth is, the first time, before the peace accords, they were like, like petty thieves, pickpockets. They just rob what you have and run away and you never see them again.

"But after the peace accords, these guys, well, completely organized, they get on the bus, and . . . just like any common everyday bus rider, and they're just sitting there, waiting a few stops, then . . . they say they're taking out their rifles, and shotguns, you know—firearms—and they make all of us get down on the floor in the bus—

"And so a lady screams, desperate you know—and then one of them comes and fires two bullets.

"And there's a big commotion. People began to scream more."

I was confused, perhaps by the sudden switch in verb tense from present to past as he arrived at a moment of horror. "They shot—her?" I asked.

"They shot her. They killed her."

He continued. "I remember I—so I lift my head, just reacting to it all, you just react, so I lift my head up and the guy, who is by my side, threatens me with a gun, and says to me, 'Don't you look at me you son-of-a-you-know-what,' and so I, right away, put my head down, and he shoots, he shoots, and hits the handrail on the bus seat."

The three thugs—young men, twenty or twenty-one years old—took everything they could from the bus passengers. Nelson gave up his camera, briefcase, and money. Swearing, swaggering, they threatened to kill everyone. As they left, the men ordered everyone to stay put. They claimed they left a grenade behind. After a few terrified moments, all the passengers rushed off the bus. Only then, Nelson admitted to me, did he realize that the woman had been killed—when he saw her body. And only then, when he heard the other passengers talking about it, did he grasp that the bandit had actually aimed his gun at *him* (his narration above includes that retrospective recognition).

He said to me, "And then I realized that, that, I could have been shot."

This story, though brief, contains much. Take the beginning: in less than a minute, Nelson mentioned the 1992 peace accords five times. It is an obsessive return, a troubled fixation. *What went wrong?* Like so many crime stories shared in El Salvador at that time, part of what Nelson's account does is critique the peace. "Peace" may mean absence of war—but it may not feel more secure than before. For Nelson, counterintuitive as it may sound, it was even more terrible.

The conclusion that *things were worse* emerges through a distinction in the duration and intensity of past and present drama: the pickpockets who quickly run away versus the organized thugs who take up positions and commandeer a bus. It is significant that Nelson described the pickpocket as the criminal icon of the 1980s, after alluding to the fact that he had nearly died in another war-era assault—indeed, after describing his brother's disappearance and the mutilated cadavers scattered across the country in the early 1980s. Even discussing the possible murder by drug dealers of his brother, Nelson downplayed the war era (yet imagined non-"political") crime by suggesting that it had only been the softer drug of marijuana, while the harder, more destructive stimulant cocaine dominated postwar drug trafficking. (His explanation for his brother's disappearance, never proven, may have helped the family refute the widespread war-era stigma of pre-sumed "guilt" [of subversion] about victims and disappeared people. But his presentation of it in the context of a postwar crime story also participates in the critical code-switching impulse in which "common" crime becomes highlighted above "political" violence.)

Nelson did not just pronounce the postwar era to be "more terrible" than the war years. Through a self-reflexive evaluation of the performance of the crime, he contributed to a popular archive of knowledge of new modes of violent action in the postwar era. He also demonstrated how individuals needed to learn to protect themselves. In his account this happens, in part, through grammatical switches transpiring below the threshold of aware-ness, as the narration moves between the past and present verb tense. In the first, pre-peace accords assault, he started in the past tense, talking about a specific case. Then he slipped into the present tense. Such a verb-tense change could indicate a general rule, keying what the sociologist Erving Goffman theorizes as an imaginary "original" event on which subsequent performances of the same kind are modeled: "The first time, . . . they were like, like petty thieves, pickpockets," Nelson began, remembering a specific incident; next, illustrating a general rule, he said, "They just rob what you have and run away and you never see them again." [13]

Then in the second, postwar story, Nelson depicted a singular event of brute force. He referred to a specific case with the present tense. This is not a general rule, however, but rather the narrative present, in which the teller re-lives the experience. [14] Nelson was doing several things here, then. Through both these stories, he was relating a specific incident. And he was analyzing a historical change in models of violence. But he was also sharing key information about the new models, new scripts, new roles in the postwar climate. Further, his realization that the woman had been killed, and that he, too, had been in jeopardy—that others knew when the gun was aimed at him—revealed his essential, separate existence. He had been in grave danger: "I could have been shot." As individuals, then, we must seek strategies for managing danger.

Stories like Nelson's, the quick and shocking murder witnessed on a bus, the terrorized passengers passing their watches and wallets to a foul-mouthed group of thugs, offered a route through which to conclude that peace was "even more terrible." And, along with many other social forces gathering in the first postwar decade, they helped sculpt a new kind of knowledge, an expertise, even, on how to survive in the new, alienating environment. Public comments on such experiences functioned to fashion late twentieth-century market subjectivities. And so such expressions as "It's worse than the war," as detachable, circulatable units, influenced the way people oriented themselves in the world: they affected how people constructed social imaginaries and how people interacted with each other as citizens. Ultimately they contributed to the quality of the emergent democracy.

What Happened Next?

Like Nelson, many people shared pre-1992 incidents when I asked about postwar violence. Clearly, such experiences had already been entextualized into transportable, tellable units of talk. But the ways 1990s-era crime stories are marked historically, as intimately linked to the postwar moment, distinguish them from other accounts. They repeat in myriad ways that somehow "today," in its openness—in the murky space to the right of the question mark, what comes next? —feels much less manageable than the past, with its utterly knowable, if sometimes horrible, antinomies. In Nelson's account of his brother's disappearance, the frightening ambiguity of war violence as practiced by the terrorist state has disappeared; the *not-knowing* that characterized the murk of war is replaced by a retrospective *knowing*. Whether or not people explicitly embedded memory of wartime terror in their crime stories, the evaluation of the postwar present had congealed into the common language of "worse." The sentiment does not turn into a shared ideology, however. Rather, in William Roseberry's useful take on hegemony, it comprises common material and a dominant framework for talking about the social order.[15]

Saskia Góngora DeVries, a Salvadoran planning director of a prominent humanitarian NGO, put it this way when we spoke in the air-conditioned relief of her elegant office in the Colonia Escalón in May 1998: "We talk about violence every day. There's always someone who knows someone who had something happen to them, who knows this guy whose son was murdered." [16] (Our mutual friend Ondina, whom I knew from the gym, had introduced us, telling me that Saskia had much to say about crime. They had been close since their days more than a quarter-century earlier in an exclusive Catholic girls' high school.)

"You know," Saskia said, "I was ill this week, I stayed home for two days, so a friend came to visit me, two friends actually. And we began to talk, and one of them began to tell us an anecdote about another case of someone kidnapped in their car at a stoplight. And you know I had already heard another version of that story from a totally different person! Imagine it, how horrible. Crime is always the topic of conversation. . . . Today I don't even walk to work. I live very close, only a few blocks away, I could walk, but I am afraid. . . .

"Today there's not even a way to know where or when one can feel safe, or not feel safe, and you have this sensation that you're just crippled. I think that there are a lot of people going around with guns, women, too—before, women never went around with pistols in their purses, now they go and get a gun and register it and put it in their purse."

Interpretations of what happened in shared stories of crime, collaborating to create new knowledge of the postwar moment, often recontextualize surrounding discourses on citizen security—whether yesterday's front-page murder, the priest's call for a just society (or for family values, often couched in terms of the Catholic church in El Salvador), or the softly lit TV spots promoting privatization of the state pension plan (claiming it would allow individuals to define their own futures). People's responses to others' words always occur in a larger context of previous utterances or texts. [17] Nelson told me that after the bus trauma, he began reading the papers to guide his movements in the city. I recall one working-class man, Juan Pablo, using the phrase "lujo de barbarie" (luxury of barbarity, or excessively savage) as characteristic of postwar crime. He was likely reentextualizing a phrase common in media reports (though not in everyday talk)—he told me he watched three news programs most evenings. "They don't simply kill a person, but first abuse and torture them," he said, describing a mode of postwar crime that had its roots in war-era practices. He believed, as did many people, that unemployed ex-combatants brought their war "skills" to the practice of crime.[18]

Entextualization, to reiterate, is the process of making a stretch of talk about an experience into a relatively malleable text that can be lifted out of its local setting, out of its context, and then repeated in new contexts.[19] These new contexts are crucial for understanding the valence of crime stories after the war. Of course before and during the war people also shared stories of experiences of violence, stories that could be read for an individualizing message of self-protection. But the meanings change in new historical circumstances.

Better Off Before?

Amparo de Valenzuela, a candid, loquacious woman in her fifties from the Soyapango church Nelson attended, compared the moment we spoke (1998) with an almost mythic past time of community harmony.[20] "My God, I remember before the war I was always like really carefree [*vaga*]. I loved to go out, I used to go out to eat, go around the city center [*el centro*]. . . . I would go around, I'd be carrying a purse and wearing high heels and everything. Now I would never be calm walking around at ten at night in *el centro* . . . I would never stay there that late. . . . This is the postwar answer—what comes is this violence. There's always been violence, this country is known for its violence. The majority of us are violent, we get angry too fast. But now . . ."

I asked if she had gone out so freely in the 1980s. I knew that during the war she and our mutual friend Caro (who had first brought me to their church) had studied together in an urban Christian base community, led by laypersons trained in liberation theology. They had worked with them to read the Bible's messages in the context of the experiences of the poor. Her answer was blunt, not reflecting the politics I had expected.

"Well, in the situation around the [1989] offensive, I wouldn't go, for fear of bullets, but really, crime wasn't so exaggerated like today."

"The fear was different?"

"The fear was if there were going to be bullets or if a bomb was going to go off, or a grenade. Or if they'd assault you. In the war there were assaults, there were, but more of businesses and banks. They left the poor people alone. But it was less [*que era menos*]. There was crime, it's true, there was, but you could wear a nice little necklace, or a watch, and now you can't.

Now even a watch worth twenty colones they'll grab, they'll even hold up children at knifepoint to take their bicycle."

Ana Lorena Palomo's thoughts paralleled Amparo's, though she was a generation younger. She too claimed to feel a kind freedom of movement in the past that she did not have after the war.[21] Her days of youthful liberty, though, occurred in the early 1980s. In 1998 when we spoke in her boyfriend's house, Ana Lorena, by then forty, was a government employee who commuted to her office by bus from Ilopango (just east of Soyapango), where she lived with her mother. We had met at the gym in the Colonia Escalón, the only place where she and her boyfriend could regularly see each other. Unlike many people I knew, she declared she always felt safer when she saw soldiers during the war. Indeed, she was a staunch supporter of ARENA (the rightist Nationalist Republican Alliance party), one who questioned whether the government should have negotiated with "terrorists."

"We were better off in the war [*estabamos mejor cuando estaba la guerra*] because at that time you could, I was in the university and I went out at eight at night. . . . I used to go out dancing, and I would go out to eat with my friends from the university, and I would arrive in my house around two in the morning. . . . But now to go out at eight at night fills me with dread [*me da pavor*]—I could be assaulted, I could be killed, I could be raped. . . . After the war, in what we are in now, what we call the postwar, it's worse [*después de la guerra, en lo que estamos hoy, lo que llamamos 'posguerra,' es peor*]."

José Roberto Aguirre, a young man in his thirties who had recently completed his medical degree, told a dramatically different story of the 1980s. We had first met at the open-air church in Soyapango. Our conversation took place in the relative privacy of our friend Caro's kitchen, while Caro prepared us a breakfast of beans, eggs, fried plantains, and tortillas. The military had detained him three times (he used the word *secuestrar* [kidnap]) while he was a student at the University of El Salvador. Once they held him for three days, beating him, insulting him, "telling me I was a guerrilla because I was a university student, that all university students were guerrillas." When I asked him about postwar experiences, he said the most dramatic thing that had happened to him was a carjacking. After he pleaded with his captors to leave his body somewhere where people could find it, they shoved him out onto an isolated road.

Then Roberto brought up the topic of rape. This was something few others talked about directly (except as a fear, as Ana Lorena indicated).

"Now in this [rural] zone where I am working, there have been a lot of rapes, too," he said. "In [the department of] Morazán . . . there's a gang, a group of ten or fifteen who go around armed with rifles and everything, and they enter the houses even in the middle of the day. . . . In the community where we work they've told us of four or five cases of rapes, so far this year. . . . These are violations of young girls and also of older women who work in their homes."

"The community must be terrorized," I said.

"Yes, a lot of them say they're worse off than during the war [*Sí muchos de ellos dicen que están peor que cuando la guerra*], because during the war when there was conflict, a lot of people, well, they didn't get involved in anything, the army would come and demand food, and the people had to give it to them, and if the guerrilla came, the same. I mean, they didn't get involved with anything. But today no, if anyone comes, they come to rape the women and kill the men." In fact rape was a weapon of war in El Salvador, especially in conflicted rural areas such as northern Morazán. It was likely, however, that people in the community still did not speak publicly of the war atrocities.[22]

"Yes, it's terrible, the situation right now, because during the war. . . . If I knew they were from the guerrilla I was never afraid that they would kill me or do something to me, because you would explain to them and that would be okay, but with the army, if you came up against them, at the checkpoints, I would be afraid, right, . . . because they didn't ask questions or wait for explanations."

He stopped.

His account left me confused: "So . . . how can you compare [now] to the situation of war?"

He said, "I think maybe it's worse [*Yo siento que quizás peor*] today. . . . The question today with crime is that you never know where it is, or who it is. It can be anyone, it can be anytime, because today you even see criminals in the newest model cars, armed to the teeth, cars with tinted windows, that suddenly stop at a corner—I mean you just don't know who it could be."[23]

These circulating stories begin to sound like each other, despite differences in the tellers' class, gender, political positioning, and even experience of war terror. Roberto, the son of a single mother who cleaned offices to support her children, told a story that resonated with that of Saskia, a woman from a family with a "known" name linked to wealth. Amparo, who had once followed liberation theology, echoed Ana Lorena, the ardent ARENA supporter. Five years after the peace accords, they revealed a common anxiety about *not-knowing*, pointing to a kind of deterritorialized, deregulated violence. In their words one finds a disorder of things: Saskia's professional women friends slipped guns in their purses while Roberto saw street criminals roam the city in late model cars.

Many people also reported a paradoxical kind of wartime security in a repertoire of survival tactics. Saskia, it turned out, had not spent the war in a posh office. She had worked in rural zones, had traveled in conflict areas. Her anxiety about walking a few blocks in the relatively safe Escalón neighborhood in the 1990s, with numerous private security guards protecting it, thus seemed particularly jarring to me. Indeed, her fear became even more perplexing to me after she later shared a story she said she thought was most emblematic of the moment. In it, she was not so much concerned with the burglars who slipped into her house late one night to steal her jewelry, as she was enraged with how police did not believe her when she reported the break-in. They implied that "one of her lovers" might have taken her necklaces.

During the 1980s, at least in retrospect, she believed she knew how to handle the authorities. She represented the war era as constructed by unambiguous forces that one simply had to manage.

"I used to work a lot in the countryside," she told me. "In the interior of the country, with the government [during the war], and I had to do a lot of work in the east, in San Vicente [where there was a lot of conflict]. You learned how to recognize when there was danger, how to act in a dangerous climate. We knew that at this place at that hour, you couldn't go to that place; we knew there were zones we couldn't get into easily. So you learned to manage different kinds of danger, at least with the kinds of things that happened at that time. To some extent you learned how to play the game.

"And now it's not like that, the sensation of violence," she continued. "Now it doesn't conform to a struggle between two groups. Before one could think if one stayed on the margin and took the precautions necessary, then nothing would happen, at least if it wasn't just random chance. Now no. Now we don't know. There's not an enemy, nor is there a friend. There's not a cause, a struggle, that generates the violence. It's just crime. So before, if you ran into the guerrillas, they could ask for a contribution, or . . . they could take your car, [or if it was a military checkpoint, they'd] check your documents. But you knew that they wouldn't kill you, or you had a level of certainty they probably wouldn't kill you. That doesn't mean that that didn't happen."

She leaned forward. Her voice dropped. "But today, to rob a car, they kill you. To steal a ring, they kill you. The sense is that if someone breaks into your house and takes your microwave oven they might rape you." [24]

It was Febe Rodas, the mother of an old school friend of my partner Evert, finally, who convinced me that this circulating sentiment of degradation was more than a gauge of comparative experience in the late 1990s. [25] "It's worse than the war" was a forceful narrative framework that pulled in diverse people. Examined closely, it was always contradictory. All accounts, of course, contain their particular kinds of misrecognition, their own mystifications. But, while exceeding postwar reality, the "worse than" feeling also had something to do with experience. It made sense. It told of people's efforts to reorient themselves in the new situation. Otherwise it would not have circulated so freely. [26]

Febe, a physical education teacher in her fifties when we spoke in a cafeteria near the University of El Salvador in 1998, had suffered tremendously in the 1980s. The decade started with the kidnapping of her husband, who had just been elected to a political post in the western town of Chalchuapa. He had been warned not to get involved. "They never found him, I mean they found him but not complete, you know, but, in pieces. They found him in El Playon, you know where all the lava is [below the San Salvador Volcano, where many death-squad victims were left]. And I had to go identify him. It really affected me for a long time. It was something, an experience, that was . . . really strong, right. And I had to get that out of my mind, to get it out, but I couldn't for so long."

The case was never solved. Soon after she confirmed he was dead, she brought her two young children and elderly father to San Salvador. They suffered violence there too: In 1986, they were held hostage in their home over night. A group of thieves tied them up and stole everything, even the children's clothes. After the war, she said (after thinking for a moment), she had only been held up at knifepoint. But she had seen a lot. Just outside her school, thieves with machetes and knives—often ex-students—preyed on teachers and students. "Since the accords began, as they say, there's been violence," she said. "I mean even right by the school—nothing's happened to me there, right, because I'm always wearing sports clothes, maybe they think I never have anything of value, which is better because they don't rob me right?—But my colleagues [have been held up]. Over there by the school there are some gangs, and they're out robbing every day."

I asked her if she thought crime had gotten worse or better since 1992.

"You know to tell you the truth I don't know what to tell you," she said. "But regarding the [teachers'] union [ANDES-21 de Junio], how can I explain this to you. It's that, before, we suffered much more, . . . well, for example, politically, right, they would go and grab a teacher in her own house and kill her. We all suffered a lot because so many of us were killed like that, right. And other organized workers, too.

"Now I don't know. But in one sense it's calmed down, really, it's gone down. But now, there's so much crime. . . . There's this license to rob in a different way, in that they just kill to kill [*hay como libertad de que roben en otra forma de que maten por matar*]. I don't know if I would say that's it's increased, for that reason. It's like they unleashed all this robbery, because—let me think—when I was robbed in 1986, yes, in that time also it was messed up, and they used to rob people on the highways, they robbed houses. But I think maybe it's gone up."

"Why?" I asked.

"Well, they rob banks, they assault people in the buses, they stab them, and just in cold blood it . . . But it was bad before. They killed teachers like they killed pigs."

Increased Intensity, Rising Depravity

"The event is not what happens," Allen Feldman declares in his book on political violence in Northern Ireland. "The event is that which can be narrated. The event is action organized by culturally situated meanings."[27] The oral histories he recorded by political prisoners in Belfast, he explains, mediated a disjuncture between political aims of violence and excesses in meanings of violence. In El Salvador after the war, I have suggested that the ways Salvadorans talked of order and disorder—the narratives of crime and violence—were marked historically after 1992 as distinctly postwar. Clearly, people telling everyday crime stories engaged in their own kind of code-switching. Politicians and social scientists and United Nations observers sought to categorize incidents as "political" and "common," or noncritical, crime. But ordinary Salvadorans, as they worked to understand the contrasts between the past and the present, sometimes felt and expressed intensities that exceeded the state taxonomy, sometimes hinted at a surplus of meaning. *Some*thing was happening, something more.[28]

In constructing narratives of events, people create coherence and causality and temporality itself.[29] Narratives are always forms of culturally specific media through which speakers assert their ideas of social form—and through which ideas of social form simultaneously assert themselves on speakers. Thus the crime stories circulating in San Salvador in the 1990s were not just reflections of the historical moment, but key sites of new knowledge production.

They were also sites of remaking meanings of the past, in bending the big stories, even if people were not necessarily talking about the same past. Some people conflated the freedom of their distant youth with a generalized national past, often before the war, as did Amparo. They seemed to be engaging in a romanticized sense of an almost precapitalist community, though the historical moments they idealized held great strife. Others suggested a more ambiguous sense of relative insecurity. Many, like Maru in the first chapter, as well as Roberto, Saskia, and Ana Lorena, missed the safety they had paradoxically felt as they had learned to maneuver well through the war—whether they sided with the guerrilla or the military or neither. After the war, they suddenly lacked the right kind of *Angstbereitschaft*, or readiness for anxiety.

The "worse than the war" proposition emerged over and over again in a trope of increased intensity and rising depravity. Amparo said "they" focused on businesses and banks and left the poor people alone during the war—but in the postwar moment "they" held up children at knifepoint to take their bicycles (the child and the bike, of course, iconic of innocence; as such the assault indexes degeneracy, but also, especially in the way Amparo framed it, a loss of class solidarity). Ana Lorena compared frolicking at 2 a.m. with her college pals in the 1980s with her terror of being killed or raped today. This gendered dread arose in several other accounts. Saskia suggested that the postwar criminals were so wicked that they would kill to steal a ring and rape to rob a microwave. Roberto offered a perspective from a poor, rural community, also echoing a loss of class consciousness: during the war groups of men asked for food on their way elsewhere, but today the groups of men came solely to rape women in their houses. (The fact that rapes also happened in the war does not come up because it does not fit into the hegemonic logic of the war-to-postwar transition.)

Both Saskia's and Roberto's examples seem strangely denuded of the big stories of history. Certainly Roberto, who easily let slip an affinity with the guerrillas, well knew war atrocities, including the El Mozote massacre in Morazán (in which the nearly thousand villagers the military slaughtered reportedly were not collaborating with the insurgency).[30] Saskia knew that anyone suspected of subversion, even those just named by a neighbor as suspicious (as she was at one point), could have been taken from their homes and disappeared. She knew no one could manage the chaos of war.[31] But their attention, like that of so many, was on the terrifying ambiguity of now rather than the sometimes nightmarish, but always imagined to be safely past, then. (And here we might recall Walter Benjamin's warning of how memory can become a tool of the ruling class: "For every image of the past that is not recognized by the present as one of its own concerns threatens to disappear irretrievably."[32]) In the historical war-to-postwar trajectory of forms of violence in El Salvador that Saskia narrated, death—murder—and rape—were more "real" and pressing *after* war. It was a narrative of change over time shared among many Salvadorans in the late 1990s.

Even Febe suggested that there was something quite incomprehensible, something ruthless and amoral, and thus worse, in the violence of the postwar moment: they kill just to kill, they kill in cold blood, as opposed to killing for political reasons. Her husband might have been cut up into pieces, but his murder fit into a (horrifying) logic—he had gotten involved in politics. Teachers might have been murdered—like pigs—but it was understood this was for their union activism and opposition to those in power. Febe did try to resist the dominant narrative force. She might have agreed with the logic of the state's critical code-switching, toggling "political" and "common" crime. But she was not sure of the issue of criticality and the state of unexception. Ultimately the *worse* may lie in the experience of not-knowing, in the uncertainty of the present.

Performing Market Subjectivities

As individual narratives, crime stories depict "a temporal transition from one state of affairs to another."[33] These small transitions reflect, comment on, and produce, larger transitions. And for the Salvadoran government and transnational elites who controlled much of the country, the postwar transition was all about disarticulating the old, polarizing political community (and class identifications). As we saw in the previous chapter, from the late 1980s the thrust of governance in El Salvador was to inculcate a market rationality in the citizenry. If the war was characterized by fear of state and paramilitary and insurgent terror, as well as by collective resistance, then the postwar era was supposed to encompass market democracy structured around individual responsibility for the management of risk. Of course, individual risk-taking and everyday insecurity, intensified but thoroughly familiar elements of late modernity's "risk climate," were already part of most poor people's ontologies.[34]

To illustrate this idea, we can look to what might be considered an extreme version of this essence in the heart of the market itself, the Chicago Board of Trade. There, speculators deal in derivatives contracts, which offer options contracts or futures contracts on underlying products (such as wheat or soy—or the debt of the American treasury). Derivatives are supposed to reduce the risk that the value of an asset will fall unexpectedly—though the financial crisis of the fall of 2007 through 2009 showed the world otherwise. In her book *Out of the Pits* the anthropologist Caitlin Zaloom follows the transition from one mode of this risk management—intense, physical, face-to-face socialization of new derivatives traders on the floor (or in the "pits") of the Chicago Board of Trade—to another—the quiet, internalized online trading of the electronic era. She describes how traders disciplined themselves to be detached, purely economic entities. As market beings, they "give up part of the self . . . rejecting the responsibilities of social connections . . . to enter into the space of economic action."

She writes, "Speculation positions traders at the edge of the present moment, a location of high uncertainty where the authority of knowledge fades as traders try to anticipate slight market movements. With this murky view of the future, traders orient themselves with charts and social knowledge, but the material that they shape the most assiduously is the self." Examples of this "work" in the post-"pits" era, when people could no longer internalize a market *habitus* through embodied interaction, include diaries required of new online traders, recording their decision process, as well as online surveillance that trained traders to be rationalized self-observers.[35]

How did crime stories help instill a market rationality in 1990s El Salvador? One way these narratives instructed in social relations in the new era was through a reflexive awareness of interactions as performances—an awareness of patterns, scripts, and even rules.[36] In stepping out of a crime (or any) experience, displacing themselves from it, to narrate it, Salvadoran storytellers engaged in self-reflexive analysis. Since the typical postwar crime experience frequently entailed material gain or loss, indeed involved risk and survival, the comparison with Zaloom's traders is not so farfetched. Salvadoran storytellers, in the way the related their experiences, seemed sometimes to distance themselves from the social implications, the causes and effects (even on themselves) of violence, and critiqued the performance of the crime. The war-era (or perhaps more generally the twentieth-century) sense of class conflict in El Salvador, girded by an (often implicit) under-standing of structural inequalities, was being displaced by a troubling, iso-lating feeling of all against all.

Performance and Risk

The folklorist and semiotician Richard Bauman tells us that performance "calls forth special attention to and heightened awareness of the act of ex-pression and gives license to the audience to regard the act of expression and the performer with special intensity."[37] Performance tends to trans-form what we think of as the "normal," the "basic referential" use of lan-guage. It sets a special, critical frame for interpretation of actions. By frame, I mean the interpretative context that helps the observer or participant understand what kind of message or action is taking place: for example, whether something is recognized as a joke and not a serious exchange.[38] As cultural beings, we become habituated to recognizing shifts in and invoca-tions of frames, signaled by "keyings." Keyings are the ways people signal to each other whether they see ongoing interaction as more or less formally modeled upon some other (imagined) "original" event, in which there is a predictable formula with a familiar pattern: an academic talk, a politician's plea for votes.[39]

I am suggesting here that this special intensity in Salvadorans' at-tention to the act of expression in the performance of crime—even as it emerged in a critique of the state's ability to manage the democratic tran-sition—reflected and indeed promoted state and global efforts to develop, disseminate and institutionalize a market rationality. It did this in part by encouraging a self-monitoring mode that focused on personal risk man-agement.[40] Salvadorans maneuvering the streets in the years just after the war were looking for a logic they could bet on for survival. They were try-ing to understand how to speculate on possibilities. Functioning like trad-ers' diaries, crime stories after the peace accords oriented people to a new climate, at the edge of the murky future (an edge that seemed particularly unknowable after the war).

People quickly recognized that they could not draw on familiar war-era social resources (witness Saskia's and Ana Lorena's realization that state security forces weren't there for them anymore; others felt social movements did not give them the same purpose as in the past). The difficult transition from the National Police to the National Civilian Police, as well as the postwar changes in the courts and other parts of the government, reinforced many people's distrust of the state, even as the peace accords had fashioned some institutions that aimed to overcome this problem (such as the Office of the Human Rights Counsel). The stories people told described both institutional failings and personal heroism—self-care, self-protection, self-responsibility—often with little reflection on differential (classed and gendered) capacity for control.

Since everyday crime itself often arises from a risk-taking market mentality, this quality of crime stories, inculcating a sense of individualized strategizing, extended far beyond the postwar context. As I have noted, this mode was already quite familiar to most poor people in El Salvador—the majority of the population. But in the past personal risk management had not necessarily been their primary orientation, as wide support for the popular movement before and during the war showed. What makes the pervasive inculcation of market subjectivity worthy of comment, then, is that in the immediate postwar decade it seemed to fill the space once occupied by hopes for democracy. The "struggle" seemed to become a private one rather than a collective one.

Thus, as I have argued, crime stories became performative, in the sense of a "discursive practice that enacts or produces that which it names"—constituting meanings through action (rather than just enacting preexisting meaning). At the same time, meanings are not "free." Public interpretations of (criminal, or any) acts and social interactions are always disciplined by cultural constraints. The disciplinary apparatus for the crime-story teller is the social nature of storytelling in which certain kinds of narrations become hegemonic. It was, again, the very contour of the speech genre of the 1990s Salvadoran crime story itself that acted, as the narrative forms became "standardized," helping to shape the way people experienced encounters with violence. As Hannah Arendt has written, one may be the hero of one's life story (telling it), but one is nonetheless not the author of that story (its form defined long beforehand).[41] In El Salvador after the war, there might have been a sense of a space for a changing story to be told about experiences in the world, but powerful social forces constrained the shape of that space.

Archiving Emergent Knowledge

How did Salvadorans critique performance in their postwar crime stories? The Soyapango photo-shop worker Nelson pointed to the rudimentary tactics of ordinary, low-level, war-era thieves (the word he used, *rateros*, translates to pilferers, pickpockets), who grab and run, and compared them to the completely organized postwar group of three men who commandeered an entire bus. The words "completely organized," to any Salvadoran in the mid- to late 1990s, gestured toward the involvement of former combatants, whether military or guerrilla. As Juan Pablo, above, suggested, they turned to a new kind of stage (and drew on a post-Cold War rationality) to continue their violent acts. By describing their experiences this way, as a critique, it was as if storytellers stepped outside the events they were telling. They sought to analyze "new" forms of social relations, archiving emergent knowledge about the world around them.

Saskia, too, analyzed a historical change in models, in her case in a self-reflexive mode. In the war, people learned how to manage danger. The old reiterations had become comforting in themselves during war—at least so they seemed in retrospect. The anthropologist Brandt Peterson describes this kind of contradictory rationalization in terms of the traumatic experiences layered in the palimpsests of Salvadoran history. Writing of descendents of survivors of the Matanza, the big story of the 1932 massacre in western El Salvador, he argues, "In spite of the acknowledgement that people who were not involved in political activities, people who were 'innocent' by any measure, were nonetheless killed, a kind of irrational rationalization is formed that insists that there is a way to insure one's safety despite the clear evidence that no one is safe in the end." [42]

The war, long past, stored as a familiar and ordered set of facts, seemed safe, at least if layers of consciousness and memory were not disturbed. What to do now? In this "postwar," unlike the retrospectively imagined "war," there were no sure boundaries, no times and places, no checkpoints, labeled safe and unsafe. In the crime stories they told in the 1990s, many Salvadorans said they only realized what was happening too late, with an abrupt gun in the back or knife in the side. This, we shall see, was what happened to both Patricia Herrera de Alemán and Teófilo Turcios Lara, who shared two dramatic crime stories with me.

Though they have never met—their social worlds far apart—I have interspersed Patricia's and Teo's stories here in order to compare their experiences. Perhaps you could imagine overhearing them in a crowded café or a neighborhood *chupadero* (bar). Sometimes one exclamation attracts your attention—then you are drawn to the intensity of the other voice. Their contrasting accounts offer us an opportunity to examine the production of knowledge of individual strategies for surviving in the postwar moment, and to investigate the emergence of shifting of subjectivities.

Being *Listo* in the Postwar World

Patricia Herrera de Alemán and I met through Ondina, who introduced me to a number of acquaintances in her circle of comfortably situated friends. Ondina joined us for our conversation in the garden of Patricia's walled-off home in the Colonia Escalón.[43] While we spoke, the silent, uniformed maid brought us lemonade, and the clinking glass and ice (as well as a yappy dog) still echo on the tape. Patricia's family, she said, was one of the founding families of ARENA. At that moment in her early forties, however, she told me she was no longer interested in politics; rather, she studied Buddhism.

I began our conversation by explaining that I was studying crime stories and was interested in how mass-mediated accounts and people's own experiences might connect.

"I read the paper," Patricia said, "but I don't pay much attention to crime news, or political news. Now I'm not interested, though I used to be really involved, a long time ago. Now I don't even watch the news. It doesn't interest me. At any rate, other people tell you, you find out what happened anyway, so why watch it."

Then she launched into her own crime story. It began when she and a friend and their two little girls were standing in the street, trying to figure out how to get the keys out of her friend's inadvertently locked car. Already, Patricia admitted to a slip in strategies for risk management. The locking of the key in the car was a big mistake. This kind of acknowledgement arose often in 1990s crime stories, as people tried to figure out what went wrong— why they were robbed or kidnapped—and considered how to rectify that error in the future. How to discipline themselves to confront risks.

In Patricia's story, the two women eventually gave up trying to figure out how to get into the car and opened the *portón*, a kind of garage door, into the enclosed property. Patricia walked in ahead toward the house while her friend and the two girls paused. She told me, "And in that moment when we were entering, my friend stopped and said, 'Oh, now I remember how to get the keys out!' . . . But I was already inside [the house.] And I heard a sound and went back to the door, and there was my friend and her little girl—

and three men. So I went over there and I said, 'You've made a mistake'—I thought they had come to the wrong house.

"Then they put a pistol to my head and began to insult me."

The frame shifted, abruptly, keyed by the gun. The undifferentiated, ongoing experience of living suddenly became stark, hard, and separate. Distinguished from the flow of life around it, its performance became prone to evaluation, culled for new knowledge.

Such surprise forms an integral part of the "standard version" of the postwar crime story. This sudden imposition of an assault-frame contrasts with remembered generic wartime situations. As we have seen, many Salvadorans retrospectively reconstructed the past as clear-cut. They believed they had been able to expect or predict the "war" at certain times and places. In the postwar decade, that people did *not* recognize the cues of danger right away, or that they misread the frame of social interaction or performance, was agonizing after so many war-era years of heightened awareness, after years of being *listos*. *Listo* translates as both "ready" and "clever, smart." Prepared. Disciplined.

Here I will bring the second storyteller, whose voice was loud and boisterous, perhaps drowning out Patricia's softer, ladylike tone for a moment in our imagined crime-story café. Teófilo Turcios Lara prided himself on being *listo*.[44] Twenty-seven years old, garrulous and gangly, Teo grew up in Ahuachapán, on the western edge of El Salvador. His father taught biology at the regional branch of the national university. In Santa Tecla, Teo rented a small sleeping room from a cousin. He attended college classes in communications at the Universidad Tecnológica while working full-time in an equipment-rental firm. He was a staunch supporter of the leftist FMLN party.

In the following conversation, tape-recorded at our mutual father-in-law Don Antonio's house and interrupted by loud dinner preparations, he had already told me three crime stories of his four ("Really, there have been four attempted assaults on me, of which three have been successful for the criminals, and one not"). His big story had a learning curve in which knowledge of postwar crime performance had slowly accumulated. At first he could not even recognize his attackers as thieves. But by the end, in this final story, he was able to manage the situation much better.

This story starts with Teo deciding to take the last bus home to Ahuachapán. It was six o'clock, getting dark. He had been at an anniversary party for his company at the well-known Restaurante Néstor in Santa Tecla.

"There was a work party, and there had been a football game, and there was a party, and then I wanted to go home to my parents," he said. These explanations, work and family, justified his choice to take the risk of traveling at night. Everyone knew more assaults happened after dark, especially on the Pan-American Highway heading west.

After about two hours on the road, one more to go, Teo said, "I was alone in a seat, half-asleep, and I didn't really notice that some strange people got on the bus." (Half-asleep, faltering on the necessary discipline of self-responsibility.)

I asked, "Strange how?"

"Like gang members," he said. "They identified themselves as from a gang, but they were trying to confuse us, blaming another gang. They said they were from the Forty-Second Street gang, they *said*. . . . Anyway, uh, they began to make a commotion, I don't remember exactly, but here they don't use words like 'This is an assault,' like in the movies. Here they just say, 'Hey give us all you got.' And so they began to point their guns at the people in front."[45]

Teo's narrative contrasts with Patricia's in many ways: Certainly their social and literal locations, a public bus at night and a walled-in mansion in the day, differ. Yet these stories have much in common. In all of the examples above, the speakers pointed to keying—recognizing when they're "on stage," and thrust into the crime-performance frame. The shift to danger happened suddenly. For Teo, it occurred just as he was drifting to sleep, forgetting to stay vigilant, *listo*.

Right away Teo, demonstrating his expertise, critiqued the crime performance by referring to other kinds of scripts. He nodded to movie versions of holdups. Then (in the present tense, indicating a general rule and thus instructing the listener on modes of crime) he described an authoritative form of postwar crime performance: "Here [in postwar El Salvador] they say, 'Hey give us all you got.'" Then he reverted to the past verb tense, describing the specific instance, the singular performance of the bus holdup. By that point Teo had already keyed the "gang" (*mara*) genre, familiar to Salvadorans as distinctly postwar. They were consummate performers, gang members, with their baggy pants and black gothic tattoos, continually staging shows of power. The porousness between "authentic" and "staged" got mixed up here, as Teo doubted they were "really" the Forty-Second Street gang. The theme of masking—of code confusion, or of duping and duplicity—was a wartime continuity; it was believed "common" criminals (or soldiers) used to claim they were guerrillas. We saw the same thing in the previous chapter in César's account of his kidnapping. Through the 1990s Salvadorans were always doubting the identities of others, not wanting to be the *maje* (the duped fool). It was common for criminals to try to pass as cops, or cops to try to pass as everyday criminals (but what was the difference?).[46]

Later, Teo would describe this assailants—two very young, two in their late twenties—as *essentially* criminal, an aspect of crime storytelling we will explore in Chapter 6. "Looking at their faces . . . they were gang members. One had long hair, the other normal hair, but you could see they had tattoos. . . . They had criminals' faces, they had the look of delinquents, and it was like they were on drugs, that was the worst."

"This That Is Happening to You Is Real"

In her story, Patricia explicitly contrasted the imagined typical experience, the authoritative version, and the moment of singular performance in her garage. "That's the first thing they do," she explained, instructing her audience in the rules of crime performance.

As she constructed her experience in words, she also began to seek a space for her own emergent subjectivity in the risk-laden postwar climate. "They told us to get ourselves on the ground, and [asked,] 'Are there more people in the house?!' My little girl was right next to me, and they went to get my two employees. We were right by the entrance, and they were yelling at us, insulting us. So I grabbed my daughter and pushed her down, I told her, 'Lie down.'

"The first thing I thought—remember I've studied philosophy, Buddhism and all this, for many years. . . . So when I saw that they were pointing the gun at my head, and heard the men yelling, insulting me, the only thing that came to my head was, 'This that is happening to you is real. You have to do exactly what is necessary in order to survive.' And in that instant I became very calm."

Patricia pointed to how she resisted the victim role imposed upon her by her assailants. She also placed her singular experience into a spiritual frame. She attained a calmness she commented on several times in her narrative— "I don't know how I stayed so calm."

"When I was lying down," Patricia continued, "the man yelled, 'Who is the whore [*puta*] owner of the house,' so I went and said, 'I am.' My daughter turned and looked at me, a face of panic, she wanted me to be quiet. So he told me, 'Give me the jewels, where are the jewels.' So I said, 'I'll get them for you.' So they grabbed me by the hair and lifted me up, and pulled me up the stairs. If I remember right, when I turned to look at him he let me go, and never again did he touch me. He was right next to me insulting me, but he didn't touch me again."

The thief's use of the word *puta*—to most Salvadorans a vulgar term—points to gendered vulnerability. There are real, embodied consequences to crime, and women in particular recognize this. Remember how Ana Lorena and Saskia pointed to rape as worse than murder through the order of emphasis.

Patricia continued: "I said to him, 'Don't yell at me like that, you're going to make me nervous. And if I get nervous, I am not going to be able to give you the things.' I grabbed a wallet and I said, "Here, take the things,' I even chose the wallet that I was going to give him. They were saying tons of things. They insult you, they say everything, they're constantly telling you what they're going to do to you if you don't give them the things." Patricia's changes in verb tense contrasted the model performance (in present tense, "They insult you," which contributed to the larger archive of information about postwar crime) and the particular event she was describing ("They were saying . . . "). As the action continued, she framed *herself* as the agent in control of the stage.[47]

"He yelled, if there was more, and then suddenly he said, 'Now give me the guns.' I told him I didn't have any guns, so he said, 'If I find a gun, I'll kill you,' and he came and opened the drawer, and there were two guns, but there was another drawer in my husband's night table, in which there was another gun. So the man took out the guns and began to shout, 'You whore, why didn't you tell me!?' [*Puta, ¿por qué no me dijiste?*]. I told him 'I don't know what my husband keeps in his drawers, I don't go looking in his drawer.' I knew they were there. I don't know how I stayed so calm.

"And so he began to insult me, saying, 'Tell me where there were more,' and suddenly the gun went off. Two bricks fell from the wall. I turned and I said to him, 'Look, sir, the gun went off.' So the man got even more nervous. And I thought, inside my head, that they'd better leave soon, because at about that hour my son always came home." Patricia was so worried about what might happen at her son's arrival, she said, that she rushed the thieves. In the end she handed them the car keys (to the one vehicle that was insured), and managed to shut the door on them when they went out to look at it. The thieves didn't try to get back in.

"Objectively" Patricia was victimized. Men invaded her house, insulted her, stole her property. At the same time she constructed herself as in control, a heroine, and portrayed her assailants as out of control, hapless. In her description, her attacker did not shoot the gun himself—it just went off (literally, a bullet left him, *se le fue un balazo*).[48] When Patricia addressed the thief after his weapon discharged, she used the formal (*Usted*) form, complete with a title (*señor*): *Mire señor*. Her sarcastic tone of voice parodied the polite form of address (especially since in her narration she had used the familiar *vos* with the thieves earlier).

Much later in her narrative, Patricia described her attackers. "They had the look of gang members, with the kind of pants that fall down below their underwear, and those big guns," she said. "Two young guys, one a bit older but not old old, maybe thirty-five, and the others much younger. And they were really nervous the whole time."

The class element of Patricia's efforts at control, at risk management, are undeniable; the *portón*, the car, the car insurance, the choice of wallets, even the sarcasm. Buddhism, too, is highly class-specific in El Salvador, generally limited to elites (our friend Ondina had traveled to Thailand to deepen her Buddhist practices). Further, in the postwar climate, practices of Buddhism echoed a distinctly individualizing market-oriented ideology.

But Patricia's crime story has much in common with others circulating throughout San Salvador at the time. She deployed a central trope of Salvadoran postwar crime narratives in her description of her attackers. She emphasized their nervousness. She criticized their substandard performance. These men did not show the "professionalism" Salvadorans knew from the war and recognized among some postwar criminals. If they were nervous—like Patricia's attackers—they lacked the efficiency and organization that could merit odd appreciative commentary (as they defied the weak state and its poor performance, its incapacity to control violence). Through retelling her experience of crime, Patricia, like many, reworked her memory of war, and as such participated in a larger process of transforming social memory.

Social memory is not about individual experiences, but about shared constructs of the past in relation to the present. Teo was much younger than Patricia, and they had different class backgrounds. Still, both of them participated in a circulating ideological narrative that modified social memory of war and also pointed to a new neoliberal subjectivity in which the individual had to manage the risks present in the marketplace of life options, governing themselves within the logic of late capitalism.

"That Wasn't the Correct Form"

In his narrative Teo did not just criticize but lampooned the poor performance of the gang members. Over what seemed like two hours, he said, they wandered up and down the aisle, demanding the passengers give them one thing after another, wallets, watches, money, shoes. "They kept on passing by, again and again, asking for one thing from one person, asking for the other things from other people. They didn't ask for everything at once, like they should have. It's like they were on drugs or something, because that isn't the correct form, right, all disorganized, and asking and threatening the people like that."

Teo exploited the anarchy. "And when they would ask for the things, someone would go and ask for other things, so one of them said to me, 'Gimme your shoes, you gimme your shoes' he said, and then another would come by with a bag. So when they asked for the shoes I didn't give them, I said, 'Yeah,' you see, and when I took them off I threw them beneath the seat and, they were hiking boots, and I had white socks, so I just lifted my feet onto the seat and they thought that I had given them to him." Teo's drama carried a hint of machismo and subterfuge rather than the individual Buddhist awakening that Patricia offered as a survival strategy.

"Then one of them said, 'I'm going to check everyone and if I find five cents on anyone I'll kill him!' You had to give them even your coins. It was pretty drastic, you know. Even the coins, you had to give your coins or they'd kill you. They were a little nervous, pretty nervous, because it was really long, the assault, like two hours, two hours kidnapped on the bus, they took us all off [the bus and made us go into a coffee grove, one by one]. Really it was horrible."

I asked him, "What would have happened if they found your shoes?"

His answer showed his talent for self-strategizing—but also revealed a break in his bravura. "I would have said, they weren't mine, but they didn't see my shoes because they were beneath the seat, and it was dark, it was night, so they didn't see them. And the thing is, the funny thing in the end was that—well everything was dramatic in this moment, I thought that they were even going to rape a girl, I don't know what I would have done, probably I would have intervened, because . . . I wanted to go over there, but they were four, and maybe among all of us—but they had guns, so, it was better that we collaborated with them."

During the long assault, the gang members hit the driver in the head with the gun and knocked him out. After the assailants left, threatening to kill anyone who followed, much like Nelson's bus holdup, Teo took over. He became the hero of his story. He told everyone to keep down, waiting, and then announced it was safe to return to the bus. Since he was the only one with shoes, he drove the rest of the way home.

The Social Within the Individual

This chapter has examined how ordinary, if differently positioned, people's narrative constructions of their experiences with violence took form and meaning in the democratic transition of the immediate postwar decade. Crime stories linked individual bodily experiences with the imagined community of the nation-state, in which a sense of "worse than the war" became a widely circulated public feeling. As such, these stories deconstructed the past national drama and the attachment people had to a lost future. For many Salvadorans, the big story of war became a predictable, almost safe, place and time, reworked through the seemingly new, out-of-control nervousness of the postwar situation, in which drugged or unstrung criminals would rob you and kill you—they could kill for a ring, or a lie about guns, or for five cents.

The stories offered new orientations for people to turn to in the aftermath of peace. These new senses of self inculcated a market subjectivity disciplined to the new rationality dominating postwar El Salvador. Thus the stories, even as they effectively critiqued the state's transition to a market democracy, pointing to how the situation had become "worse," also collaborated with the powerful efforts to transform citizen orientations from collective, war-era passions to individualized, market-oriented modes of thinking. The narrative performance of experiences with violence provided tellers—such as Patricia and Teo—a way to reinterpret their fates and to reimagine their worlds. Many of the stories I heard helped speakers regain a sense of control as they explored ways to comprehend, codify, and confront new formations of violence. The stories shared among Salvadorans told of disarticulation. They turned what could have been framed as shared experiences into individualized, private, and privatized exercises of confronting danger.

This common narrative of the postwar era also constructed a new social imaginary which created new kinds of social Others, the criminalized subjects who became bare-life biopolitical debris. In El Salvador a sovereign-declared state of exception returned by 2003, when idle adolescent boys and lost young men who found collective passions within gangs would be outlawed as a category. Antigang laws proliferated throughout Central America in the post-9/11 global context, as we will explore in Chapter 6. The young men (and some young women) themselves, of course, lived in the contradictions of the moment, too. They were as subject as everyone else to neoliberal orientations, lacking class solidarity as they ventured into the market of public streets seeking gains.[49]

Crime stories contributed to a privatizing, market-oriented ethic. But it is important to remember that they did so *socially*. Stories are always told *to* others, shared *with* audiences. What people say does not emerge in isolation. Words always occur in a larger context of previous utterances or texts. Even monologues are social and public. As these crime stories circulated, then, a sort of publicly unifying way to talk about experience of the transition emerged—a way to *share* a sense of the radical insecurity of violence after war, even if it subverted class differences and displaced material conflicts. As they circulated, and were standardized into recognizable, publicly shared shapes, crime stories also produced collective knowledge about a shared national drama, seeking to define the unknown of the postwar while also reiterating a familiar narrative of disillusion. The recontextualization of these detachable fragments of experience served as community resources in the new historical moment. The shared nature of the stories could undercut their individualizing nature. As such, they always held the potential to build new kinds of communities. They could point to alternative postwar social forms.

After sharing her experience, Patricia explicitly compared the war and postwar eras. Her coda points to the wide, cross-class nature of this form of storytelling, even as it masks class differences. It displays a larger, shared disenchantment with postwar democracy.

"There have always been assaults. But there used to be less. It's *after* [the war] that they've increased so much. I know this. I listen to people everywhere. I always go to get massages, I go to this blind woman, and I hear about all kinds of problems.

"I talk with the people there, and they tell me about other people, and they tell me, and—well, if they can even steal from her, a blind woman, on the bus—it's never been as bad as it is now. . . . I tell you, yes, before the war, in the war, people robbed, but they robbed and they might stab you and that was it. Today no, today they rob you and they kill you if they feel like it."

In the decade after the peace accords, crime stories produced new knowledge of what most people saw as a critical situation. These narratives repeated a vision of violence spiraling out of control. By reviewing, reframing and reimagining crime through their narrative performances, Salvadorans were conceptualizing the political transition to market democracy, critiquing the peace proclaimed as a state of unexception, looking for space to manipulate experiences of violence in the context of critical code-switching, and disciplining new, individual postwar selves within the social, collective form of storytelling. Within their stories they invented an agency they often could not find in the nation's unfolding historical drama. Even as they repeated the lament, "It's worse than the war," they were also insisting on another kind of space and time, a different form of the social. Not the war, not this "peace." Something not known, not *yet* known. But possible.

Chapter 4
Adventure Time in San Salvador

So she opened the window.

HONK-groan-clank. Airrr. Relief.

Yellow—Red light ahead. Slow, stop.

It was one in the afternoon on Boulevard de los Heroes, in front of Met-rocentro's vast glass-and-steel-and-brick shopping paradise.[1] All around, cars, trucks, buses, vans, SUVs, motorcycles, grumbling, gunning. Waiting. Sun beating down. And in the car no A/C—still out. Leatherette seats biting sweaty thighs.

But that window. That window, left open. Open to the world. Open to possibilities. Later, reconfiguring it all, shaping a series of actions and reactions into a crime story, Marielena would come to know she didn't simply forget to roll up the glass at the light. That's what she first claimed: a momentary lapse. Her account a cautionary tale, another crime story telling people how to handle postwar risk. But soon enough she would admit that all the warnings hadn't just slipped her mind. She hadn't suddenly misremembered all the proper counsel conveyed to well-bred young ladies who venture onto the streets of San Salvador.

The streets of San Salvador. In their unpredictability, their anarchy, their menace, metonymic, perhaps, of El Salvador itself, for some representing the rabble to be repressed, for others signifying the risks of the marketplace for which citizens had to be disciplined. Even the fantasy of order at that very moment, in the red traffic signal restraining vehicular chaos, hinged on a fragile social agreement as to the meaning of that red—not to be taken for granted—and also to an erratic power supply (better now than during the war). But as Marielena waited by that light in 1995, familiar times and spaces of danger had been shifting. The very way the world was available as a space for action—the alignment of bodies and objects in that world—was changing.[2] We have seen that the taxonomy of public violence, the meaning of risk, was transforming as the government attempted its critical code-switching to a state of unexception. At the same time, circulating crime stories were insisting the situation was "worse than the war." What would happen next? No one knew. So Marielena, like much of El Salvador at that moment in 1995, was anxiously watching and waiting. By then, the cruelty of postwar optimism had begun to set in. In the story she told me three years later, she spoke of dread, of defiance later repented, and of the dangers that lie in wait for those who leave the window open. And yet she continued to leave that window open, just a crack, granting remnant possibilities that *some*thing might come up.[3]

This chapter follows Marielena's narrative.[4] It tells a story of a kidnapping and near-rape that occurred in less than two hours' time within a ten-minute-driving radius in the city of San Salvador, and yet in retelling spiraled across time and over space. As it considers how Marielena positioned herself, the people she addressed, and other figures in and outside the communities she constructed in her talk, it explores how she tried to order the world—giving an insecure, shifting world stable meanings.[5] It reveals a tale of gender and class and even race so often submerged in the *mestizaje* myth of Central America's middle isthmus.[6] It suggests that she lived through a disorienting *queer moment*: not only "the intellectual experience of disorder, but the vital experience of giddiness and nausea, which is the awareness of our own contingency and the horror with which it fills us."[7] What becomes most compelling in her narrative is the new knowledge it produces. It rethinks, above and below the threshold of awareness, notions of solidarity and community and protection and patriarchy in the emergent era of market democracy. An analysis of her account demonstrates how Salvadoran postwar crime stories became a technology for the transformation of structures of feeling,[8] a transformation that contributed to conditions for the possibility of a return to war-era defensive security measures a few years later. It shows how public danger was finally narrated in terms of what was seen as private affect, rather than public, political, community, or national experience.[9]

This feeling of separateness, as discussed in earlier chapters, had supplanted the social imaginary of obligation, or social care, that characterized much social memory of the war and the years leading up to it. It deconstructed an idea of the world in which people imagined that others in their communities acted out of concern for one another. Chapter 3 examined how crime stories, in the emergent affective and ideological space created by the "worse than" sentiment, produced practical knowledge of how to manage social relations. It demonstrated how, as they circulated, conversational narratives about violence instructed listeners on how to conduct themselves in the new postwar environment, individually managing risk rather than thinking of themselves as part of a collective. It also suggested that these narratives, even as they merged into a "standard version," were always capable of slippage, of opening to something else as they sat at the edge of an unknown *next*.

This chapter expands that analysis, focusing less on conduct and more on affect: in particular, it attends to how postwar market orientations of self and other emerged, diverged, and merged in complicated ways in the decade after the peace accords. The concept of structures of feeling, as distinct from ideology or worldview, emphasizes "social experience still in process" often thought to be "private, idiosyncratic, and even isolating, but which . . . has its emergent, connective and dominant characteristics."[10] Marielena's story portrays, and enacts, a withdrawal from participation in public life. It finally rejects hope, dismisses the fragile, rising possibility of a modernist national democratic community. The narrative's singularity, especially the self-transformation it describes, would seem to detach it from any "standard-version" crime story circulating at that moment. Yet it is strikingly consistent with the neoliberal political project to privatize citizenship in El Salvador. That project was far from unique to El Salvador, even as it took particular form there. It corresponded to a rising rationality that, as it redefined politics in terms of self-interest, produced new imaginations of the public, the state, and the state-citizen relationship.[11]

That same kind of project has manifested across the globe in dramatically different contexts. In the United States, Lauren Berlant describes a concerted cultural movement, during the Reaganite cultural revolution, to narrow ideas of public and political and to invalidate feelings of a common public culture. "No longer valuing personhood as something directed toward public life," she writes of that cultural moment, "contemporary nationalist ideology recognizes a public good only in a particularly constricted nation of simultaneously lived private worlds."[12] In postwar El Salvador, Marielena's story corresponds to the thrust of this imaginary. It finally distrusts a national polity. Her narrative focuses not on new rules for individual survival, as do many other stories shared in the mid- to late 1990s, but rather turns back to the past, seeking a closed, safe, private world.

Marielena at first tried desperately attempting to *unqueer* it all by insisting that nothing had happened. This is why this chapter is called "Adventure Time": the Greek adventure novel, in the view of Russian philosopher and literary theorist Mikhail M. Bakhtin, offers a plot of "pure digression from the normal course of life, excluded from the kind of real duration in which additions to a normal biography are made."[13] In Adventure Time, the main characters stumble through a series of obstacles, lurching from event to event as each springs up "suddenly." In the end they return to where they began, as if nothing had ever happened.

Is this, finally, what is left after a dozen years of war (preceded by years of chaos and struggle), following a world-watched and heavily lauded peace negotiation, and a long, violent transition to democracy? If people were saying "It's worse than the war," was there no more social justice, equality, or democracy in El Salvador after the war than in 1980, the year a death-squad assassin murdered Archbishop Óscar Arnulfo Romero while he was saying mass? Could the answer to "What happened next?" be *nothing*?

This analysis takes the body seriously. It does so by considering *time* in the sense described by phenomenologist Martin Heidegger, particularly his insight that the specificity of the self lies in its relationship to temporality—its existence in a limited amount of time. Heidegger referred to this kind of consciousness with the unwieldy compound term *being-toward-death*. This concept expresses well Salvadoran ontology in the late twentieth and early twenty-first centuries. In the immediate postwar period, everyone was intimately aware of the vulnerability of the physical body. Everyone in El Salvador in the mid- to late 1990s—memories always already sated by experiences of, and images of, war—everyone moving in bodies through the streets of San Salvador—had to calculate risks for each outing. They had to contemplate the odds of death. This daily gamble fed into the postwar discourse of crime stories. Every day people negotiated their anxiety about the world as they faced the possibilities of the streets.

Bodies, never separate from minds, always incline themselves toward objects, toward others, toward places, toward time itself—ultimately toward something that could be summed as *care*.[14] The basic characteristic of care, concentrated to the more prosaic level of everydayness (and involved activity) is "within-time-ness," an orientation often expressed through narrative form itself: it is "our being thrown among things which tends to make our description of temporality dependent on the description of things about which we care."[15]

Marielena's tale is that of a privileged young woman about to move from the protection of the father to that of the husband, in a proper progression of the conventions of family and inheritance and child-rearing time. It focuses on a kind of cusp in her life, when she momentarily looked outside her world. She opened that window. It narratively orients itself toward care and illusions of care in four zones: care of the patriarch, of the community, of the state and then, perhaps, of God, or the supernatural. It is the zone of community, and its blockage, that most interests me. The postwar opening had allowed Marielena, for a moment that might be called cruel optimism in retrospect, to envisage a democratic polity as a kind of national community of care, in a broad sense. After all, such a world had been promised in state and global rhetoric. It had also been contained in a broad Salvadoran social memory of a possible future. Marielena may not have participated in the war-era passion that stimulated visions of democracy as a form of individual sovereignty and social equality. But at the time of the peace accords she clearly, if briefly, shared in the hope for more openness, inclusiveness, and social solidarity.[16]

It was the queer moment of Marielena's carjacking trauma that turned her. As she told it in her crime story, both the state and the imagined postwar community of social care abandoned her. They seemed to deny her very existence. The experience sent her fleeing risk, running from the dangers of change, back into the arms of the patriarch (her family and the Holy Family)—where she reacquainted herself with old, secure knowledge of the world: a well defined *us* and an evident *them*.

Bajo Salvador del Mundo

The story begins when Marielena crosses a deeply narrativized spatial boundary, venturing "bajo Salvador del Mundo." The phrase translates literally as "Below the Savior of the World." El Salvador del Mundo is San Salvador's patron saint. In the city his stand-in is a gray-white statue of a robed figure of Jesus Christ, arms outstretched, perched on a blue globe and balanced on a long, tall crucifix base. The monument rises up from a small, green diamond-shaped park, itself surrounded by the exhaust and creaking metal of San Salvador's perpetual traffic jam as it moves toward and away from the volcano that rises over the city. Some say that the spot has traditionally marked a psychic limit for the orientations of a small, powerful class of wealthy and near-wealthy inhabitants of the capital city, many with addresses in the large Colonia Escalón and other nearby enclaves. Moving down past the statue could indeed seem to represent a descent, away from privately patrolled, walled-in godliness, its cleanliness assured by masses of servants who usually arrived from distant rural homes very far *bajo Salvador*. In this imaginary, as Salvador del Mundo faded into the exhaust-filled distance, the traveler entered the outer rings of a Dantéesque inferno. As Salvadoran poet Oswaldo Escobar Velado wrote in 1959, in the epic poem *Patria exacta* (1959):

Bajo la sombra de "El Salvador del Mundo"
se mira el rostro de los explotadores.
Sus grandes residencias con sus ventanas que cantan.
La noche iluminada para besar en Cadillac
a una muchacha rubia.

Allá en el rostro de la Patria, un gran dolor
nocturno: allá y yo con ellos, están los explotados.
Los que nada tenemos como no sea un grito
universal y alto para espantar la noche.

[Under the shadow of El Salvador del Mundo
One sees the face of the exploiters
Their grand residences
With windows that sing the night
Illuminated
To kiss a blonde in a Cadillac

There in the rest of the country,
A great pain
Nightly:
There are the exploited
And I with them.
Those of us who have nothing
Except a scream,
Universal and loud
To frighten the night.] [17]

Marielena's story becomes such a journey of descent. It starts nestled in deep safety, in comfortable relations of care in her father's brick rampart-wrapped home in the Colonia Las Mercedes. The neighborhood sits near the national military headquarters and indeed is full of military residents, people who had always protected her privileged community.[18] Then one day she veered a little bit out of the safe circuits that had defined and circumscribed her life. Her deviation felt so small. Could a shopping trip really have been an act of rebellion? Could leaving a car window open on a hot day really have been a form of resistance?

Leaving a window open, especially at a stoplight, oriented Marielena differently from before. It interrupted a collective chant, a normalizing injunction repeated again and again, about moving through space in the ever breaking-down world of end-of-century San Salvador. When she opened her window, the *outside* entered into the imagined safety of the car. When Marielena did *not* roll up the tinted pane at the red, she became a reachable object for the inevitable hand of fate.[19]

The hand, which she described as dark and ill-clothed, reached in and took hold of the car's steering wheel. It violated her sense of herself, her class, gender, and race, in relation to others' permissible reach. It took her on a long ride. It took her to a place in which she became so invisible that even the patriarchal state she had trusted all her life could not see her—she who had always been seen, watched, watched over.

"Nothing had happened to me," she would say in her account (and accounting), "until 1995," until the stoplight. And yet by the end, after she had described the doubling of her peasant kidnapper into the devil, she repeated: "*Nothing happened to me. I was trembling, thinking of what could have happened to me. . . . Thank God nothing had happened to me. . . .*"

"Not Going Out at Night"

"Well, the truth is," Marielena told me, as we settled into the comfortable chairs of the front living room, "that in El Salvador ever since the war, we live with this feeling of insecurity."

This was already clearly a story shared with a *gringa* anthropologist in El Salvador in January 1998. It was early afternoon in a large house surrounded by thick walls. Unlike a story told to a Salvadoran friend, who likely would have shared ideas of widespread insecurity, this account needed to establish a mutual frame. Marielena reoriented herself to what she imagined was my outside vantage point. She observed her experiences as within the space of the nation and the time of the war and its aftereffects. Still, she did not make everything explicit for me. The phrase "Ever since the war" begged the question: And during the war? Like so many stories people shared in the 1990s, the war took up a known, and paradoxically safe, meaning. It was past. It had been endured.

"Logically in a period of war, we weren't allowed to go out at night, members of my generation—I'm twenty-seven—so we just lived like that, not going out at night."

What kind of Salvadoran laments about not being able to go out at night as one of the major deprivations of war? For one, Marielena Schettini—

whose surname is known in El Salvador. Her body, so named, became a token of wealth and power. She was the protected daughter of a prominent economist-businessman who ran for high political office in the 1990s.[20] We could limit our interpretation of this story, then, to that of privilege. But we must remember that stories, as they circulate, exceed the limits of their origins, drawing on larger community knowledge to make them tellable. We might also recognize that while her body, like all, is oriented in relation to power and capital, it is also subject to countless other complicated forces. At the very start of her story Marielena showed us some of the forces that intersected in her being, by pointing to a gendered and classed limit to movement: "out" at "night." This was during the war, a historical force overdetermining all experience. But after the war things got "worse": even a domestic errand at midday could fall beyond her world's permissible horizon.

We met in a vegetarian cooking class.[21] It was a proper orientation for us, as comfortably situated young women. A number of participants said they came because of their husbands' dietary needs. I had watched her in the first sessions, dressed in tailored pants suits, hair cut stylishly short, answering her little black cell phone. (This was that odd moment in history when cell phones were uncommon in the United States but seemingly ubiquitous in the rest of the world.) It was she who approached me, curious about the quiet foreigner. She had just graduated from the prestigious Universidad Centoamericana (UCA)—the Jesuit-run campus a five-minute drive from her house—with a degree in business administration. Her husband was an attorney. They had only been married a short time. I explained my anthropological "mission." Like many people, she responded immediately. "Yes, it's awful here, isn't it?"

Marielena first shared her story with me one day after class, at her house in a gated neighborhood called El Capistrano, in the Colonia Escalón near the luxury hotel that had until recently been called the Hotel El Salvador. It was known as the Sheraton when it was stormed by FMLN guerrillas in the 1989 offensive in the city. We had brought with us our cardboard takeout containers with a tofu-based dinner that our instructor, Doña Betty, had cooked for us in her demonstration. Marielena had insisted on giving me a ride after I told her I planned to take a bus home. We talked about driving as she maneuvered easily through the congested streets. Talk of traffic sparked talk of crime. Her crime experience happened in her car, when, she told me, she had inadvertently left the window open at a stoplight.

She seemed to be teaching me a rule on individual survival in the postwar environment, as so many crime storytellers did. I think she saw me as a fellow independent, educated white woman who had to go out into the streets of San Salvador alone. But her narrative differed from so many such stories told among Salvadorans. She said her brief kidnapping compelled a religious awakening. Though she was Catholic (she had laughingly shown me a picture from that week's society pages, of herself and her mother at a church event[22]), her account ended as if it were a Pentecostal witnessing God, and the Devil, come vividly to life.[23]

Some months after the first telling, in January 1998, I asked Marielena to repeat her drama for my tape recorder. At that moment she was about to leave for what she thought would be a year's stay in Washington, D.C., to join her husband, who had begun studying international law there. She had temporarily moved back into her parents' house. Meaning is emergent in the moment of telling—it is jointly produced and negotiated as interaction proceeds. So even as her experience had cohered in a particular way as she repeated it again and again to friends and family, she told it slightly differently in new circumstances.[24] In the second telling to me, she was undoubtedly thinking of her own move to a city up North.

"Never, Never Had Anything Happened to Us"

"But after the war there was a sense of, like, liberation—*Ah, everyone felt safe and everything*—"

Her voice dropped. "But as time passed, eh. . . . There came unemployment, and vagrancy, all the weapons that stayed in the hands of the people who had been in the war, and crime went up—in the UCA they have a special word for it, I don't remember what it is . . . but postwar crime, right.

"And all these armed people have caused—currently, I can't tell you exactly what situation we're in right now in 1998, but, yes, this feeling of insecurity because of violence, because of stealing, because of—something else that isn't war. . . . It's like it's gotten worse. Because before, the guerrillas never assaulted you."

"Before '92?" I asked.

"In the war."

"In the war."

"Exactly, I mean, thieves didn't exist as much because everyone was going around busy in other things. Yes, there were murders. "

"And kidnappings," I said.

"Exactly, and kidnappings, but that was more related to politics. . . . And lamentably, well, in the countryside, right."

"Right."

"It's that—They had, they have another kind of experience completely different from the people in the city."

Marielena organized time and space for her listener. There was war. There was "after." There was urban. There was rural. Quickly, though, she reconfigured these circumstances away from an academic slant, with words like "unemployment" and "vagrancy," toward less secure grounds. What happened in her narrative might be called struggle between different kinds of "voices" in which the politics of how to tell El Salvador emerged.[25] The contest emanated as *violencia* (the general, distanced, diagnostic word "violence") became the more street-level, less formal *ladronismo* (the pointedly on-the-ground act of stealing, or thievery). Other social phenomena also decayed—to "this thing that isn't war, but worse." To Marielena, critical code-switching did not render crime uncritical and unexceptional. Instead of a binary flip, and rather than a scientifically explainable movement in time, things turned back on themselves. Already we can see the possibility of concluding that nothing happened despite the war—nothing changed.

"So, well, the people in the city—this is what I think happened to me—As a little girl, educated in a private school, whose parents have a little vehicle for private transportation . . . I had certain comforts. Middle class.[26] So never, never, had anything happened to us, nor to anyone close to us.

"So I was driving around feeling very safe. This was in, it had to be—in '95, right, because in 1995 my car, it had only been a month since it had been given to me. A month since it had been bought. It was new."

Marielena's experience, the reach permitted her, had been shaped by her class-delimited neighborhood and city space. She spoke of relative safety and comfort. She hardly differentiated herself from others in her enclosed world. What that protection meant in the context of her narrative was that nothing had ever, ever happened to anyone, even in the midst of war. If something had happened, it would be coded political and thus, implicitly, understandable in the circumstances—the victim likely to blame. Or else, it was (lamentably) out in rural spaces, where different, incomprehensible codes ruled. Out there.[27]

So in her story now it was January 1995. The third anniversary of the peace accords. The answer to the question "What happened next?" should have been clear by then, but it wasn't, to most people. In fact Marielena did not describe the year in terms of national history. She did not reflect on the time that had passed since peace and democracy were supposed to have arrived. She had moved to a domestic orientation. She remembered the year because of the model of her car, which was a gift. She was calculating time through "care"—through a steel and tinted-glass prosthetic that was supposed to secure her from the uncaring otherworld.

"I Realized That I Was Abnormal"

"So," Marielena was saying, "it was exactly one in the afternoon, I think it was in January, in front of the Hotel Camino Real. That's a really well traveled area. Central."

"Mmm-hmm."

"—I mean it wasn't a place where you were afraid, right in front of Metrocentro. Well you've been there—there are a lot of people in movement there, in the middle of the day. . . . And, I was at the stoplight, and normally Salvadorans are—not everyone, right, but like the majority, you know—a little bit insecure? Which means you're always really alert.

"This I realized because I went to Costa Rica, uh, before the, the experience I had. The Salvadoran always goes around watching, looking around, as you go on your way—this is part of who you are, and the people maybe don't realize, but you are always checking out the people around you—are they suspicious or not." She demonstrated the furtive look, the glance back.

"Ah-ha, ah-ha," I responded knowingly.

"But there is already a prototype of the suspicious person, he goes around badly dressed." This kind of deracialized description was common in El Salvador.

"There in Costa Rica?"

"Here."

"Here, here."

"So when I arrived in Costa Rica I realized that I was abnormal compared to them."

I laughed. We both laughed.

"They didn't realize, but I did. Because we went to a park, in '92, to walk, with a friend at eleven at night in Alajuela *and there were a lot of young people in the streets, eating pizza, ice cream, Popsicles,* at that time—. . . And I just stood there with my mouth hanging open. Eleven at night in a park. . . . Because this—*never* does something like this, still—it does not happen in El Salvador—I mean just to eat Popsicles . . . *young guys, young people, there, in the park.* And I was—surprised. . . . And you feel so strange in an environment of security. Simply because nothing happens there, but for you it isn't normal. Here you have to be alert."

"Right," I said.

Marielena returned to El Salvador. "So, in 19—until 1995 nothing extraordinary had happened to me—"

"A-hah—"

"Well, maybe some regular guy says to you, '*¡Mamacita!*' [Hey baby!]"

I had to laugh.

"That kind of thing." She laughed, too.

"Yeah, don't I know it," I said.

"Right, then, uh, well, a woman always has to be careful, right?"

"Yes, yes."

"You have to stay away from these people, because you never know. That is the truth. You never know," she said.

She picked up her main story again. "Well. That day, well, I was going in my car at one in the afternoon in 1995, and—I mean—would you like some?" She held up her coffee cup, gesturing toward the kitchen.

I declined, though looking back now I think she must have been trying to postpone the retelling.

"Okay. So, uh, in 1995 I was in my car, taking it easy. For the first time, I didn't look in my rearview mirror"—she let a beat pass—"to make sure there wasn't anyone there because, because my car didn't have air-conditioning then. They always tell women '*Don't open your windows! Don't open the window!*'—and I used to say, '*How ridiculous.*'"

I laughed again. "Right, right."

"So, I had the window down, at the red light, and for the first time I said to myself, 'I'm tired of paying attention all the time,' checking the rearview mirrors, 'to see if someone is coming.' Oh, no. 'Today, no,' I said, right."

One in the Afternoon

Marielena visited Costa Rica in 1992. In January of that year, the peace accords had been signed. I suggest that her narrated impressions of Costa Rica, the country without an army often called the "Switzerland of Latin America," had everything to do with fact that she was there in 1992.[28] The peace accords, promising an end to war, full of hopes of democracy, had opened a window onto the world—had brought hope, however fleeting. That hope was not (not only) a procedural one, of voting in competitive elections. It was constituted by a cluster of desires about social solidarity that, in part, had to do with mingling with people in the streets. And eating Popsicles. And not having to look over your shoulder all the time.

The trip to Costa Rica, and the sudden self-reflection it compelled, became a *queering* adventure time for Marielena. It was a digression from the normal course of life—and yet when she returned (through the time-bending effects of her narrative logic), she saw herself—her nation—as abnormal. She recognized the safe, enclosed world in which she had lived for most of her life, growing up in war, as artificial. Even the simple statement "nothing happens" transformed. The carefree *nothing* in the park in Costa Rica was far different from the tense, monitored *nothing* in her life in El Salvador. Indeed, she amended her appraisal of "nothing" on her narrative return to El Salvador, to "nothing extraordinary." Her negative evaluation became a catalyst for her decision to throw aside a Salvadoran tool for living, that caution, that distrust. How strange it was: walking in a park at eleven at night, and young people (of her class and race) everywhere! Would anything like this happen in El Salvador's nascent peace? Could she return to El Salvador as if nothing had happened after eating Popsicles in Costa Rica?

Now we begin to understand the significance of her repetition of the hour, one in the afternoon, in her story. On the one hand, in Costa Rica, people dwell in a world in which social care extends to eleven at night in public parks.[29] On the other hand, in a major public place (at the stoplight by Metrocentro) in El Salvador, now postwar El Salvador, ostensibly democratic, in pure daylight, one still cannot relax. At this precise moment in her story, Maria Elena began to question—or resent—the world of assumed social care in which she had dwelt for so long.

"Nothing happens": she was safe and protected. So why were there so many rules, so many doors to lock, so many windows to shut? Her questioning should not be detemporalized. At that very moment, the few Salvadoran modernist public spaces in which people of varied orientations, of diverse material conditions, could mingle, could get close to each other, were disappearing. Even Metrocentro, an open-air mall, had functioned as a pseudo-public space in which crowds watched World Cup football matches through store windows. The limited spaces for heterogeneous sociality were giving way to privatized, separated lives: walled enclaves, patrolled parks, closed-in shopping centers with security guards. Ironically, then, precisely in the era of the hyperidealized market, where all are presumed equal, Marielena began to see incoherence and injustice and contradictions of the market ideology as practiced in El Salvador—far from "free."

Back to one in the afternoon in 1995. Marielena decided not to obey the restrictions of class and gender that suddenly seemed like antidemocratic injunctions with no place in the postwar transition. She did not check the rearview mirror. She left her window open. How absurd it was, not even to be able to lower the car window on a hot sunny day in a major public intersection in a society at peace. The narrative dialogue, in which a parental voice warned, "Don't open your windows!" suddenly felt backward, of another era, indeed an object of ridicule, to be answered in a tone and posture closer to the narrator's own reasonable, here-and-now voice: "How ridiculous."

But Marielena put it this way: she "*used to say,* 'How ridiculous.'" She had begun to make judgments on her world only when she was freed from the restrictions of her time and space, in her leap to Costa Rica (out of war, or the "something else" of postwar). But then, she was hinting, of course, that something finally *had* happened. She had changed. The world had changed. The moment of hope, the memory of the future possibility of democracy, had faded.

The Future for Which El Salvador Was Being Saved

Storytellers always talk about specific times and places. Marielena's particular "setting," the spot in front of the stoplight just outside the exit to the Metrocentro parking lot and across from the Hotel Camino Real, is not just functional to the story as a place in which a listener can situate action. It is crucial to the narrative as a crime story told in El Salvador. It helps establish Marielena's innocence. She was doing something everyone had done. Everyone went shopping at Metrocentro. It was not considered a provocative act. It was certainly not a (conventionally) political act. Everyone stopped at that traffic signal. It was a place many members of her community saw every day, a place I know well, a place most visitors to San Salvador recognize. It was as modernist a public space as El Salvador had seen.

One of the best-read popular-intellectual pieces written in the United States on El Salvador features this precise spot at the most intense time of the war. The writer, Joan Didion, has just run out of the Halazone tablets for purifying the tap water in her hotel. She goes out to buy some new pills (which she won't find):

> I walked across the street from the Camino Real to the Metrocenter [sic], which is referred to locally as "Central America's Largest Shopping Mall." . . . I became absorbed in making notes about the mall itself, about

the Muzak playing "I left My Heart in San Francisco" and "American Pie" ("*. . . singing this will be the day that I die . . .*") although the record store featured a cassette called *Classics of Paraguay*, about the paté de foie gras for sale in the supermarket, about the guard who did the weapons check on everyone who entered the supermarket, about the young matrons in tight Sergio Valente jeans, trailing maids and babies behind them and buying towels, big beach towels, printed with maps of Manhattan that featured Bloomingdale's. . . .

This was a shopping center that embodied the future for which El Salvador was presumably being saved, and I wrote it down dutifully, this being the kind of "color" I knew how to interpret, the kind of inductive irony, the detail that was supposed to illuminate the story. As I wrote it down I realized that I was no longer much interested in that kind of irony, that this was a story that would not be illuminated by such details, that this was a story that would perhaps not be illuminated at all, that this was perhaps even less a "story" than a true *noche obscura*. As I waited to cross back over the Boulevard de los Heroes to the Camino Real I noticed soldiers herding a young civilian into a van, their guns at the boy's back, and I walked straight ahead, not wanting to see anything at all.[30]

*Some*thing resonates here. The last haunting image, the "young civilian" soldiers shove into a van, occurs at precisely the same place in which—as we are about to hear—a young civilian shoved his way into Marielena's month-old car. Just as Didion decides she doesn't "want to see anything at all," Marielena, as we will see next, pointed out that "No one realized [that she was being carjacked]." (Interestingly, the people Didion *does* want to see, and take notes on, are young matrons trailing maids—the visible elite world to which Marielena had thought she belonged. Until she became invisible in her kidnapping.)

In 1995, Marielena's imagined community would reveal itself as rent, everyone strangers to each other. Some of them clutching private pill supplies to decontaminate water. Many closed off in the steel-and-glass vehicles that had been jamming Salvadoran streets ever since the war ended. Shutting their eyes to "other" pain. Perhaps what happened next was indeed *nothing*.

"He Just Took My Key"

"In this exact instant that I said, 'I want to rest—I'm tired of having to be paying attention all the time,' a person, a man, well, who looked quite humble, really dark-skinned, came up to the door and, uh, grabbed my keys—well, he just had to stick his hand in the open window. He just took my key and opened the door.

"*'Move over,'* he said."

"I didn't have any experience with this, not with—I didn't have any reaction, then. So he said, 'Move over!' he said, and I—'Who is this, who is this?'"

"*'What don't you get?'* he said. Then he showed me a gun. . . . He just showed it to me, here, and I—but because nothing like that had ever happened to me, I wasn't afraid, but, he—so he opened the door and because there wasn't a seatbelt law then—he practically pushed me, I don't know how he did it, but he sat in my seat, the driver's seat, and he pushed me to make me sit in the next seat.

"And in that moment the light turned green. *No one realized*. It's incredible, at one in the afternoon."

"So. So. I wasn't afraid, I was just surprised, but I . . . He said to me, 'Don't worry! I just need your car to transport something, I'm not going to do anything to do you, I'm not a thief.' *A big lie, right*."

I asked, "But in that moment, you believed him, or?"

"Yes, of course I believed him. I guess when you're used to people telling the truth, you think—but it's not like that." Her answer was unusual—most Salvadorans don't so fully reveal themselves as the dupe. But that is the point of her story. She had been duped in the past, but not anymore.

"So, well, uhhh, and my car was new. And he went up on all the sidewalks, well, practically treating it like it was a tractor, all . . . I was like, 'Ayy!' right, but what could I do. And I thought, right away—at the first stop I'm going to open the door and get out (like a movie because you say 'Well, I'm going to escape!')

"But would you believe that at that very instant, he said, 'If you try to get out, I'll kill you!!' I was so—"

She interrupted herself. "Of course they know, then. What would you think, when I, in this very moment, I was surprised because, it was just what I had been thinking, you know."

"So." She took a long sip of coffee, took a breath. " 'Don't worry,' he told me, 'I'm not going to do anything to you,' and he was really calm, and everything. I trusted him.

"Well. But he was going really fast—Now when I see, in 1998, someone driving really fast, and it's not some guy who looks like he's decent, well, but if it's someone who is sort of suspicious, I say, 'That's a thief.' Because, simply, look, he didn't even respect a stop sign, almost crashed into all the cars, would have hit anyone who dared to cross the street in front of him. He was going like he was fleeing, you know? And there I was inside the car.

"And you know what else? In those streets, who knows where he was driving me, a police car crossed in front of us. And I screamed, 'HEYYY!'"

She yelled. I jumped.

"But they didn't hear me. It's logical, they didn't hear me. And the thief, *'What are you trying to do?'* he said. *'If you do that again I swear I'll kill you.'*

"Then, I was like—yes, I got scared, I was like frozen in fear, right.

"Now. The big advantage that we have in Latin America is that we are very devout, we strongly believe in God. God for all of us exists, and acts. So I said, 'Oh, aah, God,' but this was all, I couldn't—think anything more."

Separated from Familiar Objects

This story, though intensely personal, is not just Marielena's. It emerged through a community of voices, all collaborating to explain her suddenly vulnerable position, yanked from the undifferentiated world of social care she had known until then. As we have seen in other crime stories, all speech is dialogic. All consciousness is social. People's words always occur in a larger context of previous utterances or texts. They always respond in some way to what has gone before. They always answer a question, whether spoken or unspoken (What happened next?).[31] Crime stories do so much more than just tell us something about postwar violence in El Salvador. They embody changes in social imaginaries, shifts in how people imagine they fit together and what they expect of each other.[32]

In her account, Marielena enacted, and reworked her ideas about, social relations through the voices in which she expressed differently placed points of view. To analyze her story I am drawing from the methodological insights on the multivoiced, heteroglossic quality of everyday speech formulated by linguistic anthropologist Jane Hill. Hill points to how conversational narratives employ a variety of laminations of voices to represent different perspectives and social positions (often in conflict). A listener perceives these stances through distinct tones of voice, styles of speaking, and vocabulary.[33] Marielena began speaking as a smooth narrator, an integrated "self" who could rise above the action. A kind of global eye observing it all. But many other voices kept breaking into her story, bringing her down to specific, local perspectives: her naïve self, hoping for peace after war and watching Costa Ricans' freedom with envy (*Ah, everyone felt safe and everything*); her rebellious self, an extension of this naïveté, sweating at the stoplight (*I'm tired of paying attention all the time*); the cloying, paternalistic social world in which she lived, warning her that things outside the house and the military neighborhood were not safe (*"Don't open the window!"*); the social scientist from the UCA who tried to explain postwar insecurity logically (*There came unemployment, and vagrancy, all the weapons that stayed in the hands of the people who had been in the war, and crime went up*); the kidnapper, who embodied the fears that had been impressed upon her, upon El Salvador, throughout her life, as he invaded what was supposed to be the safe, enclosed vessel of the parental love-gift car (*I swear I'll kill you*).

The prospective hope of the early postwar years was naïve. People should not mix. There is no real democratic public sphere. The old, conservative messages warning against the masses had to be heeded. The authority of the academic may have explained (and depoliticized) differences in the social classes. But then the man reached into Marielena's car.

The kidnapper was not just a man, but a lowly, dark-complexioned man. His reach into her world showed her, showed her El Salvador, the danger of overriding the old racial-class limits. His reach also ignored gendered proscriptions to proximity and decency. The kidnapper's color, dark, served as a marker that, in combination with other factors, identified his social class and determined his proper relation to women such as Marielena. "Bastante humilde," literally translated as quite humble or lowly, meant, in her usage, poorly dressed, probably a peasant from the countryside. Dress is usually the first key in El Salvador to judging class, given the country's complicated racial history.

Separated from familiar objects, she did not know where to reach. She did not quite comprehend what happened next. It seemed surreal. What was happening *could not*. When her kidnapper assured her that he wouldn't hurt her, that he just needed the car to transport something, Marielena (incredibly, she-the-narrator said, wryly) believed her captor's words.[34] She still hung on to a fragment of belief in a world of social care, one that might have even widened through the peace accords' promise of democracy.

But she would soon learn that she had become invisible. She was a mirage in the sweaty rush hour crush, everyone looking away.

The dark man took the wheel of the new car, the protective prosthetic-self, and drove it without care, without any understanding. He drove it up onto all the sidewalks. He drove it as if it were a tractor. The comparison of his driving with that of farm machinery cannot be casual. Once again, Marielena pointed to the spatial in her social differentiation. He was from out there in the countryside. The real otherness of her kidnapper, his bare-life location outside the polity, revealed itself to her as he broke law after law: "He didn't respect stop signs." He heedlessly fractured social boundaries, projecting his body far, far, beyond the appropriate range. Even three years later, the trauma of that moment, she said, guided her calibration of social relations with strangers on the road. Whenever she saw someone driving out of control, she thought he had to be a thief. "Unless he's a guy who looks like he's decent," she amended, returning to her old social categorization for inclusion.

Not only was this man "other," a stranger, from an-other place, a bare-life outlaw; he was other*worldly*, slowly metamorphosing into an animal-like figure with supersensory, extrasensory, perception. Just as she imagined escaping, he told her he would kill her if she tried ("as if it were a movie"; like Teo in the last chapter, Marielena nodded to how Hollywood shapes global thinking on crime performance). "Of course, they know," she commented. The "they" here is not an easily shifted deictic; it has an essential quality. It is an outside-of-us (yet known to us, defining us) *them*. Through the very process of constructing her narrative of her experience, Marielena further separated her assailant from her increasingly reified "safe" and decent community, excluding him from humanity.

When Marielena and her kidnapper found themselves behind a police car—the elusive state!—she cried out. The police officers didn't hear, didn't see. Or they ignored her. Social care, community, an imagined postwar democratic public world, gone. The thief then threatened to kill her. The lie was exposed. Life's utter instability, our own unsettledness, disclosed. She said, "And I, ah! Then yes, I was afraid, I was like frozen." As Heidegger writes of fear: "[A person's] 'environment' does not disappear, but it is encountered without his knowing his way about it any longer." [35]

At that instant Marielena recalled God. She stopped speaking of El Salvador, of her parents (the father) or the state or the community (whether the military or the postwar democratic world) that were supposed to care for her. Heidegger might call this mental move fleeing. Or perhaps this was that moment when the specificity of the self emerged in its most "extreme possibility of Being"—near death. [36]

"But They Can't Suspect Everyone"

Marielena continued. "He took me around and around, and then he said, 'I'm going to look for a friend,' and, uh, 'because we're going to transport some arms.'

"I don't know, it could have been a lie, too. We looked for the friend, and thank God, I'm telling you, we didn't find him. Because it would have been really dangerous, when—they say—it's really dangerous when there's a group of men doing an assault or whatever, because normally there's one who has another objective that isn't robbing, right."

I agreed quickly. "Yes."

"In, it wouldn't be that of robbery," she reiterated.

"So," she continued. "He didn't find the friend. Aaaand, I, afterwards, I thought, if he would have been able to go around driving and the other one [the friend he was supposed to find] would have been free, he could have taken advantage of me. So, eh . . . well.

"He went to the other side, we drove, he took me around for like two hours, going around and around."

I asked, "Where did you go?"

She thought for a minute. "And, he went over, um, to the National University? And we ended by the Department of Transit building. You know, where they give you your driver's license. Then, uh."

She paused. Then her pace quickened. Indignation rose.

"It's incredible, Transit, there are a lot of police over there, and we were like two blocks in back of Transit, and no one, no one, no one. Incredible, but it can happen. Didn't I tell you, a police car had even passed in front of me, but they, what are they going to suspect, they go around looking but they can't suspect everyone.

"Mmm."

"So, uh, in the end, well, of those two hours? Be- before we parked—because he parked by like an abandoned building. Before that, the man, I think—I don't know anything about drugs or anything—but the man changed. I mean, at first, he treated me well? 'Look, don't worry, nothing's going to happen to you,' I don't know. But then suddenly he began to insult me, to use vulgar words, and to say obscene—to say—*augh!*—as if he had become another man, you see.

"So, uh. He told me, '*Hey, cunt,*' he said, '*I'm going to kill you here, bla bla bla.*' I mean—I didn't know what happened, the man changed so suddenly, then, when we parked by this building. He took my watch, my necklace—really stupid, they're worthless things, what's a bracelet, really, and they sell them for nothing, but well, that's the way they are. They take everything from you, my money, I had like two hundred colones, he took it.[37]

"Well, also coul—The thing is that he—this was when we were parked, and, well, uh. . . ." Marielena exhibited marked disfluency here. Reliving her shock, she lost her composure. So she started again, returning to an authoritative voice, distanced, less located in a place and time.

"The women, how can I explain this, coming from different social classes, they have different customs. And apparently women from the lowest economic class store their money in their underwear. Mistake, right, you should never do that, well, you're not going to put your money next to your body."

I suddenly understood her verbal stumbling. "Aaaah."

Marielena spoke deliberately. "So what he did was go into my bra, and I didn't have anything there. But, up to that point, that was what I was expecting. But he said to me, 'Open your [pants] zipper,' and oh, 'Ay,' I said, 'no.'

"So when he saw that I didn't react, he took out his gun and he put it against, against my leg. 'Open your zipper.'

" 'It's that I don't have anything,' I told him. 'If you want, I'll open the door and show you, I'll shake myself off here.'

"And then, well. The thing is he made me open the zipper. And me, like this." She showed me how he made her lower herself. " 'Get down!' And I, then—"

"Lord, Why Have You Abandoned Me?"

She stopped for a few moments. I waited. When she resumed speaking, her smooth, fluid, global-narrator voice, the one with which she had begun her story, had returned.

"Thank God, my experience, I can say, was bad, but . . . I had a great lesson then. In this moment that I got down like that, the man stretched out his hand, I don't know what objective he had, you know, to check me out, to see if I had anything, because he had already checked here. Or I don't know why, but in this moment—it was a miracle, well.

"Because I said to him, 'Lord,' I said, 'Why have you abandoned me? Why are you going to let this man take—let such a thing happen in my life?'

"And in this exact instant the man, with his gun, I can't explain it. These are like two stories at the same time, the history that I have lived of violence in El Salvador, and at the same time it was a spiritual reality. Because I said to him, 'Lord Jesus, why'—and the man was here—'Lord, why have you abandoned me?' and in this precise instant, the man, like time stopped, began to yell at me. '*Get out of heeeere!*' And he insulted me. In this moment I opened the door, and ran away, just like that, I ran away. I left my wallet there, left everything.

"And nothing happened to me. I was trembling, thinking of what could have happened to me.

"And, well, after that I walked and walked, and ran into an office and asked for the telephone. I called home and they came to get me."

After a pause I asked, "Did you tell them what happened to you?"

"[I explained to them] what had happened to me, and that thank God nothing had happened to me? I mean, I had nothing more than having had contact with a person who is in that kind of world."

She continued after another pause, her voice a little calmer. "So, and he, these people, they have families, and they have children, but I believe, a lot of time they live a double life. They appear normal but they live in the Mafia, robbing cars, trafficking arms, who knows. I can't explain it to you why, there are so many things that happen in this country.

"So the car was found like twenty-four hours later, but they had taken a lot of parts from it."

I asked, "Car parts?"

"Car parts, from the car, right. Sometimes when cars are left alone for a long time, they even take the seats."

She concluded firmly. "And that's how it ended."

She added a coda. "Well that has been—almost you can say my only experience? Logically, since then, eh, one is more careful, then, not to wear valuable things."

"Right, right." I knew.

"And the lesson, is that you can never stop being alert. Even though you go to another country? You always have to be alert. Even if you think that you're in a place of trust."

Multiple Stories

Horrors came closer and closer. The thief claimed he was looking for a friend. All Marielena could imagine was that this friend would "have something on his mind other than stealing." They passed the University of El Salvador (a place at that time, in 1995, still covered in revolutionary graffiti, half-full of rubble and weeds. It was a potent symbol of the ruins of war, in some ways suggesting that El Salvador was not moving forward but backward, to what Marielena's parents and friends often saw as danger and disorder). They ended up by the Transit Department (actually ten minutes away from Metrocentro, but when you get there via Costa Rica it takes longer). She encountered the absent state, again. And no one—she repeated it three times—saw. She had been rendered invisible.

By now she had strayed far from the war-era illusion of a safe world inscribed by locked doors and reiterated warnings, a long way from the imagined postwar nation of democratic social solidarity to which she had thought she had opened her window. Instead she discovered an unstable world of risk and unpredictability.

The man changed abruptly, doubling, showing himself as two-faced. She imagined drugs. But the explanation was too mundane. He was not of her world. His voice, suddenly vulgar, broke into her speech: "*Look cunt, I'm gonna kill you here.*" He grabbed her watch, her necklace, her money. "Really stupid," she commented in her narrative. "And they sell them for nothing, but well, that's the way they are." Her narratively changed position in the space of Salvadoran social relations (vis-à-vis the beginning of her story) emerges much more forcefully as the climax nears. Her voice and words are harsh, judgmental. They stray far from the careful (care-full) analysis she learned at the university. They mock the optimism inspired by the peace accords. Cruel optimism. They rebuff the hopes for democracy and social care, hopes brought to life in her trip for Costa Rica.

As she continued her story, Marielena separated herself even more from the streets of San Salvador—from the masses, from the rabble. The words she used to describe the "others" became more and more objectifying as she tried to return to that world of care and safety that her parents, that the military, that the state, had erected long before the war. Each step in the descent of the narrative, each move bajo Salvador del Mundo, had laid out a fractured postwar social field of "us" and "them," subject and object. It had begun simply, with a bland observation about how people in the countryside were different from than those in the city, lamentably so. They had had a different kind of experience. When her kidnapper first appeared, she did not seem to objectify him, but rather simply to describe him: "a person, a man, well, who looked quite humble, really dark-skinned." But soon enough he showed that image to have been a lie, that identity to be false. Another self emerged from behind the mask, a dangerous stranger whose lack of location in space allowed him to read her mind, to see her thoughts about escape.[38] And so she began to divide up El Salvador again into a "constricted nation of simultaneously lived private worlds."[39] She separated here and there, us and them.

As the climax neared, this now monstrous stranger veered toward her body. She could hardly bear to repeat what had happened and what might have happened. She stepped away from him, removed herself from the stage of her performance. The narrator of events no longer pretended to be a neutral interpreter. She took a stance in the clashing consciousness represented in all the voices of the story.[40] At first she seemed to recall the professor from the UCA as she explained how women of "different social classes" (delicately worded) had different habits. Lower-class women carried their money in their underwear. But then she could not hold back, and became an arch judge, or a nun from a strict sect: "Mistake, right, you should never do that, put money against your body."

She called upon categories of social class as hard, essential, objects to differentiate herself from other women. It was a desperate move. Already her kidnapper had shown his lack of respect for the class and racial boundaries of social order. And then gender trumped all. He made her open her pants zipper. He stretched out his hand. She called for God. She described a splitting into two stories. First, that of the war, the nation, the insecurity. That was the one she began with, the one we shared. And then her own story, her spiritual discovery. Temporality transformed, from historical time to spiritual time: *being-toward-death*.

In the first story, she ran away, trembling. She left everything, left any thoughts of peace, of democracy, of social solidarity, of Costa Rica, of rebelling. "I left everything and nothing happened to me." The particular construction "No me había pasado nada" does not imply a responsible agent for what didn't happen to Marielena. She had retained the family honor. Nothing happened. No-thing, non-time, something akin to Bakhtin's Greek Adventure Time: "Time is not measured, nor does it add up. . . . Pure digression from the normal course of life, excluded from the kind of real duration in which additions to a normal biography are made."[41] But what was the normal biography for the "abnormal" that is the Salvadoran, for the young woman seeking the freedom to open the window? Marielena's sense of the future doubled back on itself, embittered. Her attachment to something like peace and democracy and hanging out late at night in the park eating Popsicles was revealed as cruel optimism. After all, her car, the love-gift that was supposed to protect her—and also her hopes for peace and democracy after war—would be found dismantled.

"I had nothing more than a moment of contact with a person from that world." A simultaneously lived private world in which, she explained, people appeared to be normal, caring humans with families, with children, but were also radically other. "I believe that often they live a double life. They appear normal but they live in the Mafia, robbing cars, trafficking arms, I can't explain, because there are so many things that happen in this country."

Her story of El Salvador ended. The war may have been over, in this version of events, but nothing had happened. People like Marielena still had to hide, to ensconce themselves in their closed communities, to keep their windows shut against the masses. Within a few years, the state would try to root out those whose bodies remained visible, defiant. "What are they going to suspect?" Marielena had asked at one point, commenting on the police impotence in front of her kidnapper. "They go around looking but they can't suspect everyone." By 2003, as we shall see, another big story, in the form of a dazzling media spectacle, would try to force itself upon the postwar social imaginary, brutally imposing itself as the answer to the query "What happened next?" *Mano dura* (iron fist) anticrime laws freed those now-tarnished peace-accords cops to join up with the military to grab whomever looked suspicious: those with sullen stares, those with dark skin and long reaches, those driving cars like tractors onto the sidewalks or those storing sweaty bills against their skin.

The voice that ended the story was different from the voice that began it. Marielena had changed. Her narrative had begun, like most, in a smooth voice, speaking from above, trying to take a global perspective. Different voices had broken in during the narrative, locating social stances (the parents, the kidnapper, the young woman dreaming of peace). But as the situation became critical and exceptional, the narrator finally lost control. Her experience, and her self, bifurcated, doubled, perhaps even became duplicitous. There was the Marielena who returned home, still insisting nothing happened, and there was the Marielena who could no longer look to the state or nation or perhaps even her father—who called on God.

The El Salvador that once stood for a big story of the Cold War, drawing thousands of news reporters, seemed to have fragmented into countless desperate local anecdotes, each imagined to be equal in the marketplace, and each imagining flight. At a moment in which the horizons of possibilities seemed to continually diminish, flight, leaving home, grasping at the fleeting, the transient, the contingent, may have been the queer time and place in which most Salvadorans—even those like Marielena—had to live in the postwar decade.[42]

I find some fugitive possibility in this fragmentation. Some hope. The central act in Marielena's narrative was her defiance of the social constraints on her movement through life. Inspired by the rhetoric of peace and democracy, she rebelled against limits defined by her particular classed, gendered, and racialized position in El Salvador. In the narrative she finally acknowledged this act—opening the window—not as an absentminded moment, but as an intentional gesture. True, it was carried out by a separate, naïve figure, a former Marielena, who believed in the promises of an inclusive democracy that all Salvadorans could share. But I want to argue that this was an agentive moment that she refused to regret yet could not quite claim.[43] That moment had brought her to a new place, at least in one of the two stories. It was that moment that transformed her story into a conversion experience, with God the agent (while she, Marielena, took responsibility for her act—for her individual, free will—of opening the window).

The second story, of spiritual awakening, was the one Marielena said she wanted to tell. Perhaps she was not only telling it to me and my tape recorder and potential audiences. Perhaps she was telling it to God, the ultimate listener, as well. As she felt the threat of death, she sensed the very temporal nature of her being, and became more intensely aware of herself. She described her experience as a "spiritual reality." This sense of revelation might emerge as what Judith Halberstam calls "Queer time," in which "futures can be imagined according to logics that lie outside of those paradigmatic markers of life experience," outside of convention.[44] In her doubled story Marielena did not fully close interpretations of her experience. She had not finished living it. The window exposing other possibilities might have still been slightly open. And as she told me her story, she was eyeing that opening. She was about to leave El Salvador.

Marielena's coda came, as it had to, at the end. She returned to our immediate world, where we sat in the front room of her father's big walled-in house. The boxes she would ship up to Washington surrounded us. Within a few days she would be leaving. Perhaps she was fleeing. Or maybe she was seeking a wider social space, the one she thought she had seen, so briefly, in Costa Rica; the one she had dared to imagine, for a moment, in postwar El Salvador. Still, she wasn't the same girl as before.

Within a few minutes I would leave, after I gathered my tape recorder, my notebook, my purse, and my keys. I would be getting into my car and driving through the city. She leaned forward and drew me closer. She told me: You must protect yourself. She spoke directly to me: You must remain vigilant. Even if you think you *know*. You don't know. Danger lurks everywhere. Even with the whole world watching.

Chapter 5
Democratic Disenchantment

What happened next? World annals say democracy. "El Salvador is a constitutional, multiparty democracy," the U.S. Department of State pronounces authoritatively in its Country Report.[1] Democracy was cropping up everywhere in the last decades of the twentieth century. By the time of El Salvador's peace accords, a "third wave" of global democratization, starting with Portugal in 1974, was cresting; 107 of 187 countries in the world at the time, 60 percent, organized official power through regular, competitive elections with universal suffrage.[2] By 2004, indeed, El Salvador had long established itself as a postconflict model of democracy, a big story held up for Afghanistan and Iraq to emulate.[3] What did that mean *in* El Salvador? How did the "worse than the war" sentiment shape expectations of politics, experiences of democracy? In previous chapters, we saw how the crime stories that dominated so much postwar talk worked to orient citizens toward the neoliberal environment of market democracy, in which risk must be privately managed. We also saw how crime stories could be vehicles of political feeling—as sentiments about self and other provoked by the thwarting of democratic expectations. In this chapter, we listen to crime stories in order to learn something more about the world Salvadorans imagined they would find after the euphoric moment in which the guerrillas and the government declared peace.

Crime stories reveal people's ideas about democracy because they are precisely about encounters between the state and citizens—even, or especially, when they address the *absence* of the state. These accounts offer us a glimpse of the perspectives of ordinary citizens on postconflict nation-formation during a time of changing state power and sovereignty in the global world order. Crime stories, arising in a moment felt as one of *not-knowing* what comes next, nonetheless reveal something about desires for, and anxieties about, the future. What circulated in El Salvador was a broad sense of loss of that future, in rising disillusion with the promises of the peace accords.

By 16 January 1992, the day the peace accords were signed, local and global ideas about democracy had shifted significantly. In the early 1970s in El Salvador, popular movements could stake a moral claim for a widely shared sense of democracy, something condensed, perhaps, in a yearning for "the felt experience of individual sovereignty and social solidarity."[4] Centrist and center-left politicians of the era, such as Christian Democrats José Napoleón Duarte and Rubén Zamora, could still openly proclaim their support for justice and equality in terms of agrarian reform and some redistribution of resources toward the majorities. The right, historically motivated by the need to discipline agricultural workers,[5] imposed an iron-fisted rule whenever it deemed necessary. Salvadorans saw as much in 1972 when Duarte was tortured and forced into exile after winning the presidency. To justify itself, the right often summoned up images of mob rule, epitomized in El Salvador by the 1932 Communist-led uprising.[6] During the 1980s, Salvadoran newspapers constantly pointed to what they saw as the horrors of life in neighboring Nicaragua under the Marxist-oriented National Sandinista Liberation Front (FSLN).

By 1992, however, these visions had blurred. Propelled by global forces in the context of the dramatic shift from socialist to capitalist economies in the former Soviet bloc, as well as the fall of the Sandinistas, a new, hegemonic concept of democracy, merging electoral freedom with philosophies of free-market economics, injected itself into all discussions of politics. The meaning of democracy had been code-switched. What to do, after the revolution? As Indian writer and activist Arundhati Roy put it: "What happens now that democracy and the free market have fused into a single predatory organism with a thin, constricted imagination that revolves almost entirely around the idea of maximizing profit? Is it possible to reverse this process? Can something that has mutated go back to being what it used to be?"[7]

For some of those who had been involved in the Salvadoran left, code-switched senses of democracy slipped surreptitiously into the slot formerly instilled with revolutionary fervor, the space once filled with socialist visions.[8] Disagreements over what the lurch toward this new democracy meant led to splits within the Farabundo Martí National Liberation Front (FMLN) in the first years after it converted into a legitimate political party. Some groups held to the spirit of their Marxist origins. Others joined up with more centrist parties and coalitions, including the Christian Democrats. Still others sought a modified, post-Cold War vision of socialism, as social democracy, as Francisco Velis had described shortly before his murder. The loss of direction was perhaps inevitable after war. It also reflected post-Cold War uncertainty within much of the left in those years, though the rise of the Zapatista Army of National Liberation (Ejército Zapatista de Liberación Nacional, EZLN) in Mexico in 1994 pointed to new alternatives. Still, while FMLN representatives could not offer a coherent program for the future, they consistently opposed privatization programs. They often explicitly, if ineffectually, worked against the government's neoliberal policies. Throughout the postwar decade, the FMLN remained the second political force in El Salvador. With time it gained more and more municipal offices, including the mayoralty of San Salvador, and increased its presence in the national legislature. Its base remained loyal even as leaders fought among themselves. Any political center got very little traction.

One day in 1995 as we watched television news reports on the disarray in the party, I asked my friend Ana Dolores why she supported the FMLN. She had grown up in Cacaopera with illiterate farming parents and then married one of Maru's cousins, a man who spent much of the 1980s running guns and other supplies to the guerrillas in Morazán. She replied with a quizzical look on her face (as if to say, "But isn't it obvious?"): "Somos pobres" ("We're poor").[9] Even as people watched individual leaders betray their intensely *felt* ideals, many still saw in the FMLN a symbol of hope and resistance against the continuing dominance of a tiny, tight group of powerful financial elites—and in the small country of El Salvador, everyone knew who these people were. The defiant red flag of the former guerrillas may have limited the party's appeal to any kind of moderate middle at that moment (or even blocked the emergence of that middle), but it bound the faithful.

Meanwhile, at the other end of the polarized political spectrum, followers of the right-wing Nationalist Republican Alliance (ARENA) took up the global cause of market democracy. Scholars have pointed to how the party transformed as elite interests were reshaped by new economic conditions in the 1980s. Two powerful factions had struggled during the second half of the war to control the party—one tied to old landed oligarchy and military cliques, the other to emergent financial, industrial, and commercial interests. The second group seemed to prevail with the nomination of the businessman Alfredo Cristiani for the presidency.[10] The party began to focus less on eradicating communists and subversives and more on getting on with the business of business.[11] As they kicked their coffee habit, financial elites began to accept minimal, procedural ideas of democracy as palatable and perhaps inevitable.[12] In 1992 they reveled in the "End of History," the post-Berlin Wall resolution of an epic ideological struggle brought by the arrival of liberal democracy as it merged with free-market capitalism.[13]

ARENA has never repudiated its origins. In 1999, I taught history and anthropology in a U.S.-accredited English-language university extension campus in San Salvador. In an exercise on semiotics, most of my privileged young students linked ARENA and its founder Roberto D'Aubuisson with the concept of democracy. When I told them that North Americans who had heard of D'Aubuisson would probably still think of him as a human rights violator, one of them, who had been all of ten years old in 1992, exclaimed, "It's that they weren't here in the war!"[14] To many of these students' parents, mostly business owners, ARENA had opened a space for political expression never before seen in the country.[15] Another student, her last name attached to a prominent national company, would declare later (in a jarring inversion of testimony from the left), "You were killed [during the war] if you spoke out against the guerrillas!"[16] Despite some political moderation, what bound ARENA's constituents was the anti-communist banner, which waved defiantly even in the 2009 elections.[17]

Definitions of Democracy

Are there commonalities in these many democracies—those imagined by public figures in the 1970s and 1990s, those of ARENA and the FMLN during and after the conflict, and those ideas circulating among ordinary citizens after the war? David Nugent, an anthropologist of political forms in Peru, describes democratization as in part a process of reentextualizing globally circulating discourses into "vernacularized" versions. Discourses of democratization, in El Salvador as elsewhere, absorb and adapt a long history, from the European encounter with its non-European Other, to the French, Haitian, U.S., and later Mexican and Russian Revolutions, as well as to the anticolonial movements of the mid-twentieth century.[18]

Scholarly discussions of how democratic forms have changed through the twentieth century often refer to the controversial minimalist definition conceived in 1942 by Joseph Schumpeter, who built from principles first laid out by Max Weber.[19] Schumpeter presumed, like Aristotle, the popular majority's incoherence and ignorance. "Democracy," he wrote, "means only that the people have the opportunity of accepting or refusing the men who are to rule them."[20] Later scholars took his ideas and slid them into a larger logic. They merged Schumpeter's democracy with principles of the competitive economic market, focusing on the *individual* as the principal unit. This technical ideal became the one promoted by most foreign policymakers and many democracy promotion professionals, indeed one insisted on by international lending agencies as a condition for loans. But, unlike Schumpeter's original formulation, this model tries to write politics out of its definition. Anthropologist Kimberley Coles, who studied emergent practices of democracy in Bosnia, notes, "Typical rhetoric expounded around the world paints democracy as holding the promise of salvation and progress but as being too often encumbered by 'politics and politicians.'"[21] Citizens' political action, in this vision, should be limited to casting periodic votes. ARENA avidly followed this market democracy model.

The grafting of the term *market* onto the word *democracy* has not gone uncontested. Salvadorans involved in social movements had struggled for democracy in its most inclusive sense, demanding equality, during the 1970s and 1980s. At the fifteenth anniversary of the peace accords, a group of social movements and NGOs called the Coalition for Peace, Dignity and Social Justice released a report that reaffirmed their commitment to a broad, substantive concept of participatory, social democracy, one they believed represented "the spirit of the accords."[22] They imagined, or they hoped for, an egalitarian coexistence in which all citizens could demand their rights— one in which contestatory voices dialogue with, but are never subsumed by, dominant forces, political parties, the state.[23] Of course the very emergence of this group statement, through an Internet report of an NGO, points to another element in the post-peace-accords governance environment (one broadly reflected across the Global South in the neoliberal era): the rise of NGOs, many with European and North American funding. This phenomenon has been called a late twentieth-century "quiet revolution," the significance of which has been compared to the rise of the nation-state in the late nineteenth century.[24] Many former opposition and leftist groups in El Salvador found refuge in NGOs after the war. But as we know, this new form of transnational governance is often shot through with neoliberal logic.

In its victorious 2009 campaign, the FMLN confirmed a more substantive vision of democracy. It proclaimed a citizen's right to a "vital minimum" of food, shelter, education, and jobs. The words and concept were lifted from the early twentieth-century Salvadoran social philosopher Alberto Masferrer's program of *vitalismo*, promoting a balance between capital and labor with some land reform.[25] Decrying the failure of neoliberal policies, the leftist party announced its priority as "overcoming unemployment, the high cost of living, social exclusion and unequal distribution in the costs and benefits of development."[26] Its candidates, however, sounded slightly dissonant notes in other forums. The vice president, former guerrilla commander

Salvador Sánchez Cerén, still faintly lined up socialist principles with democracy: "The peace accords are for us an integral part of the democratic revolution, in the sense that they represent a search for a fuller, more complete democracy," he said in his autobiography. "The goal is a democracy that is not just formal but real, not exclusive but participative." [27]

The president, lauded former television journalist Mauricio Funes (himself never part of the guerrilla movement, and strategically never wearing the party's red on the campaign trail), spoke more soberly in interviews, acknowledging the limited possibilities for addressing social inequalities even as a new left arose in Latin America. "Given the current international context, we do not aspire to build socialism in El Salvador," he told a journalist for an Internet site promoting "radical social change." "What we hope to build is a more dynamic and competitive economy, placing ourselves in the international playing field in a highly globalized and competitive world. . . . To do this we need institutions that work, and for democracy to become a symbol that also exists in our country." [28]

In El Salvador, democracy has always stood as a symbol of possibility—never-fulfilled possibility, like the project of modernity itself.[29] The popular movement's long struggle might be characterized as a *method* of hope, oriented toward a *not-yet* but ever possible future (as opposed to the ever-deferred object of desire).[30] But in the immediate postwar years, the lived experience of not only everyday violence but also low wages and limited opportunities, quickly undermined the vague but grand hopes that arose with the signing of the peace accords. For that is what democracy, at its core, had meant for so many people: hope. *Not-knowing* what would come next, however, Salvadorans did not necessarily reflect that democratization was not the same as democracy.[31] Too often, citizens of democratizing states expect rapid and dramatic changes in governance. This may be especially true in El Salvador, where people had limited practical experience with competitive democratic politics. When, inevitably, change doesn't happen the way people had imagined, disillusion can set in. A familiar distrust of politics returns.

Such a reaction could be seen in Salvadorans' frustration with the postwar approach to human rights. The peace accords had mandated an Office of Human Rights Counsel. But most of the cases citizens brought to the office in the first few years of its existence were deemed not to be admissible for investigation as human rights violations (because they were not related to state disregard for human rights).[32] A respected research institute found in a 1995 survey that 61.2 percent of the respondents agreed with the statement, "Human rights favor criminals so we'll never stop crime." [33] This feeling, common throughout Latin America at the time, could and often did provoke nostalgia for authoritarianism. It also incited calls for an "iron fist" against the new subversives of the twenty-first century, the surplus young men and women who did not fit the neoliberal economic formula.

These young men and women may not have found space in the nation. But they did crowd into the many crime stories circulating in postwar El Salvador. What more can crime stories, as they order the world, tell us about ideas of the polity, the public sphere, relations between self and other—and democracy?[34] Do they link to past imaginaries of a democracy in some not-yet future, or do they latch onto contemporary global hegemonic meanings of the concept? We know that many stories taught listeners how to manage the risk represented by those threatening figures lurking at the edges of the nation. It was a message consonant with ARENA's market ideology and the logic of global capitalism. But postwar crime stories carried multiple messages, even if they were internally contradictory. Most stories show Salvadorans had hoped for something more from the peace-accorded world. Hope was the *method* that had briefly allowed them to imagine the possibility of a more egalitarian, inclusive, and effective, democratic state.

I call the disillusion with the state, and politics, carried with the "worse than" sentiment of crime stories, *democratic disenchantment*.[35] I take the term from Weber's use of the phrase "the disenchantment of the world." Weber, writing in the early twentieth century, was concerned with modernity. He analyzed a progressive rationalization of the world as science replaced more mystical, religious conceptions of the universe. Discussing political systems, he saw this development as inevitable and yet contradictory: bureaucracy, resulting from a demand for "equality before the law," accompanied mass democracy (as opposed the participatory democracy of small homogenous units). Yet, he wrote, democracy, always seeking the most "direct rule" of the *demos* (which usually meant that of party leaders), "inevitably comes into conflict with the bureaucratic tendencies, which . . . [it] has produced."[36] Latin Americans in particular experienced these contradictions as their own failures. Achieving democracy would confirm that they were modern, and yet it seemed they could not sustain any system extending political equality and still maintain the other side of the equation, economic and industrial progress. El Salvador's feeble liberal experiment with the privatization of communal lands to modernize the Indians—ending with the Matanza fifty years later in 1932—demonstrated just such contradictions.

By the late twentieth century neoliberal discourses took up the Weberian opposing of democracy to bureaucracy, but as a contest between the market and the state. The market was supposed to offer citizens equal opportunities that the intrusive, uncomprehending, bureaucratic state ostensibly repressed. Weber, however, probably would have demurred from this formula. As he wrote in 1918, "Precisely the ultimate and most sublime values have retreated from public life either into the transcendental realm of mystic life or into the brotherliness of direct and personal human relations."[37] Salvadorans, or anyone, yearning for such a sublime state, hoping for transcendental togetherness, perhaps inevitably faced disappointment with the late twentieth-century hegemonic version of democracy. Yet that hope could also generate stronger feelings, affective conditions enabling change.

Eighty years after Weber wrote those words, many Salvadoran crime storytellers still yearned for what Weber called brotherliness and what I would call a social imaginary of obligation toward others. (The gendered term in Weber's description is apt; the state remains patriarchal.) In accounts by a range of Salvadorans in the 1990s, senses of democracy emerge in a cluster of hopes and illusions and promises. I have divided democracy-oriented notions in crime stories into three interrelated categories, perhaps representing three idealized aspects of democratic states during the twentieth century. First, *Order*, in the sense of rule of law and responsive institutions; second, *Belonging*, drawing on sociocultural factors that bind people in a feeling of community; and third, *Development*, which encompasses ideas that prospects for democracy are linked to economic well-being—and indeed hint at promises of equality that exceed the basic, no-frills equation of one person, one vote. In the rest this chapter, we will examine how these themes weave through and entangle narratives of postwar life.

I. Democracy and Order

In their stories of insecurity under democracy, Salvadorans often simply wanted working institutions. They hoped for the functioning, responsive state delineated in the text of the peace agreements. Much of their disillusion centered on the state's failure to respond—to protect citizen rights and private property (whether a car, a house, a watch—or a human body).[38] Such expectations line up with political scientists' consensus on the necessary conditions for a functioning democracy. After regular elections, key aspects of the political science definition of democracy include accountability of the state institutions to elected representatives and protection from arbitrary state action. There must also be guarantees of free expression and free association.[39] In San Salvador conversations of the 1990s, again and again people said they wanted efficient, sound, modern police as part of a democratic state.

Calls for order can be construed as craving a repressive state (just before the 1932 Matanza, demands for order filled the mass media[40]). But in the context of spiraling postwar crime rates a desire for responsive institutions was not unreasonable. The most public of changes encompassed under the rubric of post-1992 democratization was policing. The three security forces feared most during the war, the National Police, Treasury Police, and National Guard, were to be disbanded. The transformation of the police into a civilian body, subordinated to the civilian government, was considered the most important achievement of the agreements (beyond the cease-fire itself). The change in forms of national security, from the National Police (Policía Nacional, PN) to the National Civilian Police (Policía Nacional Civil, PNC) became a key institutional signifier of the new era.

Most Salvadorans I knew were conflicted about whether to trust the new police force. Their desires for democracy—something unknown—pushed against the intimately known history of state corruption and repression and police negligence and abuse.[41] The vast majority of crime storytellers I listened to did not consider reporting anything to authorities. The United Nations Development Programme (UNDP) in 1999 pointed to the main "deficiencies" in El Salvador's transition to democracy as rights violations by the police and the justice system, as well as problems in criminal investigation and in the penal system.[42] A 1999 World Bank study of San Salvador metropolitan area residents found that only 20 percent of crime victims actually reported incidents to the PNC. Of those who went to the police, less than 5 percent saw any resolution to their complaint. According to the study's authors, this outcome "plac[ed] in evidence a complete lack of efficiency in the institutional apparatus and justifying those who did not file a complaint." Many people surveyed in the project said the police did not pay attention when they filed complaints and "it [was] a waste of time."[43] So when, in recounting their crime stories, Salvadorans *did* mention the state (iconized by police), it was telling. It almost always revealed something about disillusion with the new state—about democratic disenchantment.

"Going into the Snake Pit"

Liliana Molina Pérez came back to El Salvador after the war for the celebrated peace—and for the heralded democracy.[44] She had lived in Edmonton, Alberta, for seven years as a political refugee. We first met within weeks of her return in 1995 (at an outing to watch the release of baby turtles to the sea at the Barra de Santiago in western El Salvador—we both had joined a trip funded by a German environmental NGO, though neither of us had anything to do with it). We became close friends.[45] We both turned thirty-three in late November. In the 1980s Lili had renounced her own (self-described) middle-class roots and joined the left-wing organizations that supported the insurgent FMLN. In 1988 she fled the country with her husband and tiny daughter after her husband was released from prison and told to leave or he would be killed. Back then, to her the biggest danger had always been the state and its henchmen—the National Guard, the National Police. Back then, she would never have casually entered one of the barricaded wealthy enclaves that the state security bodies, and their private counterparts, protected. Perhaps it would not have been surprising to the old, war-era leftist Lili that she would one day become imperiled in just such a place. But the postwar Lili, newly home, had believed things were different. So she went without fear to visit relatives in an exclusive neighborhood in early 1997.

She described the experience to me in a guest bedroom of her parents' comfortable condominium. A portrait of Pope John Paul II watched over us as she talked about how she had found herself in danger. "It was in March 1997, the Colonia La Mascota, on a pretty isolated street, but supposedly there are all these places around with security [guards]," she said. "In that area you know there are all those big *portones* [wide garage door-sized gates] and guards and everything. . . . It was like six at night, but it wasn't dark yet. I arrived there in my car, at my niece's house. It's an old car, not a car that's going to call attention to itself—I mean nobody would want to steal it." So she did not feel worried when a man she described as nice-looking and well dressed walked in her direction.[46] Not until he walked right to the car and looked down at her.

I asked, remembering Marielena (from Chapter 4), "Was the window open?" Actually, the car door was already slightly ajar, Lili said. "He began to push me, he said to me, 'Move over there! Move over there!' to make me change seats, right, he wanted me on the other seat, but—well—he asked me to give him everything that I had. The truth is, I didn't have much—didn't have anything of value—not even money—just my purse. I was coming from work and was wearing a little necklace—but it wasn't valuable—just a little thing. . . .

"I gave him my watch, but it was just a cheap watch, nothing great. . . . But then at that moment it occurred to me—that maybe he wanted something, *sexual*, and then—I really got scared. I thought, well I don't have anything material to give him—don't have any cash, the car isn't worth stealing, the watch is a piece of junk—and also I saw that this guy was pretty well dressed, and I had felt his shirt against me, it was soft, rayon or silk, fine material, so right there that frightened me. Because he wasn't, suspicious-looking, and I even remember he wasn't ugly or anything, it wasn't like you would say, 'Oh, gross,' or anything. So it scared me, him saying, 'Move over there!' like he wanted to get my keys and go somewhere with me, and so I just really quickly opened the door on the other side, the passenger's side, and rang the doorbell and started screaming.

". . . And he just took off running. He grabbed my necklace and took off running, insulting me."

"What did he say?"

"Like, 'Cunt, now you're gonna lose your purse, you had to scream,' like he was saying if I hadn't made a scandal he wouldn't have done anything. But I got so scared, and he was running down the street, so I just started yelling with all my strength. I thought maybe the security guard in the shopping center down the way, like two blocks down, might hear me, so I began to scream, 'He robbed me, get him!' because obviously it isn't normal to see a man running with a woman's purse, right."

A maid finally answered the door. Lili quickly explained the situation. In what might have been a show of gendered solidarity—or perhaps class deference—the maid jumped in the car. They began to chase the man. "Now in the car I was brave," Lili laughed. They lost him, though the shopping center guard admitted he had seen him. When Lili asked why he hadn't stopped a man running with a purse, he replied, "I'm here to protect the stores." "¡Que pasmado!" ("What an idiot!") she commented to me. In his narrative of the postwar era, social solidarity must defer to intensified economic realities even under the banner of democracy. The man was paid to protect property.

Part of the postwar transition was an adjustment of expectations: a new taxonomy of caution, a new circulating archive of knowledge of how to privately manage public risk. For Lili, and for many others like her returning after exile, the task was both more difficult, as they adjusted to cultural and temporal changes, and simpler, as at least some of them had already in some sense left the war behind. They came back for peace and democracy. Still, what happened next surprised Lili.

"I went to the National Civilian Police right away." (She said, in full, "National Civilian Police," not just "the police." She was explicitly indexing the new era.) "But there are . . . Well, the only thing there, the impression I remember is that when I went, they didn't really help me very much, in fact they really seemed to me to be totally inefficient, an inefficiency that's— embarrassing.

"They weren't nasty or anything, but it was, like, when *at last* somebody paid attention to me and I told him what happened, he asked me if there had been personal damage, like a death or an injury or something, and when I said, 'No,' 'Ah, well. Ah, well, what can you do?' Then, so he gave me a form to fill out, because I had had a wallet in my purse, with credit cards, I.D., driver's license, all my papers, everything. So I had to get an official letter from the police to go to get a new license, so they wouldn't fine me, and everything. That part was fine, but overall, I, I didn't feel good about what happened.

"What really struck me," Lili concluded, "was that never, never, did it occur to me that I would ever do anything like that in my life, to go file a report about something with the police. I mean my attitude then, my attitude after what happened, was to go right to the police. Before, I mean in the war, to go to the police would be to go into a snake pit. It was a terrible thing."

She might have hesitated to go the police had the same thing happened at the moment she was telling me her story, in April 1998. Over the previous year and a half the media had overflowed with news of police abuse, corruption, and impunity. The murder of former guerrilla leader Francisco Velis had returned to the headlines, after the extradition of a former police detective from the United States. Four cops accused of being part of the Sombra Negra death squad (which had killed twenty suspected criminals, mostly gang members, in 1995) had escaped trial. Three other cops had been released from charges of murdering of a radio reporter, Lorena Saravia, after a witness recanted. Seven PNC officers were being tried for the roadside beating death of a young medical student, Adriano Vilanova Velver, three years earlier (in an exception to the larger pattern, five would be convicted in October 1998).[47] A prominent family, the García Prietos, sued the state for deficient police investigation and lack of respect for human rights through the Inter-American Commission of Human Rights. In 1994, their banker son, Ramón Mauricio, had been brutally murdered in front of his wife and child in an exclusive neighborhood in the city.[48]

A year after Lili told me her story, a nine-year-old girl named Katya Miranda would be raped and murdered at her grandfather's beach house. The case became emblematic of the failures of the PNC and the judicial system. Her grandfather would be arrested but quickly released. The Human Rights

Institute of the Central American University (IDHUCA) led a long campaign demanding justice. Director Benjamín Cuellar took up the case with zeal, insisting it symbolized the problem of continued impunity in El Salvador. The girl's father was a military captain in charge of security for President Francisco Flores; several uncles were high-ranking military and PNC officials. A decade later, after intense public pressure, the grandfather and seven other men would be arrested again and charged with kidnapping.[49]

Why did Lili go to the police about her cheap watch and her almost-empty wallet? "Do you think it's because of the changes in the country, or because you lived in Canada for seven years?" I asked.

"The changes, or maybe both, a little of both, because in some ways to live in Canada, you, I don't know, try to follow the established system a little. But on the other hand, I was conscious of the changes here. The PNC, for example, is one of the changes. Before . . . you never knew if the police would grab you, or the National Guard, or whatever authority, or a person dressed in civilian clothes but armed. . . . I learned to go around really alert, to be super-careful, to watch to see if anyone stayed too long in a bus stop, or if there was anyone in the corner, or strange people in the corner store, or men with shirts out, because they could be hiding something . . . [like a gun]. So you were just really, really cautious. But I tell you I don't remember ever having been worried about crime, you know. You weren't trying to protect yourself from the thieves, you were mainly trying to protect yourself from the police, and not thieves. . . . A thief just grabs your watch and that's that."

And that's that. But it wasn't; it was so much more. Lili spoke of a nakedness, a lack of protection. During the war, she expected nothing (or rather, expected the worst) from the authorities. But now, *after* the war, as she ventured into the newly democratized public space, all had failed her: the safety of even an exclusive neighborhood, the nice-looking, well-dressed man, the image of security projected by the shopping center security guard—and then the PNC, the peace accords police. But still, one might ask: after the wartime terror of kidnappings and disappearances, how could an inefficient, slow police force spark such anger?

Lili's frustration tells us about something more than a moment of bureaucratic insensitivity. She had returned for peace. She had come back because El Salvador was not supposed to be the same repressive, authoritarian state. It was supposed to be a democracy. Indeed, she had left her husband (her daughter commuted back and forth between them) to come home. Arriving alone, she had expected in some perhaps not-quite-fully conscious way to be cared for, or at least cared about as an equal individual in the new political moment. That the new police were so inefficient, so bumbling, and nonchalant at the same time, was shameful.

Her words remind us once again that she is telling a story of the nation. To be embarrassed suggests she had had different expectations for her country. But there was something more here. In not even caring, the police were also negligent. They had not fulfilled the (imagined) state patriarchal bargain of protection in return for respect. People longed for the fulfillment of that bargain, even if they had never experienced it. This kind of state-citizen relationship has been called negligent patriarchy.[50] Democratic disenchantment built on familiar past emotions that implicitly acknowledged ongoing, and always gendered, relations of inequality.

A call for "law and order" in democratizing societies can easily be interpreted as a public demand to repress all kinds of perceived danger—whether seen in racialized minorities, impoverished majorities, the mentally ill, the politically oppositional, or communist subversives and terrorists and "common" criminals. After all, state formation has been predicated on exclusions in order to protect the privileges of the powerful, even as the liberal project imagines itself as embracing all identities (at least all disciplined, "normal" identities).[51] But it is also possible that citizens seek strong, reliable, institutions. That they actually want the kind of democratic state in which everyone feels okay about each other, everybody gets along. That they "desire belonging to the normal world," as Lauren Berlant has put it.[52] This is what I am suggesting here. Concerns about policing in a new democratic state do not necessarily index nostalgia for the mean, constricted safety of the dictatorship. They might reflect expectations about—or fantasies of—how the institutions of a democratic state should collaborate toward that perhaps incoherent social imaginary of equality, solidarity, and community.

Gold Chains and Motorcycles

And indeed one way Salvadorans imagined the experience of democracy, in an idealized rather than technical sense, was as an encompassing community of care. Lili, as well as Marielena in the last chapter, sought care at least partly in terms of a gendered sense of paternal protection and bodies and domestic spaces. In the next fragment of conversation, the words of a young, athletic, working-class man also express a desire for an inclusive, caring democratic state. His expectations relate both to a demand for protection and to a yearning for a feeling of mutual support among men. Felipe Rodriguez, a janitor in his twenties, and I met through Evert, my partner, at the Salvadoran National Sports Institute (INDES) gymnasium, in the San Salvador city center.[53] Felipe's class position and literal positioning thus contrast with that of Lili. While Lili described danger at the public/private threshold of a *portón* in the elite Colonia La Mascota, Felipe talked about wandering around in (and running through) the dreaded city center, a very public place in which many Salvadorans imagined they were most at risk. So Felipe had a lot of crime stories to tell. And almost all of Felipe's accounts point to state failure—and democratic disenchantment.

Felipe's story begins when he convinced his girlfriend to join him out on the street. "We were held up, me and my girlfriend," Felipe told me. "We were eating, in a Biggest [a popular hamburger joint], the Biggest by Cine España. We got bored being there, reading the newspaper, we always read the paper there, and we were wondering if we should go see a movie or not. I said, let's go out walking, go window-shopping. She said no, let's not, it's too crowded. It was around Christmas. And I convinced her to go.

"And so we left, and walked like some ten meters, and some guys were walking near me. I hadn't noticed them when they turned to me. 'Hey *vato* [pal],' they said, 'What's going on?' and then *Bam!* They grabbed my gold chain. My girlfriend was coming a little behind, and she began to hit the guy who'd robbed me! Then, I mean, it scared me so much because she was risking her life, . . . then because one of them took out—a huge knife. He held it to her stomach. Then that was it. 'Take it.' Then we weren't going to do that, no, no.

"In that moment I was afraid for her. So but then I said, those assholes, they got my gold chain. And I began to chase them, so . . . so in the corner, a block away, I ran into a cop. And I said to him, 'Look, I just got robbed,' and, he, 'Wait, I'll call my friend.'"

The police officer disappeared into the crowd. Felipe kept going. "And as I was running," Felipe said, "I began to think, they could beat me up and even hurt me. No, no it's not worth it. I just let them go, I started walking and I—my gold chain—my gold chain—"

Only a week or so later Felipe was robbed again. His second story, like Lili's, features danger in the form of a man standing over a vehicle. But for Felipe the real threat was embodied in another negligent police officer. "And then after that, it was the motorcycle that was robbed. We were in a Biggest again, but another one, the one by the Hula Hula [a park in the city center]. We were there but there's nowhere good to park the motorcycle because there are so many people selling on the sidewalks, and so we were worried about it. So I told her, I'm going to move the motorcycle, . . . I saw a better place, right by the police, in front of this police that was standing there, so that's where I parked it, in front of the police." He returned to his girlfriend but remembered he had to pay the electric bill, so he went out again.

"And it wasn't, maybe five minutes, and I went out. And from where I was walking I was looking for where I could see the motorcycle tire, 'That's where it should be,' I was telling myself, but as I was getting closer I saw that the motorcycle wasn't there! So I asked the cop, 'Look, where's the motorcycle that was there?' 'A guy took it,' he says, 'No man,' I said, 'How is someone going to take it in front of you?' I said. 'Yeah,' he said, 'I thought it was his,' he said. So my motorcycle was stolen."

In both of these crime stories, Felipe emphasized how the police simply weren't there for him as he ventured out into the street. In the first story, the drama of his girlfriend (humiliatingly) defending him—and the sexualized attack on her, the thief's knife on her body—was enough to make his experience something worth telling. But then he chased after them, seeking to regain not only his chain, but also his sense of manhood. The only reason he didn't succeed, in the logic of this story, was that the state would not defend the honorable citizen. The cop, undoubtedly a working-class man like Felipe, would not step up (much like the private guard who would not help Lili). Felipe had been feminized—it was his girlfriend who hit the thief—and abandoned—the state turned the other way. The second story adds a punctuation point to the first. The police agent stood right in front of the motorcycle—and for many young men like Felipe, a motorcycle is part of his physicality, his anatomy—and *watched* a thief steal it. The new postwar social imaginary left the citizen-Salvadoran alone to defend himself. Like so many others, this story becomes a technology producing the responsible, risk-managing subject in a market democracy. The explicit lesson could be, as in past chapters, that in the new postwar world, one must care for oneself. But Felipe also told a story about failed transition to democracy. He had hoped for some form of solidarity and equality.

These crime stories, those of Lili and Felipe, are exceptions, in that the police, the state, made an appearance, only to disappoint. Accounts like those shared by Salvadorans in the 1990s, decrying the state and disillusioned with promises of democracy, can be and often have been read as wanting (or demanding) order in the form of a *mano dura* (firm hand, the patriarchal metaphor clear). The common phrase in Spanish is often translated as "iron fist." Certainly the interpretive ambiguity, of a desire for firm paternal control versus nostalgia for authoritarianism (firm hand versus iron first), has been exploited by the ARENA government. In 2003, as we know, it imposed Draconian antigang legislation. In 2006 it passed an antiterrorist law used to repress political protestors.[54] The legal sociologist Angelina Snodgrass Godoy, after research on vigilante justice in postwar Guatemala in the late 1990s, has called *mano dura* a hallmark of the neoliberal era in Latin America.[55] Such laws at first proved popular among Salvadorans. In one 1999 survey, 55 percent of respondents agreed that the crime problem was a "justification for toppling democracy."[56] But did people really want a return to military rule? Certainly without respect for civil rights—foundational in a democracy—state security forces can revert to authoritarianism. But these crime stories also show that when citizens call for more order in the context of democratic disenchantment, they are not necessarily demanding antidemocratic governance.

II. Democracy and Belonging

In some crime stories, democracy emerges as an idealized, inclusive community of care. The concept does not offer analytic precision demanded by political scientists building ideal-type models but rather suggests the popular, sometimes incoherent "common sense" and hope-oriented prospective momentum that can be mobilized in hegemonic struggles.[57] It has something to do with the practice of equality and the pursuit of social justice. It draws on a social imaginary of obligation, of compassion in the sense of concern for the well being of others.[58] It supposes that as the *demos* citizens have at least one common project. These notions are not just dreamy abstractions. Political scientists today identify the importance of "civic virtue" or "the civic community" as a kind of "social capital" essential to democracies. Robert Putnam, who gained fame with the book *Bowling Alone* (decrying human disconnection in the contemporary United States), defines the civic community as "marked by an active, public-spirited citizenry, by egalitarian political relations, by a social fabric of trust and cooperation."[59]

My research suggests that this yearning for a feeling of belonging, this method of hope for *some*thing, spread far beyond participants in popular movements and the political left in El Salvador. Scholars have argued that it was mass politics of the twentieth century across much of the globe that injected a politics of hope into ideas of democracy—contra Schumpeterian minimalism— "as a response," anthropologist Arjun Appadurai writes, "to the realization that democracy without full popular participation is a form of oligarchy."[60] And in Latin America, as Greg Grandin argues, drawing on the experience of Guatemalans who participated in the 1944 October Revolution, "democracy as an ideal and practice was always much more participatory and egalitarian than it was procedural and individualistic."[61] David Nugent, too, points to how compulsory equality was to ideas of democracy with in the Popular American Revolutionary Alliance (APRA) in mid-twentieth-century Peru.[62] In such a world of possible meanings, then, democratization in El Salvador might be interpreted as a transition to a more inclusive public sphere.

Marielena's story, told several years after her kidnapping, begins with the dream of a democratic community of care. She positioned her experience as one of many. This was a story everyone recognized. This is so in part because of its iconicity. Everyone knew Metrocentro, where her abductor pushed himself into her car. There, city folk rich and poor gathered, passed by each other, perhaps paused side by side in front of shop windows (unlike the more recently built malls, lavish, air-conditioned palaces that seemed structured to exclude the majority of the population). Countless Salvadorans had likely already heard a story of a brush with danger at that very spot. But even as it draws on commonalities, the narrative ends by turning in on itself, warning that recourse to *any* community had been a momentary fantasy. Marielena had been abducted in one of the most well-traveled intersections in the city at the busiest time of the day, and no one noticed. So rather than a story of progress in which fractured communities came together after war to form a democracy, Marielena's account reveals individual anguish and separate salvation. Her story becomes another tale of democratic disenchantment. She did not analyze the operations of social injustice that underwrote the drama. Instead, she withdrew into her own realm of safety, both as a woman and as a part of the privileged classes.

When people recited the phrase, "It's worse than before," "before" (or even "the war") was *not just* the war. It could also have meant an almost mythical past. Marielena acknowledged that her memories of community were restricted to a closed, overprotected childhood and adolescence during the war era. But recall from Chapter 3, Amparo happily walking through the 1970s city center in high heels, carrying a purse "and everything," or Ana Lorena partying freely in the midst of war. While we could discuss this kind of rhetorical move in terms of nostalgia (in the sense of a fantasized past), we might also think of it as a way of describing an idealized state that we desire. We know we desire it because we think we have experienced something like it. It is not utopia, no-place, but, we think, real, something we wish for so much we imagine we have experienced it. It is an urge for a sense of community, of people (not just institutions) looking out for one another, that ties into people's emotional commitment to an ideal of democracy. This is true even as conditions for that ideal are deeply compromised—the cruel optimism we now know so well. The writer Nicholas Dawidoff evocatively depicts such a state of yearning: "The absence of a much-wanted experience is inseparable from the experience itself, is part of the experience. It's the vulnerability to loss that is the coefficient of the depth of feeling."[63]

We must be careful when analyzing popular images of belonging and caring. In general, as I have noted in earlier chapters, *distrust* still saturates social relations in El Salvador, even among those who have lived side by side for twenty years. In a working-class Ciudad Merliot neighborhood I know very well, when one family's small dog was found dead in the common passageway in 2004, rumors flew about how someone among them was poisoning the pets. These same residents had quickly organized to respond to the 2001 earthquakes (in which a neighborhood across town had collapsed), enthusiastically describing how they had come together as a collective during the disaster. Such a reaction is common—I saw the same immediate response to Hurricane Mitch in 1998. I wonder if people's desires and dreams about community come from their memories of these moments of hope.

In general, scholars have deconstructed as idealized notions of community as enforcing a constricted normativity, as protecting hierarchies of power. As such, ideals of community are often seen as backward, traditional, antimodern. A political definition of democracy is more about friction among communities, classes, groups with different interests—but one in which all have a say. Indeed these vague affective fantasies of community are predicated on exclusion: whether a nation defined against other nations; as Christian and capitalist against the Godless and Communist (a formula still relevant in El Salvador); or as civilized, modern citizens against barbaric, backward Others. The history of El Salvador could not be clearer on this point. But most people do not reflect on normalizing disciplines of unity and togetherness—requiring, as it almost always does, a willful ignorance of others' suffering—unless they are encompassed in a war in which enemies are clearly defined. That does not make any optimism after the peace accords, any desire for idealized democracy, false; only naïve, unknowing, easily jolted.[64]

The almost nostalgic way so many Salvadorans described their democratic disenchantment in the decade after the war related to this long-felt depth of yearning for the experience of democracy, which many people vaguely associated with a more egalitarian community, with a sense of belonging and purpose. In her research among former revolutionaries in Chalatenango, the anthropologist Irina Carlota Silber found an overwhelming sense not only of disillusionment, but deceit (the promises of revolution and peace forgotten or ignored), among people who had briefly felt the aura of something like a participative democracy. The bitterness of former FMLN combatant Kasandra speaks volumes. She described the powerful, prospective momentum of hope to Silber: "What one person had, all would have. For example, if somebody ate *frijoles* [beans], everybody would eat *frijoles*. If somebody ate meat, everybody would eat at least a little bit of the same. There was going to be unity. This is what the struggle was for, the search for unity." After the peace accords, she said, they realized, "That was a big lie."[65]

Ideas about what that *not-yet* community comprises may be contradictory, even as storytellers share a sense of its lack. José Luis Barahona, a middle-class accountant in his late thirties (and the husband of one of my English-language students at the American School extension program) did not dream of the participatory democracy Kasandra imagined, with everyone sharing their beans. He hoped for a liberal democracy in which all people are abstract equals belonging to the polity, interacting respectfully in the public sphere. He pictured his democracy in the literal marketplaces of the city market and air-conditioned malls. His worldview may seem distant from revolutionary visions that impelled guerrillas and committed peasants in the rural departments where much of the ground conflict took place. Yet there is some narrative resonance in their accounts of disenchantment.

Like Kasandra, José Luis spoke as if democratic expectations had been reversed over time.[66] "Before, I used to enjoy going to the city center to shop. Now, we're part of that joke, we only shop from [affluent] Escalón and above. We go to the Plaza Merliot, we go to Galerias, anyplace where there aren't as many people. And for the movies, we go to a theater where there aren't many people, and we go out to eat where there aren't people. It's not that we think we're too good. It's just that we think that wherever there are a lot of people there's going to be some kind of problem with violence. Or where people drink, where there's alcohol, where people are drinking beer for example—we used to go to the Zona Rosa . . . now we don't, because something could happen, we could be hit by a bullet, a fight could break out."

He insisted that the problem was not the fact of large numbers or even of poverty. It was how people interacted in the historical moment. Unlike Kasandra, who had lost her idealized future, José Luis mourned his idealized past. "Look, in my childhood [in the 1960s] I was raised—look, it was a block from the central market of San Salvador. I mean, I lived in the middle of enormous crowds, and it was a peaceful life. My mother left the door open. The only thing we had was a wooden rail across the door, and people would knock on that when they came by to visit." His story tells of movement from a childhood memory of an egalitarian, public world near the large municipal market (literally inhabited by the masses) to an escape from the crowds to places like the exclusive, air-conditioned and privatized Galerias (patrolled by security guards like the one who wouldn't help Lili). It is more than a narrative of upward mobility. Told in the context of a conversation of postwar insecurity, it delineates a trajectory of separation and division, away from any imagined democracy to a neoliberal order—perhaps to a market democracy, though José Luis did not seem to hold out even that much hope. He did not deny the social costs of that separation. Nor did he see a way to ameliorate them.

Such yearnings for a sense of belonging, whether shaped by well-honed revolutionary imaginaries or less conscious ideas about moral orders and abstract liberal equivalences, affected reactions to postwar insecurity. They inevitably formed the postwar narrative of democratic disenchantment. The way people share their stories—what fits into a tellable tale—points to what is important in the moment. The lack of a feeling of democratic community came up again and again in conversations about crime in the 1990s in San Salvador, sometimes in subtle and sometimes in overt ways.

"How Things Go in the Neighborhood"

Rosario Lémus and I met to talk about her experiences with crime in a small dark rowhouse in a rough neighborhood of Soyapango.[67] Her companion had been an FMLN combatant, part of a staunch revolutionary family from the western part of the country (and the older brother of a school friend of my partner Evert). In her late twenties, the mother of two, she was a humble woman, with an accent from the western countryside.

"But yeah," she told me, "you get scared, look, right over by the university, by the Parque Infantil, I don't know if you've been there, that's where these two men came out and took my watch. I didn't fight, but because I was holding on to my watch, a little piece of it stuck into me and made me start bleeding. I thought they'd cut me, but no, it was the watch that I wanted to hold on to. But he got it off me and took it. And that was all. Today what we do is, everything that they want we give them, because today, now, this year, they kill the people first, so they can rob them." The closeness of her watch to her body, part of her, tell us this theft's damage was more than material.

"Because last year," she continued, "over there in Passageway Ten, there they killed a man, they took his gun and some really thick gold chains and then shot him, here, he died right then, didn't last ten minutes, here in the neighborhood, you know. That's how things go in the neighborhood now." Rosario's story begins in the midst of the epitome of the modern public sphere, the public park, where today danger lurks. But, unlike José Luis and Marielena, she cannot withdraw to a secure, private world. She is not even safe in her own neighborhood.

I asked, picking up on the repeated "nows," "There wasn't as much crime before?"

Rosario gestured away from herself, toward the door. "Just him [her ex-guerrilla companion], he's the only one who himself lived the violence, but thank God, my family, everyone's here, you know, nothing happened to them. They are all here and thank God. It was luck that none of us died because most families had a lot, families lost their children, not for getting mixed up in politics, but when you got caught in the middle, you ran into something by mistake, that's when they got people." She paused.

"I almost died once in the city center. At least the Despensa [the Despensa de Don Juan, a grocery store chain] was open, the one by the cathedral, so when the shooting began, and bombs, they let us in, the Despensa. If they grab me in the street, I die, you see, but inside a business or a house there's less chance of that."

Here it is again, the narrative strand of people taking care of each other—and not. In his own neighborhood (and hers), a man was robbed and murdered. Her repetition of here, in the neighborhood, a place where she thought she belonged, is significant. In contrast, while during the war she recalled a generalized violence, she also pointed to a kind of community solidarity—even far from her neighborhood, in the larger public sphere. In the busy center of San Salvador, people she didn't even know in a large, anonymous grocery store opened their doors and let her in to escape a sudden shootout. The absence of the police, of the state, in this story is not remarkable in the context of most crime accounts. But it reminds us that people like Rosario were less likely to expect the protection of the patriarchal state that Lili and Marielena desired. She did hope for other people to help her, as they did in the war. But in the new, postwar democracy, people were pulling away from each other, even in the neighborhood.

I heard many descriptions of this kind of experience during the war, this care among strangers, as well as solidarity among friends and acquaintances. The stories testified to both separation and belonging. People in Escalón might recall all-night *toque de queda* (curfew) parties at the pool. Those in Soyapango might talk about sharing water with neighbors during the 1989 guerrilla offensive. We know that after the war, the category of violence that dominated public representation and experience changed—and so did the Salvadoran social imaginary, the way people (perceived each other to) interact with each other. Experiences with violence became individualized. In this widely circulating story, in peace, in democracy, many people felt less linked with each other.

Many of the crime stories circulating in the 1990s incorporated, in more or less subtle ways, a critique of the state, as the accounts of Saskia, Lili, and Felipe did. They also critiqued a loss of a public, involved community. I have discussed this sense of community in general, neighborhood terms—for example, Rosario pointing to a man's murder on his own street. But we have seen that postwar crime itself, not just reactions to it, had been privatized (though occurring in public places). In the discourse of everyday talk, the "new" violence comprised individual acts of delinquency, isolated, sudden chaotic moments of peril, rather than communal acts of revolutionary resistance or military deployment. Such street crime may not seem to us to be as dangerous as wartime violence. But it performed a warlike function on the subjectivities of citizens in a new, post-Cold War democracy—where freedom was defined in terms of a market—where private individuals competed with each other for material goods. So, when many Salvadorans said, "It's worse than the war," they weren't only talking about street insecurity. They were talking about a changing social imaginary, a loss of community, a slipping away of solidarity. They were lamenting a loss of hopes raised so high after the peace accords in 1992. They were telling each other about democratic disenchantment.

III. Democracy and Development

Most Salvadoran big stories depict divisions among people—landowners and peasants, oligarchs and the masses—rather than portray belonging and civic virtue. These differences changed form, but did not disappear after the war. Between 1990 and 2002 the per capita Gross Domestic Product of the country grew from $2,940 to $4,890. But this wealth was not spread evenly. A quarter of the population lived on a dollar a day in 1995. By 2000, it was 31 percent.[68]

How much poverty and inequality can a democracy bear? That question sits at the heart of a 2004 UNDP report, *Democracy in Latin America: Towards a Citizens' Democracy*. "For the first time in history," it says, "an entire developing region with profoundly unequal societies is, in its entirety, organized politically under democratic governments. Thus a new and unprecedented situation has emerged in Latin America; the coexistence of democracy, poverty and inequality." [69] The rise of new democracies in impoverished circumstances defies what was once common knowledge about conditions for the possibility of the political form. As Robert Putnam tells us, "Nothing is more obvious even to the casual observer than the fact that effective democracy is closely associated with socioeconomic modernity." [70]

The issue, the UN report asserts, is that social inclusion, participation in the public sphere—community—cannot sustain itself when citizens are struggling just to survive. UN polls show that many Latin Americans claim to value economic development more than democracy—that they would support an authoritarian government if it fixed their money problems.[71] (Roque Dalton captured this sentiment in a brief, brutal poem, "General Martínez": "They say he was a good president/because he allotted cheap housing/to the Salvadorans that were left"—those who survived the massacre of 1932.[72]) The solution, the report concludes, is a synthesis in which "Democracy, in its quest to curb the exclusion caused by the market, enhances the legitimacy of the economic system; [and] the market, by limiting the power that politics and the State have over the lives of citizens, encourages a greater adherence to democracy." [73]

Despite itself, however, the report seems to forget the particular history of concepts of democracy, the struggles for democracy, in Latin America as well as in much of the Global South. It was peasant and working-class movements, demanding economic and social justice, that were "absolutely indispensable to the advancement of democracy," Grandin tells us.[74] Much of that energy, he writes, was not inspired by visions of socialist utopias. It was propelled by ideas of economic development.[75]

After World War II, a consensus emerged that the democratic ideal of citizen equality (as fundamental sameness) could not be reached without addressing poverty. Development and modernization became methods for attaining equality, and thus, in this equation, democracy.[76] In El Salvador, as we saw in the 1960s, space sometimes opened up for civic organizations such as trade unions to grow and agitate for reform, to hone hopeful visions of democracy. When the military governments clamped down on movements, as we have seen, they inadvertently radicalized these groups, leading to large-scale collective action and waves of protest. In 1980, such repression led to the union of five guerrilla groups as the FMLN.[77]

It has been convincingly argued that both Soviet-supported revolutionary movements such as the FMLN and liberal development projects such as the Alliance for Progress (formulated by capitalist powers in part to contain communism, and quite active in El Salvador in the 1960s) were constructed by the same discursive apparatus, appealing to the same normative concepts of growth, progress, and modernity (only a small powerful elite truly opposed democracy) and relying on a "normative theory of transformation and agency."[78] Thus, that so much of the post war population, from businessmen to former guerrillas, evinced a similar sense of democracy—and that public discourse circulated a normative narrative of democratic disenchantment—should not be a surprise.

The "worse than before" trope has deeper roots than the disappointment of a dystopic postwar present. It has more profound origins than the democratic disenchantment implicit in so many crime stories told in the decade after the peace accords. If the very idea of becoming modern as a nation-state today implies becoming democratic (no matter how slippery the concept), then Latin American governments' antidemocratic qualities through much of the twentieth century have constantly reminded citizens of their backwardness in the world. "Worse than" is a familiar genre, then, one of constant lack. It haunts most "developing" nations, the descriptive gerund promising a never-yet-quite-there future.

In *Expectations of Modernity*, James Ferguson writes about what happens when the modernization myth that has shaped the meaning of the future for so many people "is turned upside down, shaken and shattered." The urban Zambians he knew had lost "faith in a country and a people 'going forward'"—something that they had briefly felt, until copper prices fell and the World Bank-imposed structural adjustment policies set in. By the mid-1980s, "the signs and symbols of modernity [whether cars or 'a decent necktie'] . . . had been abruptly yanked away."[79] El Salvador may never have had the resources or possibilities for progress that Zambia had. But modernity was just as much a hope in Central America as in the rapidly industrializing cities of southern Africa in the 1960s. Democratic disenchantment, and continued violence after war, confirmed to Salvadorans once again the impossibility of modernity—the elusiveness of that promised future.

When Ana Lorena and Amparo yearned to wear high heels and walk freely in the evenings, they were not just coveting impractical tokens of urban vanity distanced from barefoot-peasant modes. They wanted equal rights in the public sphere—democracy in the sense of free movement and expression. But along with (or as part of) that democracy, they wanted *things*—even high heels. That in the years after the war Salvadorans continued to emigrate, largely to the United States—indeed, that at least half of Salvadorans in 2005 said they dreamed of migrating, and that an estimated average of 1,070 left the country every day that year—dramatically bears out the "worse than the war" sentiment.[80] Postwar migration holds much less hope of return than war-era exile, except, as Susan Coutin describes it, in the "absent presence" of dollar remittances.[81]

"What They Do Is Rob to Survive"

If Salvadorans' ideas of democracy encompass equality and justice, a commentary on unemployment and poverty also becomes democratic disenchantment. When I asked people directly why they thought there was so much violence, their first answers were often formulaic, entextualized blocks of reasoning lifted from logic that circulated in mass media editorials and Sunday homilies. In the early to mid-1990s, many sources pointed to ex-combatants, cut loose, as a reason for crime. Indeed, significant involvement of former military (and some former guerrillas) in organized crime became apparent by 1994.[82] My friend Guayo, an English teacher whose own small-time drug habit put him in contact with local gang members, put it bluntly.[83] "Look," he told me. "It's lack of work, poverty, family disintegration. And it's because too many people learned how to kill and they don't have any other way to earn a living. Look, how many people were there, how many guerrillas, 10,000? I don't know, let's say 20,000 and there were some 300,000 [sic] in the army or more, we're talking about nearly half a million people trained to kill, people who are used to it." [84] It's not only that they know how to kill, he is saying. It's that there is no other way to earn a living for so many young and not-so-young, poor men whose bodies in the past had been conscripted to absorb the violence of the conflict.[85]

Many people, reflecting on the situation, began to suggest (if not precisely name) deeper failures that maintained the inequality and poverty and, most believed, contributed to high crime rates. Atilio, the well-connected lawyer who described how thieves shot his thumb as he tried to run them over in Chapter 2, believed in the government's neoliberal program, yet was troubled at the contradictions he saw.[86] "I am concerned about the levels of violence we have at this moment," he told me in a careful, technocratic voice (speaking in 1998). "It had improved and it's now gone back. I think one has to look into why. It must have something to do with the unemployment rate, the way it is in El Salvador in this moment. The salaries here in El Salvador are not very good. The salaries don't reflect the growth in the cost of the basic food basket. . . . We certainly have good macroeconomic numbers, but the typical Salvadoran doesn't feel the effects. I mean we see it in the change in the kind of crimes—I'm talking about narcotrafficking, kidnapping."

Mauricio Massis, a businessman in his late fifties from a family with a prominent surname who I met in the gym, owned several expensive retail stores.[87] Of Palestinian descent, he was part of the urban commercial class whose rising power and political moderation helped open the way for political transition in El Salvador. Yet Don Mauricio's comments were far from moderate—and insistently located the problems in and as El Salvador, pointing to national failure in the postwar climate. "It's gotten worse since the war," he told me in an interview in an office of the gym, which his brother owned. "Because I felt in the war, the problem was the guerrilla. And now, no, it's everyone, ex-guerrillas, ex-soldiers from the military, they don't have work, they know how to use weapons but nothing else, so what they do is rob to survive. Due to the poverty in this country, because there's enormous hunger in this country, there's poverty, here the salaries are miserable, in this country, the pay isn't enough to live, they have to rob." He voice was loud, full of democratic disenchantment. I wondered (but did not ask) how much he paid his own employees.

"There's also drugs, so many drugs, marijuana, cocaine, crack, all of these are factors too, and there's just the lack of culture in the people, there's no culture, people don't get married, men who just knock women up and leave them, and children grow up without their fathers . . . The social problem is tremendous, beyond poverty, the poverty is tremendous. So that's why crime is the order of the day." The message, again, is the old Latin American lack. We are backward, uncivilized, not modern, and very, very undemocratic.

"They Have No Chance"

This view that poverty and inequality are the root causes for crime, threatening the possibility of democracy, echoed across class and social position. It did so in a complicated dialectic with the conviction that there are a lot of bad people out there. Amparo, who pined for her youthful days of freedom, became pragmatic when discussing the grandchildren she was raising.

Speaking as a working-class woman committed to social change, she was one of the few crime storytellers I met who explicitly pointed to the nation's political economy. "Here they say an effect of the war is family disintegration, and it's possible, but what I think is that [the problem of postwar crime] really comes from unemployment. The parents don't have any way to maintain their children. What are they going to do when their children have needs? What are they going to do? It might not be good what they're doing, but it's a consequence of the war, and not only that, a consequence of class conflict, of our government's politics. We have to see all this neoliberalism is influencing the situation, the lack of work . . . Those who haven't studied, how are they going to do well? Because here not everyone studies—not because they don't want to but because they can't afford it, you know. I don't know if I'm going to be able to afford to send my two grandsons to the university." The promise of progress and the loss of possibilities, of a future, is palpable in Amparo's lament.

A psychologist acquaintance who had worked for the state in the prisons offered one the most poignant accounts of how failed dreams of modernity and of democracy affected the lives of citizens. Most people I interviewed, whether rich or poor, whether sympathetic to the logic of poverty-induced causes of crimes or not, could (or would) only speak abstractly of actual criminals. América Tenorio, from a leftist academic family (and an old friend of Guayo), knew many crime-story villains personally.[88]

"In the prisons there are so many people who just found themselves forced to rob. They weren't criminals, they weren't violent people, they were respectful, with manners, clean, organized, but they found themselves obligated to commit a crime. For example I remember a case that really impressed me so much. A man, a man forty-eight years old who had lost his job. I don't remember the whole story but he didn't have a job at that time, and some friends proposed putting up an illicit business—and his wife had cancer, and he had three sons, . . . So they had proposed putting up this illicit business, something to do with drugs, and so he accepted, thinking, well, my sons need to go to school, my wife needs medicine. In the prison there were hardworking people who had put up little carpentry shops and would just work all day, not mixing with anyone, really I don't think they were really criminals—or were circumstantially criminals. Of course this wasn't the most common case of crime but I knew four or five cases like that."

Though she was a psychologist, her explanation evoked less Freud and more Engels: "Immorality is fostered in every possible way by the conditions of working class life. . . . Distress due to poverty gives the worker only the choice of starving slowly, killing himself quickly or taking what he needs where he finds it—in plain English—stealing." [89]

Most of the people in prison, América said, had been dehumanized by deep structural violence long before their arrests. The majority of ex-soldiers she saw (and there were many) had become drug addicts in the military. She believed their commanders gave them amphetamines. They came in to treatment traumatized and even brain-damaged. Many others had lived long lives of deprivation. "The people there are so used to not having anyone to talk to. I remember the history of one guy who had burn marks over his whole body. Since he was eleven, the father was an alcoholic, the mother was a prostitute, and so this boy from the age of eleven his father sent him out to rob, and if he came back without money they burned him with cigarettes. His father would say, if you don't come home I'm going to kill you, and that was the school he was raised in. And there was another case, a boy whose stepfather gave him a knife, at age twelve, and would point to people and say, 'He, he's your victim, go get him,' and that was the school he grew up in.

"What can you expect from people like that? They have no chance, no way of learning other values." What can you expect in a country that has never known a durable democracy, that has a long, troubled history of authoritarianism, repression, exploitation, and murder?

Having and Losing Stuff

I have been arguing throughout this book that narratives of postwar violence, in their emergence and transmission, became technologies of citizen subjectivity in the decade after the peace accords were signed. In this chapter I contend that part of the "worse than before" sentiment drew from venerable, if not always fully coherent, understandings of democracy in Latin America. These understandings diverged from an individualistic market logic and thus from the minimalist neoliberal model of democracy. This imaginary of democracy encompassed a politics of hope. As democracy after the Cold War began to be redefined in terms of the market, hope seemed to have leeched out of the concept. Instead, Appadurai writes, "Insofar as the market is seen as one road to freedom (and thus to some version of equality), it is not especially reliant on the politics of hope, substituting for hope such virtues as risk-taking institution building, enterprise, and calculation, all prime virtues in the early lexicon of industrial capitalism." [90] And yet, on the ground, people still struggle for their rights, yearn to belong, seek ways to prosper—to develop, to grow. This struggle for democracy in El Salvador despite interruption, frustration, and failure, might be described not just as a politics but as a method of hope: a present moment ever oriented toward a future moment, as described compellingly by Hirokazu Miyazaki. "Hope in the present points to its own future moment of salvation," he writes.[91]

The stories I have shared in this chapter tell of a sense of loss, a loss of a never-quite-known object, a not-yet fantasy of order and democracy with functioning laws and institutions, a dream of belonging, a yearning for a community of care and mutual obligation among strangers, even if that care was sometimes shot through with paternalism or patriarchy. The stories reveal cruel optimism and democratic disenchantment. But they also address individual security and private safety. They tell of risks not only to human life but also to property. They are very much about having and losing stuff. This is not a small element in many crime stories.

Marielena had been shopping at a Salvadoran shrine to consumerism, Metrocentro, and drove a material manifestation of her parents' love, a car. Lili and the maid chased after the "nice-looking" thief who grabbed her purse. Rosario did not want to lose her watch. She gripped it so tightly she bled when the thieves ripped it off her wrist. Felipe openly lamented the theft of his gold chain, and even considered risking his life to get it back. Then he obsessed so much over his motorcycle that he went out to check on it several times.

None of these are people were disenchanted only because of the loss of the dream of a communitarian utopia. Not that they *shouldn't* dream. Arundhati Roy, seeking life "after" democracy, still believes that developing societies should aspire to that utopia. (She writes, "The early, idealistic phase [of democracy] can be quite heady."[92]) But in El Salvador, most people I know had yearned for something less than utopia. Rather, they had, for a moment, simply hoped for a liberal democracy. One of civility and respect in which everyone had equal rights. One that allowed for the possibility for a dignified existence. In it, they could eat beans every day. They could buy medicine for their spouse. They could pay for their grandchildren's schooling. Against the weight of their own histories, people projected in their stories hope for some kind of moral order that addressed not just violence in the street but also structural violence—the poverty and misery that many of them knew led to violence in the street. The stories they shared spoke of betrayal after the peace accords. They had dared to imagine something else.

And, as the elections of 2009 show us, they still dare to imagine *something* else.

Chapter Six
Unknowing the Other

No meaning is ever fully present. We may imagine revelation will come. Someday. Soon. We seek. We wait. The waiting can fill with dread: the barbarians, always just at the gate—or the National Guard, ever about to knock down the door. The waiting can also feel hopeful. The last chapter explored the *not-yet* meaning of the 1992 peace accords, full of democratic expectations, despite deepening disenchantment. And the waiting can be agonizing. El Salvador—living through "postwar transition," undergoing a "democratization process," or carrying out "structural adjustment"—may not kill (the same ways as before), but nonetheless lets die.[1] The goals of social justice, of human rights, of peace, are always deferred to some future ethical moment.[2]

This book, too, must concede its own deferral. The meanings of crime stories, whether as fragments of fright, or as moments of hope, can never really be settled.

This deferral is more than philosophical. This book seems to have deferred the very agencies that compel experience, suffering, stories. It has deferred (to?) the criminal. Perhaps deferral is inherent in the object itself, incessantly inciting desire. In most detective fiction the culprit is only revealed at the end. But this postponing is no literary strategy.

We have seen that in most San Salvador crime stories the assailant slips into the action as a nameless, almost featureless cipher. Often in conversations only my bumbling anthropologist's curiosity provoked people to description. They might have assumed we all *knew* the antagonist. The bad guy. But the tellers might also have feared summoning him or her in their stories. In this book I, too, have been nervous about calling up the criminal. I recoil from reconjuring powerful images of the Central American nation I have come to love and sometimes hate. I don't want to be one more white woman, or another *gringa*, reproducing the reputation of El Salvador as the "Heart of Darkness."[3] I have felt uneasy about reprising the deep history of Salvadorans as terrorists, gangsters, and vagrants. Revolutionary poet Roque Dalton wrote in the 1960s of compatriots in his "Love Poem":

> Los que se pudrieron en las cárceles de Guatemala,
> México, Honduras, Nicaragua,
> por ladrones, por contrabandistas, por estafadores,
> por hambrientos,
> los siempre sospechosos de todo
> ("me permito remitirle al interfecto
> por esquinero sospechoso
> y con el agravante de ser salvadoreño")

> [those who rotted in prisons of Guatemala,
> Mexico, Honduras, Nicaragua
> for stealing, smuggling, swindling
> for starving
> those always suspected of everything
> ("Allow me to place him in your custody
> for suspicious loitering
> aggravated by the fact of being Salvadoran")] [4]

I have argued that *not-knowing*—not just not knowing who to fear, but not knowing how to manage risk in a moment when agency seems to emanate from the spectral global rather than recognizable local forces—has incited so much postwar crime storytelling. And yet outside El Salvador, many people think the answer is obvious. Whenever I have given a talk in the United States on my research, someone has said, "What about the gangs? Those deported gangs!" Perhaps they heard a National Public Radio story, or saw a Fox News report, or live in a city where Central American-migrant-associated *maras* (gangs) operate. [5] The story told from the North is as "normalized" into a culturally coherent shape as any dominant narrative circulating in El Salvador. (The mass media love it, especially editors who cut their teeth in parachute-journalism in Central America. [6])

It is true that after the war ended the United States began to kick more and more criminalized bodies south. By 2005, planeloads with hundreds of deportees (some convicted of violent crimes, some of misdemeanors, most of them simply undocumented workers) were arriving each week at the national airport. But the fixation on gang members, north and south, far exceeds their part in postwar violence.[7] And my work is not primarily about diagnosing and solving postconflict crime (would that it could!). It is definitely not about gangs, as symbol or as victim or as perpetrator.[8] This book asks what happens to a nation, and to a tenuous democratization process, when violence continues after a war ends. It explores discourses on postwar crime. The premise is that as they circulated, crime stories—the ultimate accounts of property, security, commodities, and law—became media for San Salvadorans' perceptions and negotiations of meanings of their country's political changes. In the decade after the peace accords, the telling of crime stories produced knowledge about the new era's risk as something to manage individually. The stories oriented people, shaping the way they experienced not only their encounters with violence, but also their encounters with the concept of democracy, both in the free-market present and in the remembered Cold War-era past—as well as in *not-yet*, imagined future possibilities. How this happens tells us something about operations of knowledge production, agency, power, resistance, cooptation, optimism, love, dreams, and disenchantment. . . .

But there he is. It is almost always he, almost always imagined as the aggressive, gendered-male subject: The gang member, the criminal, the mugger, the *mañoso* (tricky thief), the terrorist, the narco, the *delincuente* (delinquent). He refuses to go away, to bow to my ethical stance on representation, to obey my intellectual protests about proximate and ultimate causes. He is the dark hand reaching into Marielena's car. He is the guy with the silky shirt brushing against Lili's skin. He is one of the "completely organized" thugs wielding a rifle and barking orders on Nelson's bus. He is the drug-addled gang member staggering through Teo's bus. And he is the knife-brandishing schoolgirl demanding Maru's backpack.

Social obsession with crime and criminals, we know, is not just about crime and criminals, as palpably real as they are in El Salvador, South Africa, and so many other points in the Global South. It is much more. Jean and John Comaroff (in post-Foucauldian mode) point to present-day police theatrics in which spectacles of crime and law enforcement aim to produce social order.[9] Certainly Émile Durkheim has it so, minus the element of fantasy. Criminals function to establish order, to control difference—the system demands violators to sustain itself.[10] Michel Foucault in his early work describes how institutional knowledge production about deviance (sexual, psychotic, material) normalizes society as it fabricates the forbidden.[11] René Girard tells us how assigning criminality to certain bodies helps to reunite a fractious society after a scapegoat is expelled.[12]

Knowing: Not-Knowing: Unknowing

This chapter explores the fixation with the criminal in postwar San Salvador—a search for knowledge that often manifested in the fierce and contradictory desire to see him in his fleshy presence. It builds on the argument I have been making throughout this book, about the need to know the not-known of the postwar. The desire for the Other becomes especially urgent in this quest. In previous chapters, the postwar unknown was democracy itself. Democracy, it could be imagined in the early 1990s, would provide a set of rules to get to know the Other, indeed to incorporate the Other into an inclusive political community. But in a market democracy, inclusion is contingent on the demands of global capital. The economy calls for certain kinds of bodies at certain times. It disposes of them at others.

The Other is also a philosophical concept in relation to which the self is constructed. This Other cannot be incorporated into the polity. For if our sense of self depends on this Other, how could we ever demystify it as an object—how could we ever really know the (constructed) unknown?[13] What we need is a concept of constructed unknowing that links this Other that cannot be empirically contained with the Other that girds capitalist regimes. This unknowing operates through processes of racialization and marginalization.

After introducing the concept of unknowing, this chapter falls into four sections. First, an analysis of an account by the psychologist América, whom we met in the previous chapter, shows how "expert" attempts to control individuals through knowledge production never fully succeed. Indeed they constitute spaces in which the Other emerges. Second, the spectacular case of a seventeen-year-old gang member known as El Directo, accused of killing seventeen people, illustrates processes of social knowledge (and unknowledge) production through mass-mediated discourses on law and criminality. Third, tropes that circulated through everyday talk in 1990s San Salvador demonstrate how this unknowing, constructed through expertise and mass mediation, collaborates in the culturally naturalized feelings about how the criminal is embodied. Finally, this chapter asks how these notions of individual criminality have become normalized in El Salvador. It looks back to how concepts of race, deviance, and bodies grew out of particular economic and social structures that were most dramatically, and horrifyingly, enacted in the pivotal moment of Salvadoran twentieth-century history, the Matanza. It ends by exploring how current ideas of criminality in Central America maintain, or stray from, these durable historical senses, in which unknowledge is constantly reproduced.

I have argued that the desire to know the Other, as criminal, in postwar El Salvador (even as the encounter with the Other is ever deferred) issued from anxiety about unnerving shifts in social relations, themselves the outcome of global and local transformations in capitalist relations of exchange. But let us pause for a moment and ask ourselves: how was this sense of *not-knowing* produced? Did people in San Salvador really feel, so flagrantly, an abrupt assault of the new in 1992? I want to think about how *knowing* and *not-knowing* implicate each other. Particular ignorances structure and enforce particular knowledges. Knowledges structure ignorances. The way we know shapes our sense of what we think we don't know.[14]

In San Salvador in the early years after the peace accords, questions about who to trust and not to trust were structured by the act of forgetting rather than the blank-slate condition of *not-knowing*. This is hardly a new phenomenon, and not just a postwar product. Pierre Bourdieu describes it as "forgetting of history which history itself produces" as it settles into the second nature of habitus (the embodied and mental dispositions acquired through life experience and cultural patterns).[15] In relation to crime and reasons for crime, I call this process the act of *unknowing*. I define this act as converting something largely known, if not acknowledged, into something circumstantially *unknown*, masquerading as a condition of *not being known*, so that it can be replaced. In El Salvador, what is originally known is that social inequality and structural violence in the late 1970s led to war and today still keep the majority of the population marginalized, impoverished, and criminalized. (These offenses stretches back more than five hundred years, of course.) What replaces this knowledge, through the process of unknowing reiterated especially through crime postwar stories, is the long-circulated idea of criminality as the result of individual, willful, and perhaps even congenital, deviance. Thus it follows the thrust of postwar crime stories, which insist that the individual—not the collective, not the state—must separately manage the new era's dangers.

Cultural critic and philosopher Slavoj Žižek puts it this way. "What [people] overlook, what they misrecognize, is not the reality but the illusion which is structuring their reality, their real social activity. They know very well how things really are, but still they are doing it as if they did not know." By "doing it" Žižek means that people interact as if they do not know that

there are "relations between people behind the relations between things"—
what Karl Marx called commodity fetishism. They in fact *know* people are
behind things. They just don't recognize that what they're doing, "acting as
if money . . . is the immediate embodiment of wealth," still enacts the illusion. It misrecognizes. "The illusion is therefore double: it consists in over-
looking the illusion which is structuring our real, effective relationship to
reality. And this overlooked, unconscious illusion is what may be called the
ideological fantasy." [16] People largely *know* that structural conditions produce
crime, criminals, Others. Yet they continue to act as if evil and subversion
inhere in those Others.

How is it that acts of forgetting about the criminalization of Others,
constructed as conditions of unknowing, of ideological fantasy, came to
particularly characterize San Salvador daily life in the immediate postwar
years? Is Žižek (through Marx and Freud) insisting that it is the default way
to confront the world? I desperately want to turn to the method of hope
here. After all, a time of transition from one state of affairs to another (war
to not-war) could become an "agentive moment," in which circumstances
open up the possibility for change, for people to see in new ways. These
moments come when "breaches in the order of things" are so enormous
that everyday explanations cannot appease. [17] Many Salvadorans enacted a
prospective hope as they tried to imagine something they could not know in
their struggles for democracy: a moment when old polarities would no longer order understandings of the world, and new kinds of social relations—of
individual sovereignty and social solidarity—would emerge. Not yet, perhaps, but soon. The market democracy that rose up in the postwar moment
of possibility offered "freedom." But not equality. In this logic there was no
place for those who could not compete.

For most crime-story tellers, taking a stance of *not-knowing*, just after
the war ended, may have been a practical extension of the effort to relearn
habits of caution inculcated by war-era threats. It was expedient to do so—to
plead ignorance, in effect—before a threat of violence. In the final pages of
this book I argue that crime stories helped produce a powerful sense of not-
knowing that abetted an individualized, depoliticized remaking of social
relations. To make this case, I will have to wrestle with my own deferral. At
last, then, I examine how the ideological fantasy of the Other emerged in
San Salvador crime stories in the first years after the peace accords, and how
this process structured knowledge and unknowledge about social relations.

The crime stories that circulated in early postwar El Salvador formed
around a feeling of absence. Nameless, often featureless, criminals slipped

through El Salvador in the 1990s indexed by things like dead bodies, stolen wallets, or loud headlines. Crime stories moved so effortlessly at this time because they addressed the widespread feeling of not-knowing. They offered new data about how to live in the postwar world. The knowledge produced fit well into the ideological fantasy. It guided nervous listeners on individual risk management. But even as these narratives attempted to grasp the seeming new and not known—the present and future—they invoked the familiar, the known. They revived durable culturally and historically constituted ideologies about bodies and social order. Many people returned to historically constituted "harder" essences of criminality, indexed and iconized as "race" and "class," underneath constantly shifting, emergent surface signs (such as the baggy pants of gang members). At the same time, the changing needs of the market economy produced new problematic bodies through racializing ideas that seeped into popular concepts of criminality.

Racism in this sense is produced through technologies, institutions, discourses, and social relations that unevenly allocate group tendencies to be made to live or allowed to die.[18] As Brandt Peterson, a scholar of race in El Salvador, has put it, "Racialization speaks to the slotting of subjects into an interpretive frame that makes use of race in its explanations, and that taps into a realm of sensibilities, fantasies, and signification that is not wholly conscious. It is the world of knowledge [German philosopher Theodor] Adorno signals when he says that no matter how completely and rationally one attests to the humanity of Jews, the Nazis know whom to kill."[19] Peterson argues that this knowledge, this idea of race as emergent in collective fantasies, led to the 1932 Matanza. Today the history of modern beliefs about an embodied, racialized threat—the inner barbarism deep within even the staunchly *mestizo*-mythologized nation of El Salvador—remains a crucial axis on which conceptions of order rely. Though most Salvadorans claim there are no "Indians" in their country anymore, everyday discourses of the 1990s revealed fantasized traces of indigeneity as stigma in conceptions of bodies and practices and essences.[20] In the postwar, postrevolutionary, post-Cold War era in El Salvador, these conceptions demanded a new (or renewed) kind of naturalization of the social structure, a misrecognition or unknowing of social inequality.

I. América: "Calm Down, You're Not Going to Touch Me"

As past chapters of this book have suggested, among the implicit understandings of democracy that circulated in San Salvadoran conversations about crime in the 1990s was that of an inclusive community of care. There, social equality would be practiced and social justice pursued. This concept draws on an imaginary of obligation, of compassion in the sense of concern for the well-being of others. In the most inclusive way of understanding democracy, the citizen and the state, must embrace the Other. The former Other must be absorbed into the nation-self. We saw this in the murder of ex-FMLN guerrilla commander Francisco Velis. The government's claims that he was a victim of street crime, and not a guerrilla murdered by death squads, would have confirmed that he was a full-fledged member of the new democratizing polity.

In the last chapter, América, the psychologist, was one of the few people I met who had had more than brief and tense encounters with the abject.[21] She had entered into dialogues with the Other. She told us of crushed humanity in the prisons of San Salvador. She described beings reduced to bare life: soldiers forced into drug addiction and violent young men abused since childhood. Listening to her, I could almost imagine the possibility of a democratic nation open to all voices, even those that had been criminalized by the state. However, unlike most crime-story tellers who encountered their Others, América held the upper hand in those interactions. She was the professional, deploying a clinical and compassionate knowledge (also a language of power). Indeed, her very embrace entailed the naming of the Other—the injury itself. She embodied the institutional line-drawing that determines who does and does not belong to a safe democratic public. The men she spoke to were already behind bars, literally excluded.

América had also met some of these same kinds of young men outside prison, where categories of citizenship (or classes of inclusion or exclusion) were not so clear. Three times, twice on the bus and once in a car, she had been robbed. Her compassion, the ethic of care that defined her as a therapeutic interlocutor, became something else outside of the institution. When we spoke (in June 1998), her most recent assault had occurred eight months earlier, outside an auto repair shop. Her friend had asked her to drive him back to work after he dropped off his car. "So I was in the car waiting for him," América told me, "and then this guy came up and said to me, 'Give me the time please?' When I noticed that he was talking to me, I said to myself, 'Oh, he's a thief,' but it was too late. I just looked at him, and he said to me, 'Give me your watch, give me your wallet, give me everything.' And then he got really nervous. So I said to him, 'Calm down, relax, yes, I'm going to give you everything, but you're not going to hurt me.' He was still really nervous. 'It's okay,' I told him. 'Calm down, you're not going to touch me,' because he had me like this, he was pushing something into me, I don't know if it was a gun or a knife but he had it right up against me, and so, 'Calm down, you're not going to do anything to me, yes, I'll give you the stuff.' And I gave my necklace to him."

Then her friend came out of the repair shop. He asked what was going on.

"But I said, 'Nothing's happening.' My friend is really rash. I said to myself, wait, if he's armed, there's going to be a shootout. 'No nothing,' I said, and the guy [the assailant] was still there. But after he left, I told my friend, 'I got held up,' and my friend went running after him. That's why I hadn't said anything when [the thief] was right there in front of me.

"[The thief] ran off, it was incredible, like a hare running. My friend almost reached him. And the police happened to pass by, and they followed him too, but the guy had thrown himself—there was an alleyway, and at the end of it, he'd thrown himself into a gorge, I don't know how he didn't break any bones, but we saw him, falling and falling. And then he got up and kept on running, what incredible agility."

As a psychologist interviewing traumatized subjects, América, in control, had found manageable categories of expert knowledge in which to contain the inmates. Outside, she had tried to maintain control as well. She had largely succeeded when her attacker was in her immediate orbit. She not only urged her assailant to calm down, but she told him he would not harm her. She would later explain to me, contributing to new, postwar survival skills, that the proper strategy in such situations is never to show fear, nor to resist. She even thought far enough ahead to lie to her friend about what was happening, avoiding a possible confrontation.

The moment her friend began to chase the thief, though, América's mode changed. The thief changed. He was not a damaged adolescent—nor an object restrained by social-scientific categories. He became animal-like, running like a wild rabbit. He morphed into something fantastical, not human, leaping into the air. In some ways the transformation América described echoes Marielena's story of her carjacker, in which she depicted the change from a humble person into something not of this world, a duplicitous and satanic stranger. Similarly, América's assailant fell outside of rationality, beyond the community of care—ultimately, in the logic of such narratives, excluded from democracy and postwar El Salvador. (The logic of América's particular story, however, does not find the lack in the state. She noted that the police tried to help, but were helpless before the inhumanly agile thief.)

América's next words leap toward a generalized nonhuman quality of Salvadoran criminals. Her stance is far removed from her commentary about the prisoners. I asked her what he looked like. He was young, she said, sixteen or eighteen, and "an ordinary, average guy, the same as—Well, two weeks ago, my mother got robbed. She was walking along minding her own business. She had her Bible with her, for mass, all she had was her Bible, and this guy came up on her. He was well dressed, with a notebook, my mama said, and he had a long-sleeved shirt, very clean."

"What did he do?" I asked.

"He took her wallet. And he took her Bible," she said. Though he looked like a decent human, he was not knowable. He was not categorizable in terms of mental disorders, past trauma, substance abuse, or simply immediate need, like her prison patients. His act went beyond rationality, to something—Other.

Structuring Ignorance: Psychology, Individuation, and Depoliticization

In other postconflict or post-authoritarian sites, scholars have shown that the practice of psychology can depoliticize state actions as it focuses on individualizing trauma. Psychologizing solutions can effectively aid neoliberal individuation.[22] At first, listening to América describe her Salvadoran prisoner-patients, I would not have thought that she engaged in the same logic of individual management of risk as I have been theorizing in much San Salvador postwar crime storytelling. I had felt América to be among the most compassionate of the people I met in an angry city. I had heard her explanations of prisoners' individual suffering as an embrace of the Other, as a hopeful gesture toward an inclusive democracy. Certainly her words contrasted with calls on some radio talk shows to throw all the gang members or criminals in jail—to burn them all alive. It was only later, reading the transcript of our interview, that I realized how she was managing these individuals. She was selecting them, disciplining them, and normalizing them, through her careful framing of them as patients, not agents. Further, only as individuals, not as members of a class or race or of a particular collective, could they be conceived of as innocent and damaged and human.

But outside their cells, when they slipped out of her control, América wrote them out of humanity. By not imagining them as whole beings with life histories, and, more importantly for my arguments here, by not rendering any histories as perpetrated within the unjust Salvadoran social structure, she unknew them. This is what many people did to the individual thieves and muggers and assailants in their crime stories. They did this even as they could step back from their particular experiences to reflect on the general political-economic structure and lament—in different languages and levels of expertise—state failure, endemic poverty, and deep, historically inscribed inequality. By focusing on individual trauma, most people unknew social forces and structural inequality. In their stories they unknew what so many of them had known. Even powerful men like Atilio (in Chapter 5), pointing to El Salvador's "good macroeconomic indicators," knew what he unknew. "The typical Salvadoran doesn't feel the effects" of those statistics that made El Salvador look so good to the big finance mega-number-crunchers, he had said, acknowledging how language and accounting used by powerful entities marginalize and criminalize the majorities. As I have said, many crime storytellers may have had to unknow situationally, to at least defer knowing, in order to make it through the day. But many of them (many of us!) also have had the privilege of unknowing, as they watched the world around them and gauged who they could trust, who they could not see, who they could hit with their car. In their privilege, they decided who could be part of a postwar democracy.

Early in this book I named the postwar affective state as a lack of *Angstbereitschaft*, an uneasy sense of not knowing when to feel anxiety—or not recognizing it in the new moment. But perhaps my turn to that concept was another strategy of deferral. Perhaps we *do* know, are ready to feel anxiety, but we don't want to know that we know. I am taking this sense of unknowing, this disavowal or refusal of knowledge, in the sense Eve Kosofsky Sedgwick describes. You are innocent if you don't know; you cannot take responsibility for what happens. She writes, "Ignorances, far from being pieces of the originary dark, are produced by and correspond to particular knowledges and circulate as part of particular regimes of truth."[23] In this way power erases its traces, in part by controlling who and what gets acknowledged. The language of psychological classification that América used, and the technicalities of macroeconomic indicators that Atilio deployed, structure the same kind of political disengagement that the state's criminal code-switching does. If this is so, then the unknowing built into crime stories told by ordinary Salvadorans—an unknowing that positioned criminal agency largely in the racialized bodies of disenfranchised young men—is more than a deficit of knowledge to be rescued with "the heroics of human cognition." This ideological fantasy, this unknowing, is what allows the state, and the market, in the late twentieth and early twenty-first centuries in their neoliberal guise, to continue to exploit and expel the refuse of used-up humans.

Still, these criminals, these gang members, these carjackers, remain defiantly *there*. They are visible, hypervisible. If seeing is knowing, then they must be eminently knowable. Yet they are not known, except in that brute moment of encounter—one quickly narrativized into something else. The literary scholar Elaine Scarry points to the difficulty of imagining *any* other people—but explains that depicting the Other (especially in great numbers, as a population, whether war enemies or racialized minorities) deepens the dilemma. Thinking of the Other as both hypervisible and spectral, overexposed and underexposed, is not contradictory. It is complementary. "Monstrosity and invisibility," Scarry writes, "are two subspecies of the other, the one overly visible and repelling attention, the other unavailable for attention and hence absent from the outset." She points to the overexposure of a monstrous, magnified caricature of Saddam Hussein (during the 1990–91 Gulf War) as standing in for the Iraqi population, which was largely absent from portrayals of the war. Either way—both ways—she writes, "The human capacity to injure other people is very great precisely because our capacity to imagine other people is very small." [24]

In the crime stories that circulated in the first years after the peace accords, the Other was necessarily at the center of the narrated action—looming, frightening, monstrous. Yet that center so often seemed empty, weightless, more a blurred, underexposed haunting than an embodied density. Though América clearly controlled her attacker with firm therapeutic orders while he stood in front of her, she could not contain him in the end as he slipped from her therapeutic grasp into a deep gorge. He inevitably reappeared, in this case to steal her mother's Bible. Similarly, though Atilio (in Chapter 2) saved himself from full-on assault with the steel armor of his car, he could not kill the two bandits who materialized in the night by the stoplight. They, too, slipped into the darkness. These stories remind us that no matter how tellers work to unknow the criminal (to not know the social structure that produced the criminal, replacing it with a mystical, mythical nonhumanity), they can never fully succeed in obliterating social knowledge.

This incomplete aspect of unknowing echoes the sociologist Avery Gordon's sense of *haunting* here, as "one way systems of power make themselves known and their impacts felt in everyday life, especially when they are supposedly over and done with (slavery, for instance) or when their oppressive nature is denied (as in free labor or national security). . . . Haunting . . . is an animated state in which a repressed or unresolved social violence is making itself known [even if not seen], sometimes very directly, sometimes more obliquely."[25] Gordon's haunting happens in crime stories when the subjects that become fetishized objects through the processes of unknowing resist the narrative force of such a fate. They break through.

The violence in postwar El Salvador hardly seems repressed. The abject, the Other, the disposable categories of humanity under the continuing force of the market economy, would not seem to need to resort to haunting to make themselves known. But again, what is being made *known* and what is *unknown*? What kinds of unknowing must be constantly reiterated in the circulation of crime stories? And what kinds of social and ideological effects does this production of unknowledge have? To explore these questions, I turn to a story of a spectacularly hypervisible, overexposed postwar criminal who could not be seen.

II. Overexposed/Underexposed: The Biospectacle of El Directo

On 7 January 1999, in a "lightning operation" fifty police officers descended on a small cinderblock row house in a neighborhood called Milagro de la Paz (Miracle of Peace) at the edge of the sweaty eastern city of San Miguel. Their target was a skinny, shaved-headed gang leader known as El Directo (the Direct One). He was suspected in the Christmas Eve execution of the nephew of a Human Rights Counsel delegate—and, rumor had it, at least seventeen other murders in the barrios that ringed the provincial capital. Police would later tell reporters that the teenaged suspect brandished an old army grenade before they could handcuff him.[26]

The dramatic capture went down at a moment when El Salvador's young civilian police force—indeed the entire postwar government—was under fire for staggering crime rates that belied the country's international identity as a model for transitions to democracy. A month after El Directo's arrest, the papers reported that El Salvador had beat out Colombia and Brazil for the highest murder rate in the Americas, with 120 homicides per 100,000.[27] The spectacle of El Directo would seize the popular imagination. While iconizing postwar fear in the racialized body of a gang leader, he also indexed the rise of seemingly inexplicable, fantastic excesses in the country: excess violence, excess population, excess commodities, and excess cash in unexpected places.[28] This sense of mystery multiplied in the case of El Directo, since new juvenile laws that had passed a few years earlier as part of an ongoing legal reform project prohibited the media from disseminating his image or printing his name. The public obsession with El Directo, the desire to *see* his legally invisible corporeal threat, grew out of that sense of

not knowing in the midst of increasing violence. As in many societies undergoing a shift to neoliberal globalization, public attention in El Salvador
focused on the problem of youth. Mass media obsessed on the surplus of
young men such as El Directo who loitered on the streets and boarded the
buses. They refused the demands of capitalism to disappear, as biopolitical
debris, when no longer needed.[29]

By 1999 the boisterous Salvadoran tabloids and TV news programs had
for some time been parading ominous images of baggy-pantsed, tattoo-
faced youths, cameras lingering in a kind of Lombrosian leer over their defiant, degenerate physicality. Most Salvadorans knew something about the
rumors of how, in 1980s Los Angeles, the *Mara Salvatrucha*, or MS-13, gang
had formed among alienated Central Americans who organized themselves
against Chicano bands—and how their rivals were called Eighteenth Street
(Dieciocho), transporting Los Angeles cartography. Many of the Salvadoran
gang members had fled the war as children.[30] As we know, the U.S. government was deporting hundreds of Salvadorans each week. This was the story
that would gain such currency post-9/11 in the United States (as the audiences to my public talks testified). It would also be taken up in El Salvador
for different reasons. It established a monstrous "foreignness" in criminal
bodies that had to be expelled from the body politic.[31] But like most gang
members in El Salvador, El Directo, even as his (invisible, but vividly imagined) image terrorized the nation, had never left the country.

Who was El Directo? Reporters uncovered a life stunted by both war and
poverty—a life *known* to the vast majority of Salvadorans, indeed intimately
lived by many. El Directo embodied the contradictions of the economic and
social structure. His mother Dora Alicia Morales recounted the birth of her
first son (later to be revealed as Gustavo Adolfo Parada Morales), when she
was sixteen years old, in January 1982. She described how when she went into
labor, she hitched a ride to the hospital in the ambulance that had arrived for
a soldier who had blown himself up in front of her neighbors, his in-laws.[32]
As a boy, her son, "Tavo," reportedly studied until he was ten—in 1992, the
year of the peace accords. "In school he was remembered as a shy child, head
down, sad and generally the center of teasing of his companions, as he was
one of the oldest students," an article in *La Prensa Gráfica* said. Another report suggested that Gustavo's mother pulled him out of school because he
was getting beat up every day. He worked a time in a bakery and "spent afternoons playing soccer in the streets with a ball of wadded rags."[33]

Then something happened. His life as one of the underexposed, suffering majorities transformed into that of the monster who would soon be-

come the racialized and even foreign savage threatening the national body. The Other. (My narrative does not deny the horror of what he did; but we must remember—we must not unknow—that he is a product of a system that slots him into that role.)

The process of unknowing had begun. "When he stopped studying, he began sniffing glue and hanging out with gang members," one account claimed. "At thirteen he was a criminal and feared." Just around that time, in 1994 and 1995, in that same neighborhood, local legend had it that some of the first postwar gangs began forming in El Salvador[34]—and the postwar death squad Sombra Negra began an extralegal extermination campaign against delinquents.[35] "They say he committed his first murder at fifteen," one journalist noted. "In other words, in two years, he killed at least seventeen, generally young girls who he raped (and cut off their breasts), or personal enemies, as in the case of the former chief of his clique of the *Mara Salvatrucha*." Psychologists who never met the boy made clinical pronouncements, categorizing him as individualized symptom or cause. One said he had never felt love as a child and thus never learned to love or forgive. Another said he was a psychopath who killed for pleasure, without feeling anything.[36]

But it was neither this Gustavo Adolfo, child of war and poverty, nor his victims, themselves refuse and refugees of armed struggle and economic restructuring, that propelled public fantasies. It was the law itself, its inability to contain the excess bodies, that provoked the mass-mediated response. A debate over law ultimately accelerated processes of unknowing. An orchestrated public rage turned on legal limits imposed by outsiders. It turned out that the longest sentence El Directo would face was seven years, the maximum allowed by the United Nations Convention on the Rights of the Child. As police said early on, "It's incredible, but this youth has killed one person for each year in his short life, and deserves a life sentence, but here in this country he is protected by the Law of Juvenile Offenders and the maximum sentence he would get would be seven years."[37] Media debates spiraled. Editorials condemned international organizations such as the United Nations as misunderstanding El Salvador's basic lack, its not-yet-modern population.[38] In a typical statement, a representative of the powerful National Association for Private Enterprise (Asociación Nacional de la Empesa Privada, ANEP) said on a television debate program, "We can't just import penal codes from Switzerland or whatever other country, without them being adapted to our national reality, our culture, our institutions, our people."[39]

With El Directo the beleaguered state created a spectacle. Elsewhere I have described this case as exemplifying a biopolitical spectacle, or biospectacle, in which the politics of managing populations becomes a sensational visual display, an exhibition of marked bodies as a form of unknowledge production.[40] In the state's narrative, these emergent Other bodies—both monstrous and invisible—were uncontrollable under laws that kept it from monopolizing the use of force. The Salvadoran mass media focused on the deportees, projecting an internal war in which society had to be defended against "foreign" contamination. El Directo had become a monster in the sense Judith Halberstam describes: "An economic form in that it condenses various racial and sexual threats to nation, capitalism, and the bourgeoisie in one body."[41] Soon after El Directo's story began circulating, *El Diario de Hoy* initiated yet another series of alarmist articles about criminal deportees from the United States, in classic "moral panic" mode.[42] The hysteria echoed the terror of red hordes before the 1932 massacre, as we shall see: "United States sends country wave of criminals"; "1,500 more criminals to be deported"; "More than 100 deportees in two days (the majority are ex-convicts)"; "Prison requested for deported criminals"; "What to do with these delinquents?"[43]

The El Directo biospectacle burst into the public sphere during the raucous political campaigns for the March 1999 presidential elections. Almost all discussions of the nation at that moment seemed to be framed through the knowledge/unknowledge of criminality. After the vote (which the ruling party's candidate, Francisco Flores, won easily), attention returned to El Directo, who was found guilty of seven of the seventeen charges of murder. It was the imposition of that maximum seven-year sentence that spun the biospectacle to the next extreme. Public debate repeated itself over and over, rapidly replicating unknowledge in the service of ideological fantasy. Such weak laws were unsuitable for savage Salvadoran reality! Much of the anti-crime and pro-law reform movement was led by groups like ANEP and the private-enterprise-oriented FUSADES. These groups knew high crime rates spooked investors calculating security, corruption, and theft costs.

Just as El Directo was sentenced, FUSADES released a report concluding that suspects were arrested in only 6 to 8 percent of murder cases. National Civilian Police Director Rodrigo Ávila blamed 40 percent of crime on "inadequate legal provisions."[44] Outgoing President Armando Calderón Sol proclaimed, "The fact that El Directo may have killed seventeen people says much about how in this country things aren't going well and we have to . . . reconceive (the laws)."[45] Again and again, in this process of unknowing, a paradoxical story of abject bodies, of populations to be contained, to be kept out of the democratic polity, was invoked: a unique Salvadoran criminal, and a uniquely Salvadoran criminality. In a country ever defined by its lack, such monsters could not be controlled in "civilized" ways conjured in those modern utopian countries with their human rights.

Fifteen days later, El Directo escaped prison with eight other juvenile inmates. The nation lurched into alert. *Who was this monster?* He was loose, a cipher, the Other, masked by juvenile laws and human rights protections, lurking anywhere and nowhere. The demand to *see* him, to behold this essence of criminality—to stare at the face of danger and thus somehow *know* it—became a national media frenzy. "¡CACERÍA HUMANA!" (MANHUNT!), headlines screamed: "Hundreds of Police after El Directo."[46] Hundreds of police, the media added, but those reformed juvenile laws meant that not a one could (legally) know what he looked like. As "María," a San Miguel waitress, told *El Diario de Hoy* the day after his escape, she didn't trust anyone "because any man who enters the business could be El Directo."[47] This was the production of a sense of *not-knowing* that propelled so many crime stories. Salvadorans could only imagine this "new" criminal type waiting in the shadows. Or on the sidewalk. Or on the bus.

Police recaptured El Directo three days after his escape. Within a day, El Directo's image and name were everywhere, filling the newspapers, taking over the news shows, invading the circulation of everyday crime stories. Then this Other spoke. It was not clear how microphones and cameras were smuggled into jail. "They see me as a monster. But inside there's a human being same as you," Gustavo Adolfo intoned.[48]

Perhaps his words, oddly distant from a sense of self (not "I'm a human being," but "there's a human being") only asserted his condition as human, however flawed—with the will to live despite the state's exclusionary logic. But at that moment everything paused. In the stillness after all the shrill headlines, he defied his media-assigned identity as fantasy object—whether overexposed or underexposed, monstrous or invisible.

For one moment, an agentive moment, possibilities for change opened up. For one moment of hope the insistent sense of not-knowing confronted another feeling, that of a shared sense of struggle, a struggle to know in a way that did not turn into unknowing. Another narrative, a stuttering, uncertain story, began to break through the public sphere to address what had happened to the bodies of so many of El Salvador's young people (and old people, and damaged people, and excess people) in the new global economy—or, indeed, in the durable old capitalist logic that had governed the old agro-export economy. This figure, El Directo, was a child, after all. María Teresa de Mejía of the Salvadoran Institute for the Protection of Minors asserted on one interview program, "He has the right to reeducation and reinsertion in society."[49] Some editorials whispered in agreement: young people, poor people, shouldn't be criminalized as a category. Much of the conversation veered toward the psychological, suggesting posttraumatic stress, pointing to the "problems" in individuals (much as América did). But a dialogue seemed to have begun.

At that moment the state stepped in. It seemed determined to reinstall the ideological fantasy. The courts threatened to sanction ninety-eight members of the mass media for revealing El Directo's name and face.[50] The possibilities of the moment passed. The state's action pushed off the front pages the brief but substantial discussions of privilege and prejudice, youth and protection, crime and corruption.

In the midst of rising crime rates, the sensationalist mass media display of Other bodies (often literally, in El Salvador, arranged for the cameras in handcuffed rows in front of police precincts) would seem to answer the postwar anxiety about knowing and not-knowing. But biospectacle must be connected in some way to common lived experience if it has any chance to become a shared point of reference, to become entextualized in a way that can circulate. Public circulation is only possible because signs—stories, images, ideas, whether fantastical or realistic—make sense to people who speak with and through them (even as they aren't the same as empirical facts of existence). Signs tell them something recognizable, familiar, if not verifiable. The ideological fantasy worked in postwar El Salvador because the El Directo story pointed to memories of past subversion, as well as anxiety about local crime and insecurity in the latest phase of capitalism. The discourse on postwar crime in 1990s El Salvador was not just the invention of a state attempting to assert its monopoly on the legitimate use of force in a new global era (by calling for new repressive laws). It was not just the functional product of an insecure regime asserting itself in a crisis of governance. Like Halberstam's monsters, El Directo also offered a dense symbolic site onto which Salvadorans could displace their fears, making the causes of violence seem knowable.

Spectacle is always performative. But any performance entails risk. Even as it is staged for ideological fantasy, it can produce unexpected kinds of knowledge. In a crisis, such as that produced through the escape of El Directo, entangled states of knowing and not-knowing can turn one into the other. Just as, through crime story-telling, the victim-audiences evaluate and create their own kinds of knowledge, audiences of mass-mediated criminal spectacles might consider alternative understandings of the world.

Breakthrough

On 6 June 1999, at 4:30 in the afternoon, a seventeen-year-old crack addict arrived at a football field in Ciudad Merliot. He took out an M-16 rifle and started shooting into a group of about twenty young men celebrating the end of a hard-played game with a pizza (a team called "La Ley" [The Law] had won). Two died. Three were injured. Everyone in the neighborhood—the working-class community where my partner Evert grew up—knew the players. "I mean I just saw him," Evert had said uncomprehendingly of "Pupusa," one of the victims, when his sister told him what happened. "It was the Semana Santa (Holy Week). We were looking at *alfombras* (the flower-petal and chalk designs that decorate the streets on Good Friday)." They had played football together as boys. Pupusa, the local star, later joined the Salvadoran team Árabe Marte.

The first story that circulated about the event was that the shooter, from a nearby marginal zone, or slum, was angry because the players had refused to give him coins. This was about a month and a half after the killings in Columbine High School in Littleton, Colorado, heavily reported in El Salvador. One news article described the Ciudad Merliot attack as "in the style of the recent school massacres in the United States." [51] The U.S.-based Spanish-language television program *Ocurrió Así* interviewed one of the survivors, "Chato," who lived a block from Evert's family (a year later he would be killed by gang members). Other newspaper articles took up the fury over the reformed juvenile laws, echoing the El Directo biospectacle. [52] But in the neighborhood the story soon turned murky. Maybe this was not a case of a lone gunman. It could have been—people said—Pupusa had been killing gang members. The kid wanted revenge. Or, the kid was carrying out someone else's orders. An older man would later be charged with providing the gun. Had Pupusa been a vigilante, aligned with a clandestine extermination squad? Or had he been a gang member himself? Was it about drug dealing? Why had that kid shot at *everyone*, after all, if he was supposed to be after Pupusa? If he really was a gang member, why didn't he have tattoos? The rumors mounted. [53] I fantasized for a moment of starting a new phase of research, of trying to understand these alienated, criminalized youth. But no one in the neighborhood—people I had known for more than a year by then—would tell me anything. Gang members are brothers, cousins, nephews, and neighbors. They play football, they eat pizza, they look at the *alfombras* on Semana Santa. I think now of Elana Zilberg's work on the political logic of *doble cara* (double/two-faced) in El Salvador: things are never what they appear.[54] Or perhaps it is that things are always more than what they appear. Meanings are never fully present.

What did appear, over and over, were bodies. While gang members materialized in mass media as the menace (monsters, El Directo said) *they* were often the ones dying in the streets. They were the ones who truly had to learn to manage their movements in an acute risk climate. (That was often one reason they joined gangs in the first place, much research has shown—to be part of a collective, to find protection.) Several deportees Zilberg knew died violently: She has written of "Gato," whose father had been assassinated in the war, shot by a gang member soon after one of their interviews. Another, "Weasel," told her that when he found himself deported to the country he had left at five, "I arrived with a lot of rumors in my mind about there's like this death squad that's going to kill you if you're all tattooed. So I'm a little nervous and scared. Then the police come and snatch you and put you in a little room, and I said, 'Oh, fuck . . . that's it, forget it. They got me. They're going to kill me.'"[55]

Photojournalist Donna DeCesare's moving documentary work with Edgar Bolaños, "Shy Boy," who took his murdered brother's gang name, testifies to the fragility of the lives of so many alienated young people in El Salvador. "There are lots of people who want to kill me," he told her. "I don't mean homeboys. I mean really bad people from the organized crime rings and other people who just hate us. They think because I used to live in Los Angeles that I am the leader here. They are wrong, but they have lots of guns, big guns, and we don't have much of anything."[56] Bolaños would die the next year, on 9 January 1999, just as the El Directo biospectacle was rising. It was a moment when human rights organizations reported increasing death squad and vigilante activity and extrajudicial killings of youth gang members. The case was never solved. But neighbors who saw the murder claim local vigilantes killed "Shy Boy."[57]

III. "Just to See Them You Know They're Thieves": The Other in Everyday Crime Stories

The discourse on postwar crime in 1990s El Salvador was not just the invention—spectacle—of a state attempting to mobilize diffuse anxiety in order to assert a monopoly on force. People sought ways to know the new situation, codes for managing the everyday reality of risk. Signs of risk were everywhere. Yet the changing "enemy," the materialization of this danger and disorder, slipped into the interstices, there and not there, monstrous, invisible. While people may have feared the group of teenagers with impassive, hard faces hanging out on the corner, defiantly overexposed, what may have generated more insecurity was the suspicion that the seemingly ordinary, unmarked individual might hide the real menace—*doble cara*.[58] Perhaps this panic impelled the frantic search for external signs of difference, for Other bodies, in the mass media and at the corner. Even as people attributed insecurity to "new" forms of violence, they were not sure what the new perpetrators looked like. Inevitably, they drew on old repertoires of reason. This was most evident in the way they told crime stories in the 1990s. As they were trying to understand the new, the unknown, their notions of what to look for echoed more durable ideas. What emerged was a hidden history of race.

Typical was Ana Lorena, a friend from the gym. We met her in Chapter 3. Explaining how to know criminals, she and her boyfriend Sergio described to me a walk to work in the crime-ridden center of Ciudad Delgado, where she worked in a government records office.[59] Her stress on the visible suggested the power of the invisible.

"Over the three blocks," she said, "in each corner you'll find five or ten guerrillas, all tattooed drug-addict gang members, I'm talking about today [1998]. You just get off the bus and there they are. It's better to . . . walk in the street, because I'd prefer to be killed by a car than be killed by a gang member. . . . I've been mugged too many times to count."

"You mean, people asking for money?" I asked, thinking of ragged kids who demand coins.[60]

"No, it's that they say, 'What time you got?' and in that second I look at my watch, they grab my wallet and run, or. . . . It's always the same, they even use the same line, I mean, just looking you can tell they're thieves."

"What tells you they're thieves?"

"The way they dress. The loose pants, the shirts hanging outside, the long hair. They look dirty, not at all neat, and the attitude . . . I mean, just to see them you know. They go around with Nikes, and that kind of clothes. Nike is expensive. Maybe in the U.S. it's cheap but here it's expensive. And they also go around with gold chains."

Sergio added, "And someone who doesn't dedicate himself to that [to crime] isn't going to go around showing himself like that."

"Just to see them you know they're thieves," Ana Lorena repeated.

Ana Lorena's terminology, haunted by war, recast the old image of the 1980s subversive/guerrilla as the 1990s gang member. She sutured past and present knowledge. This way of seeing the world hitched to old habits in the search for security. It also reentexualized the discourse of the party in power, ARENA, whose politicians frequently linked gangs, criminality, and the FMLN by recalling older insurgent "terrorism." But it was not so much the anachronism of the past as a dislocating element of the present that unhinged Ana Lorena and Sergio. Their unknowledge was more than situational; it also verged on confessing deeper dread, just at the edge of their awareness. "Just to see" they wanted to point to clear *class* boundaries. To them, the criminal's very shoes—their newness, their brand—disrupted. How could a street teenager, a common gangster (or, to them, a guerrilla) have Nike footwear—unless he was a deviant, unless he had stolen it? It was the rupture in their social world that disturbed them. Old (national, conceptual, legal) borders fell away in the new free-market, globalized world. As they talked of crime, they obsessed not on personal damage but displacement of commodities, matter out of place, much as Saskia and Roberto (also in Chapter 3) pointed to disorienting guns in purses and thieves in late model cars.[61]

So often, reconstructing events after a mugging, Salvadorans decided they really *knew*. They remembered some aspect, some vague premonition, some shadowy awareness. Psychologists suggest they may have been "right": Their seeming instinctive reactions ("Just to see") could have arisen from the "adaptive unconscious," in which the brain processes masses of data in milliseconds. It "reads the minds" and gauges intentions of others, measuring the risk they might present. The psychologist John Gottman calls this act "thin-slicing," in which the human unconscious finds knowledge in "patterns in situations and behavior based on very narrow slices of experiences."[62] Such snap judgments may well be necessary for everyday functioning, situational unknowledge. But they can go awry, especially under pressure, when culturally rooted stereotypes rear up. Salvadorans after the war inevitably thin-sliced. But, as Ana Lorena's words suggest, their perceptions were burdened by the country's long, fraught history of class and race politics as well as the distortions of war.

Norma Aragón taught English to privileged children at an evening and weekend language program at the elite American School, from which she had graduated some dozen years earlier.[63] She was about thirty, and embodied Salvadoran racial privilege. She was a slender Barbie-doll type with large brown eyes and shiny blonde hair. We had met several years earlier through our mutual friend Guayo. When I mentioned to him that I was going to interview her, he told me that I should see beyond her "good girl" act, that she was always asking him to get her marijuana.

She still vividly remembered the day of her assault five years earlier. It was at the Universidad Evangélica, where she had been studying medicine. It was in fact the only real street scare she could report, taking place at a time when she used to dare to venture out of her familiar circuit within the Colonia Escalón. Despite her inexperience, she *knew*.

"I was walking along and these two guys came, but I saw them, and I said to myself, 'They're thieves.'"

"Why did you think that?" I asked.

"I don't know. One was on the sidewalk and the other on the street and they just looked really suspicious."

"How?"

"They looked like humble people, loose pants, a little bit of a mess, loose T-shirt. So, to be exact, they got to my side and one took out a knife and put it against my waist, by my stomach, and they told me to give them everything I had. And I said, 'Look, I don't have anything,' that day I didn't even have money, nothing.

"So they said, 'Well then give me your watch.' . . . And I gave it to them, right, but they seemed to me really nervous so that I—and they said to me, 'Don't you look at us, don't turn around.'

" 'No, I won't, don't worry.' And so they just grabbed the watch . . . And that day, because it was early, I hadn't even put on my rings. So they just took the watch. When they left my legs just started trembling."

At the first encounter, people almost always realize they knew what to look for: thin-slicing, scanning sets of traits, behaviors, and expressions. In a society historically divided by class and race and gender, such habitus is rarely taught. Children learn, watching interactions, from their earliest moments. When these criteria fail them, people might become aware of their own practices. An unconscious habitual forgetting can convert from a sense of nonknowledge to sure knowledge.

Norma had only elaborated on "suspicious" at my insistence: poor, poorly dressed. "Humble" (*humilde*) could be (but in El Salvador is not necessarily) a racializing description—it often points to impoverished peasants (or people from outside the San Salvador area). People often make this judgment through physical attributes, including what I might call indigenous features. "A bit of a mess," also offers a clue—there was something *off* about them. People from the countryside are often very particular about appearance, conscious of judgmental city eyes. It was more likely that Norma sensed her assailants' intentions in the way they maneuvered. Still, her retrospective description may also reveal more about whom she thought might be a thief than about the threat she felt when she first glimpsed the two men. Her explanation is actually quite unsatisfactory. In a country as poor as El Salvador, huge numbers of young men could fit the image she offered. Her story did not instruct in the how to manage postwar crime. Rather, she could only say she knew (even if she did not know how she knew) but could do nothing.

Juan Granados, another person I met at the gym, fancied himself more conscious than people like Norma—more aware than most—of risk. He described for me an evolving knowledge of social hierarchies in his carefully honed skills of thin-slicing.[64] A knobby, middle-aged vitamin salesman, one afternoon in a loud Mr. Donut cafeteria he laid out a postwar checklist for me. His evidence for the effectiveness of his regime? He had never been assaulted.

"You're always checking everyone out, to see what kind of people could hurt you, those with long hair, those with loose clothes, loose pants, loose shirts, those that have tattoos, whether they're male or female, young, and the shoes, for example, usually they use athletic shoes to run, they don't use regular shoes . . . There's Nike, there's Fila, various brands, Puma, that they are buying through what they 'earn.'

"They also have the problem of drugs, they smoke marijuana, sniff glue, they take pills, so you should be paying attention to all of this. Look in the face more than anything, at the eyes, to see the expression they have. When you see a pair of them, together, you have to cross the street, to avoid problems, that's how you avoid them."

I asked, "Have you ever felt this kind of danger, seen danger?"

"Yes, I've seen people with long hair, two of them walking on the sidewalk, but really separated. . . . So I go to other side, and they don't usually follow me. Oh, and another thing is you have to look at the structure (*contextura*) of the people."

"The structure?"

"Yes, the physical structure, we're talking about the physical structure."

His advice echoed that of psychologists studying the unconscious: Watch the face. Look in the eyes. Yet in the taxonomy of Salvadoran dangers, this was hardly enough. Watch the hair, clothes—gauge social class.

But not *just* poor clothes, not *only* dirty hair; rebellious clothes, subversive hair, those of youth following music trends, like hip-hop (trends that gang members conspicuously followed—but so did the rich kids at the American School). Don Juan also pointed to the same shoe brand as Ana Lorena, Nike, as indexing danger—and the penetration of class lines. More confusing to me was his reference to the body. Was it race?

Another acquaintance, Guillermo Moressi (whom I met through Guayo), was more scientific in his thin-slicing terminology but equally vague in evidence of what sounded to me like racial difference. Physiognomy was the word he used.[65] In his story he recounted how his family restaurant, an exclusive eatery high up in Escalón, was robbed one day during dinner. He began by pointing to how the thieves tried to disguise themselves as restaurant clients. He claimed he had immediately noticed an essential difference:

"Three subjects appearing to be clients entered the restaurant. They sat at a table over there, and I saw them, and I noted that they seemed a little strange in the sense that they didn't seem to be the typical client in this restaurant, they didn't look like the socioeconomic status, middle class or upper class, they looked like they were of an inferior status. Not so much because of the clothes as their physiognomy, and something a little bit strange in their expressions. But I didn't pay much attention to them."

Not until one of them came up to the counter and pointed a gun at him.

Race and Unknowing in El Salvador

What is race in El Salvador? This question is relevant to the question of the criminal, if criminals are ever-racialized subjects; if criminals are the state's Other as Indians are the nation's Other. I have heard Salvadorans say that theirs is "the most *mestizo* country in Latin America." [66] A visitor familiar with other Latin American societies might tend to agree, if they think of *mestizaje* simply as biological mixing, or as separation from indigeneity. But *mestizaje* consciousness reemerged in the early twentieth century as a utopian and nationalist movement, especially in the Mexican Revolution. This moment is key to discourses on race in El Salvador, coming, as it did, just before the 1932 massacre. Mexican intellectual José Vasconcelos publicized it as *la raza cósmica* (the cosmic race), celebrating a creative, spiritual melding of the Native American, the European, and the African.[67] Intellectually, this movement not only imagined it would free people from racial difference, but also refused the European eugenic condemnation of "mixed" Latin Americans as racial degenerates. It also effectively erased the presence of Indians as anything but noble ancestors.

These ideas were taken up with enthusiasm in El Salvador. Social philosopher Alberto Masferrer lived from 1868 to 1932, precisely the time when indigenous Salvadorans were seeing dramatic changes in their position in the polity. He often wrote of his outrage at the poverty of the Salvadoran majorities, critiquing the liberal stance of equal opportunities as he pointed to power differences. He is famous for his theory of *Vitalismo*, promoting the state adoption of a "vital minimum" (of housing, food, schooling) to assure the welfare of even the poorest Salvadorans—an idea that echoed through twentieth-century popular demands, and a philosophy that would be taken up again by the FMLN's successful 2009 presidential campaign. Yet Masferrer almost never talked about Indians.[68] Even the literature of the era celebrating the countryside seems to erase any differentiation of the identities of the people working the earth. Poet Alfredo Espino's *Jícaras tristes*, for example, written in the 1920s, romanticizes the non-racially marked *peasant* (Indians are vague mytho-historical figures in his work) who "[sings] of the simple things of native soil."[69] While these intellectuals were all collaborating in the production of a modern national identity, it was in the context, we must acknowledge, of the destruction of the Indian—the expelling of *Pipil* or *Nahua, Lenca* or *Ulua,* difference, the erasure of embodied alterity.[70]

Many Salvadorans deny the existence, or the importance, of race in their country, as understood through U.S. references or in relation to neighboring Central American countries. Some people insist that the dictator-president General Maximiliano Hernández Martínez banished "races" after he took power in the 1931 coup. When they say this they are usually referring specifically to African-descended peoples, but the same kind of argument applies when they discuss the "disappearance" of Indians from El Salvador. The myth most often repeated is that those *indios* who survived the 1932 massacre dropped their native dress, their language, their customs. Indeed this discourse on lack of race *is* El Salvador's racial discourse.

The denial of race is thus in some ways the *unknowing* of the production of the Other: the unknowing of the Indian past, and especially the unknowing of the experience of the 1932 massacre. The national exception that everyone points to is fascinating. The relatively light-skinned, yet impoverished, residents of the northern department of Chalatenango—known as *cheles*, these descendants of Spaniards merit comment in El Salvador precisely because they do not fit into an implicit class/racial (and urban/rural) hierarchy.[71] On the other end of the spectrum, one of my wealthy students at a U.S.-accredited university extension campus joked that she "could be the maid," because of her skin color, slightly darker than that of most of her classmates. (The chauffeur behind tinted car windows waiting for her after class reminded us that she was no servant.) And then there was Atilio, the future high-ranking official of the Francisco Flores administration, who told me that he suspected then-candidate Flores was not "really" Salvadoran, that he must be Honduran—judging by his dark complexion and kinky hair texture. Atilio probably didn't mention this to Flores when he accepted his appointment. After all, Flores came from a "good" family, or so my elite students assured me one day in class.

Class and race identities are deeply intertwined. What Salvadorans first comment on, from quick impressions in the public sites of daily life, are dress, demeanor, and accent, as well as hygiene. They insist these aspects of a person are wholly issues of class and *educación*, a word best translated as manners (or breeding, which returns us to race).[72] Then, as Don Juan (above) eventually did, they might well point to "physical structure," especially facial features, mouths, ears, noses, as well as the condition of skin and posture and other signs of class. People are not shy about pointing to physical difference—nicknames in El Salvador veer far from U.S. anxiety about race and bodies (typically, "Chato" [flat-nosed]; "Chino" [slit-eyed]; "Chele" [light-complexioned]; "Negro" [dark-complexioned]). Salvadorans' own ethnographic readings in public places include acute observations of body as class type. They tell you that bodies that daily consume corn tortillas and beans and hard white cheese (if they can), bodies that work under the sun and in the rain, *look* different from those that ingest a variety of foods, and work in offices, and work out in the gym, or maybe don't work at all.[73] It is this form of *knowing* that puts the process of unknowing in discourses on criminals and crime into relief. It is a knowledge that tacitly recognizes a long history of embodied difference structured in a capitalist, agro-export-oriented economy. It is a knowledge that implicitly appreciates how at different moments capital requires different kinds of bodies—and rejects others.

IV. Embodiments of History

So far in this chapter, I have developed a theory of unknowing. I have discussed how an abject population—problematic bodies produced through historical social and economic forces—can be "forgotten" in everyday interactions. As such, something known and understood, if from different vantage points—most saliently here, a deep history of social inequality and structural violence that led to El Salvador's civil war and then continued in the postwar era in an aggressive neoliberal guise—is actively unknown, converted into nonknowledge. This process of ideological fantasy happens in the diagnostic categories of the psychologist. It occurs through a mass-mediated spectacle demanding the state control the uncivilized Other. It is instantiated through the everyday, thin-slicing, racializing ideas about deviance that circulate in crime stories. As is common elsewhere, what often emerges in this process is the conviction that criminality results from individual, willful—and monstrous—deviance.

But we know unknowing never completely succeeds. We have seen how the Other can break through. In an agentive moment, ideas about the excess populations, about bodies that do not fit into normative visions of the nation, can be jolted. The final section of this chapter considers how seemingly durable senses of the Other have cohered in Salvadoran history—but never fully. History is a continual process of forgetting and unknowing. We see this especially in the key moment of January 1932. In El Salvador the meaning of that massacre over time has had more to do with the contingencies of the moment in which it is remembered than the facts on the ground. A dramatic unknowing was produced in a Communist-obsessed Cold-War narrative that refused to let the indigenous Other break through.[74]

Before we arrive at the massacre (another deferral here), though, I want go a bit further back in history. I want to point to the ghost of Cesare Lombroso mingling among all the specters haunting El Salvador. During the scientific push of the mid- to late nineteenth century, and the liberal impulse toward rationally managing national populations, the Italian physician Lombroso strongly influenced Latin American intellectuals. His criminal anthropology formed part of the Latin American version of the "race science" of eugenics, in which physical features were thought to be related to how "evolved" or civilized people were.[75] Lombroso, drawing on photographs of Italian prisoners, used a phrenological method to identify the "born criminal." His theory linked the criminal's surface physicality and adornment to an inner felonious nature.[76] The signs of endemic delinquency included a pointed head, large handlebar ears, heavy jaw, receding brow, scanty beard: Dracula.[77] In criminal anthropology, abnormal bodily characteristics were read as something else, as being more than what they appeared to be. They exposed their carrier as an evolutionary throwback. To look at a man with a bulging forehead was to see—to know—a criminal.

This new form of knowledge was being produced at the moment of high liberalism, of secular rationalism and the rise of the individual as an economic unit. Lombroso's *Criminal Man* was first published in 1876. Salvadoran elites and intellectuals would take up its "scientific" and modern ideas during their frequent stays in Mexico City and bring them back home.[78] In the same historical moment, in 1881–82, the Liberal government divided up rights to communal lands (see Chapter 1). The state wanted to encourage a class of entrepreneurial peasants and farmers, incorporating them into the modern nation (as Salvadoran citizens, not Indians). We know that although smallholding increased at first, through the 1920s the oligarchy bought up most of the lands. Then the world crisis of 1929 forced the coffee barons to cut back drastically on their workforce and pay. One effect of this long-term transformation of land tenure was a loosening of community and land ties among peasants, both Indians and ladinos. The number of wandering migrant workers grew. As they often could not be linked to local families or patrons, they were viewed with suspicion (as Dalton's "Love Poem," above, reminds us). Or, as Marx wrote of the release of "free" proletariat after the passage of enclosure laws of England, "These men, suddenly dragged from their wonted mode of life, could not as suddenly adapt themselves to the discipline of their new conditions. They were turned *en masse* into beggars, robbers, vagabonds, partly from inclination, in most cases from stress of circumstances."[79] In El Salvador during the 1920s peasants, indigenous people, and rural workers were forced into an oppositional, racialized, and criminalized corner.[80]

During these same years, the rising Salvadoran police and military forces began to publish bulletins training their agents to identify criminal "types" to help them classify these wandering strangers and bandits. These journals, archived in the National Library in San Salvador, are filled with countless articles on how to read bodies. The periodicals republished studies by Argentine, Cuban, and Mexican criminologists, tutoring public security officials in the new, modern, taxonomic code of criminality that Lombroso had inspired fifty years earlier. An article in the December 1934 *Official Police Bulletin* under the heading "Criminal Anthropology," for example, explains the criminal in "scientific" terms: "He is not a normal man, but constitutes a special class, who, due to organic and psychic abnormalities represents, in the midst of modern society, primitive, savage races, in which moral ideas and sentiments, if they exist, are found in an anti-social state."[81]

It is no coincidence that these journals began to be published—that this "scientific" eugenic ideology of embodied criminality began to be disseminated in security forces—in the 1920s. The economy was changing rapidly. The demands of capital were generating new ideas about excess, unneeded bodies (much as they would seventy years later in another economic transition, when young men such as El Directo found themselves to be social detritus). And this was precisely the moment when increasingly impoverished peasants were becoming radicalized. Many rural indigenous and ladino peasants were responding to changing global conditions by collaborating with leftist and labor organizations, as we saw in Chapter 1. To recall the events: on 22 January 1932, after fraudulent elections, thousands of these organized rebels participated in an uprising. Despite wide reports of a "red terror," they killed no more than fifteen to twenty individuals. General Maximiliano Hernández Martínez had just taken power after the chaos of a collapse in coffee prices, in an oligarchy-instigated military coup. He immediately sent out the army. His order led to the killing spree known as the Matanza. To the elites, indigenous identity seemed to merge with the dreaded specter of international Communism. Most of the ten thousand dead were indigenous, though ladinos likely made up half the rebels.

These security forces, inculcated in specific ideologies of recognizable deviance in bodily forms, could not help but target bodies marked as Others. The killing fit into the Lombrosian logic. Given their training, the government agents inevitably concerned themselves more with seeking an essential propensity to subversion than with investigating acts (determining who had been involved in the rebellion and who had not). Historians Jeffrey Gould and Aldo Lauria-Santiago call the massacre a form of genocide. Racism was not explicit, they argue. But it conditioned the president's order to the soldiers to execute rebels.[82] And the history that began with land reform, with the growth of coffee farms, with the eventual dispossession and effective criminalization of thousands and thousands of indigenous and ladino peasants, and then the genocidal response to erase the national Other, became *violently unknown*, disguised as a communist threat.

It was a threat that continued to orient Salvadoran politics into the first years of the new millennium.

The Threat of the *Indio Comunista*

Brandt Peterson, drawing from trauma theory, writes that after 1932 the figure of the Indian split into two. On the one hand, a melancholic loss, an absence, something yearned for. On the other hand, "the *indio comunista* [Communist Indian], savage, backwards, an uncomfortable remainder, and a disease threatening the national body." He explains, "The *indio comunista* blends the immediate threat of the political radical with the timeless menace of the savage, the *indio* of national fantasy."[83] Through Hernández Martínez's dictatorship, the enemy that began as the *indio comunista* eventually swelled into a monstrous shape. He attacked everything "foreign," even foreign investment.[84] He imposed a series of discriminatory laws forbidding the non-European (different-looking) foreigners, " 'persons of Arab, Palestinian, Turkish, Chinese, Lebanese, Syrian, Egyptian, Persian, Hindu, and Armenian races, even though naturalized' to open new businesses of any type or to even participate in them as partners or to open branches of existing enterprises."[85] Any critic of the regime became a "communist," a category of criminal that became inscribed in the 1932 revision of the criminal code and then the 1939 constitution.[86] This categorization of objectionable bodies became performative. Alarmed Palestinian and Chinese communities in particular resented discriminatory laws. Some contributed large sums of money to the revolutionary forces that eventually forced the overthrow of the regime in 1944.[87]

The phantasmic power of the *indio comunista*, the red threat, did not fade from Salvadoran imagination after Martínez was ousted. It grew through the twentieth century, though its manifestation moved to different kinds of deviant physicality.[88] In the 1960s, the U.S. National Security Doctrine—the counterinsurgency creed of the Castro-spooked Kennedy administration—trained security agents in internal warfare. The problematic bodies they sought included urban labor activists and radical priests as well as college youth: all contaminated with "foreign" ideas—communism, liberation theology, long hair, and beards. After the nation's five guerrilla factions consolidated as the FMLN in 1980, state propaganda and "patriotic" commercial mass media represented the internal chaos as an invasion of foreigners. The military, as they sought to eliminate these enemies in individual ambushes and disappearances and massacres, were portrayed as "defenders of the people." Guerrillas and their supporters were considered "bands directed from Moscow, Cuba and Nicaragua." Human rights commissions, NGOs, and church efforts were described as answering to "foreign masters," meddling with "Salvadoran reality."[89] This is the narrative logic, replete with Cold War polarities, that would be straddled in the late 1990s and early 2000s. We see it in the biospectacle of El Directo—who as a gang member was associated with "foreign" Los Angeles-based modes. A long history of unknowing would repeat itself once again in the production of the monstrous Other.[90]

We're Not the Fools You Think We Are

In El Salvador at the cusp of war and postwar, established images of enemies, knowledge of who and what to fear, suddenly became jarred from their moorings. The state tried to harness the momentum of the moment through critical code-switching. In the murk of the unknown of the postwar era, people grasped at new definitions. They remembered historical texts (the Other as *indio comunista*) and attuned themselves to postwar novelty (the gang member). The telling of crime-experience stories became a postwar ritual, as people endeavored to learn how to navigate a new climate of risk. Such a practice helped produce individualized, neoliberal subjects. Whether the repetition of gossip in corner stores, or the public framing of incidents of violation and disorder on television, the telling of crime stories in the immediate postwar years became the very moment of the production of knowledge and unknowledge. But it could also transcend intentions. The Other could break through. Something new could emerge in an agentive moment.

These reiterations of unknowing reproduced the Other. They cast marginalized subjects and problematic bodies as alien, foreign dangers threatening the polity from within. To Engels, crime is inevitable in capitalist society. Crime enacts resistance to unknowing: "Acts of violence committed by the working classes against the bourgeoisie and their henchmen are merely frank and undisguised retaliations for the thefts and treacheries perpetrated by the middle classes against the workers." Crime stories circulating in the decade after the peace accords always carried a trace of this knowledge of the social structure, of crime and its relation to capital. Perhaps Ana Lorena was not confused when she conflated guerrillas and gang members. Perhaps Don Juan's suspicion of rebellious clothes and subversive hair was not so off base. Both storytellers knew that these signs indexed a rejection of a social structure ("social resentment" [*resentimiento social*], they might say). As Žižek writes, "They know very well how things really are, but still they are doing it as if they did not know." The young men so many storytellers pointed to were all outsiders. Through big and small acts they were challenging the state, defying the order of things.

Let us return to El Directo, a particular case of biopolitical refuse at the end of the postwar decade. Young men had been useful during the war, whether as guerrilla warriors or army soldiers. Gustavo Adolfo Paredes was born just a little bit too late. By the signing of the peace accords, at age ten, he already knew there was no place for him. He soon became El Directo. His story tells us what happened when a deeply damaged boy with a brief biography was detached from a specific place and time to become a postwar biospectacle, a new kind of enemy Other. El Directo was arrested as the state, recovering from war, was relocating itself in the global marketplace. He appeared at a moment of anxiety about seeing and not seeing. He materialized in the midst of fears of not-knowing and participated in the the production of unknowing. In his biospectacularity, his monstrosity, he was a site through which to mutually construct a nervous community, to externalize the inner fantasy of (a certain kind of) order. He also became a dense, contradictory sign of the remembered Other, a sign that in its excess simultaneously signified victim and perpetrator and defiant rebel: the *indio comunista* massacred in 1932, the labor activists targeted in the 1960s, the guerrillas disappeared and priests and peasants murdered in the 1980s. He was the monster weakening the imagined nation.

The biospectacle of El Directo, and speculation about him—undoing borders between past and present—might have invoked future as opposed to present: future as different from now. It could have opened the critical possibility to imagine other presents. Could this unknowing have converted to something beyond fear of crime? Might a public dialogue have emerged about the alienation of youth by a neoliberal economic formula whose magic makes them appear and disappear on command?

Most journalists, the police, business elites, and others in power worked to limit the way people interpreted the El Directo spectacle. But unknowing is never complete. The deep contradictions of El Salvador during "peace"— the poverty, the corruption, the everyday violence, and the criminalization of youth—made El Director a powerful site for emergent skepticism, for opposition, for refusal.

Within a month of El Directo's recapture, the Salvadoran rap group Mecate released a song that condensed other ways of reading the biospectacle and resisted the process of unknowledge. They proposed a defiant, collective identification with the figure rather than the individualized dread incited in the public debates. Their piece played over and over on radio. For a few weeks it seemed that all the speeding microbuses had agreed to play it every hour. It wasn't long before people in power heard it. And *knew.*

But unknew. The Association of Radios of El Salvador (ASDER) quickly condemned it.[91] The song's contents "make an apology for violence" said ASDER's then-president (and El Salvador's future president) Tony Saca.[92] Of course the song held nothing that had not already been said, over and over, in the mass media, in those very radio stations' news segments, over the previous months. But this song refused to collaborate with the script for the state-directed biospectacle—for the individualized, atomized orientation toward the world. They were, they said, *what comes next*—and they weren't going away.

"El Directo"[93]
(chorus)

duro, seguro, al grano	straight to the point
las cárceles más crudas ya las he visitado	I've already been in the worst jails
duro seguro, al grano	straight to the point
diecisiete años diecisiete he matado	seventeen years, I've killed seventeen
(final stanza)	
hablen diputados	you may talk, politicians
digan lo quieran	say whatever you want
no tienen evidencia	don't have no proof
y pronto tocaré tu puerta	and soon I'll knock on your door
hablen de los pozos	you may talk about the wells[94]
asusten a sus hijos	might scare your kids
¿¿¿La verdad???	The truth???
es que no soy un monstruo	I'm not a monster
salgo libre . . .	I get away with it . . .
¿A quién le doy gracias?	Who do I thank?
por salir caminando	for walking away
esas leyes tontas	these stupid laws
que me están provocando	you're provoking me
ya pronto dieciocho	soon I'm eighteen
me queda muy poco . . .	not much time left . . .
no me atrapan más	you're not trapping me no more
¡¡no soy tan maje!!	I'm not such a fool!!

Mecate stood before the state, before the country's elites, its mass media moguls and its business leaders, and insisted: *we're not monsters*—and *we're not the fools you think we are.* They alone, it seemed at that moment, rejected the production of unknowledge. They know they are the Other, biopolitical debris, neoliberal rejects—the worst jails may not just mean notorious Salvadoran prisons. And yet they speak. They break through. They refuse to be unknown. They resist the formulas of the contemporary market economy that call for individual strategies for managing risk. They insist on a social world in which all must respond, politicians, mothers, police officers, teachers, and bus drivers. They say, like El Directo, we are human. We are you. We will not disappear. We will not be deferred. We are part of the nation.

No wonder the song was censored.

What Happened Next?

The potent absent-image of El Directo would indelibly shape political possibilities over the next few years in El Salvador. It would mark the presidency of Francisco Flores, the U.S.-backed president elected in the midst of that biospectacle. Near the end of his term in 2003, gearing up for the next vote, Flores announced a series of sweeping antigang proposals called Plan Mano Dura ("Operation Iron First"). In Lombrosian fashion, they targeted certain bodies as degenerate rather than particular acts as illegal. They authorized state security agents to round up presumed gang members (which the government claimed to total 30,000) based on charges of *being visible*. The markers of gang membership became criminalized: tattoos, hand signs, "illicit association," carrying a rock. Flores declared he was not worried about criminals' rights—only the rights of "honorable" Salvadorans.[95] The post-Cold War knowledge produced in this moment defined who to make live and who to let die.

The police began enforcing the initiative as soon it was announced—long before it became law. It was enormously popular. Polls showed 75 percent of Salvadorans approved.[96] But many judges refused to cooperate. They sent most of the young tattooed men back into the street.[97] After the proposal finally became law, Amnesty International condemned it as discriminatory, in that it focused on controlling bodies and excluding populations rather then confronting crime.[98] Still, many such hard-line security measures, part of a "new Latin American model of public security,"[99] or *mano dura* politics, were enacted across the continent in the late 1990s and first years of the 2000s.[100] Public clamor for state repression often rises in moments of rapid social change, of social insecurity, of not knowing what comes next.

What came next in the next few years in El Salvador was, it seemed, more of the same—or maybe, as some people told me, even "worse," though references to the war were less definitive.[101] In 2004, ARENA, led by Tony Saca—the young radio magnate who had censored the El Directo rap—handily won elections. One of President Saca's first acts was to introduce Plan Súper Mano

Dura.[102] It sent more police and military into the streets. It filled jails far beyond capacity, turning them into what some called resorts for gang networking.[103] The crime rates began to spiral back up. By 2005 the murder rate was the highest in seven years and the highest in Latin America.[104]

Epilogue

What happened next? I first posed this insistent query to provoke those who lost interest in El Salvador after 1992. So many of us wanted the story to end with the peace agreements that the Farabundo Martí National Liberation front (FMLN) guerrillas and the government signed that year. The surge of violence that followed was not in the script for peace. It was not the narrative for postwar reconstruction plotted by the United Nations. It was not the model for postconflict democracy promoted by the United States.

What happens next? This was also the question Salvadorans were asking in 1992. I have argued that in an atmosphere of not-knowing, of wondering what "peace" would mean, people described postwar danger in terms of increasingly personal, or private, experience. Telling crime stories in this way became (unevenly) performative, sometimes unwittingly collaborating with broad state and global efforts to convert people into proper citizens of a market democracy. Recast in this neoliberal mold, Salvadorans were no longer supposed to dwell in a social imaginary of obligation to others. As they began to sense the situation as "worse than the war," their orientations toward the world around them started to transform. Individual risk-taking and everyday insecurity—already part of most poor people's ontologies—became sanctified features of life in postwar El Salvador. This anxious mode operated in part through an ideological fantasy of unknowing, a process through which crime was not recognized as the product of any kind of structural violence—a practice through which crime was signified as emergent in the willful deviance of Others.

What happens now? The question intrudes, again, with fresh urgency. Ethnography never ends. No honest anthropologist can offer anything more than tentative conclusions.[1] But books must eventually close. So I am uneasy about this question.

What now? Things are changing. It seems I am finishing this project at an agentive moment in Salvadoran history.

On 15 March 2009, the FMLN candidate won the presidency. Mauricio Funes, the former television journalist who has appeared now and again on these pages, got just over 51 percent of the ballots. The results overturned twenty years of dominance by the radically free-market Nationalist Republican Alliance party (ARENA). The vote upended a long history of right-wing governance in a country that had only occasionally glimpsed democratic openings in the past century. But, as we know, a lack of democratic tradition does not purge yearnings for the promises of democracy. The continually thwarted struggle for democracy, defined by equality and sovereignty, may be the biggest story in twentieth-century Salvadoran history.

So we are all asking, Salvadorans and El Salvador-watchers alike, about the next big story. Is this the happy ending that wasn't seventeen years ago? The images of thousands and thousands (and *thousands)* of jubilant Salvadorans in the streets, dressed in red, waving FMLN flags—the euphoria transmitted by cellphone cameras in San Salvador and Ahuachapán, in Silver Spring, Maryland, and Stockholm—almost overwhelm memories archived in the still photographs of 16 January 1992, the fading icon of the once-illegal guerrilla acronym FMLN unfurled in a banner across the steeple of the Metropolitan Cathedral. On the U.S. news program *Democracy Now!* journalist Roberto Lovato, himself a son of Salvadoran migrants, exclaimed breathlessly, "You're talking about ending not just the ARENA party's rule, but you're talking about one hundred and thirty years of oligarchy and military dictatorship, by and large, that's just ended last night. You're talking about $6 billion that the United States used to defeat the FMLN. [You're talking about] the utter failure of not just the ARENA party but of somebody in particular, too, who has a special place in many of our hearts: Ronald Reagan. This is the defeat of Ronald Reagan, nothing less!" [2]

Funes himself invoked assassinated revolutionary poet Roque Dalton in his celebratory speech, declaring, "Now it's the turn of the offended!" [3] The phrase comes from Dalton's poem (and book title) *El turno del ofendido*, which he wrote in 1962, exiled in Mexico after escaping a death sentence. He dedicated the book of poetry in part to the police chief who had filed the charges against him.

> Ahora es la hora de mi turno
> el turno del ofendido por años silencioso
> a pesar de los gritos.
> Callad
> callad
> Oíd

[Now it's my turn
the turn of the offended after years of silence
in spite of the screams
Be quiet
be quiet
Listen][4]

The words refuse any code conflating criminality and the demands of the poor, any politics confusing the left and the outlaw. By Funes' inauguration on 1 June 2009, polls showed that 81 percent of Salvadorans supported him.[5]

As I write in July 2009, I try to resist recalling "cruel optimism." Are we attached to a compromised vision?[6] Can we still aspire to justice and inclusion and solidarity, the causes for which so many gave their lives in the Salvadoran civil war, in this post-Cold War, postrevolutionary moment? Can we dream in the midst of a global economic crisis? But then I think of the "method of hope": "Moments of hope can only be apprehended as other moments of hope," as Hirokazu Miyazaki writes.[7] The sparks of hope flying up in the streets of San Salvador today will flash up again in moments of danger tomorrow.

What does this turn of events mean for how people experience crime and violence in El Salvador? I suggest that another effort to code-switch violence had something to do with the change of political fortunes in 2009.

Crime rates remained high in the country through the first years of the new millennium. However, public signification of—efforts to impose meaning on—this phenomenon began to shift mid-decade. Stuttering attempts at a new critical code-switching of crime seemed, by 2008, to have settled on a new tactic: denial. Crime had all but disappeared from the nation's front pages. Spectacles of defiant, tattooed gang members had practically been erased from the mass-mediated public sphere. Blood-soaked bodies in the aisles of the buses were no longer stock images in the daily television news agenda.[8]

Dead bodies are hard to hide in the absence of war. The electronic newspaper *El Faro* counted 14,003 Salvadorans killed in criminal violence during the first four years of President Antonio Saca's tenure—a term which had begun with the immodest promise to "turn El Salvador into the safest country in Latin America." That total added up to more bodies than had fallen during the entire five years under Saca's predecessor, Francisco Flores, the man who launched the first *mano dura* scheme. Still, that year police would proclaim a fall in violence. Only nine dead a day. Even with likely doctored numbers, El Salvador's murder rate was about 60 per 100,000 population. The highest in the Americas.[9]

A funny thing happened just after Funes won the elections in March 2009. The dominant news media—most long aligned with ARENA—stopped staunching the blood. They announced: every day at least thirteen people are murdered in the country.[10] They claimed: shop owners who refuse to pay extortion, boys who refuse to join gangs, couples eating dinner, workers waiting at the bus stop—they could die right now.[11] They accused: organized criminals have imposed a curfew on the city center; street vendors must close by 7 p.m., when the "law of the jungle" takes over and no one is safe.[12] They announced (while tattooed Salvatruchas once again strutted across TV screens): gangs, now part of a monstrous regional organized-crime network, have made a pact called "Plan 503" (after El Salvador's country code), in which they swear to commit more murders, execute more express kidnappings, and perpetrate more robberies and assaults.[13]

Most Salvadorans don't rely only on TV screens and newsprint for knowledge of the moment. Even before the post-election media bloodbath, when pro-ARENA editors were suppressing the carnage, people knew things were pretty bad. I heard many warnings from family and friends as I prepared for my yearly trips. I usually just went about my various projects the way most Salvadorans must go about their daily lives, high crime rate or not. Finally, though, in 2008, I decided to listen more carefully to their laments. I sought out some of the storytellers I had met in the previous decade. I wanted to ask about changes in their everyday experiences of insecurity. Some of them had died. Others had disappeared, perhaps migrating north. But almost everyone I found insisted the situation was, yet again, "worse." The word, more open-ended now (the chronological marker "the war" not uttered as often),[14] sounded somehow more tragic to me—less historical, more ontological. Ondina, now in her mid-fifties (but, unlike me, clearly still working out at the gym), said most of the small shops that sell bread and pastries from her family's large industrial bakery were being forced by crime bosses to pay weekly or monthly "taxes" (*renta* [income]). Her firm had reluctantly stopped delivering to some zones. "It's worse than ever!" she told me. "And did you hear about the murders in Guatemala [three Salvadoran Central American Parliament representatives, well-known national elites, were murdered on a highway]? Everyone knows they were into drug trafficking. No one will say it, but they were. It was never like this before!"[15]

Perhaps the most revealing conversation took place with three people I had never before interviewed. We had first met in 1993. Back then Juan, Alfredo, and Daniel were mischievous boys, aged seven, five, and two. Their parents had recently brought them from Cacaopera to San Salvador; they lived near my friend Maru. Our only previous conversations about crime had centered on their favorite television show, the Spanish-dubbed Americanized Japanese program *The Power Rangers*. The name, in English, had been taken up by a criminal gang in El Salvador at the time.

I had not seen the boys for more than ten years. Now they were university students—their undeniable adulthood offering me an unsettling measure of the temporality of the project described in this book. Their mother, my good friend Ana Dolores, sent them money each month from North Bergen, New Jersey, where she now lived, caring for other people's children. She had left El Salvador in 1997, guided by her *coyote* (migrant-smuggler) brother. She had not been able to return home since then, but they talked almost daily on cell phones.

We met at the Café de Don Pedro in Santa Tecla, some of us drinking milky-tan *horchata* (a sweet native drink made of ground seeds) and others dark Modelo beer. Rumbling buses and gunning cars occasionally drowned out our conversation. The three of them spilled crime stories carelessly, nonchalantly, perhaps their youth and bravura on display, perhaps a more recent San Salvador habitus in evidence.[16] They evinced no need to evaluate modes of performance. They made little effort to lecture each other on how to manage risk. Maybe there was no need to do so. It could be they already embodied the ideal neoliberal subjects, maneuvering among the necessary dangers of market "freedom." This was, after all, everyday life for so many people in the city, petty crime, mundane insecurity, flashes of dread. What could "worse than the war" mean today, after all, in a country with a median age of twenty-two years—the majority barely born when peace was declared?[17]

Alfredo, the family joker, laughed when I asked him to tell me his stories. A few days earlier he had mistakenly pulled out all of his money when a kid asked him for some change. He had to hand everything over. The youngster wielded no knife, no weapon, he said. But he had been intimidated. Still, he said, he was not overly vigilant in his movements across the city. "What good will it do? I don't have a gun!"

I commented that a decade ago, some people were telling me they feared for their lives just leaving their homes: that I had heard, over and over, phrases like, "Now they rob you and they kill you."

He shrugged. "I don't think people get on the bus planning to kill. They rob because they have to survive."

Daniel, the quietest of the three, said he *did* watch people. He admitted he sometimes felt afraid. All three agreed on the type to avoid, at last reiterating a trope I recognized: "You can see in the way they dress, in the attitude, in the haircut, if they're wearing earrings, if they have baggy pants, tattoos," Daniel said. "You know, you just know."

Juan, a law student at the José Matias Delgado University, turned thoughtful as the others spoke. He described how one coworker at the bakery where he held a part-time job had become involved with a gang member who often talked by cell phone to his "boss" in Mariona, the big prison in San Salvador. Juan's brothers agreed that a deep network of organized crime survived by shaking down street-level businesses, from buses to bakeries. What had him more worried, though, Juan said, was politics. Just a week earlier (in May 2008), a student had been kidnapped from the Central American University (UCA). "That was a Thursday. They called on a Friday. And then he was found dead. His back had been destroyed by a beating and his throat had been cut. He was a big FMLN activist. From Santo Tomás. It might have been personal grudges, who knows, but everyone is talking about it in the law school. It wasn't in the news, you know—wouldn't fit into the mass media's agenda, they don't want to report on murders of FMLN. It might give the wrong message, you know? The FMLN as victims." [18]

The news just then was full of rumors about links between the FMLN and the Revolutionary Armed Forces of Colombia (Fuerzas Armadas Revolucionarias de Colombia, FARC), supposedly found on the hard drives of computers seized in a controversial raid into Ecuador by the Colombian military.[19] Not coincidentally, my young friends insisted, this news came out just as Mauricio Funes, already campaigning six months by then news, was topping the polls. They repeated rumors that the government was gearing up to declare the FMLN a terrorist organization, which would outlaw the party's participation in elections. Their words, so detached when talking of "common" crime, now echoed those of their elders—parents and grandparents who remembered the fraudulent elections of 1972 and 1977, when center-left coalitions were denied victories and soldiers shot into protesting crowds.

This logic was not just a haunted return of history. Since around 2002, the government and dominant media had been warning of the resurgence of terrorism, not only in their old enemies the FMLN, but also in gang members.[20] After the rise of *mano dura* in 2003, the state of unexception the government had struggled to conjure ten years earlier was suddenly re-code-switched. Crime on the streets was not common but critical.[21]

Why was now different? How was it that the FMLN, that Mauricio Funes, had won?

I wonder if in the end ARENA simply exhausted its one-note tactic of fear mongering (like circulating rumors about a link between the FARC and the FMLN). Of course the previous twenty years of failed governance, of deepening poverty and sharpening social exclusion and record-breaking rates of violence, explains a lot. But those problems had pressed on the electorate in 1999 and 2004 as well, and political power stayed in the same hands. It probably did not help ARENA that its 2009 presidential candidate, Rodrigo Ávila, had been in charge of the police for many of the postwar years—and owned a large private security firm (thus benefiting from the failure of the very police he led). And the election of Barack Obama in the United States a few months earlier injected tremendous hope about the possibilities for change everywhere (Funes had campaigned for "change," too, but called it "safe change"). Further, the FMLN and election observers were vigilant about preventing fraud this time.[22]

But I believe one crucial, agentive moment—a tipping point—occurred a year and a half before the vote, in the middle of 2007.

To tell this story, I need to jump back a few years. It is no coincidence that those in power began warning of terror in the first years of the new decade. There was, of course, the global post-9/11 mood. But also, by 2002, a popular, collective struggle had begun to emerge in El Salvador after years of postwar anomie. It manifested most dramatically during a series of "white marches." For nine months in 2002 and 2003, the state health care workers' unions went on strike, protesting the selling off of public hospitals run by the Salvadoran Institute for Social Security.[23] As many as 200,000 supporters filled the streets of San Salvador. They donned white to show solidarity with the doctors' demand for a law forbidding privatization. Many of the participants were organized by civil-society organizations, but overwhelming public sentiment propelled thousands of angry, unaffiliated marchers to join the protests. Polls said 80 percent of the population opposed the privatization of health care.[24]

Fast-forward to the rainy season of 2006. Protests were breaking out across San Salvador over proposals to increase bus fares. In one such event, on 5 July, workers and students at the University of El Salvador staged a massive demonstration. Police, long ago primed by the white marches, were ready for such "disturbances." The Unit for the Maintenance of Order (UMO) opened fire with rubber bullets and tear gas, dispersing the crowds. In the chaos, a man named José Mario Belloso, part of an ultra-left group but also a member of the FMLN, apparently killed two police officers. His image, hunched over an M-16, was caught on news cameras. It played over and over across television screens. State officials and the right-wing mass media merged the sniper fire and the protests into one, labeling it all as terrorist. News commentators quickly began to refer to the events as "5 J" for the 5 July date. Belloso, though indentified in the film, slipped away.

Immediately the government proposed a new antiterrorism law. One observer, María Silvia Guillén, director of the Salvadoran Foundation for the Study of the Application of Law (FESPAD), would later say that the law created "wildcards that allow the concepts and penalties of the law to be invoked or left aside at any given time, influenced by any political motive." [25] The law covered a number of acts already illegal. But by retaxonomizing them as terrorist, by engaging in critical code-switching, it upped the penalties to sixty years in prison.

Almost exactly a year later, on 2 July 2007, the country's "most wanted" criminal, Belloso, was captured in a spectacular operation involving more than three hundred police officers and soldiers as well as a phalanx of television cameras. This, I contend, was the tipping point. I arrived in El Salvador a few days later. That night the big news was Belloso's videotaped confession. Dressed in rags (in which he had been arrested), his wide-eyed face half-obscured by ratted tangles of hair, his voice rambling almost incoherently, he claimed to be part of a clandestine network of revolutionaries led by the FMLN. They aimed, he said, to spawn chaos and anarchy across the country.

For a moment, I flashed on the opening lines of Marx's pamphlet *The Eighteenth Brumaire of Louis Bonaparte*, his famous analysis of the 1851 coup d'état of Napoleon's nephew in France: "Hegel remarks somewhere that all great world-historic facts and personages appear, so to speak, twice. He forgot to add: the first time as tragedy, the second time as farce." [26] In the logic of a market democracy, Belloso's ludicrous figure seemed to be a ragged remnant stand-in for the impassioned revolutionary that once inspired many thousands of Salvadorans to struggle for a better future. Like so much revolutionary rhetoric and ideology, he literally *made no sense* in the neoliberal moment.

Looking back, I now believe this tragicomedy—this farce!—finally pushed ARENA's credibility over the edge. At that moment, it appeared inevitable that the public face of the FMLN would become Mauricio Funes, the clean-shaven, bespectacled intellectual who had never gone to *el monte* (to the bush, as they said of those who joined the guerrilla forces). He might never have taken up arms, but he had been speaking "truth to power" as a television journalist for nearly a quarter century, starting while El Salvador was deep in war.

But to return to that tipping point in mid-2007: the story does not end with Belloso's arrest.[27] The same day the police "discovered" Belloso, activists were marching in the town of Suchitoto. President Saca had arrived there to inaugurate a plan to decentralize a water system, a step toward privatization. Protestors rallied, blocking some streets, burning trash, throwing rocks. UMO forces arrived and opened fire with rubber bullets and tear gas. Within hours, cellphone users had uploaded images of the violent events onto YouTube.

Fourteen people were arrested, many from CRIPDES (the Association of Rural Communities for the Development of El Salvador), a leftist NGO with roots in the war. In news reports one protestor said that police took them in a helicopter high above the reservoir and told them that they would throw them into the water. After the suspects were eventually delivered—dry—to jail, they were charged under the new terrorism laws.[28] The protestors faced sixty years in prison for blocking roads and throwing stones.

Debates exploded across the country. The Belloso spectacle played simultaneously across media forums with the case of the Suchitoto Fourteen (later Thirteen). The powerful National Association of Private Enterprise (Asociacion National de la Empresa Privada, ANEP) insisted on an investigation into whether the FMLN was out to destabilize the country. The minister of public security claimed that Belloso had been recruiting gang members into social movements. But others called the labeling of protestors as "terrorist" absurd. One judge condemned the antiterrorist law as "totally disproportionate" even as ARENA demanded stiffer sentences for "the disturbances."[29] Supporters of the arrested protestors marched in the streets, demanding they be let out of prison. Some started a hunger strike.

Eventually the prisoners were released from pretrial detention (later charges were dropped). Both the human rights counsel and the Salvadoran attorney general questioned the application of the antiterrorism law for acts of "free expression" and of "social disorder." The word "show" echoed through dozens of San Salvador conversations I heard.[30] A taxi driver told me one night—presciently: "It's like ARENA is scared—that things will happen like in Brazil, with [President Luiz Inacio] Lula [da Silva], or in

Ecuador, or in Bolivia. That the left will come in. But there are too many co-incidences. How is it that Belloso was arrested exactly a year after the event? It's like they purposely waited to arrest him." [31]

I had come to the country that year for a conference on Salvadoran history at the University of El Salvador. The talk I gave rehearsed the theories of critical code-switching outlined in Chapter 2, arguing that taxonomies of violence often shift in moments of historical change. My case study was the war-to-postwar cusp, in which the state began calling all crime "common" and not "political." I reiterated my claim that this move followed the logic of the postwar push toward depoliticization, toward individualizing subjec-tivities. [32]

Quite literally as I was saying all this in front of a small audience, just the opposite, it seems, was happening outside. The government's reactions to Belloso and the Suchitoto protests inverted the logic I was laying out. As it captured Belloso, as it charged activists with terror, the state recognized the existence of collective political actions, of social movements, of community protest. It granted them legitimacy as it identified their threat. The state was *not* naming the protests—or the disorder and vandalism resulting from the protests—as "common" crime, as dismissible everyday problems in a mod-ern democracy, as it had done in 1993.

What it was doing was naming an opposition. It was effectively opening a space for resurgence of solidarity and activism—for the very left it feared. Or, better said, it had been forced to cede that space.

By that moment the harsh headlines and the grim TV pronouncements seemed so distant from the action. They felt so remote from the rapidly replicating discourses of the day. As we know, since the early 2000s, public activism and political protest had been rising again in the country. The old powers, the state and major mass media, tried to code these actions as sub-version and terror. But things had changed. Now there were YouTube videos and text messages, electronic mail and electronic newspapers. Everyone had cell phones. And everyone still shared stories.

They all told of *some*thing, something else, something new in El Salva-dor. Something new in Latin America, too; perhaps something new across the globe.

No one can know just what will happen next. But in that gap between senses of knowing and not-knowing, a great, swollen hope propels the moment.

Notes

Introduction

1. Robinson, *Transnational Conflicts*, 89.

2. Call, "Democratization, War and State-Building," 827.

3. On the limits to FMLN agency in the agreements, see Wood, "The Peace Accords and Reconstruction," 79. In fact, "structural adjustment" (the term generally used to refer to the transition to neoliberal economic policies) was written into the peace accords, in the sense of vague promises of "necessary measures to relieve the social costs of structural adjustment" (ONUSAL, *Los Acuerdos de Paz*, 39). The accords also included a plan for the formation of a Forum for Economic and Social Concertation to discuss economic and social problems deriving from the end of the conflict and reconstruction (87). It is important to point out here that even as the FMLN could not change the economic structure of the state, demilitarization and the creation of the National Civilian Police were absolutely crucial for the transition. The old security forces had been trained for political repression, not crime prevention. As José Miguel Cruz writes, "Democratic transitions must entail a reform of the coercive apparatus: the police, among others" ("Violence, Citizen Insecurity, and Elite Maneuvering," 149–50).

4. ONUSAL's *Acuerdos de Paz* outlines each set of agreements made, beginning in Caracas on 21 May 1990. Important discussions of the accords process are offered in Holiday and Stanley, "Under the Best of Circumstances " and Call, "Democratization, War and State-Building."

5. For evaluations of various aspects of Central America's and El Salvador's peace (and related) processes, see Boyce, ed., *Economic Policy for Building Peace*; Call, "Democratization, War and State-Building"; Córdova Macías, *El Salvador en transición*; Doyle et al., *Keeping the Peace*; Karl, "El Salvador's Negotiated Revolution"; Lauria-Santiago and Binford, eds., *Landscapes of Struggle*; Montgomery, *Revolution in El Salvador*; Oakley et al., eds., *Policing the New World Disorder*; Popkin, *Peace Without Justice*; Robinson, *Transnational Conflicts*; Stahler-Sholk, "El Salvador's Negotiated Transition"; Stephen and Tula, *Hear My Testimony*; Williams and Walter, *Militarization and Demilitarization*; Wood, *Forging Democracy from Below*. The majority of these authors examine political actors and political institutions and their roles in the peace process. My contribution is to tell how the political process has bled into things that we would not necessarily consider political. This book speaks to how these institutional, political processes enter into the experiences of everyday life.

6. Definition of "ordinary citizen" from Berlant, *The Queen of America Goes to Washington City*, 3.

7. Taylor, *Modern Social Imaginaries*, 23.

8. Briggs, "Mediating Infanticide," 315–56.

9. El Salvador underwent "expansive adjustment" from 1989 to 1994, often attributed to a postwar "bounce" in investments and increased remittances as well as reforms. But in the second half of the decade the economy stagnated and inequality increased. Segovia, *Transformación estructural y reforma económica*.

10. By 2003, at least 70 percent of the country got its news primarily from television, even in rural areas, according to Rockwell and Janus, *Media Power in Central America*, 44.

11. See Moodie, "El Capitán Cinchazo."

12. Commission on the Truth for El Salvador, *De la locura a la esperanza*.

13. José María Tojeira, rector of Central American University José Simeón Cañas (UCA), has made this argument on numerous occasions. See, for example, volumes 625–26 of *Estudios Centroamericanos* (November–December 2000), a publication of the UCA. The featured editorial opening the journal, "Recognize and Take Responsibility," states, referring to the Amnesty Law of 1993, "The impunity of the past impedes us from demanding that today's criminals be called to account." http://www.uca.edu.sv/publica/eca/eca625.html (accessed 11 October 2008; my translation). More recently Tojeira and human rights groups have called for the state to abolish the Amnesty Law and replace it with a Reconciliation Law. See *La Prensa Gráfica*, "UCA propone ley de reconciliación en lugar de la ley de amnistía," 12 September 2008, http://www.laprensagrafica.com/lodeldia/20080912/18072.asp (accessed 11 October 2008).

14. Ries, *Russian Talk*.

15. "White collar" crime and bureaucratic corruption were pervasive, but rarely sparked the anger that street crime did. In retrospect, I realize that almost everyone I knew was, in some sense, implicated in some level of petty bureaucratic fraud and crime, whether not paying taxes or actual bribery or simply slipping some of a factory's product into pockets to take home. Many people went to the city center markets, looking for cheap and often stolen goods. The exception to remarking on such activity seemed to be when an already prosperous individual took advantage of those less fortunate; an example I heard several times was of the politically appointed head of the national electricity agency in the early 1990s. The story went that he pushed up the rates and then began selling generators.

16. In interviews, news directors and newspaper editors told me that they learned about stories not just from the police, but from telephone calls from readers or viewers.

17. Hall et al., *Policing the Crisis*, 220, 69.

18. Hall et al., *Policing the Crisis*, 16.

19. Cohen, *Folk Devils and Moral Panics*.

20. Numerous critics of Hall's work have pointed out that there was in fact a noticeable (and statistically confirmed) increase in assaults and robberies in England at the time, justifying public concern, if not alarm. Carol A. Stabile suggests that media representations of "public opinion," especially on crime, race,

and law-and-order issues, may well be "an industrial product rather than some authentic expression of public sentiment" (Hall et al., *Policing the Crisis*, 220, 69). She asserts, "a safer assumption to make about public opinion is that the vast majority of television viewers do not trust what they see and hear on the screen," a view that works well in the weak state of El Salvador, in which most viewers and readers—citizens—are poor and marginalized, hardly the interpellated "public" represented in and by mass media. See Stabile, "Conspiracy or Consensus?" 261–62.

21. Briggs, "Mediating Infanticide," 333. My own work, following different kinds of crime story narratives across varying contexts, ultimately has lead me to form distinct ideas about what crime stories produce and are produced by, but I find Briggs's concepts useful.

22. The three channels of Telecorporación Salvadoreña (TCS), owned by media mogul Boris Eserski, reached about a 90 percent share of the television audience in the decade after the war. See Moodie, "Wretched Bodies, White Marches and the *CuatroVisión* Public."

23. Wachs, *Crime-Victim Stories*, xv.

24. Briggs, "Mediating Infanticide," 326.

25. See Briggs and Bauman, "Genre, Intertextuality and Social Power." Greg Urban further develops this idea: "Entextualization is understood as the process of rendering a given instance of discourse a text, detachable from its local context." See Urban, "Entextualization, Replication and Power," 21.

26. Mannheim and Van Vleet, "The Dialogics of Southern Quechua Narrative"; Kristeva, "Word, Dialogue, and Novel."

27. Peterson, *Martyrdom and the Politics of Religion*, 168.

28. Das, *Life and Words*, 8–9.

29. Behar, *The Vulnerable Observer*, 27.

30. Urban, *Metaphysical Community*, xii.

31. Malkki, *Purity and Exile*, 106.

32. The stories of war-era and postwar violence that I heard during my years in El Salvador do not always parallel the accounts reported of war-related terror by social scientists involved with migrants/refugees in the United States. Legal anthropologist Susan Coutin and medical anthropologist Janis Jenkins, for example, describe dramatic and painful narratives of terror (whether the terror was personally experienced, fulfilling the demands for the granting of political asylum status, or was more communally lived, a generalized terror in which "everyone" felt at risk). Those are the kinds of stories many readers might associate with El Salvador. There are many possible reasons for this difference in our findings. First, the context in which I heard stories of violence, both of war and postwar, was radically different than that of a U.S. or European courtroom or legal office, or a hospital or clinic. Second, it could be that the people I knew in El Salvador did *not* leave their country in part because they weren't as affected by the violence, or experienced it differently, than those who left and testified to their experiences (though I am skeptical that this would explain more than a few cases): third, I was listening to stories in the flow of daily life, after the war—so war-era experiences weren't as isolable but rather constantly reworked in meaning in the context of present experiences in the same

place and possibly among the same people. Finally, my work was in San Salvador, the capital. While many people I knew had come to live in the city from the countryside, the urban experience was different from the rural. For analyses of refugees' testimonies, see Coutin, "The Oppressed, the Suspect and the Citizen," and Jenkins, "The State Construction of Affect."

33. I was involved with the Committee in Solidarity with the People of El Salvador, CISPES, which the FBI investigated during the 1980s under "foreign intelligence-international terrorism" guidelines. The premise of the investigation was that CISPES, which advocated for change in El Salvador through demonstrations, lobbying, public speaking, newsletters, etc., was a front for a terrorist group. Two investigations—which included break-ins into churches, offices, and homes of Reagan administration opponents—were closed with no charges filed. Theoharis, et al., *The FBI*, 134.

34. Montoya, "Socialist Scenarios, Power, and State Formation."

35. De Certeau, *The Practice of Everyday Life*, 214.

36. Ferguson, *Expectations of Modernity*, 21.

37. New Jersey-Los Amates Sister City Coalition. I participated in the first trip to a resettled village near the municipality of San José Las Flores in the department of Chalatenango in March 1993.

38. In the working-class Colonia Dolores and Residencial Holanda, in the southwest part of the city; in a hidden, humble pocket of San Antonio Abad, climbing up the volcano from the University of El Salvador; briefly in the comfortable, middle-class neighborhood the Colonia Roma; and in different sections of Santa Tecla and Ciudad Merliot (a walled-in middle-class neighborhood and a crowded working-class community).

39. Quinn, "Introduction."

40. Cruz and González, "Magnitud de la violencia en El Salvador," 956. The Instituto Universitario de Opinión Pública (IUDOP) of San Salvador's Central American University and the Interamerican Development Bank (IADB) found between 1994 and 1996 an average 131 intentional murders for every 100,000 citizens, compared with an estimated 130 violent deaths per 100,000 during the twelve-year war. Cruz and González, *Sociedad y violencia*. Cruz today questions the accuracy of the high homicide figures, but confirms that rates reached a minimum of approximately 80 per 100,000 between 1994 and 1997. Cruz, "Violence, Citizen Insecurity, and Elite Maneuvering in El Salvador," 152.

41. I have since reencountered this man, at a talk I gave in early 2009. While he reiterated the same kinds of materialist challenges to some of my ideas, he listened respectfully and seemed to appreciate my perspective. He also had no memory of our past conversation, which had been so anxiety-provoking for me!

42. Silber, "Mothers/Fighters/Citizens." In another example, Mike O'Connor, in "A New U.S. Import in El Salvador," *New York Times*, 3 July 1994 (one of the first in the U.S. media to point out how deportation of criminals from the United States to El Salvador was affecting the postwar transition), quotes a man named Julio Diaz saying, "It has become worse than the war," reflecting on the impact of gangs on his village in central El Salvador. More recently, Susan Coutin reports, "[One] woman remarked that many Salvadorans were frustrated because they could not visit beau-

tiful or tourist spots in El Salvador. 'It was safer to go to those places during the war,' she said." Coutin, *Nations of Emigrants*, 163.

43. I began to understand my experience more clearly after reading Bridget Hayden's reflections on research among Salvadoran refugees in Costa Rica. See her *Salvadorans in Costa Rica*, xxix–xxxii.

44. I use the word "rapport" in the sense of spun out in my Roget's: "agreeability, complaisance, rapport, harmoniousness, compatibility; welcomeness; geniality; congeniality." People who liked me, who said "sos buena gente" ("You're good people"), might relax with me, talk a little more, tell me a story, although I know they wouldn't fully trust me, tell me "everything." George Marcus rightly critiques the figure of rapport as "too simplistic to stand in for the actual complexities of fieldwork" though it has been "a regulative ideal in professional culture." Marcus, "The Uses of Complicity," 127.

45. Briggs, *Learning How to Ask*.

46. Lemon, "Your Eyes Are Green like Dollars."

47. Scheper-Hughes, "Violence and the Politics of Remorse," 202.

48. Povinelli, "The Child in the Broom Closet."

49. Fragment of poem "El país (II) los extranjeros: Sir Thomas," from Dalton, *Taberna y otros lugares*, 70, trans. Ellen Moodie.

50. See Goldstein, *Laughter Out of Place*, for an account of humor in the midst of crisis in Brazil.

Chapter 1. Big Stories and the Stories Behind the Stories

1. The title Niña, literally "girl," often pronounced *ña*, is commonly used in the Salvadoran countryside as an honorific for older women in place of the more formal Doña, used in most Spanish-speaking countries; see Argueta's *Un día en la vida* for an example. In this book, all personal names have been changed except those of most of my family and some public figures, including media representatives. Translations from Spanish are mine except where indicated.

2. These words are reconstructed from memory and field notes (June–July 1994). When I directly quote a person based on (my translations of) a recording and transcript of their own words, I indicate the time and place of the recording in a footnote.

3. So anthropologists would describe it, in the oldest (often maligned) trope of their ethnographic genre. See Behar, "Ethnography: Cherishing Our Second-Fiddle Genre"; Pratt, "Fieldwork in Common Places." As a nod to the limits of my discipline and my position within it, I offer one of many possible such stories from my research. Within this opening vignette, I have also gestured toward the inevitable incompleteness in any account, the limits to any authority I claim. This account, like any, is partial—partial, as in incomplete, and partial, as in biased toward my own perspective. See Clifford, "Introduction: Partial Truths," in *Writing Culture*, 1–26.

4. Das and Kleinman, "Introduction," 7–8.

5. I am gesturing toward the usage of the word "murk" by Michael Taussig, in

Shamanism, Colonialism and the Wild Man, who refers to *epistemic murk*. Epistemic murk addresses "not whether facts are real but . . . the politics of their interpretation and representation" (xiii).

6. Salvadoran currency was measured in the colon until early 2001, when the economy dollarized. The currency value had been tied to the dollar in postwar years before then, about 8.75 colones per dollar. The ONUSAL Human Rights Division filed reports each quarter in the first years after the war. The writers from the beginning acknowledged some concern with crime, but at first attributed it to technical problems to be worked out. "The situation has been aggravated by the fact that no public security plan was designed and therefore implemented for the transitional period [nor were] emergency measures [taken] for combating ordinary crime." By the end of that first year, though, the report said, common crime had "reached disturbing levels which, although not dramatic, are causing a pervasive feeling of insecurity among the population" (UN, "Report of the ONUSAL Human Rights Division for the Period from July 1992 to 31 January 1993," 416).

7. Aided by field notes, 16 June 1994.

8. The idea of a "standard version" of a narrative comes from Malkki, *Purity and Exile*, 106.

9. Marx, *The Eighteenth Brumaire*, 15.

10. References for Salvadoran history consulted for this chapter include Almeida, *Waves of Protest*; Alvarenga, *Cultura y ética de la violencia*; Anderson, *Matanza*; Binford, "Violence in El Salvador"; Bland, "Assessing the Transition to Democracy"; Baloyra, *El Salvador in Transition*; Brockett, *Political Movements and Violence in Central America*; Commission on the Truth, *De la locura a la esperanza*; Gould and Lauria-Santiago, *To Rise in Darkness*; Grandin, *Empire's Workshop*; Lauria-Santiago, *An Agrarian Republic*; Grande, *Our Own Backyard*; Lindo-Fuentes, *Weak Foundations*; Lindo-Fuentes et al., *Remembering a Massacre in El Salvador*; Montgomery, *Revolution in El Salvador*; Peterson, *Martyrdom and the Politics of Religion*; Robinson, *Transnational Conflicts*; Williams, *Export Agriculture and the Crisis in Central America*; Stanley, *The Protection Racket State*; Vickers, "The Political Reality After Eleven Years of War"; Wood, *Forging Democracy from Below*; Wood, *Insurgent Collective Action and Civil War*.

11. Though the number of victims has frequently been given as 30,000, historians today generally agree on the lower figure. (Lauria-Santiago, personal communication, 23 July 2007, explains that the population could not have sustained the 30,000 statistic.) My use of "peasant" translates the term *campesino* so common in Salvadoran forms of identification; I follow Marc Edelman's assertion of the relevance of the term in the late twentieth century (*Peasants Against Globalization*, 189–93).

12. In *An Agrarian Republic*, Lauria-Santiago writes that members of Indian communities already involved in commercial agriculture supported the move, which gave them more secure ownership, but carrying out the partition, usually by local and communal leaders (since the state did not have the technical, administrative, juridical, or police resources to do it), often led to internal strife and violence. He stresses the variability in these processes across El Salvador.

13. Lauria-Santiago, *An Agrarian Republic*, 62.

14. It is important to point out that all suitable coffee land had been planted by the end of the 1920s. Population increases further magnified the inequalities, especially in land ownership. See Durham, *Scarcity and Survival in Central America*.

15. Alvarenga, *Cultura y ética de la violencia*, 27, 34, 88.

16. Gould and Lauria-Santiago, *To Rise in Darkness*, 42, 302 n. 26.

17. Guidos Véjar, *Acenso del militarism en El Salvador*, 143, cited in Almeida, *Waves of Protest*.

18. Historians dispute the extent of Communist party involvement. See Ching, "In Search of the Party." Ching's interpretation of materials in Moscow archives suggests that the disorganization of the Salvadoran Communist Party hardly put it in a position to "dupe" the Indians who participated in the revolt (the dominant story in El Salvador). Lauria-Santiago and Gould add that though the Salvadoran Communist Party had planned the insurrection, its key supporters and leaders were either dead or in jail when the revolt began; see " 'They Call Us Thieves and Steal Our Wage'." In their more recent *To Rise in Darkness*, Gould and Lauria-Santiago emphasize that many of the participants in the uprising were involved with Socorro Rojo, a Communist-linked organization; they stress that the categories of indigenous and communist were not contradictory, as much Salvadoran discourse (including that of the indigenous community) has insisted.

19. Indigenous and ladino are fluid categories; I follow the historians' use of the word, recognizing that both are social constructions. For discussions of "the Indian" and indigenous peoples in El Salvador, see Peterson, "Consuming Histories" and Tilley, *Seeing Indians*.

20. For an analysis of ongoing anticommunist rhetoric at the center of the Salvadoran right's ethos, and later, the core of ARENA's political campaigns, see López Bernal, "Lecturas desde la derecha y la izquierda." See also Gould, "Revolutionary Nationalism and Local Memories."

21. Peterson, "Unsettled Remains," 214.

22. Wood, *Forging Democracy from Below*, 77.

23. Bland, "Assessing the Transition," 165, 171. See also, for example, Williams and Walter, *Militarization and Demilitarization*.

24. Parkman, *Nonviolent Insurrection in El Salvador*.

25. Emphasis mine. Grandin, *The Last Colonial Massacre*, 4.

26. Lindo-Fuentes et al., *Remembering a Massacre*, 108–14, 103. They note that members of Committed Generation represented a spectrum of political positions, not just the revolutionary leftism of Dalton and Manlio Argueta.

27. Lindo-Fuentes et al., *Remembering a Massacre*, 88.

28. LeFeber, *Inevitable Revolutions*, 174.

29. Pelupessy, *The Limits of Economic Reform in El Salvador*, 99.

30. Data from Mitchell A. Seligson, "Thirty Years of Transformation in the Agrarian Structure of El Salvador," Table 5, 62, cited in Wood, *Forging Democracy from Below*, 35.

31. Lavine and Editors of *Life*, *Central America*, 106–7.

32. Urias Betoel Escobar, personal communication, Champaign, Ill., 24 March and 13 April 2009.

33. See the important work by Cynthia Arnson, "Window on the Past." Digging

through declassified documents from the CIA, U.S. Embassy, and other sources, she found evidence of the deep structure of the death squads (they weren't a "spontaneous phenomenon," as a senior U.S. administration official claimed in the early 1980s): "Death squads in El Salvador were deeply rooted in official security bodies, particularly the intelligence sections of the Treasury Police, National Police, and National Guard, but also the army and air force. Privately constituted groups, especially the one headed by Roberto D'Aubuisson, distinguished themselves less for their independence from than for their degree of contact, and at times, coordination with state security bodies" (113, 110).

34. Field notes, Santa Tecla, 6 June 1999.

35. Father Rogelio Ponseele, a Belgian cleric who in the 1980s gained his own fifteen minutes of mass-mediated world fame as a guerrilla priest in the rebel-occupied part of Morazán, recalls that he had never heard of El Salvador until 1969: "Before the 'football war,' I didn't know that El Salvador even existed. El Salvador was unknown for us in Belgium. All I heard in my life about El Salvador was when this 'football war' happened with Honduras. Before then, nothing. After, not a mention. Never" (López Vigil, *Muerte y vida en Morazán*, 15). For another bemused account, offering the apocryphal tale of a young Salvadoran football fan killing herself after her country's defeat in the game, see Kapuscinski, *The Soccer War*.

36. The war is known in El Salvador as "The War of 100 Hours." See Dalton, *Las historias prohibidas del pulgarcito*, for analysis of press coverage—and press creation—of the "football war." See also Anderson, *The War of the Dispossessed*; Durham, *Scarcity and Survival*; and Montgomery, *Revolution in El Salvador*, 59–60. For estimates on how many died in the war, see White, "Death Tolls for the Man-Made Megadeaths of the Twentieth Century." The lowest estimate comes from Small and Singer in *Resort to Arms*, 1,900; Joseph Bercovitch and Richard Jackson in *International Encyclopedia of Conflicts* suggest 5,000.

37. The execution is widely blamed on an order from Joaquín Villalobos, who became a top FMLN commander in the war and now lives in England, writing frequently on Latin American politics. His editorial columns run in Salvadoran newspapers. Lindo-Fuentes et al. describe the murder as the result of "a combination of internal ideological disputes within the ERP, accusations of indiscipline, and even the suggestion that he was a CIA agent." They point to Dalton's prescience in a poem written shortly before he returned to El Salvador, in which he "defended the right of a leftist comrade to disagree with his superiors without being accused of treason." The event sent dissenters to form another guerrilla group, the National Resistance (RN) (Lindo-Fuentes et al., *Remembering a Massacre*, 107).

38. Lindo-Fuentes et al., *Remembering a Massacre*, 92.

39. "I was kept out of the plaza, so I could hear only the screaming and shooting," a North American journalist is quoted as saying. "Then when it was over, I got in and found it literally covered with blood, although the bodies had been removed. But perhaps the most horrible thing was when I returned an hour after THAT to find they had hosed down the plaza and there was a chill as though nothing had happened at all" (Geyer, "From Here to Eternity," quoted in Armstrong and Shenk, *El Salvador*, 88).

40. Salvadoran writer David Escobar Galindo has called the Regalado Dueñas

kidnapping "the first act of revolutionary violence of this nature" in the country, but points to how economic elites desperately wanted to blame the military (which ultimately they could control) rather than accept the "unknown enemy" of revolution. See "El duelo por el 'Duelo . . .'.", *La Prensa Gráfica*, 20 May 2006, http://archive.laprensa.com.sv/20060520/opinion/483679.asp. For the Poma kidnapping, see Martínez, *Las cárceles clandestines*, 379.

41. See Inter-American Commission on Human Rights, "Report on the Situation of Human Rights in El Salvador."

42. Guidos Véjar, "La crisis política en El Salvador," 151.

43. Sol, *El Salvador*, 53–54.

44. These names remain powerful in El Salvador. The Viera Altamirano and Dutriz families own *El Diario de Hoy* and *La Prensa Gráfica*, still the biggest papers in El Salvador. Dalton, "Statistics on Freedom," in Dalton, *Poems*, 50 (originally published in 1975).

45. In 1979, El Salvador had just 275,000 television sets and 5 million people, about 65 per 1,000 people. Statistic from *El Salvador de Hoy*, a publication of the Secretary of Information of the President's Office, 15 August 1979, 117.

46. López Vigil, *Las mil y una historias de Radio Venceremos*, 13.

47. According to the human rights office of the Catholic archdiocese, Socorro Jurídico. See Arnson, "Review of Lawrence Ladutke's *Freedom of Expression*," 200. Nearly forty reporters and photographers were killed covering the war, most Salvadorans (Pedelty, *War Stories*, 48).

48. Montgomery, *Revolution in El Salvador*, 132–33; Panamá Sandoval, *Los guerreros de la libertad*, 49, 55. Panamá offers an insider's version of the founding and mission of ARENA. As we shall see, ARENA's extremist rhetoric had moderated some by the late 1980s when Alfredo Cristiani became president.

49. The Truth Commission report found that members of a state security force killed Zamora. Commission on the Truth, *De la locura a la esperanza*.

50. Cardenal et al., *La voz de los sin voz*, 454, translation from Sobrino, *Archbishop Romero*, 25.

51. Sobrino, *Archbishop Romero*, 111.

52. Commission on the Truth, *De la locura a la esperanza*, n. 21, translation from U.S. Institute of Peace, http://www.usip.org/resources/truth-commission-el-salvador (accessed 24 June 2009).

53. Americas Watch Committee and American Civil Liberties Union, *Report on Human Rights in El Salvador*, 26 January 1982, xxvi–xxvii, cited in Bland, *Assessing the Transition*, 171.

54. Commission on the Truth, *De la locura a la esperanza*.

55. Commission on the Truth, *De la locura a la esperanza*. The men killed were Enrique Alvarez Córdoba, Juan Chacón, Enrique Escobar Barrera, Manuel de Jesús Franco Ramírez, Humberto Mendoza, and Doroteo Hernández.

56. National Guardsman arrested Maryknoll nuns Ita Ford and Maura Clarke, Ursuline nun Dorothy Kazel, and laywoman Jean Donovan on 2 December 1980, as they left the International Airport, drove them to an isolated spot, beat and raped them, shot them, and buried them in shallow graves.

57. Wood, *Insurgent Collective Action*, 18.

58. National Security Archives, *El Salvador: The Making of U.S. Policy*, 34, cited in Commission on the Truth, *De la locura a la esperanza*, n. 34.

59. See Binford, *The El Mozote Massacre*; Danner, *The Massacre at El Mozote*; and Commission on the Truth, *De la locura a la esperanza*. More recently a former soldier of the Atlacatl Battalion has opened up about his experiences at El Mozote and other war-era massacres. Efraín Antonio Fuentes was only 17 when he was forcibly recruited into the military. As soldiers arrived at El Mozote, he said, they were told "Whatever moves must die." Everyone was supposed to be a guerrilla, "from mothers even to children." See Diego Murcia, " 'En El Mozote, la orden fue: Lo que se mueva se muere," *El Faro* (15 December 2008), http://www.elfaro.net/secciones/Noticias/20081215/noticias1_20081215.asp (accessed 21 July 2009).

60. See Andersen, "Images of War"; Pedelty, *War Stories*.

61. Stanley, *The Protection Racket State*.

62. See Coutin, *The Culture of Protest*; Smith, *Resisting Reagan*.

63. Forché, "The Coronel," 16.

64. Stone, *Salvador* (MGM, 1986); Didion, *Salvador*.

65. *The Battle of Algiers* (Casbah Films, 1966), "Pontecorvo and the Film," Disc Two in Criterion Collection edition of the film, 2004. Pontecorvo mentions his desire to make a film about Romero in an interview shown on the DVD in which he discusses the difficulty of finding projects he felt passionate about.

66. Robinson, *Transnational Conflicts*, 88–89; see the important book by Herman Rosa, *AID y las transformaciones globales en El Salvador*.

67. Martín-Baró, "Los medios de comunicación masiva y la opinión pública," 1082.

68. Many sources document the wartime broadcast news *apertura* (opening). In English they include chapter 10, "Dialogue Was a Crime" in Whitfield, *Paying the Price*, and Lindsey Gruson, "Salvadoran TV Dares Tell the News," *New York Times*, 27 September 1988. One clear analysis in Spanish is an unpublished paper by UCA students Marcos Antonio Rivera and Claudia Evelyn Perla, "El surgimiento y posterior modernización." They write, "If we take into consideration that the population was anxious to inform itself about what was happening on the war front, and the news programs fulfilled this function, and, . . . , that the vision of some businessmen permitted the perception of the profitability of these businesses, we can deduce the basic criteria that motivated the 'boom' of news programs in El Salvador." That kind of profit-loss balance sheet is often said to have figured into some power elites' calculation of the profitability for private enterprise of an end of military conflict, and thus their support for the peace negotiations.

69. Statistics are from a survey by the Instituto Universitario de Opinión Pública (IUDOP) of the UCA, published in Martín-Baró, *Así piensan los salvadoreños urbanos*. Ethnographic research suggests that the circulation of news through mass media was extremely limited through most of the twentieth century in El Salvador; newspapers did not make it out of urban areas, and the few radio frequencies that reached rural areas were dominated by government/military sources. My father-in-law Don Antonio, for example, recalls a kind of "town crier" calling out the "news" in a cantón of San Pablo Tacachicas in La Libertad in the early 1940s.

70. Taussig, *Shamanism, Colonialism and the Wild Man*; Margold, "From 'Cultures of Fear and Terror'."

71. On truth-effects, see Foucault, "Truth and Power," 118.

72. Edgar Rivas (longtime journalist and professor of journalism, University of El Salvador), interview by author, San Salvador, July 1994.

73. Green, *Fear as a Way of Life*.

74. Coutin, "The Oppressed, the Suspect and the Citizen," 75.

75. Commission on the Truth, *De la locura a la esperanza*. Along with UCA rector Ignacio Ellacuría, and vice-rector Ignacio Martín-Baró, the victims were Segundo Montes, director of the UCA Human Rights Institute; Amado López, Joaquín López y López, and Juan Ramón Moreno, teachers at the UCA; and Julia Elba Ramos and Celina Mariceth Ramos.

76. The two men were released in the amnesty declared by President Cristiani after the Truth Commission report was made public in March 1993. In late 2008, a criminal complaint filed in the Spanish High Court revived hopes that those behind the massacre could face trial. Human rights lawyers filed a complaint against Cristiani and fourteen former members of the Salvadoran military (Victoria Burnett, "Jesuit Killings in El Salvador Could Reach Trial in Spain," *New York Times*, 13 November 2008).

77. United Nations, "El Salvador-ONUSAL Background."

78. Boutros-Ghali, "Democracy: A Newly Recognized Imperative," cited in Holiday and Stanley, "Under the Best of Circumstances," 38.

79. Holiday and Stanley, "Under the Best of Circumstances," 37. In the same vein, the political scientist Charles T. Call has called the Salvadoran case "among the most successful implementations of a peace agreement in the post-Cold War period" ("Democratization, War and State-Building," 827).

80. Karl, "El Salvador's Negotiated Revolution," appropriating Boutros-Ghali, "La larga noche de El Salvador llega a su fin," Mexico City, 16 January 1992, published in the edited collection *Acuerdos hacia nueva nación* (San Salvador: FMLN, 1992), 151, cited (and translated into English) in Holiday and Stanley, "Under the Best of Circumstances," 37–38. George Vickers published a similarly titled article at the same time, "A Negotiated Revolution," 4–8. For other early academic assessments, see Holiday and Stanley, "Building the Peace"; Stahler-Sholk, "El Salvador's Negotiated Transition." It is important to note that many scholars recognized shortcomings as well, though those concerns were not generally picked up in the political, policy, and diplomatic communities. Indeed Jack Spence, George Vickers et al. added a question mark to Boutros-Ghali's enthusiastic assessment in their 1994 report, *A Negotiated Revolution?* The positive overall assessment, however, continued to dominate accounts of the process.

81. Wood, *Forging Democracy from Below*, 3, 12.

82. Robinson, *Transnational Conflicts*, 70. The original theory of polyarchal democracy was put forward by political scientist Robert Dahl in *A Preface to Democratic Theory*, further developed in *Polyarchy: Participation and Opposition*.

83. The majority of people in the country did not participate as active combatants, of course; and, as we will explore throughout this book, that people said they *felt* the conditions were worse than the war is a function of the way memory works in the present rather than an objective measurement of danger and risk at any historical moment.

84. Binford, "Violence in El Salvador," 205.

85. Borrowing the language from Naomi Klein in her talk, "Shock Doctine: The Rise of Disaster Capitalism in Latin America," University of Illinois, Urbana, 29 October 2008.

86. Giddens, *Modernity and Self-Identity*, 123.

87. Klein, *The Shock Doctrine*.

88. Herman Rosa documents the strengthening of the private sector through USAID monies channeled through FUSADES in his *AID y las transformaciones globales*, 75–95. Between 1983 and 1994, FUSADES received at least $150 million and became the main outlet for USAID monies to civil society, according to Robinson in *Transnational Conflicts*, 90. Thus, FUSADES, though promoting "free trade," echoed economic restructuring in Chile, which, in its very enunciation as a North-South exchange—with the North the authority—undermined the notion of the free market as a liberalizing impulse. See Cárcamo-Huechante, "Milton Friedman," 429–30.

89. Segovia, *Transformación structural y reforma económica*, 24; see also Pedersen, "The Storm We Call Dollars," for an investigation of changing values between the U.S. and El Salvador in relation to the flow of dollars. Pedersen points to a 1982 $87 million IMF loan, in exchange for conditions including fiscal austerity and the creation of a "parallel" foreign currency exchange market (not controlled by the Central Bank), particularly for remittances, as important to this transformation.

90. In order to revitalize banks, the government effectively bought up bad (nonperforming, overdue) debts that had been held by the nationalized banks, increasing national debt in order to increase the appeal of stocks in the privatized banks (authorized by Article 137 of the Ley del Régimen Monetario). Alexander Segovia points to "irregularities" in the privatization process that essentially permitted a kind of return of oligopolistic banking practices and *greater* concentration of wealth, rather than a spread of wealth and the increasing competition that Smithian capitalism prescribes (*Transformación structural y reforma económica*, and "La actuación y las políticas macroeconómicas a partir de 1989," 92). Boyce, in *Ajuste hacia la paz*, describes the financial sector reform being carried out without proper oversight or restrictions on speculation (358–59). Thanks to Anna Jefferson and Brandt Peterson for help on these references.

91. Friedman, *Capitalism and Freedom*.

92. Paley, "Introduction," 13.

93. Nelson, *Reckoning*, 27.

94. Rose, "Governing 'Advanced' Liberal Democracies"; Brown, "Neoliberalism and the End of Liberal Democracy," 7, 1.

95. Mendez, "Gender and Citizenship in a Global Context," 24, citing in part Schild, "New Subject of Rights?" 96.

96. See excellent discussion of historical and local specificities of neoliberal governance in Ong, *Neoliberalism as Exception*, 11–13.

97. Hale, *Más que un indio*, 34–35.

98. Fukuyama, *The End of History*.

99. Thanks to Fernando Coronil for reminding us of the limits of a critique of neoliberalism—if neoliberalism is a "bubble" in the big story of the advance of capi-

talism in world history, then manifestos narrowly homing in on neoliberalism will hardly matter. Coronil made the statement in a roundtable discussion, "The Rise of Current Social Movements and Protests in Latin America," 30 October 2008, Center for Latin American and Caribbean Studies, University of Illinois, Urbana.

100. Braier, "Market Reforms in El Salvador Mean New Opportunities for U.S. Business."

101. United Nations Development Programme, *Report on Human Development in El Salvador 2001*, chap. 4. "Since the beginning of the 1990s El Salvador has been implementing an aggressive agenda of international trade negotiations that has allowed the country to incorporate to the GATT [1991] and later to the WTO [1995]; reactivate the process of economic integration in Central America; sign free-trade agreements with the Dominican Republic and Mexico; participate in negotiations of the AFTA, follow up negotiations with Chile, Panama and Canada, and hold expectations to negotiate a free-trade agreement with the United States."

102. See Hernandez and Coutin, "Remitting Subjects"; Coutin, *Nations of Emigrant*; Pedersen, "In the Stream of Money"; Baker-Cristales, *Salvadoran Migration to Southern California*.

103. Descriptions of structural violence and symbolic violence from Bourgois, "The Power of Violence in War and Peace," 8, based on the work of Galtung, "Violence, Peace and Peace Research"; Bourdieu, *Pascalian Meditations*; and Scheper-Hughes, "Small Wars and Invisible Genocides."

104. Montgomery and Reitan, "The Good, the Bad and the Ugly," 143; Spence et al., *El Salvador*, 7.

105. On the route many took from the airport to the city, it welcomed returning "brothers [and sisters] from afar" (or "distant brothers"). Migrants later began protesting the inference that they were "distant"; President Tony Saca later began referring to them as *hermanos cercanos* (close brothers). See Baker-Cristales, "Magical Pursuits," 357.

106. Cruz and González, "Magnitud de la violencia en El Salvador," 956. The Instituto Universitario de Opinión Pública (IUDOP, University Institute of Public Opinion) of San Salvador's Central American University and the Interamerican Development Bank (IADB) found between 1994 and 1996 an average 131 intentional murders for every 100,000 citizens, compared with an estimated 130 violent deaths per 100,000 during the twelve-year war. See Cruz and González, *Sociedad y violencia*. Cruz today questions the accuracy of the high homicide figures, but confirms that rates reached a minimum of approximately 80 per 100,000 between 1994 and 1997 (Cruz, "Violence, Citizen Insecurity, and Elite Maneuvering," 152). For comparison, in the mid-1990s, Colombia's figure was 65 per 100,000 people, the U.S. rate 11 (Douglas Farah, "Killing in Salvadoran Crime Wave Outpaces Deaths During Civil War," *Washington Post*, 16 March 1996); Canada, 2.3; Costa Rica, 3.9, and Mexico, 19.4 (Cruz, "La violencia en El Salvador"). For comparison with South Africa, made by the Inter-American Development Bank, see Cristian Villalta, "Violencia: Un deporte nacional," *El Diario de Hoy*, 28 September 1997, 5.

107. Caldeira, *City of Walls*, 19.

108. IUDOP, "La delincuencia urbana."

109. Cruz, "Los factores posibilitadores y las expresiones de la violencia," 981.

According to Cruz, that 45 percent figure was the highest among surveys in cities across the Americas. Margaret Popkin notes the second such poll in *Peace Without Justice*, 1.

110. Cruz and González, "Magnitud de la violencia en El Salvador," 956. Surveys by IUDOP record a fall in the reports of crime victimization between 1994 (with a high of 39.5 percent) to 1999 (14.7 percent), but the perception of crime as the country's principal problem rose during those years (Cruz et al., "The Social and Economic Factors Associated with Violent Crime in El Salvador"). A May 1999 IUDOP poll found that 45 percent of Salvadorans thought the government's priority should be to combat crime, more than twice as many as those who would eradicate poverty, an attitude that is linked to a call for *mano dura* politics (Cruz, *¿Elecciones para qué?*, 52–53). Cruz suggests that accumulation of experiences of violence convinced citizens of increasing criminality, despite some evidence to the contrary.

111. Popkin in *Peace Without Justice*, 1. Popkin describes failures of the Salvadoran judicial system to establish itself as fully independent and credible after the war, despite the high priority the FMLN had placed on human rights and the judicial system in the negotiating agenda.

112. *Estudios Centroamericanos*, "Editorial: ¿Quince años de paz?"

113. Warner, "What like a Bullet Can Undeceive?" 44.

114. Martín-Baró, "Monseñor: Una voz para un pueblo pisoteado," 17–18.

115. Peterson, *Martyrdom and the Politics of Religion*, 145; see also Peterson and Peterson, "Martyrdom, Sacrifice, and Political Memory."

116. *Estudios Centroamericanos*, Edición Monográfica, "La cultura de la violencia en El Salvador."

117. Weber, "Politics as a Vocation."

118. Davis, "The Age of Insecurity," and Frühling, Tulchin, and Golding, *Crime and Violence in Latin America*.

119. Comaroff and Comaroff, "Law and Disorder in the Postcolony," 1, 4–5.

120. Friedman, "Globalization, Dis-Integration, Re-Organization," 19–20. For a lucid discussion of globalization in relation to Central America, see Robinson, *Transnational Conflicts*.

121. Giddens, *Modernity and Self-Identity*, 12.

122. Marx and Engels, *Manifesto of the Communist Party*.

123. Freud, *Introductory Lectures on Psychoanalysis*, 395, cited in Giddens, *Modernity and Self-Identity*, 43–44. Thank you to Yasemin Yildiz for the word and analysis.

Chapter 2. Critical Code-Switching and the State of Unexception

Epigraph: Reuters, "El Salvador Rebel Leader Gunned Down in Capital." *Toronto Star*, 26 October 1993, A19.

1. Later the police officers would be charged with negligence. Quote from Serrano, "Reaparecen escuadrones de la muerte." Other references used for reconstructing the events include *El Mundo*, "Dirigente del FMLN asesinado esta mañana," 25 October 1993; "Cristiani pide a CIHD investigue asesinato del FMLN," 26 October

1993; *La Prensa Gráfica*, "Asesinan a miembro de Comisión Política FMLN," "FMLN pide captura de asesinos," "Editorial: Contra todo tipo de violencia," "Iglesia participa en estrategia política," 26 October 1993; "3 entidades inician exhaustivas investigaciones," 27 October 1993; "Miembros de ONUSAL infórmanse de la autopsia practicada a Velis," "Movimiento Solidaridad condena ola de violencia," 29 October 1993; *El Diario de Hoy*, "Matan ex-comandante del FMLN," 26 October 1993.

2. In *Homer Sacer*, Giorgio Agamben describes how, through history, law has separate political beings, citizens, from "bare life," bodies without rights. A guerrilla or terrorist in the Salvadoran civil war was banned from society; as a body he was "included in the juridical order solely in the form of its exclusion (that is, of its capacity to be killed)."

3. I use the term *interpellate* in a variation of the sense first articulated by Louis Althusser in "Ideology and Ideological State Apparatuses" (1970; http://www.marxists.org/reference/archive/althusser/1970/ideology.htm, accessed September 2007): the ideological production of a subject through a process of "hailing," in which a person recognizes himself as always already defined within an ideological paradigm. The example Althusser uses is a police officer calling out "Hey you!" to a person on the street, who turns, and is thus "produced" as an already guilty subject. The example in my text does not quite follow this pattern, as the reporters in the news conference did not have to, and indeed often didn't, respond as Cristiani would have liked, to his "hailing"; but that is the process he *attempted* to incite. I follow thinkers who develop these ideas in other realms, particularly Judith Butler in work on performativity and gender (see *Gender Trouble* and *Bodies That Matter*).

4. And, thus, fabricate its very state-ness through another staged drama—if we consider the state as an entity reified through multiple discourses and practices proclaiming that they represent the nation. As Fernando Coronil has written, "The national state is the fetish of itself and of the nation; its mystifying form of representing the nation and representing itself is an essential part of its constitution as the nation's representative." Coronil argues against Philip Abrams's formula of the state as a "mask" disguising the political system in Abrams, "Notes on the Difficulty of Studying the State." Rather, Coronil theorizes the "mystified union of mask and what is being masked." In other words, Cristiani, declaring a "state of unexception," both offered the "mask" intending to constrain interpretations of the event, and at the same time, by *stating* the state of affairs, brought the state of affairs into being (though in this case the state could not control the force of "brute reality"—indeed, as we shall learn, other elements within the state still insisted on a state of exception that refused people like Velis their citizenship status). See Coronil, "State and Nation in Chávez's Venezuela: Reflections on the State, Illuminating the 2002 Coup," unpublished revised version of an article in *Anuario de Estudios Americanos*. Coronil develops his insights on the state form in *The Magical State*.

5. Serrano, "La reveladora huelga de salud."

6. American Hospital Association, "HIPAA Updated Guidelines."

7. Das, *Critical Events*, 6.

8. By "performative," I refer to a genealogy of theorizing performative speech acts, which starts with the proposition that words do not merely describe the world but *act* on it, changing it, starting with a recognition of institutionally sanctioned

speech ("I now pronounce you husband and wife") and moving to the realization that language itself is always performing—language itself is social action (for example, in languages that differentiate levels of intimacy or respect in the pronoun "you," the differentiation is constantly reiterated, performed, and shapes the way people see the world). See Austin, *How to Do Things with Words*; Derrida, "Signature Event Context"; Butler, *Bodies that Matter*.

9. Agamben, *State of Exception*, 2.

10. This is not to say that senses of "normal" are only imposed through dominant discourse, as theories of embodiment and *habitus* tell us; rather, in the hegemonic struggle for the meaning of postwar senses of reality, there were efforts to direct citizens toward a more individualistic, strategizing, neoliberal rationality.

11. Calhoun, "The Privatization of Risk," 262.

12. Guha, *Elementary Aspects of Peasant Insurgency*.

13. Guha, *Elementary Aspects of Peasant Insurgency*, 79, 109.

14. Indeed the title of Guha's book, *Elementary Aspects of Peasant Insurgency in Colonial India*, echoes Emile Durkheim's *The Elementary Forms of the Religious Life*.

15. Benjamin, "Theses on the Philosophy of History," 257.

16. Scheper-Hughes, *Death Without Weeping*, 219.

17. By "common sense," I am referring to the Gramscian concept that the values of the bourgeoisie, as those in power—those in control of the means of production—become the values of all, even if not in the majority's best interest. This allows the state to rule through consent rather than coercion. If concepts of violence are limited to individual acts and not structural or symbolic (capitalist exploitation, class exclusion, etc., that have real effects such as difference in health and infant mortality, etc.), then the (in this case capitalist) state can rule much more effectively. Anthropologist Andrea Smith has succinctly described "common sense" as "an unreflected and largely unconscious conception of the world shared by the 'mass of people.'" See Gramsci, *Selections from the Prison Notebooks*, 324, and Smith, "Heteroglossia, 'Common Sense,' and Social Memory," 252.

18. See Bourgois, "The Power of Violence in War and Peace," 8.

19. Hume, "The Myths of Violence." Focusing on interpersonal, "masculinist" violence and gendered socialization in two marginal San Salvador-area communities, she writes, "the role of the state and elite groups in embedding violence in Salvadoran political, social and economic life should not be underestimated" (69).

20. Povinelli, "The Child in the Broom Closet," 528.

21. Scheper-Hughes, *Death Without Weeping*, 219–20.

22. See Samuel Moyn, "On the Genealogy of Morals," *The Nation* 284 (15), 16 April 2007, 29. See Grandin's *Empire's Workshop*, for how neoconservatives in the Reagan administration appropriated the language of human rights for Central American conflicts.

23. Cristiani, "Address by Mr. Alfredo Félix Cristiani-Burkard," 3.

24. Guha, *Elementary Aspects of Peasant Insurgency*, 39–40.

25. Benjamin, "Theses on the Philosophy of History," 255.

26. *El Mundo*, "Dirigente del FMLN asesinado esta mañana," 25 October 1993.

27. *El Mundo*, "Gobierno de EUA condena asesinato de miembro FMLN," 26 October 1993; *La Prensa Gráfica*, "ONUSAL muestra preocupación," 26 October 1993.

28. *La Prensa Gráfica*, "Condenan asesinato de Velis: Gobierno de E.U. y Procuraduría de D.H.," 26 October 1993; *El Mundo*, "Procuraduría califica de 'ejecución sumaria' asesinato de politico Velis," 26 October 1993.

29. *La Prensa Gráfica*, "FBI investigara asesinato de miembro del FMLN," 27 October 1993.

30. *La Prensa Gráfica*, "Sería lamentable una escalada de violencia por asesinato de Velis, afirma Ministro de Defensa," "Director PNC dice se investiga," "Pdte Cristiani ordena investigación," 26 October 1993; See also *El Mundo*, "Cristiani pide a CIHD investigue asesinato del FMLN," 26 October 1993; *La Prensa Gráfica*, 26 October 1993; "3 entidades inician exhaustivas investigaciones," 27 October 1993; *El Diario de Hoy*, "FMLN pide comisión investigue asesinato," "F.A. llama a izquiera a no politizar asesinato," 27 October 1993.

31. Cristiani, "Address by Mr. Alfredo Félix Cristiani-Burkard," 4.

32. The Legislative Assembly majority (led by Cristiani's party, ARENA) had voted to grant amnesty to the named perpetrators in the Truth Commission Report—85 percent of them affiliated with state agents—military and state security bodies (including paramilitary death squads)—5 percent FMLN, and 10 percent civilian. The report was based on 44,000 accusations received over three months.

33. Alonso, *The Burden of Modernity*.

34. Agamben, *State of Exception*, 2.

35. Gould and Lauria-Santiago quote one 1930s coffee planter saying, "The lower class [which most elites thought of all as Indians] . . . has no civilization . . . is a primitive mass that instead of forming the basis for progress is a drag on it and a denial of it." In *To Rise in Darkness*, 12.

36. Paradoxically, at that same moment Indians were being welcomed back into the nation. Some Salvadorans had begun reclaiming indigenous identities through quincentennial indigenous movements, as race seemed to displace class as a mobilizer of politics. In El Salvador the anthropologist Brandt Peterson has argued that for some activists this desire for indigeneity filled the lack left by the loss of a revolutionary future. See Peterson, "Consuming Histories."

37. *La Prensa Gráfica*, "Banda de secuestradores y asaltantes desbaratan," 25 October 1993.

38. *El Diario de Hoy*, "Cafeteleros piden a Cristiani protección militar en fincas," 25 October 1993.

39. *The Battle of Algiers* (1966), dir. Gillo Pontecorvo, Criterion 3–DVD Collection release (2005), with accompanying booklet.

40. See Guha, *Elementary Aspects*; Tilly, *From Mobilization to Revolution*; Hobsbawm, *Primitive Rebels*.

41. Guha, *Elementary Aspects of Peasant Insurgency*, 12.

42. Gould and Lauria-Santiago, *To Rise in Darkness*.

43. *Amores Perros* (2000), dir. Alejandro González Iñárritu, Altavista Films.

44. In "Microbus Crashes and Coca-Cola Cash," I pose an argument as to the political nature of traffic accidents in the context of economic structures.

45. Fukuyama, *The End of History and the Last Man.*

46. *La Prensa Gráfica*, "FBI investigara asesinato de miembro del FMLN," 27 October 1993.

47. Marx, *On the Jewish Question.*

48. Ueltzen, ed., *Conversatorio con los hijos del siglo*, 75–98.

49. Babb, *After Revolution*, 154–55.

50. Grandin, *The Last Colonial Massacre*, 4.

51. Comaroff and Comaroff, "Law and Disorder in the Postcolony," 31, referring to Benjamin, "Critique of Violence."

52. Marx, "The Usefulness of Crime," 52.

53. Pressured by ONUSAL after Velis's murder and that of another FMLN leader, Heleno Castro, on 8 December 1994, Cristiani announced that Salvadoran Human Rights Counsel Carlos Molina Fonseca, and ONUSAL Human Rights Division director Diego García Sayan, along with Salvadoran jurists José Leandro Echeverría and Juan Jerónimo Castillo, would form the commission, referred to as the Joint Group. They would have six months to investigate "illegal armed groups." They would only investigate acts that occurred after 16 January 1992. They released their report 28 July 1994. Grupo Conjunto, *Informe del Grupo Conjunto para la Investigación de Grupos Armados Ilegales*, 7.

54. Castellanos Moya, *El arma en el hombre*. In a German-language interview for the online version of the Zürich-based weekly journal *WOZ Die Wochenzeitung*, the author responded to a question about the relation of the Velis case to the incident described in the book. Castellanos Moya conceded some similarities, noting that he worked as a journalist and read extensively of the situation in early 1990s El Salvador, but insisted on the literary nature of his inquiry and the fiction of his character "Robocop." See Schönherr, "Schlicht überleben."

55. Concertación por la Paz, la Dignidad y la Justicia Social, "Evaluación de 15 años después de la firma de los Acuerdos de Paz en El Salvador."

56. Pedelty, *War Stories*, 4.

57. See *El sector justicia de El Salvador en números*, quoted in Stanley and Loosle, "El Salvador," available at http://www.ndu.edu/inss/books/policing/cont.html (accessed August 2000); and Stanley, Vickers and Spence, *Risking Failure.*

58. Anonymous, interview with author, San Salvador, 29 June 1999.

59. Francisco Elías Valencia, interview with author, San Salvador, June 1999.

60. Mauricio Funes (*Entrevista Al Día*, Channel 12), interviews by author, Santa Elena, June 1996 and 22 June 1999. True to his origins as a reporter in the midwar news "boom," Funes was always accessible to scholars and journalists, at least through the early 2000s. He was generous and thoughtful and intense in both recorded interviews he gave me.

61. Narciso Castillo (*Teleprensa*, Channel 33, radio RCS), interviews by author, San Salvador, June 1996 and 21 June 1999; David Rivas (*Megavisión*, Channel 21), interview by author, San Salvador, 24 June 1999; Julio Rank and Walter Hernández (*El Noticiero*, Channel 6), interview by author, 17 June 1999; other 1999 anonymous interviews from editors at the newspapers *La Prensa Gráfica, El Diario de Hoy, El Mundo*; from radios *Mayavisión*, YSUCA, YSR, YSU, YSKL; from television network TCS.

62. In South Africa, the white government's failure to prosecute nonpolitical crime in the townships during the Apartheid era, along with the African National Congress "policy of ungovernability" during the struggle, has been suggested as another reason for the tremendous rise in crime in post-Apartheid South Africa. See Morris, "The Mute and the Unspeakable," 58. While the cultural and political differences between South Africa and El Salvador are many, the two transitions are often compared. See, for example, Wood, *Forging Democracy from Below.*

63. *La Prensa Gráfica,* Editorial, 1 January 1993, 5.

64. *El Diario de Hoy,* "Sigue incontenible el incremento de la violencia," 12 February 1993, 7.

65. *La Prensa Gráfica,* Editorial, 30 December 1993.

66. For example, on 11 July 1993, in the Legislative Assembly Diputado René Calderón of the Partido de Conciliación Nacional (PCN) said the government couldn't counter crime because it had lost that capacity with the abolishment of the National Guard and the Treasury Police, and this legitimized the collaboration of the army in the crime fight (Cristiani had sent out the military as a "dissuasive presence" on the highways) (*Estudios Centroamericanos* [ECA], "Crónica del mes: julio–agosto," 537–38 [July–August 1993], 766).

67. Stanley, *Protectors or Perpetrators?,* 9.

68. Steiner, "Criminalidad en El Salvador."

69. Foucault, *Discipline and Punish,* 192–93.

70. Anonymous, interview with author, San Salvador, 5 June 1999; author's field notes, 11 June 1999.

71. *La Prensa Gráfica,* "Sería lamentable una escalada de violencia por asesinato de Velis, afirma Ministro de Defensa," 26 October 1993.

72. United Nations, "Report of the ONUSAL Human Rights Division for the period from 1 January to 30 April 1992," 247.

73. United Nations, "Report of the ONUSAL Human Rights Division for the period from 1 July 1992 to 31 January 1993," 432.

74. See Doyle et al., eds., *Keeping the Peace;* or Oakley et al., eds., *Policing the New World Disorder.*

75. Boutros-Ghali, "Introduction," 36.

76. United Nations, "El Salvador-ONUSAL: Background."

77. Douglas Farah, "Killing in Salvadoran Crime Wave Outpaces Deaths During Civil War," *Washington Post,* 16 March 1996. Comparing the number to other murder rates, Farah asserted, "The figures make El Salvador one of the most violent countries in the world."

78. Charles Call notes that even by the signing of Chapultepec accords, the official army numbers had fallen from 60,000 to 31,000. Call, "From Soldiers to Cops," 145.

79. Stanley, Vickers, and Spence, *Risking Failure,* 16. Charles Call's numbers differ slightly from Stanley's though he ends with the same approximate reduction, from 60,000 public security personnel to 6,000 PN by mid-1992. Call also excludes from his numbers "the 30,000 troops and 11,000 FMLN troops who were NOT dedicated to policing-type functions." Call, "From Soldiers to Cops," 146.

80. Castellanos Moya, *El arma en el hombre,* 12.

81. Castellanos Moya, *El arma en el hombre*, 32.

82. Castellanos Moya, *El arma en el hombre*, 39.

83. Anonymous, interview by author, San Salvador, 8 June 1998, tape recording.

84. Would the "same incident" have happened two years earlier, during the war? According to some sources, crime was actually increasing in El Salvador before the war ended—in 1990 and 1991. The Salvadoran Ministry of Justice reported that crime increased 83 percent in the two years *prior to* the accords, and these statistics continued to increase before the cease-fire. See Stanley et al., *Risking Failure*.

85. Anonymous, interview with author, San Salvador, 6 June 1998, tape recording.

86. For example, the murder of journalist Lorena Saravia in August 1997 generated countless rumors. In the widely publicized case, the three police officers arrested for the murder were released from custody when a key witness recanted, saying she had been forced to testify against them. One television program suggested that Saravia had been the lover of a higher-up police official; other news sources implied links to narcotics trafficking. Later eight suspects were arrested but the case was dropped in 2001 for lack of evidence.

87. *El Salvador Proceso* 593 (30 December 1993).

88. Mike Reid, "FMLN Murders 'Prove the Return' of Death Squads," *The Guardian*, 5 November 1993; Tracy Wilkinson, "Salvadoran President Vows to Get Full Truth Behind Surge in Political Violence; Cristiani Reacts to Leftist's Assassination," *Los Angeles Times*, 28 October 1993.

89. Boutros Boutros-Ghali, "Introduction."

90. *Teleprensa Noticias*, Channel 2, 1 November 1993; reported in *Fundación Flor de Izote/El Rescate Report from El Salvador* 4 (40) (1–8 November 1993).

91. *Cadena de Oro*, 1 November 1993. Reported in *Fundación Flor de Izote/El Rescate Report from El Salvador* 4 (40).

92. Grupo Conjunto, *Informe del Grupo Conjunto para la Investigación de Grupos Armados Ilegales* (English), Annex 3, 78.

93. *La Prensa Gráfica*, "Aplicar mano dura," 4 November 1992, 1.

94. *Miami Herald*, "Salvador's Bloody Sequel," 1 November 1993.

95. *New York Times*, "Salvador Killings Bring a Warning of Terror," 31 October 1993.

96. Reid, "FMLN Murders 'Prove the Return' of Death Squads."

97. *Frente a Frente*, interview with Nidia Díaz, TCS Channels 2–4–6, 10 December 1993. Transcribed by INSISTEM.

98. *El Diario de Hoy*, "Vuelven las turbas," 11 December 1993, 1.

99. *El Diario de Hoy*, "Comprueben López murió a manos de asaltantes: Izquierda manipula sucesos para justificar violencia," 11 December 1993, 2.

100. Howard French, "As the Elections Near, Killings Shake El Salvador," *New York Times*, 10 December 1993. See also, for example, Pamela Constable, "Salvadoran Deaths Spur New Worries; Election, Peace Seen at Risk," *Boston Globe*, 19 December 1993.

101. Quote from *Noticiero Al Día*, Canal 12, 12 December 1993. Transcribed by INSISTEM.

102. The government never wavered from its assertion that the act was common crime. The Joint Group would not come to any conclusions in the case. See Joint Group, Annex 3, 87.

103. Povinelli, "The Child in the Broom Closet," 527.

104. Author's field notes while watching archived videos of news programs in the offices of Teleprensa Channel 33, San Salvador, El Salvador (unrecorded date), 1999. Transcription and translation by author.

105. United Nations, "Report of the ONUSAL Human Rights Division covering the period from 1 March to 30 June 1994," 574.

106. The ONUSAL Human Rights Division declared, "Following the investigation into other cases, it has been determined that the murder of [H]eleno Castro was a criminal act resulting from an altercation and that responsibility can be attributed to common criminals" (United Nations, "Report of the ONUSAL Human Rights Division covering the period from 1 November 1993 to 28 February 1994," 535).

107. Grupo Conjunto, *Informe del Grupo Conjunto para la Investigación de Grupos Armados Ilegales*, 57–58.

108. As British Prime Minister Margaret Thatcher declared in 1987, in what became a famous statement of the neoliberal philosophy, "and who is society? There is no such thing! There are individual men and women and there are families and no government can do anything except through people and people look to themselves first." Margaret Thatcher, "Interview for 'Women's Own,'" 23 September 1987, http://www.margaretthatcher.org/speeches/displaydocument.asp?docid=106689 (accessed 4 April 2007).

109. Klein, *The Shock Doctrine*, 16.

110. Dunkerley, *The Pacification of Central America*, Appendix 7.

111. Robinson, *Transnational Conflicts*, 87, 95–96.

112. Perhaps for this reason, this sense of the world watching their national drama, a group of Salvadoran migrant activists began holding annual meetings they called "International Conventions of Salvadorans in the World": they met in Los Angeles in 2003, in Washington, D.C., in 2004, Boston in 2005, and San Salvador in 2006. See Baker-Cristales, "Magical Pursuits."

113. Foucault, "Truth and Subjectivity," cited in Burchell, "Liberal Government and Techniques of the Self," 20.

114. Brown, "Neoliberalism and the End of Liberal Democracy."

115. David Pedersen, "The Storm We Call Dollars," 431–59.

116. The designation "The Fifteenth Department" draws on the fact that there are fourteen departments (territorial administrative units in El Salvador). The newspaper *Prensa Gráfica*, for example, has long had a section about Salvadorans in the exterior called "Departamento 15." See DeLugan, "Census, Map and Museum (Revisited)"; Baker-Cristales, *Salvadoran Migration to Southern California*; Coutin, *Nations of Emigrants*, 7. Coutin writes that the one in four figure comes from the Salvadoran Ministry of Foreign Affairs (Ministerio de Relaciones Exteriores) web site, which reported that 94 percent of Salvadoran emigrants live in the United States (2.3 million); the Banco Central de Reserva de El Salvador proffered the 13.6 percent GNP figure.

117. Salvadorans critique remittances from both left and right. On the left

they are often seen as leading to a vapid, passive television-culture consumerism. On the right, they are often seen as a *threat* to a neoliberal orientation; Coutin writes that critics' "anxieties center, among other things, on whether remitting enables people to act as the enterprising subjects of neoliberalism" (*Nations of Emigrants*, 136).

118. Gupta and Ferguson, "Spatializing States"; Babb, *After Revolution*, 248.

119. Edelman, *Peasants Against Globalization*, 188.

120. Brockett, "The Structure of Political Opportunities and Peasant Mobilization in Central America," cited in Flint, "Social Movements, NGOs and the State," 5. Flint notes critiques of Brockett's definition of political space as "northern theory" not always appropriate for "southern projects," but he asserts, based on his long-term research, it is appropriate for 1990s El Salvador.

121. Flint, "Social Movements, NGOs and the State," 15.

122. Almeida, *Waves of Protest*, 201, 205.

123. Hammond, "Politics and Publishing in Transition in El Salvador," 219.

124. Translated quote from Joaquín Villalobos's *A Revolution in the Left for a Democratic Revolution*, in Zielinski, "Starting Over in El Salvador."

125. Brown, "Neoliberalism and the End of Liberal Democracy."

126. Engels, "Crime in Communist Society," 51.

Chapter 3. "Today They Rob You and They Kill You"

1. Anna L. Peterson, in *Martyrdom and the Politics of Religion*, describes how political murders paradoxically contributed to the construction of an affective community of hope during the war in El Salvador. "The resurrection is true," a member of a Christian base community explained to Peterson, "because there are people like Monseñor [Monsignor] Romero who gave their lives [in his 1980 assassination]. This shows that the resurrection lives and that there is no other hope except that of resurrection." The political killings could become comprehensible (even "normalized" and assimilated into culture) if they could be reinterpreted in terms of Christ's passion and God's plan for mankind. Funerals of these martyrs, such as that of Romero, which was attended by tens of thousands, became public celebrations of faith and resurrection.

2. I am drawing on theorizations of governmentality influenced by Michel Foucault. As Graham Burchell writes, "Defining it in general as the conduct of conduct, Foucault presents government as a more or less methodological and rationally reflected 'way of doing things,' or 'art,' for acting on the actions of individuals, taken either singly or collectively, so as to shape, guide, correct or modify the ways in which they conduct themselves. . . . The rationality of government must be pegged to a form of the rational self-conduct of the governed themselves, but a form that is not so much a given of human nature as a consciously contrived style of conduct" (Burchell, "Liberal Government and Techniques of the Self," 19, 24).

3. Berlant, "Cruel Optimism," 21.

4. Williams, *Marxism and Literature*, 132.

5. Ahmed, *Queer Phenomenology*, 109.

6. In Chapter 6 I develop further the issue of race in El Salvador; in general class and gender were much more salient aspects of people's identities than race.

7. Interview with author, February 1998, tape recording, San Salvador.

8. Interview with author, 9 July 1999, tape recording, Santa Tecla.

9. Austin, *How to Do Things with Words*.

10. Derrida, "Signature Event Context"; Butler, *Bodies That Matter*.

11. Our first conversation, without a tape recorder, took place in the Soyapango church (I took notes); a follow-up recorded interview occurred in a park in the town of Nuevo Cuscatlán, in the San Salvador metropolitan area, 26 October 1998.

12. First figure from Instituto Geográfico Nacional, "Ingeniero Pablo Arnoldo Guzmán," 135; the second a projection by the División del Gobierno de Estadisticas y el Censo, http://www.digestyc.gob.sv/DigestycWeb/Estad_Demograficas/ProyeccionesAMSS.htm (accessed 30 June 2009).

13. On general rule, Goffman, *Frame Analysis*, 10; Lemon, *Between Two Fires*, 23; Bateson, "A Theory of Play and Fantasy," in *Steps to an Ecology of Mind*.

14. Labov, *Language in the Inner City*, 355.

15. Roseberry, "Hegemony, Power, and the Language of Contention," 80.

16. Interview with author, tape recording, San Salvador, 15 May 1998.

17. Mannheim and Tedlock, "Introduction" in *The Dialogic Emergence of Culture*, 15; Kristeva, "Word, Dialogue, and Novel."

18. Interview with author, tape recording, San Salvador, 26 January 1999.

19. I use the term "entextualization" in the sense of the movement of detached text through transformations in genre, first developed by Briggs and Bauman in "Genre, Intertextuality and Social Power." See also Urban, "Entextualization, Replication, and Power," 21.

20. Interview with author, tape recording, Soyapango, August 1998.

21. Interview with author, tape recording, San Salvador, 14 February 1998.

22. For example, "On 12 March 1981, units of the Military Detachment at Sonsonate and members of the civil defence unit at Cacaopera indiscriminately attacked and summarily executed men, women and children of El Junquillo canton in the district of Cacaopera, Department of Morazán"; they "raped a number of women and little girls under the age of 12." Commission on the Truth, *From Madness to Hope*.

23. Interview with author, tape recording, Soyapango, 30 August 1998.

24. Susan Coutin reports similar words from one of her informants: "One woman, who had been active on the Salvadoran Left, told me that during the war she understood the risk associated with particular actions as well as how to minimize the chance of being detained. In the postwar period, she commented apprehensively, it was completely unclear why certain people were targets of kidnappings" (*Nations of Emigrants*, 163).

25. Interview with author, tape recording, San Salvador, 1 February 1999.

26. Urban, *Metaphysical Community*.

27. Feldman, *Formations of Violence*, 14.

28. Stewart, *Ordinary Affects*, 3.

29. Ochs and Capps, "Narrating the Self," 23; Ricoeur, *Time and Narrative*; White, "The Value of Narrativity."

30. Binford, *The El Mozote Massacre*; Danner, *The Massacre at El Mozote*.

31. Saskia found out she had been named because she asked a high-up military official to investigate why her house, which she was renting in a middle-class neighborhood, had been searched several times. He told her that a neighbor reported a "foreign woman" (she is fair-skinned and could be seen as foreign) who wore heavy boots and came and went at strange hours. See Franco, "Killing Priests, Nuns, Women, Children," for a theorization of the dirty wars as invading the domestic.

32. Benjamin, "Theses on the Philosophy of History," 255.

33. Ochs and Capps, "Narrating the Self," 23.

34. Giddens, *Modernity and Self-Identity*, 123.

35. Zaloom, *Out of the Pits*, 173–74.

36. In the sense of *habitus* as "the durably installed generative principle of regulated improvisations," subject to an "art of performance" in order to be successfully reproduced. See Bourdieu, *Outline of a Theory of Practice*, 78, 20.

37. Bauman, *Verbal Art as Performance*, 11.

38. Goffman, *Frame Analysis*, 10.

39. Lemon, *Between Two Fires*, 23.

40. The war, too, produced a kind of self-monitoring as people wanted to be perceived as nonthreatening, noninvolved individuals who would not attract the attention of the security forces. I am suggesting here that the historically specific postwar form of self-monitoring could contribute to an individualistic subject with a market rationality.

41. Arendt, *The Human Condition*, cited in Joseph, *Against the Romance of Community*, 33.

42   Peterson, "Unsettled Remains."

43. Interview with author, tape recording, San Salvador, February 1998.

44. Interview with author, tape recording, Santa Tecla, November 1998.

45. Although I had imagined that Teo had made up the name—he was prone to exaggeration and embellishment—it turns out that, at least according to a 1994 article in the *New York Times*, there was a 42nd Street Gang. Mike O'Connor, in "A New U.S. Export in El Salvador: Street Gangs" (3 July 1994), one of the first U.S. reports on a phenomenon that has fascinated the mass media, writes of a group of young men in the village of San Bartolo. "None of the youths have been to the United States, but in [naming themselves, the gang] reached north for an appropriate image. They decided on 42nd Street, after seeing a movie that portrayed the street as running through an especially rough part of New York." The reference to movies demonstrates their global relevance (as in Teo's descriptions of movie holdups).

46. Diane M. Nelson in *Reckoning* describes postwar Guatemala as suffused with "duping discourses," and in her book she explores efforts to "reckon," or "to be in the know" in the face of suspicions that everyone is full of duplicity. A similar dynamic echoes among many people I know in El Salvador; Elana Zilberg's work points to the phenomenon of *doble cara*, or two-facedness, in Salvadoran political culture, in which "things are never as they appear" ("Gangster in Guerrilla Face," 39).

47. To stress her own control of the situation, in the Spanish, Patricia used the nonobligatory first-person pronoun *yo* frequently here (thus indicating a high level

of grammatical animacy). She also unevenly used the familiar form of you, *vos*, indexing, I would suggest, the forced intimacy of the moment, since her reporting of her assailant's speech toward her also takes the *vos* form: "Yo todavia le dije, 'No me grites, porque me va a poner nerviosa,' le dije yo, 'y si me pone nerviosa no le voy a poder dar las cosas' Agarré una cartera y le dije, 'Aquí llévese las cosas,' hasta yo escogí la cartera que le iba a dar."

48. Patricia used a grammatically agentive form of speaking, mildly more notable in Spanish than in English, since Spanish construction tends toward grammatical passivity. The passive *se me* construction (*se le fue un balazo*), which has no parallel in English, is generally "used in Spanish to expressed unplanned or involuntary happening" (Solé and Solé, *Modern Spanish Syntax*, 82).

49. See Rodgers, "Living in the Shadow of Death." Rodgers carried out participant-observation with a street gang in urban Nicaragua, and over time saw transformations from gangs constituting a form of local social solidarity in the face of insecure sociopolitical conditions to "a more individually and economically motivated type of brutality," a change related to wider structural processes in Nicaragua. For an account of similar processes in Guatemala, see Burrell, "Intergenerational Conflict in the Postwar Era."

Chapter 4. Adventure Time in San Salvador

1. The enormous Metrocentro shopping complex was developed by one of El Salvador's elite families, the Pomas. Roberto Poma's kidnapping and death in guerrilla custody in 1977, mentioned in Chapter 1, was an event marked as bringing the nation closer to war.

2. Ahmed, *Queer Phenomenology*, 109.

3. *Some*thing, not quite nameable, but possible, its presence palpable in intensity of interaction, as Kathleen Stewart might write. "It's ordinary affects that give things the quality of a *some*thing to inhabit and animate," she does write. "There's a politics to ways of watching and waiting for something to happen" (*Ordinary Affects*, 15–16).

4. Interview with author, San Salvador, tape recording, January 1998.

5. Teresa P. R. Caldeira, in her book *City of Walls*, demonstrates how through their narratives middle-class crime storytellers reorder a world they perceive as contaminated and disrupted.

6. In the middle isthmus, Honduras, El Salvador, and Nicaragua, in the early twentieth century "an emerging discourse of ethnic homogeneity supported ladino [non-Indian] efforts to appropriate land and political power from indigenous minorities. All three countries . . . underwent real or perceived processes of cultural *mestizaje*, defined here as a nation-building myth of racial mixture and a cultural process of de-Indianization that often accompanied the advance of agrarian capitalism" (Gould and Lauria-Santiago, *To Rise in Darkness*, xv, 101).

7. Merleau-Ponty, *The Phenomenology of Perception*, 296, cited in Ahmed, "Orientations," 544.

8. Williams, *Marxism and Literature*, 128–35.

9. I do not mean to reify separation between private and public, but rather to recognize their social construction. Feminist scholars point to the political act of negotiating the line between the two spheres. See Gal, "A Semiotics of the Public/ Private Distinction."

10. Williams, *Marxism and Literature*, 132.

11. Özyürek, *Nostalgia for the Modern*, 5.

12. Berlant, *The Queen of America Goes to Washington City*, 5.

13. Bakhtin, *The Dialogic Imagination*, 90–92.

14. Ahmed, "Orientations," 543.

15. Ricoeur, *Time and Narrative*, 62. Ricoeur concedes he has condensed care to the more prosaic level of concern, or preoccupation—*besorgen*.

16. This description of hopes for democracy is based on a popular post–World War II sense as described by historian Greg Grandin in *The Last Colonial Massacre*, 4.

17. Original Spanish fragment of poetry, Escobar Velado, "Patria exacta," in Escobar Velado, *Patria exacta y otros poemas*, 149; trans. in Armstrong and Shenk, *El Salvador*, 9.

18. Stanley, *The Protection Racket State*.

19. Ahmed, "Orientations," 543.

20. Marielena identifies herself by her paternal surname (not augmented with her husband's family name, as in "de X"). The choice is common among educated Latin American women, though not among Salvadoran elites. She claims to some vanity: while hers is an Italian name with some cachet in El Salvador (changed in this book), her husband's is a common Spanish one. Her husband's surname does link to her father-in-law, a widely respected man appointed to an important position as part of the reforms dictated by the peace accords in the early 1990s.

21. It turned out that Marielena's husband and my close friend Guayo were old friends, linked through some real estate transaction, so she accidentally fit into my network of crime storytellers described in the introduction. That's how the San Salvador metropolis works, I soon found—the city is hyperlinked in the most unexpected ways.

22. Marielena was a member of a charismatic Catholic praise group at a church known for its upper-class congregation, the Iglesia del Sagrado Corazón in the Colonia Escalón.

23. See Harding, *The Book of Jerry Falwell*, 24–38.

24. Johnstone, *Stories, Community and Place*, 62.

25. Bakhtin, *The Dialogic Imagination*, 354–55.

26. A Latin American friend who grew up among elites in Guatemala, reading a draft of this chapter, questioned how a woman of such privilege would call herself "middle class," given common understanding of class in Central America. It could be that she was "translating" herself for me. But certainly, while cosmopolitan, she was not of the most economically elite in the country. No one of that class would have had to drive around with a car with broken air-conditioning. They likely would have used another car. And perhaps would have had a driver.

27. Halberstam, *In a Queer Time and Place*, 22.

28. See Marc Edelman's careful historical review showing how Costa Rica's

"beguiling" imagined past as an egalitarian outpost is partly accurate and partly fanciful in *Peasants Against Globalization*, 44–90.

29. Setha M. Low in *On the Plaza* describes a much more complicated, class-segregated and gendered scenario in public parks and plazas in late twentieth-century San José, Costa Rica; of course, Marielena's description is novelistic, utopian, idealized, functioning to move forward her story about postwar El Salvador.

30. Didion, *Salvador*, 35–36. This book has been heavily criticized, specifically these paragraphs, precisely for its ("postmodern") disengagement. Didion never contemplates who the young civilian was, she never tries to get in touch with people involved in resisting this kind of abuse, and she never "mixes with the masses." See Yúdice, "*Testimonio* and Postmodernism."

31. Mannheim and Tedlock, "Introduction" in *The Dialogic Emergence of Culture*, 15; Julia Kristeva, "Word, Dialogue and Novel," in *Desire in Language*, 64–91.

32. Taylor, *Modern Social Imaginaries*, 23.

33. Hill, "The Voices of Don Gabriel," in *The Dialogic Emergence of Culture*, 108. Among the theoretical inspirations for her method are Bakhtin, *The Dialogic Imagination*, and Goffman, *Frame Analysis*.

34. This citation instantly indexes history for Salvadorans. During the war, people of all social classes told me, guerrillas would "borrow" vehicles for deliveries, usually of arms, and let the owner know where they left it the next day. Indeed, later in this narrative the kidnapper will explicitly say, "We're going to transport arms." Recall, too, that Marielena said earlier, "The guerrillas never assaulted you." At some level, this kind of act—"borrowing" a vehicle—could be linked to a kind of "social care," in the sense that the FMLN's stated—whether believed or not by all—goal was to revolutionize the state, make it more responsive to the needs of the majority.

35. Dreyfus, *Being in the World*, 141.

36. Dreyfus, *Being in the World*, 141.

37. Two hundred colones would have been about $23.

38. Simmel, "The Stranger," in *The Sociology of Georg Simmel*.

39. Berlant, *The Queen of America Goes to Washington City*, 5.

40. Hill, *The Voices of Don Gabriel*, 97; Bakhtin, *The Dialogic Imagination*, 295.

41. Bakhtin, *The Dialogic Imagination*, 90–92.

42. Halberstam, *In a Queer Time and Place*, 2.

43. An "agentive moment," in E. Valentine Daniel's definition, is a coming together of enabling circumstances (and limiting constraints, especially in the tensions and contradictions of cultural predispositions) that open up the possibility for change. See *Charred Lullabies*, 191.

44. Halberstam, *In a Queer Time and Place*, 2.

Chapter 5. Democratic Disenchantment

1. U.S. Department of State Bureau of Democracy, Human Rights and Labor, "El Salvador Country Report."

2. Huntington, *The Third Wave*; Borón, "Faulty Democracies?" 43.

3. See Mark Engler, "El Salvador No Model for the Future of Iraq," *Newsday*, 1 December 2004; David Brooks, "Insurgency Busting," *New York Times*, 28 September 2004; Boutros-Ghali, "Democracy," cited in Holiday and Stanley, "Under the Best of Circumstances," 37.

4. Past chapters have pointed to historian Greg Grandin's discussions of the meaning of democracy to Latin Americans in the post–World War II world. See *The Last Colonial Massacre*, 4.

5. Elisabeth Jean Wood writes, "[Salvadoran] elites long opposed to democratization not only for the usual reason—that the many might expropriate or heavily tax the wealth of the few—but because the economic privileges of the elite depended on state-enforced procedures unlikely to be sustainable under democratic rule. In El Salvador, these measures included the torture and disappearance of labor activists and sometimes their families by death squads allied to state security forces and paramilitary groups, coercive workplace practices that long prevented any labor organizing, and close local alliances between landlords and representatives of the state that preempted political organization in the countryside." *Forging Democracy from Below*, 4.

6. Héctor Lindo-Fuentes, Rafael Lara-Martínez, and Erik Ching point to various examples of how the right coded the events (in which ten to fifteen people were killed by rebels and at least 10,000 died by the hand the military): For example, a 1984 book by Mariano Castro Morán, a colonel who had been part of the 1961 military junta, states, "The murder of peaceful and unarmed citizens, the rape and pillaging, the vandalism in the destruction of property, will figure in Salvadoran history as an example of what would have happened throughout the Republic had the subversive communist movement triumphed." See *Remembering a Massacre in El Salvador*, 243, citing Castro Morán, *Función política del ejército salvadoreño en el presente siglo*, 138.

7. Roy, "Into the Inferno."

8. Through the next decade different FMLN members would leave, or be expelled after tribunals. But the disintegration of the war-era unity was signaled most dramatically by the defection of the guerrilla commander Joaquín Villalobos, leader of the People's Revolutionary Army (ERP), in 1995. He founded the centrist Partido Demócrato, but it did not draw a strong following and disappeared within a few years.

9. Field notes, San Salvador, October 1995.

10. The diversified Cristiani family financial interests, in pharmaceuticals, sugar, and cotton as well as coffee, typified the new generation of financial leaders that took the reins of ARENA in the late 1980s. Struggles within the party would continue over the next twenty years, however, even as it continued winning presidential elections. See Robinson, *Transnational Conflicts*, 95–97.

11. Wood, *Forging Democracy from Below*, 72–73.

12. Paige, *Coffee and Power*.

13. Fukuyama, *The End of History and the Last Man*.

14. Field notes, San Salvador, April 1999.

15. This is Mario Lungo Uclés's thesis about the rise of ARENA—that it de-

veloped for the bourgeoisie "a political class with its own organic expression." See Lungo Uclés, *El Salvador in the Eighties*, 120–21.

16. Field notes, San Salvador, 22 June 1999.

17. Despite its transformation from a virulently right-wing, death-squad-linked party to more moderate, neoliberal representatives of business, ARENA continued demonizing the FMLN as "communists" and "terrorists," dredging up images of their opponents in guerrilla mode. Up to and including the 2004 elections, when the vigorous young businessman Tony Saca ran against the old Communist guerrilla leader Schafik Handal, the strategy was successful.

18. Nugent, "Democracy Otherwise," 22.

19. In *Wirtschaft und Gesellschaft*, likely written before 1914 and published posthumously in 1921, Weber writes, "The *demos* itself, in the sense of an inarticulate mass, never 'governs' larger associations; rather, it is governed, and its existence only changes the way in which the executive leaders are selected and the measure of influence which the *demos*, or better, which social circles from its midst are able to exert upon the content and the direction of administrative activities by supplementing what is called 'public opinion'" (quoted in "Bureaucracy," in *From Max Weber*, 225). Weber's oeuvre clearly demonstrates that he did applaud this development but rather saw it as part of the larger process of rationalization and bureaucratization of human relations.

20. Schumpeter, *Capitalism, Socialism and Democracy*, 284–85.

21. Coles, *Democratic Designs*, 20–21.

22. Concertación por la Paz, la Dignidad y la Justicia Social, "Evaluación de 15 años después de la firma de los Acuerdos de Paz en El Salvador."

23. For an insightful discussion of struggles over these ideas of the state and democratization see Frazier, *Salt in the Sand*, 16; for a discussion on how social movements in a neoliberal environment deploy citizens' rights discourse, see Mendez, "Gender and Citizenship in a Global Context."

24. Fisher, "Doing Good?" 440, citing Salamon, *The Global Associational Revolution*, 1.

25. Gould and Lauria-Santiago, "'They Call Us Thieves and They Steal Our Wage,'" 208. Alberto Masferrer's program of *Vitalismo*, which called for housing, food, and schooling for all, inspired people across Central America and was integrated into President Arturo Araujo's campaign in 1931. See Masferrer, "El mínimum vital," in *Páginas Escogidas*.

26. FMLN, *Cambio en El Salvador para vivir mejor: Programa del gobierno 2009–2014*, San Salvador, 2008, 3.

27. Sánchez Cerén, *Con sueños se escribe la vida*, 274.

28. Amanda Shank, "El Salvador: The UDW Interview with FMLN Presidential Candidate Mauricio Funes (Part I)," http://upsidedownworld.org/main/content/view/1282/1/ (accessed 30 August 2008).

29. Alonso, *The Burden of Modernity*; see Cohen, *Bordering Modernities*, for a compelling account of another Latin America country's (Mexico's) efforts to overcome its always-already lack.

30. Miyazaki, *The Method of Hope*, 5.

31. Dankwart A. Rustow's statement, "The factors that keep a democracy stable

may not be the ones that brought it into existence" has been influential in political science. It came in the article, "Transitions to Democracy: Toward a Dynamic Model." His focus on agency, process, and bargaining broke from functionalist approaches at the time, which sought to determine when prerequisites for a democracy—economic, sociopolitical, psychological—had been met.

32. The number of cases reported increased dramatically over the first half of the 1990s, as more people gained confidence in the Human Rights Counsel. In 1993, 2,454 cases were admitted; in 1994, 1,840; and in 1995, 4,696. In 1996, 8,365 of 12,810 accusations, 65 percent, were not admitted (of cases presented and admitted, 780 provided the evidence for concluding with a resolution of state responsibility; many investigations were archived). Velásquez de Avilés, *Evolución de los derechos humanos.*

33. IUDOP, "Los derechos humanos en la opinión pública salvadoreña." IUDOP's polls are considered the most reliable in Central America.

34. Caldeira, *City of Walls,* 28–30.

35. Evelyne Huber, Dietrich Rueschemeyer, and John Stephens have also referred to disenchantment in democratizing societies, pointing to a decline in social movements after the first democratic elections, due "in part to disenchantment with the failure of democratic rule to bring about significant improvements in the material situation of most citizens." See Huber et al., "The Paradoxes of Contemporary Democracy," 331.

36. Weber, "Bureaucracy," in *From Max Weber,* 224, 226.

37. Weber, "Science as a Vocation," in *From Max Weber,* 155, also "Religious Rejections of the World and Their Directions," 357.

38. This sense of protection is characteristic of the patriarchal state, which considers women property to be protected. See Elshtain, *Public Man, Private Woman*; Molyneux, "Twentieth-Century State Formations in Latin America," 35.

39. Huber et al., "The Paradoxes of Contemporary Democracy."

40. For example, one letter published in the *Diario Latino* newspaper in 1931, commenting on the chaos of protests and strikes at the time, denounced the Arturo Araujo government for "leniency toward 'the criminal elements'" (Anderson, *Matanza*). A military coup soon followed, and then, after the January 1932 uprising, the massacre.

41. Indeed, the process of demobilizing the three bodies was fraught with problems, and the rising crime rate added to the government's reasons to resist the timetable. Obviously, habitual interpretations of police actions continued into the transition. Some newspaper editorials on the left were especially concerned about the makeup of the new police force, negotiated in the peace accords. It was supposed to be 20 percent former FMLN combatants, 20 percent former military, and 60 percent new recruits. People's political perspectives shaped their interactions with police. For example, in 1996, a friend of mine who was stopped for a traffic infraction told the police the name of his in-law, a former ARENA mayor of San Salvador. The officer responded, "Things aren't like that any more." Rather than concluding that the police force was less corrupt than in the past, my friend told me, "That guy had to be a guerrilla."

42. UNDP, *El Salvador: The State of the Nation: Human Development 1999*

(Spanish language version), hdr.undp.org/en/reports/nationalreports/latinameri-cathecaribbean/elsalvador/name,2998,en.html, 85 (accessed 1 March 2001).

43. Cruz et al., "The Social and Economic Factors Associated with Violent Crime," 38.

44. Interview with author, San Salvador, tape recording, 18 April 1998.

45. Lili introduced me to Guayo; they had taught English together in the past. He, too, quickly became a good friend and the center of one of my networks of crime-story-tellers, as described in the introduction.

46. Again, Lili, like most Salvadorans, did not use explicit racial or ethnic markers in her description, though "nice-looking" may have signaled more European features (while "well-dressed" pointed to class). Her trust in him may have been amplified by the fact that he looked like he belonged in the neighborhood rather than that he was "nice-looking" and therefore trustworthy.

47. The case had been revealed by investigative reporters from *El Diario de Hoy*. But it had taken three years, and ongoing pressure by the Human Rights Institute of the Central American University (IDHUCA), the Office of the Counsel for Human Rights, as well as other human rights-oriented NGOs in the media, and Vilanova's family, to bring the case to a conclusion. Political scientist Lawrence Ladutke details the case in *Freedom of Expression in El Salvador*. See also IDHUCA, "Los derechos humanos en El Salvador 1997."

48. In 2007, the García Prieto family announced plans to reopen the case with the Inter-American Court of Human Rights, charging the Salvadoran state with negation of access to justice and violation of human rights. See Alicia Miranda, "El Salvador a las puertas de una nueva demanda internacional," *El Faro* 19–25 March 2007, http://www.elfaro.net/Secciones/noticias/20051121/noticias8_20051121.asp (accessed 26 March 2007).

49. See Daniel Valencia and Rosarlin Hernández, "Capturan a abuelo por secuestro," *El Faro*, 21 March 2009, http://www.elfaro.net/secciones/Noticias/20090323/noticias1_20090323.asp (accessed 18 July 2009). For a study of the entire case, see the IDHUCA web site dedicated to Katya Miranda: http://www.uca.edu.sv/publica/idhuca/katya.html (accessed 18 July 2009).

50. Hurtig, *Coming of Age in Times of Crisis*.

51. As we have seen in previous chapters, the liberal state in El Salvador converted other Others to citizens by erasing them—through a process of *ladinoización*, turning Indians into ladinos or mestizos, in part by eliminating communal land, or by outright killing as in the 1932 Matanza.

52. Berlant, *The Female Complaint*, 9.

53. Interview with author, San Salvador, tape recording, 18 January 1999.

54. See Concertación por la Paz, la Dignidad y la Justicia Social, "Parte III, Retrocesos y Deterioros," 64–69, in *Evaluación de 15 años después de la firma de los acuerdos de paz en El Salvador*, which summarizes laws passed since the peace accords that have authoritarian qualities. For background on anti-terrorism laws, see *Proceso* 1248, 1249, and 1250 (4, 11, 18 July 2007), http://www.uca.edu.sv/publica/pubind.html (accessed July 2007). See also U.S.-El Salvador Sister Cities, "The Salvadoran Anti-Terrorism Law and Its Mirror Image," http://elsalvadorsolidarity.

org/joomla/index.php?option=com_content&task=view&id=61&Itemid=43 (accessed 20 August 2007).

55. Godoy, *Popular Injustice*, 12.

56. Call, "Democratization, War and State-Building," 842, 828.

57. Gramsci, *Selections from the Cultural Writings*, 188–90.

58. Woodward, "Calculating Compassion," 59–86.

59. Quote from Putnam, *Making Democracy Work*, 15; also see Putnam, *Bowling Alone*.

60. Appadurai, "Hope and Democracy," 30.

61. Grandin, *The Last Colonial Massacre*, 14. Charles R. Hale, however, points to how participants in the October Revolution, and in much of the twentieth-century Latin American left, never overcame a racialized logic in which indigenous peoples still needed to be "developed." See *Más que un indio*.

62. Nugent, "Democracy Otherwise."

63. Nicholas Dawidoff, "The Man Who Wasn't There," *New York Times*, 15 June 2008, 12.

64. See Joseph, *Against the Romance of Community*, for an incisive discussion of these issues.

65. Silber, "Not Revolutionary Enough?" 179.

66. Interview with author, San Salvador, tape recording, 19 January 1999.

67. Interview with author, Soyapango, tape recording, 27 November 1998.

68. Source for this data is the United Nations Common Database, http://globalis.gvu.unu.edu/indicator_detail.cfm?IndicatorID=50&Country=SV.

69. UNDP, *Democracy in Latin America*, 39.

70. Putnam, *Making Democracy Work*, 11.

71. UNDP, *Democracy in Latin America*, 131.

72. Dalton, "General Martínez" (1962), trans. in Dalton, *Poems*, 24. Spanish original in Dalton, *El turno del ofendido*, 103.

73. UNDP, *Democracy in Latin America*, 189.

74. Grandin, *The Last Colonial Massacre*, xiv.

75. I use the word "development" with care, cognizant of the critique by Arturo Escobar and others. While I recognize the discursive production of underdevelopment as an important element in to North-South dynamics, I prefer Marc Edelman's take on the debate, recognizing, with him, that many people (at least many people I know in El Salvador) think of it in terms of "improved well-being" or "rising living standards"—and they want those things. See Edelman, *Peasants Against Globalization*, 10.

76. Appadurai, "Hope and Democracy," 31.

77. Almeida, *Waves of Protest*, 10.

78. Saldaña-Portillo, *The Revolutionary Imagination in the Americas and the Age of Development*, 6–7.

79. Ferguson, *Expectations of Modernity*, 10, 13.

80. As the UNDP describes it, by 1996, "once the bubble of peace passed, old problems reappeared": lack of job opportunities, increasing inequality, rising political polarization, crime. Hurricane Mitch in 1998 and two 2001 earthquakes made things worse. But by then people had heard many success stories from migrants who

had traveled North. Estimates of how much emigration increased between 1990 and 2000 range from 70 to 400 percent. UNDP, *Informe sobre el desarrollo humano El Salvador 2005*.

81. Coutin, *Nations of Emigrants*, 123.

82. Grupo Conjunto, *Informe del Grupo Conjunto para la Investigación de Grupos Armados Ilegales con Motivación Política en El Salvador*. See Chapter 2.

83. Interview with author, San Salvador, tape recording, 3 June 1998.

84. Political scientist William Stanley estimates the war-era regular army as comprising about 20,000, and noted 30,000 part-time civil defense and village patrols in the countryside, as well as about 10,000 FMLN in areas the guerrillas controlled. After the war, he writes, "in effect, forces of vigilance abruptly dropped from roughly 75,000 during wartime to around 6,000" (Stanley et al., *Risking Failure*, 16).

85. The peace accords contained provisions for job training and land redistribution to ex-combatants, but these were limited in scope and poorly administered. Given the economic realities in the country, even well carried out programs had limited possibilities of success.

86. Interview with author, San Salvador, tape recording, 12 June 1998.

87. Interview with author, San Salvador, tape recording, March 1998.

88. Interview with author, San Salvador, tape recording, June 1998.

89. Engels, "The Demoralization of the English Working Class," 48.

90. Appadurai, "Hope and Democracy," 31.

91. Miyazaki, *The Method of Hope*, 23.

92. Roy, "Into the Inferno."

Chapter 6. Unknowing the Other

1. In the biopolitical sense in which governance entails managing populations as biological entities, killing through death squads is not quite the same as letting die through bus accidents (in poorly managed public transportation and infrastructure) or childhood pneumonia (as a result of poverty and lack of access to health care). For the theory, see Foucault, "*Society Must Be Defended*", 240–44. For illustrations, see Moodie, "Microbus Crashes and Coca-Cola Cash."

2. Povinelli, "The Child in the Broom Closet."

3. Joan Didion had no such qualms, invoking Joseph Conrad directly in her *noir*-ish war-era volume *Salvador*. I still admire the essay.

4. Though Roque Dalton, a committed Marxist, wrote this in the 1960s in a different political moment, the poem has reinvigorated resonance in the contemporary diaspora. It circulates on Salvadoran-American blogs and web sites, pointing to the suffering of undocumented migrants. "Love Poem," in Dalton, *Poems*, 47. Spanish original in Dalton, *Las historias prohibidas del pulgarcito*, 199–200.

5. I offer a typical, if hyperbolic, slice of commentary, by the television pundit Bill O'Reilly, interviewing Lisa Ling, who made a documentary for the National Geographic Explorer television channel on Salvadoran gangs: "Now, I spent some time in El Salvador in the war down there in the early '80s, and that was the most

vicious war you can imagine. So, there is a vicious strain in that society for whatever reasons, poverty, whatever. But these MS-13 guys [gang members] are particularly nasty, are they not?" (Bill O'Reilly, "Gangs Migrating Between Nations," a segment on *The O'Reilly Factor*, 10 February 2006, Fox News Network, transcript uploaded 14 March 2006 through database Academic Search Premiere).

6. For an article in this mode, see, for example, Wallace, "You Must Go Home Again."

7. Deportations from the United States surged after the passage of the 1996 Illegal Immigration Reform and Immigrant Responsibility Act and the Antiterrorism and Effective Death Penalty Act. Both laws allowed expulsion of permanent residents for minor offenses such as drunk driving, gambling, or shoplifting. The coincidence of deportations and the appearance of gangs gave rise to a powerful belief, seen especially in sensational U.S. media reports, that these gangs organized across borders (in the United States, this conviction intensified in an increasingly anti-immigrant climate, especially after the events of 11 September 2001). However, long-term research suggests that the transnational nature of the gangs is limited. Deportees brought a certain transnational cultural model—a distinctly identifiable image—of youth gangs. But the vast majority of gang members in the 1990s had never left Central America, according to Cruz and Portillo in *Solidaridad y violencia en las pandillas de gran San Salvador*. They found that "only 16.3 percent of [one thousand] interviewed gang members mentioned having been in the United States . . . [and of those who had been deported], only 15.5 percent maintained contact with gangs." See also Washington Office on Latin America (WOLA), "Executive Summary."

8. For research that takes gang members as a point of understanding links between transnationalism, migration, and U.S. security, see Zilberg, "Refugee Gang Youth," 61–89, and Coutin, *Nations of Emigrants*, especially 149–75.

9. Comaroff and Comaroff, "Criminal Obsessions After Foucault." They discuss a seeming reversal of Foucault's genealogy of penality. Foucault theorized a trajectory from public spectacles of torture to enclosed, regimented prisons that would create docile bodies (*Discipline and Punish*).

10. Durkheim, *The Division of Labor in Society*; Comaroff and Comaroff, "Law and Disorder in the Postcolony," 21.

11. Foucault, *Discipline and Punish*; Foucault, *History of Sexuality*.

12. Girard, *The Scapegoat*.

13. For thinking on the self-Other relationship, consult Sartre, *Being and Nothingness*; de Beauvoir, *The Second Sex*; Said, *Orientalism*.

14. See Sedgwick, "Privilege of Unknowing: Diderot's *The Nun*," 25.

15. Bourdieu, *Outline of a Theory of Practice*, 78.

16. Žižek, *The Essential Žižek*, 17–30 (emphasis original). Thanks to an anonymous reviewer for pointing this quote out to me.

17. Daniel, *Charred Lullabies*, 191.

18. See Chari and Verdery, "Thinking Between the Posts," 35; also Gilmore, *Golden Gulag.*

19. Peterson, "Unsettled Remains," 214.

20. See Tilley, *Seeing*; Peterson, "The Politics of Misrecognition"; Peterson, "Unsettled Remains."

21. Interview with author, San Salvador, tape recording, June 1998.

22. Frazier, *Salt in the Sand*, 219.

23. Sedgwick, "Privilege of Unknowing," 25.

24. Scarry, "The Difficulty of Imagining Other Persons," 285, 288.

25. Gordon, "Introduction to the New Edition," in *Ghostly Matters*, xvi.

26. *La Prensa Gráfica*, "'El Directo autor de 17 homicidios," 10 February 1999, 68.

27. Carlos Ramos, "El Salvador con el más alto índice de homicidios en A.L.," *La Prensa Gráfica*, 9 February 1999.

28. Godoy, in *Popular Injustice*, makes a parallel argument about Guatemala, a similar postwar site experiencing high crime rates. Jean and John Comaroff have discussed crime along these lines as well. See "Criminal Obsessions After Foucault." See also Rosas, "The Biopolitical Violences of the U.S.-Mexico Borderlands and Other 'Criminal' Knowledges."

29. Comaroff and Comaroff, "Millennial Capitalism"; Scheper-Hughes, "Specificities."

30. Smutt and Miranda, *El fenómeno de las pandillas en El Salvador*; Cruz and Portillo, *Solidaridad y violencia en las pandillas de gran San Salvador*; DeCesare, "From Civil War to Gang War," 283–313; Zilberg, "Fools Banished from the Kingdom"; Yngvesson and Coutin, "Backed by Papers"; Coutin, *Nations of Emigrants*, 17–45.

31. See Halberstam, *Skin Shows*, for an examination of how monstrous criminal bodies such as Dracula or Mr. Hyde are imagined as foreign.

32. *Vertice*, "El hijo de Dora Alicia," Sunday supplement of *El Diario de Hoy*, 9 May 1999.

33. Marcos Aleman, "Seventeen-Year-Old Killer Stuns Violence-Numbed El Salvador," Associated Press article published in *Idaho Falls Post-Register*, 23 May 1999.

34. See *El Diario de Hoy*, "Flores lleva mano dura a San Miguel," 28 November 2003; Daniel Valencia and Sergio Arauz, "'Para mí era ridículo que metieron presa a la gente sólo porque tiene tatuajes': Entrevista Rodrigo Ávila," *El Faro*, 9 January 2006, http://www.elfaro.net (accessed 30 May 2006).

35. In July 1995 four police agents were arrested along with local businessmen and accused of forming the vigilante antidelinquent squad (they were later exonerated under suspicious circumstances).

36. *La Prensa Gráfica*, "'El Directo' autor de 17 homicidios," 10 February 1999, 68; *Vertice*, "El hijo de Dora Alicia."

37. *La Prensa Gráfica*, "A sus 16 años de edad: 17 homicidios," 12 January 1999, 24. (El Directo turned seventeen soon after his arrest.)

38. In 1998 a new Criminal Code and Criminal Procedures Code went into effect, to much criticism from government leaders. As Edgardo Alberto Amaya of El Salvador's FESPAD (Fundación de Estudios para la Aplicación del Derecho) writes, "These new conditions transformed public opinion. . . . After 1998, the public began to think that the new legislation was a factor in the growth of ordinary crime, and the perception led to a major shift in public support for authoritarian postures" (Amaya, "Security Policies in El Salvador," 137).

39. *Teleprensa*, 20 April 1999, Channel 33 (San Salvador). See Zilberg, "Gangster in Guerrilla Face," 37–57, for another commentary on this ongoing trope of laws from Switzerland.

40. Moodie, "Seventeen Years, Seventeen Murders."

41. Halberstam, *Skin Shows*, 3.

42. Moral panic is a mass-mediated reaction "out of all proportion to the actual threat offered." In Stuart Hall's analysis, the source of hegemonic elite agreement on the problems of crime (of mugging in early 1970s England, in his particular case) is capitalist crisis manifesting in class polarization and intensified racism. See Hall et al., *Policing the Crisis*.

43. These are all headlines from Salvadoran newspapers in 1998–99. Such articles date back to at least 1995.

44. Popkin, *Peace Without Justice*, 240.

45. *La Prensa Gráfica*, "Funcionarios coinciden en reformar ley del menor infractor," 4 May 1999, 5.

46. *El Diario de Hoy*, "Cacería humana: Cientos de policías tras El Directo; Juró vengarse de sus acusadores," 1 May 1999, 1.

47. *El Diario de Hoy*, "San Miguel demanda conocer a 'El Directo,'" 2 May 1999, 3.

48. *CuatroVisión*, Channel 4 (TCS), 3 May 1999 (San Salvador).

49. *Entrevista Al Día*, Channel 12, 5 May 1999 (San Salvador).

50. *El Salvador Proceso* 854, "Opinions," 12 May 1999, http://www.uca.edu.sv/publica/proceso/ (accessed 5 May 2000).

51. Jenny Cruz, "Menor acribilla a deportistas," *La Prensa Gráfica*, 7 June 1999, 18.

52. *La Prensa Gráfica*, "La ley borra los antecedentes," 8 June 1999, 5.

53. Author's field notes, 7–11 June 1999. Articles consulted include Roberto Alas and David Marroquín, "Menor acabó con la vida de dos futbolistas," *La Prensa Gráfica*, 8 June 1999; Roberto Alas, "Interamiento a menor acusado de homicidios," *La Prensa Gráfica*, 10 June 1999, 20; José Zometa, "Identifican a cómplice de menor acusado de crímenes," *La Prensa Gráfica*, 22 June 1999, 12. One article, "Pandillas, drogas, pobreza: Heriberto," and an accompanying sidebar, "La Margaritas, una comunidad en olvido" (Carlos Ramos, *La Prensa Gráfica*, 11 June 1999, 8), does explore the possibilities opened up in the agentive moment of the El Directo biospectacle: it attempts to understand how the suspect, "Heriberto M.," became what he did. It points to the desperate conditions of the suspect's life, noting that he lived in a six-by-three-meter shack in a crowded illegal settlement where the average family earned less than $100 a month (coincidentally, it was Las Margaritas, a slum on the road to the volcano just next to my rented house in Santa Tecla). He had been a good student, reportedly, until he turned to the gangs. "Here, the majority [of young people] are ruined," his brother said, alluding to gangs and drugs.

54. Zilberg, "Gangster in Guerrilla Face."

55. Zilberg, "Fools Banished from the Kingdom," 767.

56. DeCesare, "How Edgar Bolaños Became Shy Boy in El Salvador."

57. DeCesare, "From Civil War to Gang War," 291.

58. James Siegel writes of a similar kind of phenomenon in Indonesia in the 1990s, thirty years after large-scale massacres of suspected Marxists. Indonesians, he writes, have a "fear of something they cannot locate." He explains, "They cannot

find a name or face for their fears. The people they fear appear as ordinary and like themselves" (Siegel, *A New Criminal Type in Jakarta*, 5–6).

59. Interview with author, tape recording, San Salvador, 14 February 1998.

60. Donna DeCesare found that youth, including gang members, consider this act "begging" if they are unarmed; but, she notes, most Salvadorans, terrified of tattoos, feel too threatened to say "no." DeCesare, "How Edgar Bolaños Became 'Shy Boy' in El Salvador."

61. Migrants from humble origins who returned flush with cash, with Nikes on their feet, were often critiqued in the same way, or even blamed for increasing crime. See Coutin, *Nations of Emigrants,* 165, 167.

62. Gladwell, *Blink*, 23, 43.

63. Interview with author, tape recording, San Salvador, May 1998.

64. Interview with author, tape recording, San Salvador, 1 May 1998.

65. Interview with author, tape recording, San Salvador, February 1998.

66. Virginia Tilley writes that Salvadoran scholar Rodolfo Barón Castro was the first to say this. In 1956 he reported in a Madrid conference that, with only 10 percent of the people indigenous (and those atomized), "El Salvador is the country that has the highest degree of *mestizaje* in America." Tilley, *Seeing Indians,* 216.

67. Vasconcelos, *La raza cósmica.*

68. See Masferrer, "El mínimum vital." The idea echoed over the next century in Salvadoran politics—including the FMLN's 2009 presidential campaign.

69. López Vallecillos, "La sensibilidad lírica de Alfredo Espino," 7. The poems, written before his death at age twenty-eight in 1928, were published in 1936.

70. See Tilley, *Seeing Indians*, xvii–xviii, for a discussion on terminology in reference to Salvadoran indigenous groups.

71. Brandt Peterson points to the term *indio chele* as evidence of the tremendous fluidity of the term "indio" and race itself as a social construction. He suggests that by the time of the 1932 massacre "indio" was "a labile term no longer anchored to specific people or places, perhaps best thought of as a way of looking at society and the complicated grammars of difference and sameness of mestizo nationalism." Peterson, "Unsettled Remains," 77, drawing from de Guevara, "El añil de los 'indios cheles.'"

72. For an insightful discussion of these intertwined categories (in the context of Cuzco, Peru), see De la Cadena, *Indigenous Mestizos.*

73. Pierre Bourdieu writes in *Distinction*, "Taste, a class culture turned into nature, that is *embodied*, helps to shape the class body." The classifying principle is that everything the body ingests becomes "the most indisputable materialization of class taste, . . . first in the seemingly most natural features of the body, the dimensions (volume, height, weight) and shapes (round or square, stiff or supple, straight or curved) or its visible forms" (190). Of course "taste" is not merely a choice among poor Salvadorans.

74. Lindo-Fuentes et al., *Remembering a Massacre in El Salvador.*

75. Stepan and Lawrence Taylor agree that "Lombroso's influence, and generally that of the Italian school of criminology, is apparent in the many references to Lombroso in Latin American anthropological and criminological writing" (Stepan, *The Hour of Eugenics*, n. 34, 51). See also Taylor, *Born to Crime.*

76. See Lombroso and Lombroso, *Criminal Man*; Lombroso, *Crime, Its Causes and Remedies*.

77. Judith Halberstam demonstrates how well modeled on the Lombrosian "born criminal" Dracula was. She points to specific references to Lombroso in Bram Stoker's original 1897 text. She argues that the fact that the provincial schoolteacher Mina cites Lombroso indicates that such ideas of criminality and degeneracy were widespread in Europe—at least to an educated readership. See Halberstam, *Skin Shows*, 93. Gould, in *The Mismeasure of Man*, documents the connection as well.

78. Historian Sajid Alfredo Herrera Mena has found references to Lombroso in Salvadoran newspapers in the 1890s. See his " 'No me muera, sino que se arrepienta el criminal y viva' " in *Los rostros de la violencia*, 189–223.

79. Marx, "Crime and Primitive Accumulation," 47.

80. Gould and Lauria-Santiago, *To Rise in Darkness*; Lauria-Santiago, *An Agrarian Republic*, 229, 220.

81. *Boletín Oficial de la Policia*, "Los factores del delito," December 1934, 43.

82. Gould and Lauria-Santiago, *To Rise in Darkness*.

83. Peterson, "Unsettled Remains," 77, drawing from Marroquín, "El problema indígena en El Salvador."

84. Parkman, *Nonviolent Insurrection in El Salvador*, 21.

85. Parkman, *Nonviolent Insurrection*, 21.

86. Parkman, *Nonviolent Insurrection*, 26.

87. Parkman, *Nonviolent Insurrection*, 56.

88. José Alfredo Ramirez Fuentes, "El anticomunismo en El Salvador: Las acciones del estado y los sectores de la derecha salvadoreña como factores de la guerra civil de los años ochenta."

89 Commission for the Truth in El Salvador, 4–5, 54.

90. And the *indio* is not irrelevant here; Brandt Peterson reports that the National Civilian Police, in 2002, posted on its web site an explanation of postwar violence that said, in part, "El Salvador has a long history of violence, beginning with the fact that the indigenous race that peopled these lands of hundreds of years ago possessed violent characteristics. One can suppose that these genes have passed on from generation to generation, a situation increased through the mixes with other races. Given this, it is not surprising that we currently suffer from attacks of rage so common among our population, which in most cases end in violent acts against the self and against the other." Translation from Peterson, "Unsettled Remains," 221, citing Policía Nacional Civil, "La violencia social en El Salvador." The site was quickly taken down after protests.

91. *El Diario de Hoy*, "Censuran canciones vulgares," 29 June 1999, 1.

92. *El Diario de Hoy*, "Radios se autoregularán," 30 June 1999, 1.

93. J. Dutriz, E. Schaeuffler and E. Luna, "El Directo" (1999), http://www.geocities.com/Yosemite/2507 (accessed October 2001).

94. The first suspected victims were found in wells in the marginal barrios of San Miguel.

95. Hallett, in "Operation Super Iron First," offers an insightful discursive analysis of the war of words that accompanied the war on gangs in 2003 El Salvador,

in which the state produces its enemies in order to produce itself. Other critical analyses of *mano dura* and antigang initiatives as a state-building act (the "body through which the body politic is being constructed") include Gema Santamaria, "Gangs as *Homo Sacer*" and Hume, "Mano Dura."

96. El Faro, "Flores propone reformas a ley antimaras," *El Faro*, 10 November 2003, http://www.elfaro.net (accessed 11 November 2003).

97. They released 91 percent of arrestees (19,275 in the first year) for unconstitutionality and lack of evidence. Francisco Hernández Cáceres, "Arrancó plan Súper Mano Dura," *El Faro* 10 March 2005, http://www.elfaro.net (accessed 26 May 2006); Washington Office on Latin America (WOLA), "Youth Gangs in Central America," 11, citing Martínez Ventura, *Limites democráticos al poder penal*, 401.

98. Amnesty International, *El Salvador Report 2005*.

99. Kincaid, "Demilitarization and Security in El Salvador and Guatemala."

100. Godoy, *Popular Injustice*; Kincaid, "Demilitarization and Security in El Salvador and Guatemala."

101. In late July 2007 the electronic journal *Contrapunto Revista Latinoamericana* published an article on recent horrific murders that began, "In the daily conversations of hundreds of Salvadorans on the increase in violence and murder in Salvador, there's a popular phrase: 'Today we're worse off than before [*hoy estamos peor que antes*]—at least during the war we knew who was guilty,'" http://www.contrapunto.com.ec/contrapuntoNew/foro_detalle.php?IDPAGINA=2000 (accessed 28 September 2007).

102. The Súper Mano Dura package of antigang reforms, passed in July 2005, was negotiated over two months in a national forum, which included Saca, the judicial branch, the police, and human rights agencies—but no group representing gangs or ex-gang members. It attempted to circumvent the constitutional limitations that killed the original Plan Mano Dura and its proposed legislation through the revival of older laws on illicit association, and focused on narcotrafficking and murder for hire. It created new antigang police and military units and raised sentencing limits (Francisco Hernández Cáceres, "Arrancó plan Súper Mano Dura," *El Faro*, 10 March 2005). See Coutin, *Nations of Emigrants*, 167–75, for an analysis of how Súper Mano Dura was carried out under Saca.

103. César Castro Fagoaga, Raúl Benítez and Edu Ponces, "'Los mareros han hecho de las cárceles auténticos resorts': Entrevista con Pepe Morataya," *El Faro*, 29 May 2006, http://www.elfaro.net (accessed May 2006).

104. OSAC, *2006 Crime and Safety Report*; Daniel Valenica, "El Salvador arrasa en informe sobre violencia," 15 December 2008, http://www.elfaro.net/secciones/Noticias/20081215/noticias2_20081215.asp (accessed 21 July 2009).

Epilogue

1. Such a realization sent anthropologist Billie Jean Isbell to write a novel, as she describes in *Finding Cholita*, x.

2. *Democracy Now!* Interview by Amy Goodman with Roberto Lovato.

3. Luis Romero Pineda, "Gobierno de Funes será 'el turno del ofendido,'" *Dia-*

rio CoLatino, 17 March 2009, http://www.diariocolatino.com/es/20090317/nacio-nales/64867/ (accessed 21 July 2009).

4. Fragment of Dalton, "The Turn of the Offended," in Freedman, "A Grass-roots Drive Pushes ARENA Out of Government." Spanish original in Dalton, *El turno del ofendido*, 10.

5. CID-Gallup Latinoamérica found 81 percent support for Funes in a survey during May 2009, higher than any incoming president had had in the previous 20 years (*ContraPunto*, "Funes con más de 81 por ciento de aprobación," 22–26 May 2009 (accessed 21 July 2009).

6. Berlant, "Cruel Optimism," 21. I also write this epilogue watching ongoing news of the aftermath of the June 2009 coup in Honduras, which at this moment seems to be threatening any sense of durable democratic transitions in the region.

7. Miyazaki, *The Method of Hope*, 23.

8. In my field notes of August 2006 (Santa Tecla), I wrote of a conversation with Doña Griselda, a longtime friend: "[She says] television news has cut down on crime. Order of Rodrigo Ávila [the head of the National Civilian Police] (rumor, not proven). Censorship. Even in [the sensationalist television news program] *Cuatro-Visión*. Hiding things, except arrests of *maras* [gangs]. *Maras, maras, maras. Pandillas* [gangs]. And the *mano dur* was a total failure, it just made the *mareros más bravos* [the gang members more fierce]. Now they're focusing on terrorism."

9. The PNC would proclaim a decrease in violence in the first half of the year, with 220 fewer killings than in the same period the year before (for a total of 1,672 homicides between January and June 2008; about nine dead a day in a country of six million). See *ContraPunto*, "Menos asesinatos en primer semestre," 17 July 2008; "Bajan los homicidios en El Salvador," 1 August 2008, http://www.contrapunto.com.sv (accessed 17 July and 1 August 2008); Daniel Valencia, "14 mil salvadoreños asesinados en País Seguro," *El Faro*, 2 June 2008, http://www.elfaro.net (accessed 2 June 2008). The *El Faro* article, reporting on 14,003 murders between June 2004 and April 2007, also points to the continued weakness of the judicial system, noting that, according to the UNDP, only 14 percent of murder cases went to trial during that time, and only 3 percent of those trials ended in conviction.

10. O. Iraheta, J. López, L. Ábrego, "Asesinan a 13 personas diarias en el país," *El Diario de Hoy*, 16 June 2009, http://www.elsalvador.com (accessed 21 July 2009).

11. Most of these cases appear in one article in *El Diario de Hoy*, "Asesinan a dos víctimas de extorsiones el fin de semana," 19 July 2009 (accessed 21 July 2009); see also Iris Lima and Gerardo Orellana, "Matan a menor por negarse a entrar pandilla," *El Diario de Hoy*, 14 July 2009 (accessed 21 July 2009).

12. *La Prensa Gráfica*, editorial, "La ley de la selva," 26 June 2009, http://www.laprensa.com.sv (accessed 21 July 2009).

13. David Marroquín, "Maras y narcos entre prioridades," *El Diario de Hoy*, 1 June 2009, (accessed 21 July 2009). Predictably, this news was accompanied by demands that the new government *do something*. On 11 June 2009, the Funes administration announced a plan that involved improving policing (including better compensation and depuration of the forces) (Stefany Jovel, "Funes promete alivio económico a policies y mejorar condiciones laborales," *La Prensa Gráfica*, 11 June 2009, http://www.laprensagrafica.com/el-salvador/judicial/38845–funes-promete-

alivio-economico-policias-y-mejorar-condiciones-laborales.html (accessed 21 July 2009); within a month critics pounced. "The plan announced by the authorities of the government to stop the national killing spree still has not produced any results. Between Thursday night and yesterday [Friday] afternoon, police sources registered the murders of 16 people in different parts of the country," one article in *El Diario de Hoy* announced. The new security and justice minister, Manuel Melgar, insisted crime was slowly decreasing. "PNC registra 16 asesinatos en menos de 24 horas," 10 July 2009, http://www.elsalvador.com/mwedh/nota/nota_completa.asp?idCat=8613&idArt=3813415 (accessed 21 July 2009).

14. Anthropologist Ainhoa Montoya, carrying out fieldwork on Salvadoran postwar violence in 2008–2009, tells me that in her research "the war" remained an explicit comparative reference in discussions of contemporary crime in El Salvador (personal communication, 13 June 2009, Rio de Janeiro).

15. Field notes from interview with author, Santa Tecla, 31 May 2008. Three Salvadoran congressmen from the ARENA party, representatives to the Central American Parliament (PARLACEN), and their driver, were murdered on 19 February 2007; the four Guatemalan police officers who confessed to the killings were murdered in prison soon after. See James McKinley, Jr., "In Guatemala, Officers' Killings Echo Dirty War," *New York Times*, 5 March 2007, http://www.nytimes.com (accessed 20 April 2009). We must recall that references to memory and history ("It was never like this before!") are about feelings in the present, not objective measures of violence in the past. Ondina may have been referring to a "before" that incorporated my project ("before when you were here doing your research on crime").

16. Political scientist Mo Hume theorizes a normalization or banalization of violence in her San Salvador-based research of the middle of the first decade of 2000. See Hume, "The Myths of Violence." During my research in El Salvador each year in 2003–2008, I continued to find much fear and anxiety among people I knew in a variety of economic situations, but perhaps younger people such as Juan, Alfredo and Daniel represent a different attitude in the postwar generation.

17. The Salvadoran population distribution is 35.4 percent under age 14, with a median age of 22.5, according to 2009 estimates in the CIA World Factbook.

18. Field notes during and after our conversation in Santa Tecla, 29 May 2008. FESPAD compiled a list, "Probable Political Assassinations in El Salvador, March 2006–July 2008," translated into English through CISPES: http://www.cispes.org/index.php?option=com_content&task=view&id=444&Itemid=31 (accessed 21 July 2009). It includes a report of the murder of Walter Ayala Ulloa of the FMLN Youth of Santo Tomás, who had reportedly been publicly threatened by the ARENA mayor of the town days before his disappearance on 21 May 2008. His body appeared the next day in a cemetery in Ciudad Delgado. CISPES reports that a number of assassinations of FMLN activists went uninvestigated or unreported during the campaign. See CISPES, "El Salvador Elections Observation Report, January 18 Elections."

19. See Alexei Barrionuevo, "U.S. Studies Rebels' Data for Chávez Link," *New York Times*, 14 March 2007 (accessed 20 April 2009).

20. In June 2005, as crime rates spiraled upward, discussions of whether or not gang activities could be considered terrorism came out in the open. See the quality

of public alarm over violence in the 21 June 2005 *La Prensa Gráfica* editorial, "The Unstoppable Wave of Homicidal Violence" (*La imparable ola de violencia homicida*). In field notes on 22 June 2005, I note that people all around were discussing the case of William López, a popular football player murdered by gang members in the city of Quetzaltepeque. When two suspects were arraigned in court, the judge refused to charge them with terrorism, despite police demands. See Milton Grimaldi and David Marroquín, "FGR y jueces no aplicarán terrorismo," *La Prensa Gráfica*, 22 June 2005, 12. See also, for example, Wilfredo Salamanca, "Terrorismo: Nuevo cargo contra pandilleros," *El Diario de Hoy*, 21 June 2005 (accessed 20 April 2009): "Facing the wave of homicides committed with excessive barbarity (*lujo de barbarie*) by gang members, the National Civilian Police confirmed today that it would charge gang members who have committed murder and illegal arms possession with acts of terrorism." This discussion arose in the midst of the U.S. debate on whether to pass the Central American-Dominican Republic Free Trade Agreement (CAFTA), and, in El Salvador, whether anyone would want to invest in such a violent country— indeed, whether terrorism charges would make things worse since terrorist violence might also turn off investors. In a semiotic stream of associations, on the same day (22 June) an article appeared describing how at an Organization of American States meeting, a U.S. trade representative linked Venezuela's Hugo Chávez to terrorist movements across the continent ("Acusan Chávez de instigar crisis," *El Diario de Hoy*, 22 June 2005). On television, William Meléndez conducted an interview with PNC subdirector Pedro González, who was adamant that gang members were terrorists; a numbers of telephone callers pointed to the use of the term to scare political opponents, refusing a return to past practices (*Entrevista al día*, 22 June 2005, Channel 12). Another element contributing to the state's focus on violence and threat at the time was the quiet opening of the International Law Enforcement Academy (ILEA), part of a U.S.-sponsored network of police schools that critics fear will reproduce the kinds of graduates that the notorious School of the Americas in Fort Benning, Georgia (now the Western Hemisphere Institute for Security Cooperation), once did. The network began in 1995 under President Bill Clinton, who saw it as a way to combat international drug trafficking, and terrorism. See Enzinna, "Another SOA?" See also debate over Enzinna's article in the CISPES web site, "Getting Personal: Cuéllar and the ILEA," http://www.cispes.org/index.php?option=com_content&task=view&id=438&Itemid=80 (accessed 21 July 2009).

21. See Chapter 2 for extended discussion of the term "critical." For an example of the new critical code-switching, in December 2008, government security bodies came out with a sensationalist report that there were forty armed illegal groups roaming the countryside, especially in the areas where the guerrilla forces of the FMLN had once been in power (and also in some areas where in 2007 FMLN municipal governments had just been elected). As journalist Juan José Dalton wrote of the sudden revelation, "In a territory as small as El Salvador, with more and more highways crossing it and with the institutional presence of the State, how can forty illegal groups with weapons of war move about freely without even one having been arrested? This can mean one of two things: either it's an absurd political campaign or it's another demonstration of the incapacity public security bodies. . . . Another question is why this 'exploded' right in the middle of a political campaign." "Hasta

40 grupos armados hay en El Salvador," *ContraPunto* (15 December 2008), http://www.contrapunto.com.sv (accessed 21 July 2009).

22. For description of anti-fraud vigilance in the March 2009 elections, see Freedman, "A Grassroots Drive Pushes ARENA Out of Government." Freedman reports widespread belief that the January 2009 legislative and municipal elections (in which the FMLN lost the mayoralty of San Salvador for the first time since 1997) had been filled with fraud. Many Salvadorans I know insisted that the previous (2004) presidential elections were fraudulent.

23. The strikes were against the privatization of the Salvadoran Institute for Social Security (ISSS), which provided health care for about 15 percent of Salvadorans (generally those employed in the formal economy) (Selva Sutter, "La decentralización y la reforma de salud neoliberal," 1031). Public hospitals for the poor, mainly administered by the Ministry of Public Health and Social Assistance, attended to about 80 percent of the population. A system of private clinics served about 5 percent. Since 1992, the government had been proposing reforms to state-run medical systems (along the lines of structural adjustment promoted by the World Bank and Interamerican Development Bank) (see Smith-Nonini, "Health 'Anti-Reform' in El Salvador"). There had been smaller protests before 2002, including mobilizations in 1999.

24. Schuld, "Who Will Have the Hospitals?"; Estudios Centroamericanos, "Crónica del mes: Noviember-diciembre"; Almeida, *Waves of Protest.*

25. U.S.-El Salvador Sister Cities Network, "The Salvadoran Anti-Terrorism Law and Its Mirror Image." The legislation, which passed 21 September 2006, has been compared to the USA Patriot Act.

26. Marx, *The Eighteenth Brumaire of Louis Bonaparte*, 15. See http://www.youtube.com/watch?v=jAxy4RTsv0I for images of Belloso's arrest, and http://www.youtube.com/watch?v=s-O2FUDjBZc for the videotape of his confession (accessed 20 April 2009).

27. Belloso would be sentenced to 35 years in prison for aggravated homicide on 15 August 2007.

28. There are many accounts of these arrests and debates: see, for example, *El Salvador Proceso 1250*, "¿Actos de terrorismo en El Salvador?" 18 July 2007, http://www.uca.edu.sv/publica/proceso/proceso/proceso.php?id=1250 (accessed 20 April 2009), and *El Salvador Proceso 1251*, "Hablar de terrorismo en El Salvador," 25 July 2007, http://www.uca.edu.sv/publica/proceso/proceso/proceso.php?id=1251 (accessed 20 April 2009). For television reports on the arrests, including images, see http://www.youtube.com/watch?v=-e9Npsw4Xl8 (accessed 20 April 2009).

29. *El Diario de Hoy*, "Los ex-militantes critican al FMLN," 7 July 2007, 8; Geraldine Varela, "ANEP pide profundizar en las investigaciones," 7 July 2007, 4; Karen Molina, "Polémica por la ley contra el terrorismo," 11 July 2007, 4; R. Mendoza and J. Zometa, "Debate: Comisión contra grupos armadas," 13 July 2007; José Zometa, "Saca propone ampliar penas por disturbios," 15 July 2007, 2; C. Monti and D. Marroquín, "Crece apoyo para más penas por disturbios," 16 July 2007, 4; Mirna Jiménez, "Ley Antiterrorista totalmente desproporcionada, asegura Jueza de Paz," *Diario CoLatino*, 18 July 2007, 2; *El Diario de Hoy*, "Seguridad: Mario Belloso reclutaba a pandilleros," 20 July 2007, 4.

30. See for example, "Caso Belloso 'Show': Montaje político," the front-page

headline in a short-lived left-wing weekly *El Independiente*, 16 July 2007. The caption on a photo of Belloso read, "Belloso, la confabulación de la derecha" (Belloso, the invention of the right).

31. Field notes, 17 July 2007, Santa Tecla.

32. Moodie, "'No es una situación crítica'."

Bibliography

Abrams, Philip. "Notes on the Difficulty of Studying the State." *Journal of Historical Sociology* 1, no. 1 (1988): 58–89.

Agamben, Giorgio. *Homo Sacer: Sovereign Power and Bare Life*. Stanford, Calif.: Stanford University Press, 1998.

———. *State of Exception*. Chicago: University of Chicago Press, 2005.

Ahmed, Sarah. "Orientations: Toward a Queer Phenomenology." *GLQ* 12, no. 4 (2006): 543–74.

———. *Queer Phenomenology: Orientations, Objects, Others*. Durham, N.C.: Duke University Press, 2007.

Almeida, Paul D. *Waves of Protest: Popular Struggle in El Salvador, 1925–2005*. Minneapolis: University of Minnesota Press, 2008.

Alonso, Carlos J. *The Burden of Modernity: The Rhetoric of Cultural Discourse in Spanish America*. Oxford: Oxford University Press, 1998.

Alvarenga, Patricia. *Cultura y ética de la violencia: El Salvador 1880–1932*. San José: EDUCA, 1996.

Amaya, Edgardo Alberto. "Security Policies in El Salvador, 1992–2002." In *Public Security and Police Reform in the Americas*, ed. John Bailey and Lucia Dammert. Pittsburgh: University of Pittsburgh Press, 2006.

American Hospital Association. "HIPAA Updated Guidelines for Releasing Information on the Condition of Patients," 1 February 2003. http://www.aha.org/aha/advisory/2003/030201–media-adv.html (accessed 28 February 2008).

Americas Watch Committee and American Civil Liberties Union. *Report on Human Rights in El Salvador*. New York: Vintage, 1982.

Amnesty International. *El Salvador Report 2005*. http://web.amnesty.org/report2005/slv-summary-eng (accessed 15 April 2006).

Anderson, Robin. "Images of War: Photojournalism, Ideology, and Central America." *Latin American Perspectives* 16, no. 2 (1989): 96–114.

Anderson, Thomas P. *Matanza*. Willimantic, Conn.: Curbstone Press, 1992.

———. *The War of the Dispossessed: Honduras and El Salvador, 1969*. Lincoln: University of Nebraska Press, 1981.

Appadurai, Arjun. "Hope and Democracy." *Public Culture* 19, no. 1 (2007): 29–34.

Arendt, Hannah. *The Human Condition*. Chicago: University of Chicago Press, 1958.

Argueta, Manlio. *Un día en la vida*. San Salvador: UCA, 2007.

Armstrong, Robert, and Janet Shenk. *El Salvador: The Face of Revolution*. Boston: South End Press, 1982.

Arnson, Cynthia. "Review of Lawrence Ladukte, *Freedom of Expression in El Sal-

vador: The Struggle for Human Rights and Democracy." *Latin American Politics and Society* 48, no. 1 (2006): 200–204.

———. "Window on the Past: A Declassified History of Death Squads in El Salvador." In *Death Squads in Global Perspective: Murder with Deniability*, ed. Bruce Campbell and Arthur Brenner. New York: St. Martin's, 2000.

Austin, J. L. *How to Do Things with Words.* Cambridge, Mass.: Harvard University Press, 1962.

Babb, Florence. *After Revolution: Mapping Gender and Cultural Politics in Neoliberal Nicaragua.* Austin: University of Texas Press, 2001.

Baker-Cristales, Beth. "Magical Pursuits: Legitimacy and Representation in a Transnational Social Field." *American Anthropologist* 110, no. 3 (2008): 349–59.

———. *Salvadoran Migration to Southern California: Redefining El Hermano Lejano.* Gainesville: University Press of Florida, 2004.

Bakhtin, Mikhail M. *The Dialogic Imagination.* Trans. Michael Holquist. Austin: University of Texas Press, 1981.

Baloyra, Enrique A. *El Salvador in Transition.* Chapel Hill: University of North Carolina Press, 1982.

Bateson, Gregory. *Steps to an Ecology of Mind.* New York: Ballantine, 1972.

Bauman, Richard. *Verbal Art as Performance.* Prospect Heights, Ill.: Waveland Press, 1977.

Beauvoir, Simone de. *The Second Sex.* New York: Vintage, 1989.

Behar, Ruth. "Ethnography: Cherishing Our Second-Fiddle Genre." *Journal of Contemporary Ethnography* 28, no. 5 (1999): 472–84.

———. *The Vulnerable Observer: Anthropology That Breaks Your Heart.* Boston: Beacon Press, 1996.

Benjamin, Walter. "Critique of Violence." In *Reflections: Essays, Aphorisms, Autobiographical Writings*, ed. Peter Demetz. New York: Schocken, 1978.

———. "Theses on the Philosophy of History." In *Illluminations: Essays and Reflections*, ed. Hannah Arendt. New York: Schocken, 1969.

Bercovitch, Joseph, and Richard Jackson. *International Conflict: A Chronological Encyclopedia of Conflicts and Their Management 1945–1995.* Washington, D.C.: Congressional Quarterly, 1997.

Berlant, Lauren. "Cruel Optimism." *differences* 17, no. 3 (2006): 20–36.

———. *The Female Complaint: The Unfinished Business of Sentimentality in American Culture.* Durham, N.C.: Duke University Press, 2008.

———. *The Queen of America Goes to Washington City: Essays on Sex and Citizenship.* Durham, N.C.: Duke University Press, 1997.

Binford, Leigh. *The El Mozote Massacre: Anthropology and Human Righs.* Tuscon: University of Arizona Press, 1996.

———. "Violence in El Salvador: A Rejoinder to Philippe Bourgois's 'The Power of Violence in War and Peace.'" *Ethnography* 3, no. 2 (2002): 201–19.

Bland, Gary. "Assessing the Transition to Democracy." In *Is There a Transition to Democracy in El Salvador?* ed. Joseph S. Tulchin with Gary Bland. Boulder, Colo.: Lynne Reinner, 1992.

Borón, Atilio. "Faulty Democracies? A Reflection on the Capitalist 'Fault Lines' in Latin America." In *Fault Lines of Democracy in Post-Transition Latin Amer-*

ica, ed. Felipe Agüero and Jeffrey Stark. Miami: North-South Center Press, 1998.

Bourdieu, Pierre. *Distinction: A Social Critique of the Judgment of Taste.* Cambridge, Mass.: Harvard University Press, 1984.

———. *Outline of a Theory of Practice.* Trans. Richard Nice. Cambridge: Cambridge University Press, 1977.

———. *Pascalian Meditations.* Stanford, Calif.: Stanford University Press, 1997.

Bourgois, Philippe. "The Power of Violence in War and Peace: Post-Cold War Lessons from El Salvador." *Ethnography* 2, no. 1 (2001): 5–34.

Boutros-Ghali, Boutros. "Democracy: A Newly Recognized Imperative." *Global Governance* 1, no. 1 (1995).

———. "Introduction." In *United Nations and El Salvador 1990–1995.* UN Blue Books Series 4. New York: United Nations, 1995.

Boyce, James K., ed. *Economic Policy for Building Peace: The Lessons of El Salvador.* Boulder, Colo.: Lynne Rienner, 1996.

Braier, Alexander. "Market Reforms in El Salvador Mean New Opportunities for U.S. Business." *Business America* (25 March 1991). http://www.findarticles.com/p/articles/mi_m1052/is_n6_v112/ai_10591878 (accessed 31 January 2007).

Briggs, Charles L. *Learning How to Ask: A Sociolinguistic Appraisal of the Role of the Interview in Social Science Research.* Cambridge: Cambridge University Press, 1986.

———. "Mediating Infanticide: Theorizing Relations Between Narrative and Violence." *Cultural Anthropology* 22, no. 3 (2007): 315–56.

Briggs, Charles L., and Richard Bauman. "Genre, Intertextuality and Social Power." *Journal of Linguistic Anthropology* 2, no. 1 (1992): 131–72.

Brockett, Charles, D. *Political Movements and Violence in Central America.* Cambridge: Cambridge University Press, 2005.

———. "The Structure of Political Opportunities and Peasant Mobilization in Central America." *Comparative Politics* 23 (1991): 253–74.

Brown, Wendy. "Neoliberalism and the End of Liberal Democracy." *Theory and Event* 7, no. 1 (2003): 1–19.

Burchell, Graham. "Liberal Goverent and Techniques of the Self." In *Foucault and Political Reason: Liberalism, Neoliberalism and the Rationalities of Government,* ed. Andrew Barry, Thomas Osborne, and Nikolas Rose. Chicago: University of Chicago Press, 1996.

Burrell, Jennifer L. "Intergenerational Conflict in the Postwar Era." In *Mayas in Postwar Guatemala: Harvest of Violence Revisited,* ed. Walter E. Little and Timothy J. Smith. Tuscaloosa: University of Alabama Press, 2009.

Butler, Judith. *Bodies That Matter: On the Discursive Limits of "Sex".* New York: Routledge, 1993.

———. *Gender Trouble: Feminism and the Subversion of Identity.* New York: Routledge, 1990.

Caldeira, Teresa P. R. *City of Walls: Crime, Segregation and Citizenship in São Paulo.* Berkeley: University of California Press, 1999.

Calhoun, Craig. "The Privatization of Risk." *Public Culture* 18, no. 2 (2006): 257–63.

Call, Charles. "Democratization, War and State-Building: Constructing the Rule of Law in El Salvador." *Journal of Latin American Studies* 35, no. 4 (2003): 827–62.

———. "From Soldiers to Cops: 'War Transitions' and the Demilitarization of Policing in Latin America and the Carribean." Ph.D. dissertation, Stanford University, 1999.

Cárcamo-Huechante, Luis E. "Milton Friedman: Knowledge, Public Culture, and Market Economy in the Chile of Pinochet." *Public Culture* 18, no. 2 (2006): 413–35.

Cardenal, Rodolfo, Ignacio Martin-Baró, and Jon Sobrino, eds. *La voz de los sin voz: La palabra viva de Monseñor Óscar Arnulfo Romero.* San Salvador: UCA, 1980.

Castellanos Moya, Horacio. *El arma en el hombre.* Barcelona: Tusquets, 2001.

Castro Fagoaga, César, Raúl Benítez, and Edu Ponces. " 'Los mareros han hecho de las cárceles auténticos resorts': Entrevista con Pepe Morataya." *El Faro* (29 May 2006). http://www.elfaro.net (accessed 29 May 2006).

Castro Morán, Mariano. *Función politica del ejército salvadoreño en el presente siglo.* San Salvador: UCA, 1984.

Certeau, Michel de. *The Practice of Everyday Life.* Trans. Steven Rendall. Berkeley: University of California Press, 1999.

Chari, Sharad, and Katherine Verdery. "Thinking Between the Posts: Postcolonialism, Postsocialism, and Ethnography After the Cold War." *Comparative Studies in Society and History* 51, no. 1 (2009): 6–34.

Ching, Erik. "Comunismo, indígenas, y la insurreción de 1932." In *Las masas, la matanza y el martinato en El Salvador,* ed. Erik Ching, Carlos Gregorio López Bernal, and Virginia Tilley. San Salvador: UCA, 2007.

———. "In Search of the Party: The Communist Party, the Comintern, and the Peasant Rebellion of 1932 in El Salvador." *Americas* 55, no. 2 (1998): 204–39.

CIA World Factbook. "El Salvador." http://www.cia.gov/library/publications/the-world-factbook/print/es.html (accessed 10 April 2009).

CISPES (Committee in Solidarity with the People of El Salvador). "El Salvador Elections Observation Report, January 18 Elections," 13 February 2009. http://www.cispes.org/index.php?option=com_content&task=view&id=518&Itemid=30 (accessed 21 July 2009).

Clifford, James. "Introduction: Partial Truths." In *Writing Culture: The Poetics and Politics of Ethnography,* ed. James Clifford and George Marcus. Berkeley: University of California Press, 1986.

Cohen, Deborah. *Bordering Modernities: Race, Masculinity, and the Cultural Politics of Mexico-U.S. Migration.* Chapel Hill: University of North Carolina Press, forthcoming.

Cohen, Stanley. *Folk Devils and Moral Panics: The Construction of Mods and Rockers.* London: MacGibbon, 1972.

Coles, Kimberley. *Democratic Designs: International Intervention and Electoral Practices in Postwar Bosnia-Herzegovina.* Ann Arbor: University of Michigan Press, 2007.

Comaroff, Jean, and John L. Comaroff. "Criminal Obsessions After Foucault: Postcoloniality, Policing, and the Metaphysics of Disorder." *Critical Inquiry* 30 (2004): 800–824.

———. "Law and Disorder in the Postcolony: An Introduction." In *Law and Disorder in the Postcolony*, ed. Jean Comaroff and John L. Comaroff. Chicago: University of Chicago Press, 2006.

Comaroff, John L., and Jean Comaroff. "Millennial Capitalism: First Thoughts on Second Comings." *Public Culture* 12, no. 2 (2000): 291–343.

Commission on the Truth for El Salvador (Truth Commission). *De la locura a la esperanza: La guerra de 12 años en El Salvador: Informe de la Comisión de la Verdad para El Salvador.* New York: United Nations, 1993.

———. *From Madness to Hope: The 12–Year War in El Salvador: Report of the Commission on the Truth for El Salvador.* New York: United Nations, 1993. U.S. Institute of Peace, http://www.usip.org/resources/truth-commission-el-salvador (accessed 30 June 2009).

Concertación por la Paz, la Dignidad y la Justicia Social. "Evaluación de 15 años después de la firma de los Acuerdos de Paz en El Salvador." San Salvador, 16 January 2007. http://www.redes.org/scroll/scroller.php (accessed March 2007).

Córdova Macías, Ricardo. *El Salvador en transición: El proceso de paz, las elecciones generales de 1994, y los retos de la gobernabilidad democrática.* San Salvador: FundaUngo, 1994.

Coronil, Fernando. *The Magical State: Nature, Money and Modernity in Venezuela.* Chicago: University of Chicago Press, 1997.

———. "State and Nation in Chávez's Venezuela: Reflections on the State, Illuminating the 2002 Coup." *Anuario de Estudios Americanos* 62, no. 1 (2005).

Coutin, Susan Bibler. *The Culture of Protest: Religious Activism and the U.S. Sanctuary Movement.* Boulder, Colo.: Westview Press, 1993.

———. *Nations of Emigrants: Shifting Boundaries of Citizenship in El Salvador and the United States.* Ithaca, N.Y.: Cornell University Press, 2007.

———. "The Oppressed, the Suspect and the Citizen: Subjectivity in Competing Accounts of Political Violence." *Law and Social Inquiry* 26, no. 1 (2001): 63–94.

Cristiani Burkard, Alfredo Félix. "Address by Mr. Alfredo Félix Cristiani-Burkard, President of the Republic of El Salvador, to the Forty-Eighth Session of the United Nations General Assembly, Fifth Plenary Meeting," 27 September 1993. UN Bibliographic Information System, Dag Hammarskjöld Library Index to Speeches, Meeting Record Symbol A/48/PV.5.

Cruz, José Miguel. *¿Elecciones para qué? El impacto del ciclo electoral en la cultura política salvadoreña.* San Salvador: FLACSO, 2001.

———. "Los factores posibilitadores y las expresiones de la violencia en los noventa." *Estudios Centroamericanos* 588 (1997): 977–91.

———. "La violencia en El Salvador." *Estudios Centroamericanos* 569 (1996): 240–49.

———. "Violence, Citizen Insecurity, and Elite Maneuvering in El Salvador." In *Public Security and Police Reform in the Americas*, ed. John Bailey and Lucia Dammert. Pittsburgh: University of Pittsburgh Press, 2006.

Cruz, José Miguel, and Luis Armando González. "Magnitud de la violencia en El Salvador." *Estudios Centroamericanos* 588 (1997): 953–66.

———. *Sociedad y violencia: El Salvador en la post-guerra*. San Salvador: UCA, 1997.

Cruz, José Miguel, and Nelson Portillo. *Solidaridad y violencia en las pandillas de gran San Salvador: Más allá de la vida loca*. San Salvador: UCA, 1998.

Cruz, José Miguel, Alvaro Trigueros Argüello, and Francisco González. "The Social and Economic Factors Associated with Violent Crime in El Salvador." Paper presented at conference, "Crime and Violence: Causes and Policy Responses," Bogotá, Universidad de los Andes, 4–5 May 1999, part of World Bank project Crime and Violence in Latin America, November 1999. http://www.wblnoo18.worldbank.org/lac/lacinfoclient.nsf (accessed 1 August 2001).

Dahl, Robert. *Polyarchy: Participation and Oppposition*. New Haven, Conn.: Yale University Press, 1972.

———. *A Preface to Democratic Theory*. Chicago: University of Chicago Press, 1956.

Dalton, Roque. *El turno del ofendido*. San Salvador: UCA, 2000.

———. *Las historias prohibidas del pulgarcito*. San Salvador: UCA, 1988.

———. *Poems*. Trans. Richard Schaaf. Willimantic, Conn.: Curbstone, 1984.

———. *Taberna y otros lugares*. San Salvador: UCA, 2000.

Daniel, E. Valentine. *Charred Lullabies: Chapters in an Anthropography of Violence*. Princeton, N.J.: Princeton University Press, 1996.

Danner, Mark. *The Massacre at El Mozote: A Parable of the Cold War*. New York: Vintage, 1994.

Das, Veena. *Critical Events: An Anthropological Perspective on Contemporary India*. Delhi: Oxford University Press, 1995.

———. *Life and Words: Violence and the Descent into the Ordinary*. Berkeley: University of California Press, 2007.

Das, Veena, and Arthur Kleinman. "Introduction." In *Violence and Subjectivity*, ed. Veena Das, Arthur Kleinman, Mamphela Ramphele, and Pamela Reynolds. Berkeley: University of California Press, 2000.

Davis, Diane E. "The Age of Insecurity: Violence and Disorder in the New Latin America." *Latin American Research Review* 41, no. 1 (2006): 178–97.

DeCesare, Donna. "From Civil War to Gang War: The Tragedy of Edgar Bolaños." In *Gangs and Society: Alternative Perspectives*, ed. Louis Kontos, David Brotherton, and Luis Barrios. New York: Columbia University Press, 2003.

———. "How Edgar Bolaños Became Shy Boy in El Salvador." *APF Reporter* 18, no. 4 (1998). http://www.aliciapatterson.org/APF1804/DeCesare/DeCesare.html (accessed 10 April 2009).

De la Cadena, Marisol. *Indigenous Mestizos: The Politics of Race and Culture in Cuzco, Peru, 1919–1991*. Durham, N.C.: Duke University Press, 2000.

DeLugan, Robin. "Census, Map and Museum (Revisted): El Salvador's Postwar Transnational Imagination." *Identities: Global Studies in Cutlure and Power* 15, no. 2 (2008): 171–93.

Derrida, Jacques. "Signature Event Context." In *Limited, Inc.*, ed. Gerald Graff. Evanston, Ill.: Northwestern University Press, 1988.

Didion, Joan. *Salvador*. New York: Washington Square Press, 1983.

Dutriz, J., E. Schaeuffler and E. Luna. "El Directo." 1999. http://www.geocities. com/Yosemite/2507 (accessed October 2001).

División del Gobierno de Estadisticas y el Censo. "El Salvador proyecciones de población del área metropolitana de San Salvador." http://www.digestyc.gob.sv/ DigestycWeb/Estad_Demograficas/ProyeccionesAMSS.htm (accessed 30 June 2009).

Doyle, Michael, Robert Orr, and Ian Johnstone, eds. *Keeping the Peace: Lessons from Multidimensional U.N. Operations in Cambodia and El Salvador.* Cambridge: Cambridge University Press, 1997.

Dreyfus, Hubert. *Being in the World: A Commentary on Heidegger's Being in Time, Division I.* Cambridge, Mass.: MIT Press, 1991.

Dunkerley, James. *The Pacification of Central America: Political Change in the Isthmus, 1987–1993.* New York: Verso, 1994.

Durham, William. *Scarcity and Survival in Central America: Ecological Origins of the Soccer War.* Stanford, Calif.: Stanford University Press, 1979.

Durkheim, Émile. *The Division of Labor in Society.* Trans. George Simpson. New York: Free Press, 1933.

———. *The Elementary Forms of Religious Life.* Trans. Joseph Ward Swain. New York: Free Press, 1965.

Edelman, Marc. *Peasants Against Globalization: Rural Social Movements in Costa Rica.* Stanford, Calif.: Stanford University Press, 1999.

Elshtain, Jean Bethke. *Public Man, Private Woman.* Princeton, N.J.: Princeton University Press, 1981.

Engels, Friedrich. "Crime in Commuist Society." In *Crime and Capitalism: Readings in Marxist Criminology,* ed. David F. Greenberg. Philadelphia: Temple University Press, 1993.

———. "The Demoralization of the English Working Class." In *Crime and Capitalism: Readings in Marxist Criminology,* ed. David F. Greenberg. Philadelphia: Temple University Press, 1993.

Enzinna, Wez. "Another SOA? A Police Academy in El Salvador Worries Critics." *NACLA* 41, no. 2 (2008).

Escobar Velado, Oswaldo. *Patria exacta y otros poemas.* San Salvador: UCA, 2002.

Estudios Centroamericanos. "Editorial: ¿Quince años de paz?" In Edición monográfica, "Problemas de la paz: Violencia, impunidad, deficit institucional . . ." *Estudios Centroamericanos* 701–2 (2007): 195–201.

———. Edición monográfica, "La cultura de la violencia en El Salvador: La violencia y su magnitud, sus costos y los factores posibilitadores." *Estudios Centroamericanos* 588 (1997).

———. "Crónica del mes: Julio–agosto." *Estudios Centroamericanos* 537–38 (1993): 763–73.

———. "Crónica del mes: Noviembre–diciembre." *Estudios Centroamericanos* 649–50 (2002): 1145–51.

Feldman, Allen. *Formations of Violence: The Narrative of the Body and Political Terror in Northern Ireland.* Chicago: University of Chicago Press, 1991.

Ferguson, James. *Expectations of Modernity: Myths and Meanings of Urban Life in the Zambian Copperbelt.* Berkeley: University of California Press, 1999.

Fisher, William F. "Doing Good? The Politics and Antipolitics of NGO Practice." *Annual Review of Anthropology* 26 (1997): 439–64.

Flint, Adam. "Social Movements, NGOs and the State: Contesting Political Space in the Transition to Democracy in El Salvador." Paper presented at Latin American Studies Association Meetings, Chicago, 26 September 1998.

Forché, Carolyn. *The Country Between Us.* New York: HarperCollins, 1981.

Foucault, Michel. *Discipline and Punish: The Birth of the Prison.* Trans. Alan Sheridan. New York: Vintage, 1979.

———. *History of Sexuality.* Vol. 1, *An Introduction.* New York: Vintage, 1990.

———. *Power/Knowledge: Selected Interviews and Other Writings, 1972–1977.* Ed. Colin Gordon. New York: Pantheon, 1980.

———. *"Society Must Be Defended": Lectures at the Collège de France, 1975–76.* Trans. David Macey. New York: Picador, 2003.

Franco, Jean. "Killing Priests, Nuns, Women, Children." In *On Signs,* ed. Marshall Blonsky. Baltimore: Johns Hopkins University Press, 1985.

Frazier, Lessie Jo. *Salt in the Sand: Memory, Violence and the Nation-State in Chile, 1890 to the Present.* Durham, N.C.: Duke University Press, 2007.

Freedman, Elaine, "A Grassroots Drive Pushes ARENA Out of Government," *Revista Envio* 33, April 2009. http://www.envio.org/ni/articulo/3983 (accessed 21 July 2009).

Freud, Sigmund. *Introductory Lectures on Psychoanalysis.* Harmondsworth: Penguin, 1974.

Friedman, Jonathan. "Globalization, Dis-Integration, Re-Organization: The Transformations of Violence." In *Globalization, the State, and Violence,* ed. Jonathan Friedman. Walnut Creek, Calif.: AltaMira Press, 2003.

Friedman, Milton. *Capitalism and Freedom.* Chicago: University of Chicago Press, 1962.

Frühling, Hugo, Joseph S. Tulchin, and Heather A. Golding, eds. *Crime and Violence in Latin America: Citizen Security, Democracy, and the State.* Baltimore and Washington, D.C.: Woodrow Wilson Center Press and Johns Hopkins University Press, 2003.

Fukuyama, Francis. *The End of History and the Last Man.* New York: Free Press, 1992.

Gal, Susan. "A Semiotics of the Public/Private Distinction." *differences* 3, no. 1 (2002): 77–95.

Galtung, Johan. "Violence, Peace and Peace Research." *Journal of Peace Research* 6 (1969): 167–91.

Giddens, Anthony. *Modernity and Self-Identity: Self and Society in the Late Modern Age.* Stanford, Calif.: Stanford University Press, 1991.

Gilmore, Ruth Wilson. *Golden Gulag: Prisons, Surplus, Crisis and Opposition in Globalizing California.* Berkeley: University of California Press, 2006.

Girard, René. *The Scapegoat.* Baltimore: Johns Hopkins University Press, 1986.

Gladwell, Malcolm. *Blink: The Power of Thinking Without Thinking.* New York: Little, Brown, 2005.

Godoy, Angelina Snodgrass. *Popular Injustice: Violence, Community and Law in Latin America.* Stanford, Calif.: Stanford University Press, 2006.

Goffman, Erving. *Frame Analysis: An Essay on the Organization of Experience*. 1974. Boston: Northeastern University Press, 1988.

Goldstein, Donna. *Laughter Out of Place: Race, Class, Violence and Sexuality in a Rio Shantytown*. Berkeley: University of California Press, 2003.

González Iñárritu, Alejandro. *Amores Perros*. Altavista Films, 2000.

Gordon, Avery. "Introduction to the New Edition." In *Ghostly Matters: Haunting and the Sociological Imagination*. Minneapolis: University of Minnesota Press, 2008.

Gould, Jeffrey L. "Revolutionary Nationalism and Local Memories in El Salvador." In *Reclaiming the Political in Latin American History: Essays from the North*, ed. Gilbert M. Joseph. Durham, N.C.: Duke University Press, 2001.

———. *To Rise in Darkness: Revolution, Repression, and Memory in El Salvador, 1920–1932*. Durham, N.C.: Duke University Press, 2008.

Gould, Stephen Jay. *The Mismeasure of Man*. New York: Norton, 1981.

Gramsci, Antonio. *Selections from the Cultural Writings*. Ed. and trans. David Forgacs and Geoffrey Nowell-Smith. London: Lawrence and Wishart, 1985.

———. *Selections from the Prison Notebooks*. Ed. and trans. Quintin Hoare and Geoffrey Smith. New York: International, 1971.

Grandin, Greg. *Empire's Workshop: Latin America, the United States, and the Rise of the New Imperialism*. New York: Metropolitan Books, 2006.

———. *The Last Colonial Massacre: Latin America and the Cold War*. Chicago: University of Chicago Press, 2004.

Green, Linda. *Fear as a Way of Life: Mayan Widows in Rural Guatemala*. New York: Columbia University Press, 1999.

Grupo Conjunto. *Informe del Grupo Conjunto para la Investigación de Grupos Armados Ilegales con Motivación Política en El Salvador*. New York: United Nations, 1994. UN Doc. S/1994/989 (28 July 1994).

de Guevara, Concepción Clara. "El añil de los 'indios cheles.'" *América Indígena* 34, no. 4 (1975).

Guha, Ranajit. *Elementary Aspects of Peasant Insurgency in Colonial India*. Oxford: Oxford University Press, 1983.

Guidos Véjar, Rafael. *Acenso del militarismo en El Salvador*. 2nd ed. San José: UCA, 1982.

———. "La crisis política en El Salvador (1976–1979)." *Estudios Centroamericanos* 369–70 (1979): 507–26.

Gupta, Akhil, and James Ferguson. "Spatializing States: Towards an Ethnography of Neoliberal Governmentality." *American Ethnologist* 29, no. 4 (2002): 981–1002.

Halberstam, Judith. *In a Queer Time and Place: Transgender Bodies, Subcultural Lives*. New York: New York University Press, 2005.

———. *Skin Shows: Gothic Horror and the Technology of Monsters*. Durham, N.C.: Duke University Press, 1995.

Hale, Charles R. *Más que un indio (More Than an Indian): Racial Ambivalence and Neoliberal Multiculturalism in Guatemala*. Santa Fe, N.M.: School of American Research Press, 2006.

Hall, Stuart, Charles Crichter, Tony Jefferson, John Clarke, and Brian Roberts. *Po-

licing the Crisis: Mugging, the State and Law and Order. London: Macmillan, 1978.

Hallett, Miranda Cady. "Operation Super Iron Fist." Manuscript.

Hammond, John L. "Politics and Publishing in Transition in El Salvador." *Latin American Research Review* 30, no. 3 (1995): 210–23.

Harding, Susan Friend. *The Book of Jerry Falwell: Fundamentalist Language and Politics*. Princeton, N.J.: Princeton University Press, 2000.

Hayden, Bridget. *Salvadorans in Costa Rica: Displaced Lives*. Tucson: University of Arizona Press, 2003.

Hernandez, Ester, and Susan Bibler Coutin. "Remitting Subjects: Migrants, Money and States." *Economy and Society* 35, no. 2 (2006): 185–208.

Herrera Mena, Sajid Alfredo. "'No me muera, sino que se arrepienta el criminal y viva': El debate sobre el trabajo penitenciario en los impresos salvadoreños, 1880–1990." In *Los rostos de la violencia*, ed. Ana Margarita Gómez and Sajid Alfredo Herrera Mena. San Salvador: UCA, 2007.

Hill, Jane H. "The Voices of Don Gabriel: Responsibility and Self in a Modern Mexicano Narrative." In *The Dialogic Emergence of Culture*, ed. Dennis Tedlock and Bruce Mannheim. Urbana: University of Illinois Press, 1995.

Hobsbawm, Eric. *Primitive Rebels: Studies of Archaic Forms of Social Movements in the 19th and 20th Centuries*. Manchester: Manchester University Press, 1959.

Holiday, David, and William Stanley. "Building the Peace: Preliminary Lessons from El Salvador." *Journal of International Affairs* 46, no. 2 (1993): 415–38.

———. "Under the Best of Circumstances: ONUSAL and the Challenges of Verification and Institution Building in El Salvador." In *Peacemaking and Democratization in the Western Hemisphere*, ed. Tommie Sue Montgomery. Miami: North-South Center Press, 2000.

Huber, Evelyne, Dietrich Rueschemeyer, and John Stephens. "The Paradoxes of Contemporary Democracy: Formal, Participatory and Social Dimensions." *Comparative Politics* 29, no. 3 (1997): 323–42.

Hume, Mo. "Mano Dura: El Salvador Responds to Gangs." *Development in Practice* 17, no. 6 (2007): 739–51.

———. "The Myths of Violence: Gender, Conflict and Community in El Salvador." *Latin American Perspectives* 35 (2008): 59–76.

Huntington, Samuel. *The Third Wave: Democratization in the Late Twentieth Century*. Norman: University of Oklahoma Press, 1991.

Hurtig, Janise. *Coming of Age in Times of Crisis: Youth, Schooling and Patriarchy in a Venezuelan Town*. New York: Palgrave Macmillan, 2008.

Instituto de Derechos Humanos de la Universidad Centroamericana (IDHUCA). "Los derechos humanos en El Salvador 1997." San Salvador: UCA, 1998.

Instituto Geográfico Nacional Ingeniero Pablo Arnoldo Guzmán. *San Salvador: Monografías del departamento y sus municipos*. San Salvador: Ministerio de Obras Públicas, 1982.

Instituto Universitario de Opinión Pública (IUDOP). "La delincuencia urbana." *Estudios Centroamericanos* 534–35 (1993): 471–79.

———. "Los derechos humanos en la opinión pública salvadoreña." *Estudios Centroamericanos* 558 (1995): 351–66.

Inter-American Commission on Human Rights. *Report on the Situation of Human Rights in El Salvador.* Chap. 2: "Right to Life". Washington, D.C.: OAS, 1978. http://www.cidh.org/countryrep/ElSalvador78eng/chap.2.htm (accessed 24 October 2008).

Isbell, Billie Jean. *Finding Cholita.* Urbana: University of Illinois Press, 2009.

Jenkins, Janis H. "The State Construction of Affect: Political Ethos and Mental Health Among Salvadoran Refugees." *Culture, Medicine and Pscyhiatry* 15 (1991): 139–65.

Johnstone, Barbara. *Stories, Community and Place: Narratives from Middle America.* Bloomington: Indiana University Press, 1990.

Joseph, Miranda. *Against the Romance of Community.* Minneapolis: University of Minnesota Press, 2002.

Kapuscinski, Ryszard. *The Soccer War.* Trans. William Brand. New York: Vintage Books, 1992.

Karl, Terry Lynn. "El Salvador's Negotiated Revolution." *Foreign Affairs* 71, no. 2 (Spring 1992): 47–64.

Kincaid, Douglas. "Demilitarization and Security in El Salvador and Guatemala: Convergences of Success and Crisis." *Journal of Interamerican Studies and World Affairs* 42, no. 4 (2000): 39–58.

Klein, Naomi. *The Shock Doctrine: The Rise of Disaster Capitalism.* New York: Metropolitan Books, 2007.

Kristeva, Julia. "Word, Dialogue, and Novel." In *Desire in Language: A Semiotic Approach to Literature and Art*, ed. Leon S. Roudiez. New York: Columbia University Press, 1980.

Labov, William. *Language in the Inner City: Studies in the Black English Vernacular.* Philadelphia: University of Pennsylvania Press, 1972.

Ladutke, Lawrence. *Freedom of Expression in El Salvador: The Struggle for Human Rights and Democracy.* New York: MacFarland, 2004.

Lauria-Santiago, Aldo. *An Agrarian Republic: Commercial Agriculture and the Politics of Peasant Communities in El Salvador, 1823–1914.* Pittsburgh: University of Pittsburgh Press, 1999.

Lauria-Santiago, Aldo, and Leigh Binford, eds. *Landscapes of Struggle: Politics, Society and Community in El Salvador.* Pittsburgh: University of Pittsburgh Press, 2004.

Lauria-Santiago, Aldo, and Jeffrey L. Gould. " 'They Call Us Thieves and Steal Our Wage': Toward a Reinterpretation of the Salvadoran Rural Mobilization." *Hispanic American Historical Review* 84, no. 2 (2004): 191–237.

Lavine, Harold, and the Editors of *Life. Central America.* Life World Library. New York: Time Inc., 1964.

LeFeber, Walter. *Inevitable Revolutions: The United States in Central America.* New York: Norton, 1984.

Lemon, Alaina. *Between Two Fires: Gypsy Performance and Romani Memory from Pushkin to Postsocialism.* Durham, N.C.: Duke University Press, 2000.

———. "Your Eyes Are Green like Dollars: Counterfeit Cash, National Substance and Currency Apartheid in 1990s Russia." *Cultural Anthropology* 13, no. 1 (1998): 22–55.

LeoGrande, William M. *Our Own Backyard: The United States in Central America, 1977–1992.* Chapel Hill: University of North Carolina Press, 2000.

Lindo-Fuentes, Héctor. *Weak Foundations: The Economy of El Salvador in the Nineteenth Century, 1821–1898.* Berkeley: University of California Press, 1990.

Lindo-Fuentes, Héctor, Erik Ching, and Rafael Lara-Martínez. *Remembering a Massacre in El Salvador: The Insurrection of 1932, Roque Dalton, and the Politics of Historical Memory.* Albuquerque: University of New Mexico Press, 2007.

Lombroso, Cesare. *Crime, Its Causes and Remedies.* Trans. Henry P. Horton. Boston: Little, Brown, 1912.

Lombroso, Gina, and Cesare Lombroso. *Criminal Man.* New York: Putnam's Sons, 1911.

López Vallecillos, Italo. "La sensibilidad lírica de Alfredo Espino." In *Alfredo Espino, Jícaras tristes.* San Salvador: UCA, 1994.

López Vigil, María. *Las mil y una historias de Radio Venceremos.* San Salvador: UCA, 1991.

———. *Muerte y vida en Morazán: testimonio de un sacerdote.* San Salvador: UCA, 1987.

Lovato, Roberto. Interview by Amy Goodman, *Democracy Now!* (16 March 2009). Transcript at http://www.democracynow.org/2009/3/16/fmln_ candidate_ mauricio_funes_wins_el (accessed 10 April 2009).

Low, Setha M. *On the Plaza: The Politics of Public Space and Culture.* Austin: University of Texas Press, 2000.

Lungo Uclés, Mario. *El Salvador in the Eighties: Counterinsurgency and Revolution.* Philadelphia: Temple University Press, 1996.

Malkki, Liisa H. *Purity and Exile: Violence, Memory, and National Cosmology Among Hutu Refugees in Tanzania.* Chicago: University of Chicago Press, 1995.

Mannheim, Bruce, and Dennis Tedlock. "Introduction." In *The Dialogic Emergence of Culture,* ed. Dennis Tedlock and Bruce Mannheim. Urbana: University of Illinois Press, 1995.

Mannheim, Bruce, and Krista Van Vleet. "The Dialogics of Southern Quechua Narrative." *American Anthropologist* 100, no. 2 (1998): 326–46.

Marcus, George. "The Uses of Complicity in the Changing Mise-en-Scène of Anthropological Fieldwork." In *Ethnography Through Thick and Thin,* ed. George Marcus. Princeton, N.J.: Princeton University Press, 1998.

Margold, Jane. "From 'Cultures of Fear and Terror' to the Normalization of Violence: An Ethnographic Case." *Critique of Anthropology* 19, no. 1 (1999): 63–88.

Marroquín, Alejandro. "El problema indígena en El Salvador." *América Indígena* 35, no. 4 (1975): 747–71.

Martin-Baró, Ignacio. *Así piensan los salvadoreños urbanos (1986–7).* San Salvador: UCA, 1989.

———. "Los medios de comunicación masiva y la opinión pública en El Salvador de 1979 a 1989." *Estudios Centroamericanos* 496–97 (1989): 1081–93.

———. "Monseñor: Una voz para un pueblo pisoteado." In *La voz de los sin voz: La palabra viva de Monseñor Óscar Arnulfo Romero,* ed. Rodolfo Cardenal, Ignacio Martin-Baró, and Jon Sobrino. San Salvador: UCA, 1980.

Martínez, Ana Guadalupe. *Las cárceles clandestines de El Salvador: Libertad por el secuestro de un oligarca.* San Salvador: UCA, 1996.

Martínez Ventura, Jaime. *Limites democráticos al poder penal: Reformas de la seguridad pública y la justicia penal.* San Salvador: FESPAD, 2005.

Marx, Karl. *Capital: A Critique of Political Economy, Vol. 1.* Ed. and trans. Friedrich Engels and Samuel Moore. London: Sonnenschein, Lowry, 1967.

———. "Crime and Primitive Accumulation." In *Crime and Capitalism: Readings in Marxist Criminology,* ed. David F. Greenberg. Philadelphia: Temple University Press, 1993.

———. *The Eighteenth Brumaire of Louis Bonaparte.* New York: International Publishers, 1963.

———. *On the Jewish Question.* 1844. http://www.marxists.org/archive/marx/works/1844/jewish-question/ (accessed 14 February 2007).

———. "The Usefulness of Crime." In *Crime and Capitalism: Readings in Marxist Criminology,* ed. David F. Greenberg. Philadelphia: Temple University Press, 1993.

Masferrer, Alberto. *Páginas escogidas.* 2nd ed. San Salvador: Ministerio de Educación, 1961.

Mendez, Jennifer Bickham. "Gender and Citizenship in a Global Context: The Struggle for Maquila Workers' Rights in Nicaragua." *Identities: Global Studies in Culture and Power* 9, no. 24 (2002): 7–38.

Merleau-Ponty, Maurice. *The Phenomenology of Perception.* Trans. Colin Smith. London: Routledge, 2002.

Miyazaki, Hirokazu. *The Method of Hope: Anthropology, Philosophy, and Fijian Knowledge.* Stanford, Calif.: Stanford University Press, 2004.

Molyneux, Maxine. "Twentieth-Century State Formations in Latin America." In *Hidden Histories of Gender and the State in Latin America,* ed. Maxine Molyneux. Durham, N.C.: Duke University Press, 2000.

Montgomery, Tommie Sue. "Getting to Peace in El Salvador: The Roles of the United Nations Secretariat and Onusal." *Journal of Interamerican Studies and World Affairs* 37, no. 1 (1995): 139–72.

———. *Revolution in El Salvador: From Civil Strife to Civil Peace.* Boulder, Colo.: Westview Press, 1995.

Montgomery, Tommie Sue, and Ruth Reitan. "The Good, the Bad and the Ugly: Observing Elections in El Salvador." In *Peacemaking and Democracy in the Western Hemisphere,* ed. Tommie Sue Montgomery. Miami: North-South Center Press, 2000.

Montoya, Rosario. "Socialist Scenarios, Power, and State Formation in Sandinista Nicaragua." *American Ethnologist* 34, no. 1 (2008): 71–90.

Moodie, Ellen. "El Capitán Cinchazo: Blood and Meaning in Postwar El Salvador." In *Landscapes of Struggle: Politics, Society and Community in El Salvador,* ed. Leigh Binford and Aldo Lauria-Santiago. Pittsburgh: University of Pittsburgh Press, 2004.

———. "Microbus Crashes and Coca-Cola Cash: The Value of Death in 'Free-Market' El Salvador." *American Ethnologist* 32, no. 1 (2006): 63–80.

———. " 'No es una situación critica': La despoliticización de la violencia en la situación salvadoreña (1992–1995)." Paper presented at Second Conference on Salvadoran History, University of El Salvador, San Salvador, 19 July 2007.

―――. "Seventeen Years, Seventeen Murders: Biospectacularity and the Production of Post-Cold War Knowledge in El Salvador." *Social Text* 99 (2009): 77–103.

―――. "Wretched Bodies, White Marches and the *CuatroVisión* Public in El Salvador." *Journal of Latin American and Caribbean Anthropology,* forthcoming.

Morris, Rosalind. "The Mute and the Unspeakable: Political Subjectivity, Violence, Crime, and 'the Sexual Thing' in a South African Mining Community." In *Law and Disorder in the Postcolony,* ed. Jean Comaroff and John L. Comaroff. Chicago: University of Chicago Press, 2006.

National Security Archives. *El Salvador: The Making of U.S. Policy, 1977–1984.* Alexandria, Va.: Chadwick-Healey, 1984.

Nelson, Diane M. *Reckoning: The Ends of War in Guatemala.* Durham, N.C.: Duke University Press, 2009.

Nugent, David. "Democracy Otherwise: Struggles over Popular Rule in the Northern Peruvian Andes." In *Democracy: Anthropological Approaches,* ed. Julia Paley. Santa Fe, N.M.: School for Advanced Research Press, 2008.

Oakley, Robert, Michael Dziedzic, and Eliot Goldberg, eds. *Policing the New World Disorder: Peace Operations and Public Security.* Washington, D.C.: National Defense University Press, 1998.

Ochs, Elinor, and Lisa Capps. "Narrating the Self." *Annual Review of Anthropology* 25 (1996): 19–43.

Ong, Aihwa. *Neoliberalism as Exception: Mutations in Citizenship and Soveriegnty.* Durham, N.C.: Duke University Press, 2006.

ONUSAL. *Los Acuerdos de Paz.* San Salvador: Arcoiris, 1992.

Overseas Security Advisory Council (OSAC). *San Salvador: 2006 Crime and Safety Report.* 19 April 2006. http://www.osac.gov/Reports/report.cfm?contentID=45275 (accessed 1 August 2006).

Özyürek, Esra. *Nostalgia for the Modern: State Secularism and Everyday Politics in Turkey.* Durham, N.C.: Duke University Press, 2006.

Paige, Jeffrey M. *Coffee and Power: Revolution and the Rise of Democracy in Central America.* Cambridge: Cambridge University Press, 1997.

Paley, Julia. "Introduction." In *Democracy: Anthropological Approaches,* ed. Julia Paley. Santa Fe, N.M.: School for Advanced Research Press, 2008.

Panamá Sandoval, David Ernesto. *Los guerreros de la libertad.* Andover, Mass.: Versal Books, 2005.

Parkman, Patricia. *Nonviolent Insurrection in El Salvador: The Fall of Maximiliano Hernández Martínez.* Tucson: University of Arizona Press, 1988.

Pedelty, Mark. *War Stories: The Culture of Foreign Correspondents.* New York: Routledge, 1995.

Pedersen, David. "In the Stream of Money: Contradictions of Migrant Remittances and Development in El Salvador." In *Landscapes of Struggle: Politics, Society and Community in El Salvador,* ed. Aldo Lauria-Santiago and Leigh Binford. Pittsburgh: University of Pittsburgh Press, 2004.

―――. "The Storm We Call Dollars: Determining Value and Belief in El Salvador and the United States." *Cultural Anthropology* 17, no. 3 (2002): 431–59.

Pelupessy, Wim. *The Limits of Economic Reform in El Salvador.* New York: St. Martin's, 1997.

Peterson, Anna L. *Martyrdom and the Politics of Religion: Progressive Catholicism in El Salvador's Civil War.* Albany: State University of New York Press, 1997.

Peterson, Anna L., and Brandt G. Peterson. "Martyrdom, Sacrifice, and Political Memory in El Salvador." *Social Research* 75, no. 2 (2008): 511–42.

Peterson, Brandt G. "Consuming Histories: The Return of the Indian in Neoliberal El Salvador." *Cultural Dynamics* 18 (2006): 163–88.

———. "The Politics of Misrecognition: Taking the Measure of Indigeneity in El Salvador." Manuscript.

———. "Unsettled Remains: Race, Trauma and Nationalism in Millennial El Salvador." Ph.D. dissertation, University of Texas, 2005.

Pontecorvo, Gillo. *The Battle of Algiers.* Casbah Films, 1966.

Popkin, Margaret. *Peace Without Justice: Obstacles to Building the Rule of Law in El Salvador.* University Park: Pennsylvania State University Press, 2000.

Policía Nacional Civil. "La violencia social en El Salvador." 2002. http://www.pncelsalvador.gov.sv/violencia/capitulo2.htm (accessed 2002).

Povinelli, Elizabeth A. "The Child in the Broom Closet: State of Killing and Letting Die." *South Atlantic Quarterly* 107, no. 3 (2008): 509–30.

Pratt, Mary Louise. "Fieldwork in Common Places." In *Writing Culture: The Poetics and Politics of Ethnography,* ed. James Clifford and George Marcus. Berkeley: University of California Press, 1986.

Putnam, Robert D. *Bowling Alone: The Collapse and Revival of American Community.* New York: Simon and Schuster, 2000.

———. *Making Democracy Work: Civil Traditions in Modern Italy.* Princeton, N.J.: Princeton University Press, 1993.

Quinn, Naomi. "Introduction." In *Finding Culture in Talk: A Collection of Methods,* ed. Naomi Quinn. New York: Palgrave Macmillan, 2005.

Ramírez, José Alfredo. "El anticomunismo en El Salvador: Las acciones del estado y los sectores de la derecha salvadoreña como factores de la guerra civil de los años 80." Paper presented at Second Conference on Salvadoran History, University of El Salvador, San Salvador, 19 July 2007.

Ricoeur, Paul. *Time and Narrative.* Vol. 1. Chicago: University of Chicago Press, 1984.

Ries, Nancy. *Russian Talk: Culture and Conversation During Perestroika.* Ithaca, N.Y.: Cornell University Press, 1997.

Rivera, Marcos Antonio, and Claudia Evelyn Perla. "El surgimiento y posterior modernización de los noticieros televisivos el el período de 1985 a 1989." Manuscript.

Robinson, William I. *Transnational Conflicts: Central America, Social Change and Globalization.* London: Verso, 2003.

Rockwell, Rick, and Noreene Janus. *Media Power in Central America.* Urbana: University of Illinois Press, 2003.

Rodgers, Dennis. "Living in the Shadow of Death: Gangs, Violence and Social Order in Urban Nicaragua, 1996–2002." *Journal of Latin American Studies* 38, no. 2 (2000): 267–93.

Rosa Chávez, Herman. *AID y las transformaciones globales en El Salvador: El papel de la política de asistencia económica de los Estados Unidos desde 1980.* Managua: CRIES, 1993.

Rosas, Gilberto. "The Biopolitical Violences of the U.S.-Mexico Borderlands and Other 'Criminal Knowledges.'" Manuscript.

Rose, Nikolas. "Governing 'Advanced' Liberal Democracies." In *Foucault and Political Reason: Liberalism, Neoliberalism, and Rationalities of Government*, ed. Nikolas Rose, Andrew Barry, and Thomas Osborne. London: UCL Press, 1996.

Roseberry, William. "Hegemony, Power, and the Language of Contention." In *The Politics of Difference: Ethnic Premises in a World of Power*, ed. Edwin N. Wilmsen and Patrick McAllister. Chicago: University of Chicago Press, 1996.

Roy, Arundhati. "Into the Inferno." *New Statesman* (16 July 2009). http://www.newstatesman.com/international-politics/2009/07/india-democracy-market (accessed 21 July 2009).

Rustow, Dankwart A. "Transitions to Democracy: Toward a Dynamic Model." *Comparative Politics* 2 (1970): 337–63.

Said, Edward. *Orientalism*. New York: Vintage, 1979.

Salamon, L. M. *The Global Associational Revolution: The Rise of Third Sector on the World Scene*. Baltimore: Institute for Policy Studies, Johns Hopkins University, 1993.

Saldaña-Portillo, María Josefina. *The Revolutionary Imagination in the Americas and the Age of Development*. Durham, N.C.: Duke University Press, 2003.

Sánchez Cerén, Salvador. *Con sueños se escribe la vida: Autobiografía de un revolucionario salvadoreño*. México, D.F.: Ocean Sur, 2008.

Santamaria, Gema. "Gangs as *Homo Sacer*: Violence and Contemporary Power in El Salvador." Master's thesis, London School of Economics, 2008.

Sartre, Jean-Paul. *Being and Nothingness: A Phenomenological Essay on Ontology*. Trans. Hazel E. Barnes. New York: Routledge, 2003.

Scarry, Elaine. "The Difficulty of Imagining Other Persons." In *Human Rights in Political Transition: Gettysburg to Bosnia*, ed. Carla Hesse and Robert Post. New York: Zone Books, 1999.

Scheper-Hughes, Nancy. *Death Without Weeping: The Violence of Everyday Life in Brazil*. Berkeley: University of California Press, 1992.

———. "Small Wars and Invisible Genocides." *Social Science and Medicine* 43, no. 5 (2003): 889–900.

———. "Specificities: Peace-Time Crimes." *Social Identities* 3, no. 3 (1997): 471–97.

———. "Violence and the Politics of Remorse: Lessons from South Afirca." In *Subjectivity: Ethnographic Investigations*, ed. Joao Biehl, Byron Good, and Arthur Kleinman. Berkeley: University of California Press, 2006.

Schild, Veronica. "New Subject of Rights: Women's Movements and the Construction of Citizenship in the 'New Democracies'." In *Culture of Politics, Politics of Culture: Re-Visioning Latin American Social Movements*, ed. Sonia E. Alvarez, Evelina Dagnino, and Arturo Escobar. Boulder, Colo.: Westview Press.

Schönherr, Valentin. "Schlicht überleben." WOZ-Online, 2003. http://www.woz.ch/archiv/old/03/49/6178.html (accessed 3 April 2007).

Schuld, Leslie. "Who Will Have the Hospitals?" *NACLA: Report on the Americas*

36, no. 4 (January/February 2003): 42–45. www.cis-elsalvador.org/archive/ NACLE%20 JanFeb%Article.htm (accessed 11 January 2008).

Schumpeter, Joseph. *Capitalism, Socialism and Democracy.* New York: Harper & Row, 1942.

Sedgwick, Eve Kosofsky. "Privilege of Unknowing: Diderot's *the Nun.*" In *Tendencies,* ed. Eve Kosofsky Sedgwick. Durham, N.C.: Duke University Press, 1993.

Segovia, Alexander. "La actuación y las politicas macroeconómica y la reconstrucción de postguerra en El Salvador." San Salvador: UNDP, 1995.

———. *Transformación estructural y reforma económica en El Salvador: El funcionamiento económico de los noventa y sus efectos sobre el crecimiento, la pobreza y la distribución del ingreso.* Guatemala: F&G, 2002.

Seligson, Mitchell A. "Thirty Years of Transformation in the Agrarian Structure of El Salvador." *Latin American Research Review* 30, no. 3 (1995): 43–74.

Selva Sutter, Ernesto A. "La decentralización y la reforma de salud neoliberal." *Estudios Centroamericanos* (ECA) 660 (2003): 1029–47.

Serrano, Omar. "Reaparecen escuadrones de la muerte." *Revista Envio* (November 1993). http://www.envio.org.ni/articulo/814 (accessed 28 February 2008).

———. "La reveladora huelga de salud." *Revista Envio* (October 1993). http://www. envio.org.ni/articulo/814 (accessed 28 February 2008).

Shank, Amanda. "El Salvador: The UDW Interview with FMLN Presidential Candidate Mauricio Funes (Part I)." http://upsidedownworld.org/main/content/view/1282/1/ (accessed 30 August 2008).

Siegel, James. *A New Criminal Type in Jakarta: Counter-Revolution Today.* Durham, N.C.: Duke University Press, 1998.

Silber, Irina Carlota. "Mothers/Fighters/Citizens: Violence and Disillusionment in Post-War El Salvador." *Gender and History* 16, no. 3 (2004): 561–87.

———. "Not Revolutionary Enough? Community Rebuilding in Postwar Chalatenango." In *Landscapes of Struggle: Politics, Society and Community in El Salvador,* ed. Leigh Binford and Aldo Lauria-Santiago. Pittsburgh: University of Pittsburgh Press, 2004.

Simmel, Georg. "The Stranger." In *The Sociology of Georg Simmel.* New York: Free Press, 1950.

Smith, Andrea. "Heteroglossia, 'Common Sense,' and Social Memory." *American Ethnologist* 31, no. 2 (2004): 251–69.

Smith, Christian. *Resisting Reagan: The U.S. Central America Peace Movement.* Chicago: University of Chicago Press, 1996.

Smith-Nonini, Sandy. "Health 'Anti-Reform' in El Salvador: Community Health NGOs and the State in the Neoliberal Era." *Political and Legal Anthropology Review* 21, no. 1 (1998): 99–111.

Smutt, Marcella, and Jenny Lissette E. Miranda. *El fenómeno de las pandillas en El Salvador.* San Salvador: FLACSO and UNICEF, 1998.

Sobrino, Jon, ed. *Archbishop Romero: Memories and Reflections.* Maryknoll, N.Y.: Orbis, 1990.

Sol, Ricardo. *El Salvador: Medios masivos y comunicación popular.* San Salvador: Porvenir, Collección Minuto, 1984.

Solé, Yolanda R., and Carlos A. Solé. *Modern Spanish Syntax: A Study in Contrast.* Lexington, Mass.: D.C. Heath, 1977.

Spence, Jack, and George R. Vickers, eds. *A Negotiated Revolution? A Two-Year Progress Report on the Salvadoran Peace Accords.* Cambridge, Mass.: Hemisphere Initiatives, 1994.

Stabile, Carol A. "Conspiracy or Consensus? Reconsidering Moral Panic." *Journal of Communication Inquiry* 25, no. 3 (2001): 258–78.

Stahler-Sholk, Richard. "El Salvador's Negotiated Transition: From Low-Intensity Conflict to Low-Intensity Democracy." *Journal of Interamerican Studies and World Affairs* 36, no. 4 (1994): 1–59.

Stanley, William. *The Protection Racket State: Elite Politics, Military Extortion and Civil War in El Salvador.* Philadelphia: Temple University Press, 1996.

———. *Protectors or Perpetrators? The Institutional Crisis of the Salvadoran Civilian Police.* Washington, D.C.: WOLA and Hemisphere Initiatives, 1996.

Stanley, William, and Robert Loosle. "El Salvador: The Civilian Police Component of Peace Operations." In *Policing the New World Order: Peace Operations and Public Security*, ed. Robert Oakley, Michael Dziedzic, and Eliot Goldberg. Washington, D.C.: National Defense University, 1998.

Stanley, William, George R. Vickers, and Jack Spence. *Risking Failure: The Problems and Promise of the New Civilian Police in El Salvador.* Cambridge, Mass. and Washington, D.C.: Hemisphere Initiatives and Washington Office on Latin America, 1993.

Steiner, Roberto. "Criminalidad en El Salvador: Diagnóstico y recomendaciones de política." Unpublished consultant's report elaborated for the Fundación Salvadoreña de Desarrolla Sconómica y Social, 1999.

Stepan, Nancy Leys. *"The Hour of Eugenics": Race, Gender and Nation in Latin America.* Ithaca, N.Y.: Cornell University Press, 1991.

Stephen, Lynn, and María Teresa Tula. *Hear My Testimony: María Teresa Tula, Human Rights Activist in El Salvador.* Boston: South End Press, 1999.

Stewart, Kathleen. *Ordinary Affects.* Durham, N.C.: Duke University Press, 2007.

Stone, Oliver. *Salvador.* MGM, 1986.

Taussig, Michael. *Shamanism, Colonialism and the Wild Man: A Study in Terror and Healing.* Chicago: University of Chicago Press, 1987.

Taylor, Charles. *Modern Social Imaginaries.* Durham, N.C.: Duke University Press, 2004.

Taylor, Lawrence. *Born to Crime: The Genetic Causes of Human Behavior.* Westport, Conn.: Greenwood Press, 1984.

Theoharis, Athan G., Tony G. Povidea, Susan Rosenfeld, and Richard Gid Powers, eds. *The FBI: A Comprehensive Reference Guide.* Westport, Conn.: Greenwood Press, 1999.

Tilley, Virginia. *Seeing Indians: A Study of Race, Nation and Power in El Salvador.* Albuquerque: University of New Mexico Press, 2005.

Tilly, Charles. *From Mobilization to Revolution.* Reading, Mass.: Addison-Wesley, 1978.

Tojeira, José María. "Dar cuenta y asumir responsabilidades." *Estudios Centroamericanos* 625–26 (2000). http://www.uca.edu.sv/publica/eca/eca625.html (accessed 11 October 2008).

Ueltzen, Stefan, ed. *Conversatorio con los hijos del siglo: El Salvador del siglo XX al siglo XXI*. San Salvador: III Milenio, 1994.

United Nations. "El Salvador-ONUSAL Background." http://www.un.org/Depts/dpko/dpko/co_mission/onusalbackgr2.html (accessed 1 June 2007).

―――. "Report of the ONUSAL Human Rights Division for the Period from 1 January to 30 April 1992." A/46/935–S/24066, 5 June 1992, Document 43 in UN Blue Book Series 4. New York: United Nations, 1995.

―――. "Report of the ONUSAL Human Rights Division for the Period from 1 July 1992 to 31 January 1993." A/47/912-S/25521, 5 April 1993, Document 70 in UN Blue Book Series 4. New York: United Nations, 1995.

―――. "Report of the ONUSAL Human Rights Division Covering the Period from 1 March to 30 June 1994." A/49/281-S/1994/886, 18 July 1994. Document 114 in UN Blue Book Series 4. New York: United Nations, 1995.

―――. "Report of the ONUSAL Human Rights Division Covering the Period from 1 November 1993 to 28 February 1994." A/49/116–S/1994/385, April 1994. Document 105 in UN Blue Book Series 4. New York: United Nations, 1995.

United Nations Development Programme (UNDP). *Democracy in Latin America: Towards a Citizens' Democracy*. New York: UNDP, 2004.

―――. *Informe sobre el desarrollo humano El Salvador 2005: Una mirada al nuevo nosotros: El impacto de las migraciones*. San Salvador: UNDP, 2005. http://hdr.undp.org/en/reports/nationalreports/latinamericathecaribbean/elsalvador/name 3307, en.html (accessed 1 January 2006).

―――. *Report on Human Development in El Salvador 2001*. New York: UNDP, 2001. http://www.desarrollohumano.org.sv (accessed 10 July 2001).

Urban, Greg. "Entextualization, Replication, and Power." In *Natural Histories of Discourse*, ed. Michael Silverstein and Greg Urban. Chicago: University of Chicago Press, 1996.

―――. *Metaphysical Community: The Interplay of the Senses and the Intellect*. Austin: University of Texas Press, 1996.

U.S. Department of State Bureau of Democracy, Human Rights and Labor. "El Salvador Country Report on Human Rights Practices," 31 March 2003. http://www.state.gov/g/drl/rls/hrrpt/2002/18331.htm (accessed April 2003).

U.S.-El Salvador Sister Cities Network. "The Salvadoran Anti-Terrorism Law and Its Mirror Image," 3 March 2007. http://elsalvadorsolidarity.org/joomla/index.php? (accessed 20 August 2007).

Vasconcelos, José. *La raza cósmica: Misión de la raza iberoamericana*. Paris: Agencia Municipal de Liberia, 1925.

Velásquez de Avilés, Victoria. *Evolución de los derechos humanos en El Salvador: Informe anual 1996*. San Salvador: Procuraduría para la Defensa de los Derechos Humanos, 1997.

Vickers, George R. "A Negotiated Revolution." *NACLA Report on the Americas* 25, no. 5 (1992): 4–8.

―――. "The Political Reality After Eleven Years of War." In *Is There a Transition to Democracy in El Salvador?* ed. Joseph S. Tulchin. Boulder, Colo.: Lynne Rienner Publishers, 1992.

Wachs, Eleanor. *Crime-Victim Stories: New York City's Urban Folklore*. Bloomington: Indiana University Press, 1988.

Wallace, Scott. "You Must Go Home Again: Deported L.A. Gangbangers Take over
El Salvador." *Harper's* (August 2000): 47–56.

Warner, Michael. "What like a Bullet Can Undeceive?" *Public Culture* 15, no. 1
(2003): 41–54.

Washington Office on Latin America (WOLA). "Executive Summary: Transnational Youth Gangs in Central America, the United States and Mexico." 30
March 2007. http://www.wola.org/index.php?option=com_content&task=vie
wp&id=272&Itemid=2 (accessed 14 February 2007).

———. "Youth Gangs in Central America: Issues in Human Rights, Effective Policing, and Prevention." *WOLA Special Report*, November 2006. http://www.
wola.org/index.php?option=com_content&task=view&id=80&Itemid=2 (accessed January 2007).

Weber, Max. "Bureaucracy." In *From Max Weber: Essays in Sociology*, ed. H. H. Gerth
and C. Wright Mills. Oxford: Oxford University Press, 1946.

———. "Politics as a Vocation." In *From Max Weber: Essays in Sociology*, ed. H. H.
Gerth and C. Wright Mills. Oxford: Oxford University Press, 1946.

White, Hayden. "The Value of Narrativity in the Representation of Reality." In *On
Narrative*, ed. W. J. T. Mitchell. Chicago: University of Chicago Press, 1981.

White, Matthew. "Death Tolls for the Man-Made Megadeaths of the Twentieth
Century." http://users.erols.com/mwhite28/warstatx.htm#d (accessed 30 June
2009).

Whitfeld, Teresa. *Playing the Price: Ignacio Ellacuría and the Murdered Jesuits of El
Salvador*. Philadelphia: Temple University Press, 1995.

Williams, Philip, and Knut Walter. *Militarization and Demilitarization in El Salvador's Transition to Democracy*. Pittsburgh: University of Pittsburgh Press, 1997.

Williams, Raymond. *Marxism and Literature*. Oxford: Oxford University Press,
1978.

Williams, Robert G. *Export Agriculture and the Crisis in Central America*. Chapel
Hill: University of North Carolina Press, 1986.

Wood, Elisabeth Jean. *Forging Democracy from Below: Insurgent Transitions in South
Africa and El Salvador*. Cambridge: Cambridge University Press, 2000.

———. *Insurgent Collective Action and Civil War in El Salvador*. Cambridge: Cambridge University Press, 2003.

———. "The Peace Accords and Reconstruction." In *Economic Policy for Building
Peace: The Lessons of El Salvador*, ed. James K. Boyce. Boulder, Colo.: Lynne
Rienner, 1996.

Woodward, Kathleen. "Calculating Compassion." In *Compassion: The Culture and
Politics of an Emotion*, ed. Lauren Berlant. New York: Routledge, 2004.

Yngvesson, Barbara, and Susan Bibler Coutin. "Backed by Papers: Undoing Persons,
Histories, Return." *American Ethnologist* 33, no. 2 (2006): 177–90.

Yúdice, George. "*Testimonio* and Postmodernism." *Latin American Perspectives* 18,
no. 3 (1991): 15–31.

Zaloom, Caitlin. *Out of the Pits: Traders and Technology from Chicago to London*.
Chicago: University of Chicago Press, 2006.

Zielinski, Michael. "Starting Over in El Salvador." *Z Magazine*, June 1995. http://www.zmag.org/zmag/articles/june95zielinski.htm   (accessed   10   February 2007).

Zilberg, Elana. "Fools Banished from the Kingdom: Remapping Geographies of Gang Violence Between the Americas (Los Angeles and San Salvador)." *American Quarterly* 56, no. 3 (2004): 759–79.

———. "Gangster in Guerrilla Face: A Transnational Mirror of Production Between the U.S.A. and El Salvador." *Anthropological Theory* 7, no. 1 (2007): 37–57.

———. "Refugee Gang Youth: Zero Tolerance and the Security State in Contemporary U.S.-Salvadoran Relations." In *Youth, Globalization, and the Law*, ed. Sudhir Venkatech and Ron Kassimir. Stanford, Calif.: Stanford University Press, 2007.

Žižek, Slavoj. *The Sublime Object of Ideology: The Essential Žižek*. London: Verso, 2008.

Periodicals Referenced

APF Reporter
Boston Globe
ContraPunto
Diario CoLatino
Diario Latino
El Diario de Hoy
El Faro
Foreign Affairs
Fundación Flor de Izote/El Rescate Report from El Salvador
The Guardian
Harper's
Idaho Falls Post-Register
El Independiente
Miami Herald
El Mundo
The Nation
New York Times
Newsday
La Prensa Gráfica
El Salvador Proceso
Toronto Star
Vértice
Washington Post

Index

Acknowledgments

In this book I argue that in the aftermath of peace, people were forced to turn to individual strategies for survival. *El Salvador in the Aftermath of Peace* is anything but an individual achievement; it is the product of a wonderful, if cacophonous, collective effort. If I have succeeded in anything, it is because so many people have helped me along the way.

I must start by thanking Blanca Molina and Denis Johnston, who first welcomed me to El Salvador in New Jersey. In my first visits to Central America, Conchy Molina, along with Asunción, Idalia, Eli and Nubia Molina, as well as Fidencio Rios, Rosa Emma Canales, and David, Ricardo, Rene and Emma Antonia Rios, all made me feel at home. Rene Contreras, Guillermo Mejía, Gregorio Bello Suazo, Sergio Leonel Estrada, Milton Martínez, Anna Keene, Santiago (Carlos Henríquez Consalvi) and Georgina Hernández Rivas all helped me find my feet and voice in the early years. Later Olga Zepeda, Paty Morales, Carlos Benjamín Lara Martínez, Edith Saíz de Lara, José Roberto Lara Martínez and Patricia Guirola gave me many insights on life in postwar El Salvador. José Miguel Cruz, Luis Armando González, Rafael Guidos Véjar, and Knut Walter offered good advice at key junctures. Cledys Molina, Vilma Rivera, Cecy Marroquín and Claudia Anay García assisted me as able research assistants. I am also grateful to the many other Salvadorans whose names I cannot use.

I met my husband in El Salvador. His knowledge and skepticism and anger have taught me too much. Antonio Rivera, Vilma Guadalupe Rivera, Rosa María de los Angeles Rivera, Karen Rivera and Arnoldo Amaya let me into their lives in ways that profoundly affected me. I also thank Jesús Landaverde. María Elisa Pineda de Rivera, Julián Rivera and Elvira Palomo kept me laughing in difficult times.

I would not have become the anthropologist I am if Ruth Behar at the University of Michigan had not been my adviser. Her approach to ethnography freed me. While Ruth taught me about writing and relationships, Bruce Mannheim taught me about language and meaning. This book would have been very different without his influence. I also thank Alaina Lemon and Sueann Caulfield, along with E. Valentine Daniel, Brinkley Messick, Roger Rouse, Fernando Coronil, Webb Keane, Crisca Bierwert and Janet Hart, University of Michigan faculty who inspired me at different moments. Stefan Senders, briefly at Michigan, nudged me in unexpected directions. My Michigan cohort motivated me to think in ways I would never have imagined back in my newspaper reporter days. I am especially grateful to Esra Özyürek's wisdom and sympathy and Carla Daughtry's determination and humor. Lourdes Gutiérrez supported me (and still supports me!) in countless ways. Charo Montoya, Bridget Hayden, Bethany Grenald and Tomomi Yamaguchi read some of my early work. Viviana Quintero listened like no one else. Erica Lehrer understood. Along the way, Penelope Papailias, Jennifer Dickinson, Laura Kunreuther and Jim Herron (in the amazing Language as Social Action cohort), as well as Rachel Heiman, John Collins, Adrienne Young, Laura Ahearn, Mani Limbert, Susan Frekko, David Pedersen, and Bianet Castellanos, among many others, contributed something to the project that became this book.

Writing groups and readers have become crucial to my creative process. I have learned much from noisy get-togethers with Lessie Jo Frazier, Deborah Cohen, Charo Montoya, and Emily Maguire; and the critical reading skills of my literary writing group Yasemin Yildiz, Ericka Beckman and Anna Stenport have vastly improved this book. Others who have offered helpful commentary include Erica Lehrer, Laura Roush, Gilberto Rosas, Matt Tomlinson, Kimberley Coles, Bianet Castellanos, and Hinda Seif. Many scholars of El Salvador have proved to be important critics: they include Leigh Binford, Brandt Peterson, Aldo Lauria-Santiago, Bridget Hayden, and Susan Coutin. Conversations with Héctor Lindo, Jeff Gould, Robin DeLugan, Lotti Silber, Elana Zilberg, Sajid Herrera, Carlos Gregorio López, Ana Patricia Rodríguez, Douglas Carranza, David Pedersen, Jason Cross, Ainhoa Montoya, and Joe Wiltberger have brought more clarity to my thinking.

At the University of Illinois I have found an intellectual home. I cannot imagine what this book would look like without the support of my mentors and friends on the anthropology faculty. Matti Bunzl was always ready to read my work, and I am so grateful for emergency aid on more than one occasion. Martin Manalansan was also there for me at key moments; and Andy Orta, Nancy Abelmann, Alma Gottlieb, and Gilberto Rosas have lent me their critical eyes. I also want to thank Marc Perry, Alejandro Lugo, Brenda Farnell, Janet Keller, Steve Leigh, Virginia Dominguez, Bill Kelleher, and

Sasha Newell. Outside my department, Michael Rothberg gave me a forum through the Unit for Criticism and Interpretive Theory that pushed me to write a crucial chapter. Stephen Hartnett, William Castro, Nils Jacobsen, and Angelina Cotler offered helpful insights. Recent conversations with Betoel Escobar have helped to personalize Salvadoran history. I am indebted to my research assistants here: William Hope, Edwin Vega, Charles Taylor, and Jason Ritchie. Jason and Edwin, along with Cristobal Valencia and María del Mar González-González were in a class on Central America that helped me think through my ideas. More recently readers who have encouraged me in the final stages of this work include participants in the "After the Handshakes" Wenner-Gren workshop, especially Jennifer Burrell, Mark Anderson, Jennifer Bickham Mendez, Florence Babb, Leigh Binford, Marc Edelman, and Ciska Raventós. Rob Borofsky became an inspiration near the end, and Penn Press's Peter Agree's enthusiasm got me over the last obstacles.

I must add a word of special appreciation to my brother and sister, Gordon Moodie and Ginger Moodie-Woodward, and my stepmother and father, Eileen Moodie and Colin Linton Moodie, as well as the memory of my mother, Patricia Hartshorn Moodie. This book is dedicated to her.

I had a number of generous fellowships for this project. At the University of Michigan, the Rackham School of Graduate Studies, the Latin American and Caribbean Studies Program, the International Institute, the Gayle Morris Sweetland Writing Center and the Department of Anthropology have all funded parts of my fieldwork research and write-up. The National Science Foundation paid for my 1994 trip. The Social Science Research Council and American Council of Learned Societies funded my year in El Salvador in 1995–1996. Fellowships for two more years of fieldwork between 1997 and 1999 came from the Fulbright-Hays Doctoral Research Abroad Program, the Jennings-Randolph Peace Scholar Fellowship Program of the U.S. Institute of Peace, the Social Science Research Council, and the Organization of American States. A Fletcher Family Research Grant from Bowdoin College, a Mellon Post-doctoral Fellowship in the Humanities at the University of Illinois, and (also at the U of I) the Campus Research Board, the Center for Latin American and Caribbean Studies, and the Department of Anthropology have funded return trips to El Salvador each year between 2003 and 2008.

A small portion of Chapter 6 was published in a different version as "Seventeen Years, Seventeen Murders: Biospectacularity and the Production of Post-Cold War Knowledge in El Salvador" in the journal *Social Text 99*

(Summer 2009). Permission to publish portions of Roque Dalton's poetry was generously granted by the family of Roque Dalton (personal communication, Juan José Dalton, 6 May 2009). Curbstone Press allowed publication of English translations of the poems. South End Press permitted reprinting of Oswaldo Escobar Velado's poem. Permission to republish the Reuters article "El Salvador Rebel Leader Gunned Down in Capital" was granted by Thomson Reuters (personal communication, Morene Stark, 6 May 2009). After Agustin Anaya (Omnionn) directed me to him, Enrique Luna kindly allowed me to use excerpts of the rap song "El Directo" (personal communication, 10 May 2009).